Economic Outlook for Southeast Asia, China and India 2015

STRENGTHENING INSTITUTIONAL CAPACITY

OECD
BETTER POLICIES FOR BETTER LIVES

Please cite this publication as:

OECD (2015), *Economic Outlook for Southeast Asia, China and India: Strengthening Institutional Capacity*, OECD Publishing, Paris, *http://dx.doi.org/10.1787/saeo-2015-en.*

ISBN 978-92-64-21086-8 (print)

ISBN 978-92-64-17441-2 (PDF)

Annual: Economic Outlook for Southeast Asia, China and India

ISSN 2310-1105 (print)

ISSN 2310-1113 (online)

Photo credits: Cover design by the OECD Development Centre based on images of Dirk Ott, TTstudio, Hoang Cong Thanh, Hoang Cong Thanh/Shutterstock.com.

Corrigenda to OECD publications may be found on line at: *www.oecd.org/publishinig/corrigenda.*

Foreword

The *Economic Outlook for Southeast Asia, China and India* is an annual publication on Asia's regional economic growth, development and regional integration processes. It focuses on the economic conditions of the Association of Southeast Asian Nations (ASEAN) member countries (Brunei Darussalam, Cambodia, Indonesia, Lao PDR, Malaysia, Myanmar, the Philippines, Singapore, Thailand and Viet Nam) and two large economies in the region, China and India. This Outlook evolved from the *Southeast Asian Economic Outlook*.

This Outlook was initially proposed at an informal reflection group on Southeast Asia in 2008 as a follow-up of the Council Meeting at Ministerial level (MCM) in 2007 and was accepted by ministers/senior officials from ASEAN countries at the occasion of the 2nd OECD-Southeast Asia Regional Forum in Bangkok in 2009. The Outlook project was officially launched in 2010 and each edition is regularly presented at the occasion of the ASEAN/East Asia Summit.

The 2015 edition highlights the importance of institutional capacities to development in the Emerging Asian economies. In particular, it reviews indicators of governments' planning and implementation, the recent history of public sector reforms, and experiences with informality and support for formal markets.

The OECD Development Centre is committed to working alongside governments of developing and emerging economies and regional actors to identify key areas of intervention in order to address these challenges. The Centre enjoys the full membership of three Southeast Asian countries, namely Indonesia, Thailand and Viet Nam, as well as India. This project also benefitted from the generous support of other Emerging Asian countries.

This Outlook is the result of policy dialogue and consultation at the regional level, at the *3rd OECD-AMRO-ADB Joint Asian Regional Roundtable on Near-term Macroeconomic and Medium-term Structural Policy Challenges*, held in Manila, the Philippines, in July 2014.

Like other regional economic outlooks produced by the OECD Development Centre, the report was prepared in collaboration with a regional partner, in this case the ASEAN Secretariat. The OECD is committed to supporting Asian countries in their efforts to promote economic and social well-being through rigorous analysis, peer learning and best practices.

Acknowledgements

The 2015 edition of the *Economic Outlook for Southeast Asia, China and India: Strengthening Institutional Capacity* was prepared by the Asia Desk of the OECD Development Centre in Paris, in co-operation with the ASEAN Secretariat in Jakarta.

The team was led by Kensuke Tanaka, Head of the Asia Desk and overall guidance was provided by Mario Pezzini, Director of the OECD Development Centre. This volume was drafted by a team composed of Kensuke Tanaka, Derek Carnegie, Prasiwi Ibrahim, Charles Pigott, Pitchaya Sirivunnabood, Anna Mae Tuazon and Rony Soerakoesoemah. Edouward Turkisch, Masakazu Someya and Yoki Okawa provided useful inputs in preparing the publication. Important inputs were received from Mari Imada, participant of the OECD Corporate Traineeship Programme. Mireille Benicke provided useful administrative support for relevant mission arrangements of this project. Elizabeth Nash, Delphine Grandrieux, Studio Pykha and Aida Buendia turned the manuscript into the publication.

This publication benefited from discussions with OECD Delegations at three informal consultation group meetings in April, July and November, 2014 in Paris and with experts in the region at the *3nd OECD-AMRO-ADB Asian Regional Roundtable on Near-term Macroeconomic and Medium-term Structural Policy challenges*, jointly organised by the ASEAN+3 Macroeconomic Research Office (AMRO), the Asian Development Bank (ADB) and the OECD, in Manila in July 2014. The Outlook was launched at the occasion of the ASEAN/East Asia Summit in Nay Pyi Taw, Myanmar in November 2014 in a joint session with ERIA (Economic Research Institute for ASEAN and East Asia). The authors are grateful to Rintaro Tamaki, Deputy Secretary-General of the OECD, Yoichi Nemoto, Director of the AMRO, and Juzhong Zhuang, Deputy Chief Economist of the ADB as well as Munenari Nomura, Chaipat Poonpatpibul, Joseph E. Zveglich, Forametee Vimolsiri, Thurgha Govindasamy, Shikha Jha, Maung Maung Win, Petar Vujanovic, Shanaka Jayanath Peiris, Jon Blondal, Peter Jarrett, Rizal A. Djaafara, Yumiko Murakami, Hidetoshi Nishimura, Yasushi Iwata, Fukunari Kimura and Yoshifumi Fukunaga.

Support from OECD Delegations and Embassies of ASEAN countries in Paris, in particular, Ambassador Apichart Chinwanno, Ambassador Hans-Juergen Heimsoeth, Ambassador Kazuo Kodama, Ambassador Rezlan Ishar Jenie, Ambassador Si-hyung Lee, as well as Rapunzel Acop, Wasana Honboonheum, Nefertiti Hindratmo, Fajar Har, Sang Hee Hong, Anindita Kosala, Tran Phan Linh, Chanol Rith, Widya Sadnovic, Jürg Schneider, Rakesh Sharma, Natsuko Sakata, Asami Takeda, Sirichada Thongtan and Kang-hyeon Yun is gratefully acknowledged.

A large number of government officials and experts in Emerging Asian countries were involved in successive consultations during OECD Development Centre's missions, seminars and meetings. Particular thanks go to Masato Abe, Luky Alfirman, Juda Agung, Armida S. Alisjahbana, Irfa Ampri, Allauddin Bin Anuar, Prijambodo Bambang, Bui Tat Thang, Chonlatee Chanrachakul, Rosemarie Edillon, Emmanuel Esguerra, Rodrigo Garcia, Carla Hernandez, Mohamad Ikhsan, Asnawi Kamis, Le Luong Minh, Don Nakomthab, Paul van den Noord, Nguyen Duc Thanh, Nguyen Hoang Ha, Nguyen Thi Lan Huong, Kunta W.D. Nugraha, Aung Naing Oo, Phan Ngoc Mai Phuong, Pham Minh. Thao, Pradit Phataraprasit, Bambang Prijambodo, Zakariah Abdul Rashid,

Purbaya Yudhi Sadewa, Mahendra Siregar, Thammanoon Sodsrichai, Wismana Adi Suryabrata, Syaifullah, Pattama Teanravisitsagool, Teresa Peralta, Li Jun Tan, Arkhom Termpittayapaisith, Leonard Thampubolon, Thia Jang Ping, Tran Anh Vu, Trang Thu Vu, Ma. Cyd n. Tuano-amador, Suthirat Vansrisawasd, Prasetijono Widjojo, Perry Warjiyo, Adininggar Widyasanti, Wongwan and Kan Zaw.

The Medium-term Projection Framework for Growth and Development (MPF) used in this publication was prepared by a team managed by Kensuke Tanaka, Masakazu Someya and Yasuo Hirose.

Last but not least, the OECD Development Centre would like to acknowledge gratefully the financial support received from the Governments of Japan, Korea and Switzerland.

Table of contents

Tables

Main findings and policy recommendations

Chapter 1

Chapter 2

Chapter 3

Figures

Chapter 2

Chapter 3

Chapter 4

Boxes

Chapter 1

Chapter 3

Chapter 4

Acronyms and abbreviations

ADB	Asian Development Bank
AEC	ASEAN Economic Community
AFTA	ASEAN Free Trade Area
APEC	Asia-Pacific Economic Co-operation
ASEAN	Association of Southeast Asian Nations
ASEAN-5	Indonesia, Malaysia, the Philippines, Thailand and Viet Nam
ASSOCHAM	Associated Chambers of Commerce and Industry of India
BAU	Business-as-usual
BPO	Business process outsourcing
BPS	Statistics Indonesia
BSM	Poor Students' Assistance Programme
BSP	Philippine Central Bank
BTA	Border tax adjustment
CCT	Conditional cash transfer
CGIF	Credit Guarantee and Investment Facility
CPC	Communist Party of China
CPI	Consumer price index
CPIA	Country Policy and Institutional Assessment Indicators
CPS	Country Partnership Strategy
DepEd	Department of Education, Philippines
DOSM	Department of Statistics, Malaysia
EC	European Community
ECEC	Early childhood education and care
EITI	Extractive Industries Transparency Initiative
EMEAP	Executives Meeting of East Asia-Pacific Central Banks
EPPO	Energy Policy and Planning Office
ETI	Environmental tax instrument
ETP	Economic Transformation Programme
EU	European Union
FAO	Food and Agriculture Organization
FDI	Foreign Direct Investment
FESR	Framework for Social and Economic Reforms
FPDFs	Forest Protection and Development Funds
FTA	Free trade agreement
GDP	Gross domestic product
GERD	Government expenditure on R&D
GHI	Green and Happiness Index
GMS	Greater Mekong Subregion
GNI	Gross national income
GST	Goods and services tax
GTP	Government Transformation Programme
GVA	Gross value added
HTA	Health Technology Assessment
IAI	Initiative for ASEAN Integration
ICT	Information and communication technology
IDR	Indonesia Rupiah
IEA	International Energy Agency
IFAD	International Fund for Agricultural Development

ILO International Labour Organization
IMF International Monetary Fund
IPR Intellectual property right
IRBM Integrated results-based management
ISO International Organization for Standardization
JICA Japan International Cooperation Agency
JKN Jaminan Kesehatan Nasional
KPK Corruption Eradication Commission
LDCs Least developed countries
LPG Liquefied petroleum gas
MADB Myanmar Agriculture Development Bank
MARD Ministry of Agriculture and Rural Development
MP3EI Master Plan for the Acceleration and Expansion of Indonesia's Economic Development
MPA Marine Protected Areas
MPC Malaysia Productivity Corporation
MPF Medium-Term Projection Framework for Growth and Development
MPI Ministry of Planning and Investment
MSME Micro, small, medium-sized enterprise
MTBF Medium-term budgetary frameworks
MTDP Medium-term development plan
MTFF Medium-term fiscal framework
MTPF Medium-term performance framework
MYR Malaysian Ringgit
NCPO National Council for Peace and Order
NDGIs Narrowing Development Gaps Indicators
NDRC National Development and Reform Commission
NEDA National Economic and Development Authority
NEM New Economic Model
NESDB National Economic and Social Development Board
NFHS National Family Health Survey
NGO Non-governmental organisation
NHTS-PR National Household Targeting System for Poverty Reduction
NIPAS National Integrated Protected Areas System
NKEA National Key Economic Area
NLD National League for Democracy
NPC National People's Congress
NPL Non-performing loan
NPM New public management
NREGA National Rural Employment Guarantee Act
NSDC National SME Development Council, Malaysia
NSDCB National Skill Development Co-ordination Board
NUEPA National University of Education Planning and Administration
OBC Other Backward Classes
OECD Organisation for Economic Co-operation and Development
OWWA Overseas Workers Welfare Administration
PDP Philippines' Development Plan 2011-16
PEFA Public Expenditure and Financial Assessment
PEM Public expenditure management
PFES Payments for Forest Environmental Services
PFM Public financial management
PHP Philippine Peso
PISA Programme for International Student Assessment

PITA	Petroleum Income Tax
PKH	Family Hope Programme
PNPM	National Programme for Community Empowerment
PPBS	Programme Performance Budget System
PPP	Public-private partnership
PPP	Purchasing power parity
PRC	People's Republic of China
PSC	Public Sector Comparator
PSR	Public sector reform
QE	Quantitative Easing
R&D	Research and development
RBI	Reserve Bank of India
RCA	Revealed Comparative Advantage
RMSA	Rashtriya Madhyamik Shiksha Abhiyan
RP JMN 2010-14	Indonesia's National Medium-Term Development Plan
RP JPN 2005-25	Indonesia's National Long-Term Development Plan
RTA	Regional Trade Arrangement
RTE	Right to Free Education
SBV	State Bank of Vietnam
SC	Scheduled caste
SEDP	Socio-Economic Development Plan
SEDS	Socio-Economic Development Strategy
SITC	Standard International Trade Classification
SLM	Sustainable Land Management
SMEs	Small and medium-sized enterprises
SOCB	State-Owned Commercial Bank
SOE	State-owned enterprise
ST	Scheduled tribe
Stranas PPK	Indonesian National Strategy to Prevent and Eradicate Corruption
THB	Thailand Baht
TMS	Target Management System
TNP2K	National Team for the Acceleration of Poverty Reduction
TSeKaP	Tamang Serbisyong Kalusugang Pampamilya
TVET	Technical vocational education and training
UN	United Nations
UNCTAD	United Nations Conference on Trade and Development
UNDP	United Nations Development Programme
UNESCAP	United Nations Economic and Social Commission for Asia and the Pacific
UNFCCC	United Nations Framework Convention on Climate Change
UNSO	United Nations Statistical Office
UNWTO	United Nations World Tourism Organization
USD	United States Dollar
VAS	Vietnamese Accounting Standard
VAT	Value-Added Tax
VNEN	Vietnam Escuela Nueva
WB-IEG	World Bank Independent Evaluation Group
WEF	World Economic Forum
WEO	World Economic Outlook
WGI	World Governance Indicator
WIPO	World Intellectual Property Organization
WTO	World Trade Organization

Editorial

Growth in Emerging Asia – Southeast Asia, China and India – is expected, in general, to remain strong over the medium term as these economies continue to shift from a reliance on exports to a broader base of new growth drivers. This rebalancing will boost consumption and investment and is helping the region to adjust to changing international conditions. While monetary policy normalisation in the United States has some worried, other risks persist. The prospect of continued slowing growth in China and the advanced economies, along with increased competition in export manufacturing among emerging economies, poses a serious threat to the export-led growth model. The implementation of "Abenomics" reforms will also be felt in the region's economies with close trade and investment links to Japan.

More fundamental reforms are needed to support sustainable and resilient growth, however. This 2015 edition of the *Economic Outlook for Southeast Asia, China and India* highlights the central role of public-sector institutional capacities in fostering development. I believe that this topic highlights an issue of great importance throughout the region, particularly as these economies look for ways to implement the deep reforms needed to adjust to new development strategies. Nevertheless, the challenges faced in improving institutions are diverse; fiscal management, bureaucratic efficiency and corruption are among the major issues that have to be addressed.

This edition of the Outlook discusses the multifaceted issue of institutional capacity in terms of current performance in implementing plans, Emerging Asia's experiences in building the institutions that underpin markets and help address informality, and lessons learned from past reform efforts. Evaluating the progress made in achieving national development plan targets offers new ways of looking at the region's institutional capacities, in terms of how well governments set and fulfil the goals to which they have committed. While most countries express their priorities well, performance in turning these targets into results has varied greatly between countries and between policy areas within countries. Shortcomings therefore highlight issues that may be deserving of greater attention. Similarly, Emerging Asia has had varied success in building the institutions on which markets rely – such as the rule of law and contract enforcement – and in enforcing tax and regulatory demands on the private sector; areas of potential weakness that will need to be addressed to limit informality and encourage the expansion of flexible formal markets.

The creation of strong institutions is rarely a straightforward task, however. Governments that recognise the importance of improving their own capacities to develop and implement policy may be impeded in pursuing reform by that very lack of capacity or by entrenched interests in the public sector. The lessons learned from past reforms in the region discussed in this Outlook help to illustrate the importance of comprehensive, well-designed and appropriately paced reforms. At the same time, this discussion recognises the limits of good design in overcoming contextual factors, offering a valuable reminder of the interconnectedness of institutions and political and economic development.

In exploring these topics and related policy options, I am hopeful that this edition of the Outlook will, like past editions, encourage a better understanding of, and provoke fruitful discussion on, the development of the Emerging Asian economies.

Mario Pezzini

Director

OECD Development Centre

Executive summary

Key findings

Growth prospects look favourable overall in Emerging Asia (Southeast Asia, China and India) over the medium term. Gross domestic product (GDP) growth in the region is forecast to average 6.5% per year over 2015-19. Although growth in Emerging Asia will moderate gradually due to the slowdown in China, for the ten ASEAN countries as a whole, growth momentum remains robust and broadly similar to that of the past ten years, averaging 5.6% over 2015-19.

The large ASEAN-5 economies – Indonesia, Malaysia, the Philippines, Thailand and Viet Nam – will sustain their growth momentum in the medium term, led particularly by Indonesia and the Philippines with an average annual growth of 6.0% and 6.2% respectively, over 2015-19. Stable economic prospects are also foreseen for Brunei Darussalam and Singapore. Cambodia, Lao PDR and Myanmar (CLM) should see more rapid growth exceeding 7% over the next five years. Improvements in the agricultural sector and the business environment will also be engines of growth in these countries.

China and India face significant challenges: China's growth is slowing (6.8% over 2015-19, compared with 8.2% over 2011-13) as it seeks to adjust to an ageing population, switches its growth focus from investment to consumption, and copes with agricultural, environmental and educational issues. India's growth should be stable over 2015-19 (6.7% compared with 5.5% over 2011-13), but this could change as the new government carries out ambitious plans for investment and reform.

External and domestic risks remain. Potential external risks include changes to US monetary policy, the Chinese economic slowdown, structural policy changes in Japan, and growth prospects in the euro area. However, these factors will have only a moderate impact on the region (as of November 2014). Domestic political risks include those related to the newly elected governments in India and Indonesia, and the current unrest in Thailand.

Further acceleration of regional integration towards the goal of the ASEAN Economic Community by 2015 is essential. Growth depends on the success of key regional initiatives, such as reducing the Common Effective Preferential Tariffs and improving trade facilitation, accelerating the development of institutional arrangements like investment frameworks, deeper financial integration, education, infrastructure and greater progress on narrowing regional disparities. Integration should also address a broader range of issues in future, including topics like the environment and green growth.

Main policy messages

Improved government capacity is needed to achieve policy goals more consistently. Medium-term development plans can be valuable tools to help governments guide and co-ordinate their policies in pursuit of strategic goals and to signal these intentions to the private sector and other domestic and international actors. Technical expertise, appropriate budgeting systems, inter-ministry co-operation and strong statistical systems are essential for the effective design and implementation of such plans.

National plans need to be improved. This Outlook includes country case studies on medium-term development plans for the large ASEAN-5 countries, plus Myanmar, China and India. While these countries are focussing on appropriate priority areas for their development, actual performance with respect to plan targets has been uneven. In many cases, reforms to improve competitiveness, education and inclusive and sustainable growth are in particular need of greater attention.

Policy lessons from public sector reform

Emerging Asian economies have undertaken a wide range of public sector reforms in recent decades, with varying levels of success. Further reform is needed. Public spending management systems and tax administrations are more advanced in middle-income countries like China and India than in the lower-income countries in ASEAN, but are still less advanced than in OECD countries. Corruption remains a significant concern, particularly in the CLM countries.

Experiences in Emerging Asia do not provide any magic bullets for ensuring that public sector reforms are effective but they do suggest some guidelines that should help to increase the prospects of success:

- Public sector reforms must be carefully adapted to existing institutional capacities and evolve as local circumstances change.
- The pacing of reform is important. Starting a public sector reform programme with a few relatively easy to implement measures with high short-term pay-offs can help to improve the credibility of the overall programme and provide lessons for implementing the subsequent and potentially more difficult steps.
- On-going commitment to public sector reform from the highest level of political leadership is essential.
- Public sector reform is likely to make more rapid and ultimately greater progress when the concerns of key stakeholders are taken into account.

Reducing the informal sector to boost growth

The informal sector is a barrier to growth and development. A significant informal sector is quite common in Emerging Asia's lower-income economies with weaker institutional capacity. Although informality appears to be declining across the region with continued development, it remains a barrier to growth as it limits the reach of government and lowers productivity levels.

Policy makers need to implement comprehensive solutions that reduce harmful informal activity without affecting the livelihoods of the poor and marginalised workers who depend on informal income sources. Four policy areas are particularly important in this regard:

- Institutional and judicial reforms are needed in several countries to address shortcomings in areas like contract enforcement and protection of property rights that help to make the formal sector more attractive.
- Support for small and medium enterprise (SME) development can be helpful, as informal firms tend to be small and this sector has great potential to contribute to growth. Providing expanded access to training and finance for these firms can help to encourage them to operate formally and to improve their productivity.

- Tax and regulatory reform may also be needed where excessive burdens on the private sector push workers and employers into the informal sector. This may include restructured tax systems and reduced administrative barriers, particularly for new and small firms.
- Targeted enforcement and, possibly, concessions for sectors with high levels of informality should be carefully considered. Such targeted strategies could seek to simultaneously formalise firms, suppliers, customers and even lenders from the informal financial sector.

Main findings and policy recommendations

While the growth prospects of the OECD countries continue to moderate, they look favourable overall in the 12 Emerging Asian economies (i.e. ASEAN-10, China and India) for 2015-19, averaging 6.5% per year, according to this Outlook's Medium-term Projection Framework (MPF-2015). Although growth in Emerging Asia will moderate gradually due to the slowdown in China, for the ten ASEAN countries as a whole, growth momentum remains robust and broadly similar to the past ten years, averaging 5.6% in 2015-19. The year 2014 saw major transformations in the region's political landscape, with economies being impacted differently. Indonesia's presidential election brought Joko Widodo to power, while India's general election ushered in Narendra Modi as the new Prime Minister. The electoral processes in both countries were widely regarded as successful, peaceful changes of government. However, territorial disputes over the sovereignty of the South China Sea affected tourism and exports in some countries, while political unrest in Thailand has had relatively strong economic impacts

Table 1. **Real GDP growth of Southeast Asia, China and India**

Annual percentage change

Country	2013	2019	2003-07	2011-13	2015-19
ASEAN-10 countries					
ASEAN-5 countries					
Indonesia	5.8	6.3	5.5	6.2	6.0
Malaysia	4.7	5.6	6.0	5.2	5.6
Philippines	7.2	6.3	5.7	5.9	6.2
Thailand	2.9	4.6	5.6	3.2	4.1
Viet Nam	5.4	5.8	7.2	5.6	5.7
Brunei Darussalam	-1.8	1.9	1.7	0.9	1.6
Cambodia	7.5	7.3	10.6	7.3	7.1
Lao PDR	8.0	7.7	7.1	8.1	7.6
Myanmar	7.5	7.8	-	6.9	7.8
Singapore	3.9	3.6	7.9	4.1	3.5
Two large economies in the region					
China	7.7	6.6	11.7	8.2	6.8
India	5.0	6.8	8.8	5.5	6.7
Average of ASEAN-10 countries	5.2	5.8	5.9	5.4	5.6
Average of Emerging Asia	6.5	6.5	9.5	7.0	6.5

Notes: The cut-off date of data is 6 October 2014. Emerging Asia denotes ASEAN-10 countries plus China and India. ASEAN-5 includes Indonesia, Malaysia, the Philippines, Thailand and Viet Nam.

Source: OECD Development Centre, MPF-2015 (Medium-term Projection Framework). For more information on MPF, please see www.oecd.org/dev/asiapacific/mpf.

Individual countries' growth paths point in different directions. The large **ASEAN-5** economies – Indonesia, Malaysia, the Philippines, Thailand and Viet Nam – will sustain their growth momentum in the medium term, led by **Indonesia** and **the Philippines** (averaging 6.0% and 6.2% annually, respectively). Indonesia's economy will be supported by robust domestic demand and expectations of reform – with the Widodo administration possibly rationalising the fuel subsidy. Another economy driven by domestic demand, strongly supported by remittances from overseas and political stability is the Philippines, where growth is expected to be favourable in the medium term. The success of measures to create jobs, reduce unemployment and improve infrastructure will be key to its sustained growth.

Malaysia's vigorous domestic demand, supported by the rise of the middle class and the growing export-oriented sector, will remain resilient despite still weak demand in the OECD economies. Political unrest in **Thailand** adversely affects growth prospects in the near term, as consumer and investor confidence and the country's trade performance weaken amid uncertainty related to the new economic roadmap. With declining but long-lasting high inflationary pressures, **Viet Nam** could enjoy stable economic growth in the medium term, although risk remains in the banking sector.

Economic growth prospects are mostly stable for **Brunei Darussalam** and **Singapore**. Brunei's growth performance will depend on the energy sector and the volatility of oil and gas prices, however, while smooth economic transformation in healthcare and social services and effective land use will be challenges for the Singaporean economy.

More rapid growth is expected for the **CLM** countries (Cambodia, Lao PDR, and Myanmar) than for the ASEAN-5. Their annual growth is slated to exceed 7% over the next five years. Improvement in the agriculture sector and the business environment will be engines of the growth of **Cambodia** and **Lao PDR**. As for **Myanmar**, it has seen rapid progress in many areas, which will keep it on a favourable path in the medium term. The performance of the new CLM growth engine in Emerging Asia will also affect the speed of the ASEAN integration initiative.

The region's two largest economies, **China** and **India**, face significant challenges. China's growth is slowing as it seeks to adjust to its changing demographic landscape, switch its hub of growth from investment to consumption, and cope with environmental, agricultural and educational issues. India's growth should be stable over 2015-19, but these prospects could change depending on the implementation of the reforms of the new Modi government. These plans include promoting domestic and foreign investment, creating jobs, improving food security, raising the standards of education and skills development, building new key infrastructure, enhancing water governance and increasing India's overall competitiveness, particularly in the manufacturing sector.

The key points of the medium-term economic outlook are as follows:

- Despite slight moderation in the first quarter of this year, growth in Emerging Asia should remain robust, at 6.5% over 2015-19. The Chinese economy is slowing, but the large ASEAN economies are showing resilience and growth momentum remains broadly similar to the past ten years (5.6% over 2015-19). The CLM countries are expected to become the new centres of growth in ASEAN, with average annual growth in each exceeding 7%.
- Overall, current account imbalances are gradually improving, particularly in the ASEAN-5. The CLM countries will continue to show deficits in the medium term. There are signs that foreign direct investment (FDI) is slowing in the region. Additional efforts to attract and retain investors will be required.
- Generally speaking, there will be no dramatic changes in fiscal conditions, though trends will differ by country. While fiscal balances in Malaysia and the Philippines may improve, those in Thailand and Viet Nam will worsen in the medium term. Overall, fiscal reforms need to be strengthened further in the region.
- Emerging Asian countries may have to contend with external risks. For instance, the normalisation of US monetary policy, the slowdown in the Chinese economy, the implementation of structural policies related to "Abenomics" in Japan and uncertainties concerning the growth prospects of the euro area. However, the impact of these factors on the region will be moderate, since markets have already factored these changes in their expectations (as of November 2014). Transformations

in the political landscape will affect different countries in different ways. There are worries over the current political unrest in Thailand in particular. Overall, effective capital flow management (of both inflows and outflows) will remain a challenge in the region in the medium term.

- Further acceleration of regional integration by 2015, in furtherance of the goal of the ASEAN Economic Community (AEC), will be necessary – particularly to narrow disparities within the region.

Challenges of regional integration

The medium-term outlook for Emerging Asia could be less favourable than the projections imply for a number of reasons concerning not only the success of the countries themselves in their national economic policies, but the success of key regional initiatives towards the goal of the ASEAN Economic Community.

- A notable achievement is the reduction of tariffs, which has supported the steady increase in intra-regional trade. The current Common Effective Preferential Tariffs (CEPT) rates are close to 0% for advanced ASEAN economies, though slightly higher rates of 2.6% are applied by Cambodia, Myanmar, Lao PDR and Viet Nam (Figures 1 and 2). Trade facilitation is also being strengthened through the implementation of National Single Windows (NSWs) and their streamlining and integration to develop the ASEAN Single Window as a single platform for electronic trade. Although improvements have been made in trade facilitation initiatives, there is still a wide disparity within ASEAN.
- Institutional arrangements for regional integration have gradually been established recently, though there is still room to accelerate this progress overall. On the free flow of investment, the ASEAN Comprehensive Investment Agreement (ACIA), which came into effect in 2012 and built upon the past two ASEAN investment frameworks – the ASEAN Investment Area Agreement (AIA) and the Investment Guarantee Agreement (IGA) – lays out the rules for investment to enhance the business environment and to attract more domestic and international investment.
- Financial integration under the Roadmap for the Integration of ASEAN in Finance is crucial to achieve the goal of the AEC. Capital market development has been advanced with the launch of the marketing and branding campaign for the ASEAN Exchanges initiative and the development of an ASEAN Bond Market Development Scorecard. To strengthen the integration of the banking sector, two frameworks for the banking sector integration are in place: the ASEAN Framework Agreement on Services (AFAS) and the ASEAN Banking Integration Framework, which compliments the AFAS. In addition, the multilateral currency swap arrangement among the ASEAN+3 (China, Japan and Korea) countries through the recently amended Chiang Mai Initiative Multilateralisation (CMIM), of which the total size amounted to an enlarged USD 240 billion, with the IMF de-linked portion raised to 30%, will strengthen the region's ability to respond to liquidity problems in times of urgency.
- Progress in the implementation of programmes related to narrowing disparities in the region needs to be accelerated. In particular, greater efforts will be required on information and communication technology (ICT), education and infrastructure. Higher education could improve through the strengthening of the ASEAN University Network (AUN) and, overall, quality of education in ASEAN countries could be emphasised further. There will be room to speed up the implementation of large-scale infrastructure projects, such as the ASEAN Highway Network (AHN)

programme. Integration should also continue with a broader range of issues addressed, including topics like environmental protection that have so far been mostly left aside.

Figure 1. **Average of the Common Effective Preferential Tariff rates for ASEAN**

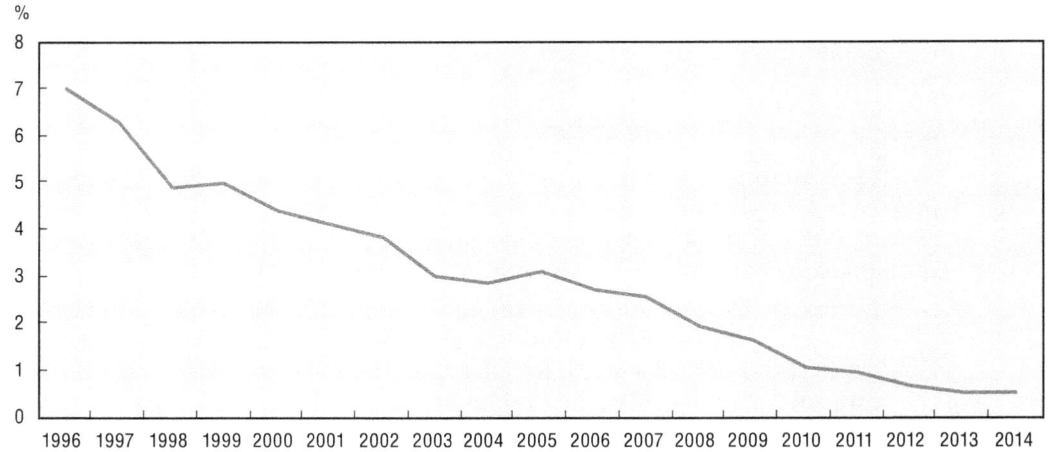

Source: ASEAN Secretariat.
StatLink http://dx.doi.org/10.1787/888933179295

Figure 2. **Share of intra-regional trade as percentage of total trade**

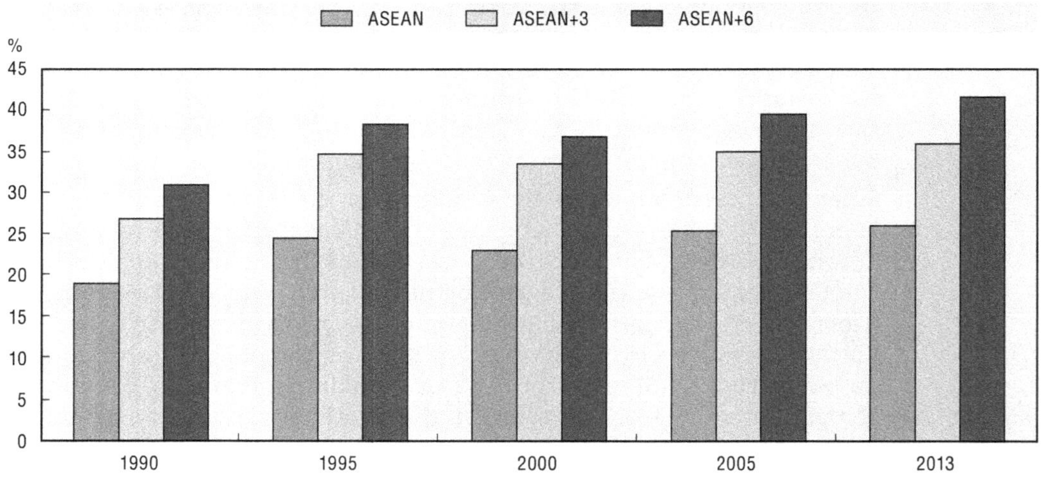

Note: ASEAN+3 includes ASEAN-10 countries plus China, Japan and Korea. ASEAN+6 includes ASEAN+3 plus Australia, India and New Zealand
Source: CEIC, OECD Development Centre calculations.
StatLink http://dx.doi.org/10.1787/888933179309

Institutions for effective policy implementation: What are the barriers to achieving medium-term plan targets?

Institutional capacity is needed to design and implement national development plans

Medium-term development plans can be valuable tools for governments looking to guide and co-ordinate their own policies in pursuit of strategic goals and to signal these intentions to the private sector and other domestic and international actors. They can cover a wide range of development goals and policy areas, from growth and macroeconomic stablility to inclusiveness, sustainability and well-being. Despite their widespread use in Emerging Asia and around the world and the need for these plans to remain credible, however, targets are sometimes unrealised. This can be the result of contextual and political factors but also of institutional weakness in plan design and implementation, reflecting poor data availability, the lack of skilled staff, barriers to inter-ministry co-operation, and disconnection between planning and budgeting. The achievement of plans' targets therefore offers a useful way of measuring governments' institutional capacities in broad terms.

Capacity is needed throughout the planning process to produce relevant, reasonable and ambitious targets and to ensure their timely implementation (Figure 3). The designing of plans also needs to balance inclusiveness with technical expertise. The leadership and expertise of officials in agencies in charge of producing plans may have to weigh competing costs and benefits against each other when trying to determine what constitutes the public good. Planning requires these agencies to have – or have access to – strong technical capacities. Budgeting strategies may also be needed to manage multiple projects, because successfully implementing development plans is largely dependent on matching programmes of work with appropriate funding. As line ministries tend to be less concerned about their overall budget impacts, budgeting strategies can offset their tendency to propose too many projects and make large expenditure requests, which could otherwise lead to unsustainable deficits, poor resource allocation, and inefficient spending on public goods and services.

Figure 3. **The planning process comprises design, implementation and evaluation**

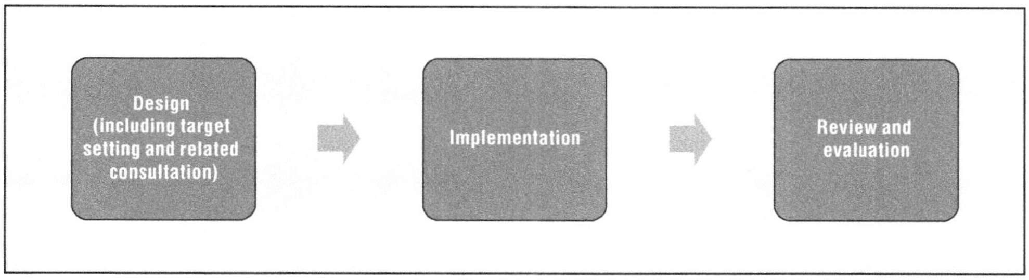

Source: OECD Development Centre.

Effective planning also relies on broader institutional capacities across government. Reliable statistics are needed where targets are quantified to establish baselines and historical trends and, as the plan is put in place, to monitor on-going and final progress. Additionally, the targets established by medium-term plans may often be unfeasible because they are disconnected from annual budgets which, unlike development plans, are binding on government. Reconciling planning and budgeting over annual and medium-term timeframes may be facilitated through medium-term budgetary frameworks (MTBFs) which use projected expenditure for guidance in preparing annual budgets. Most Emerging Asian economies use MTBFs – or the related medium-term fiscal frameworks (MTFFs) and medium-term performance frameworks (MTPFs).

After the plan is set and assuming that the government is in fact committed to it, the government becomes responsible for implementing the plan and striving to meet its targets. However, this process is complicated by the multiple actors involved and the limited resources available to them. Public expenditure management (PEM) systems are a useful tool to facilitate the supervision of line ministries. Supervision may be carried out directly by the ministry of finance, either *ex ante* or *ex post*. Whatever the approach, mismanagement may be dealt with through internal disciplinary action or, in cases of corruption, through the courts. Co-ordination and management in plan implementation are not only the responsibilities of the ministry of finance and other central agencies; these organisational responsibilities are also needed to direct cross-ministry co-operation and within-ministry operations. There must consequently be effective co-ordination between central agencies and line ministries, between ministries, and within them. Capable and motivated staff and flexible institutions are then needed to implement plans.

The implementation of development plans in Emerging Asia can be improved

This *Outlook* includes country case studies on medium-term development plan targets and implementation for the large ASEAN-5 countries (Indonesia, Malaysia, the Philippines, Thailand and Viet Nam), Myanmar, China and India. Each study summarises the key targets set in the country's current plan, the original status of these indicators and progress made thus far toward the targets. The targets themselves and the patterns in the achievement of these targets are discussed in terms of their implications for the country's development and for where greater attention may need to be paid by governments (Table 2). While countries are paying attention to the areas that should be priorities for their development, actual performance with respect to plan targets has been uneven across countries and across policy areas within countries. The recognition of areas of relative weakness may be used to help identify where targets can be rethought or where greater implementation efforts are needed.

Indonesia is near the end of the period of its *2010-14 National Medium-term Development Plan*, which aims to create a prosperous, just and democratic country through reforms in the areas of macroeconomic growth and stability, poverty reduction, education, health, food production, energy production and distribution, infrastructure development and good governance. Overall, the country is making good progress towards its targets, particularly in macroeconomic performance and junior high school enrolment.

A number of important gaps remain, however. Progress toward goals for health outcomes in Indonesia has been particularly weak and has even worsened in some cases. Poverty rates remain high in some areas and inequalities are not being adequately addressed (Figure 4). While continued growth requires the expansion of knowledge-based industries, access to advanced education remains low. Greater investment in and attention to infrastructure development and anti-corruption will also be needed to continue to attract investment and encourage the growth of new businesses.

The *Tenth* ***Malaysia*** *Plan* (2011-15) focuses on growing to a high-income economy while ensuring inclusiveness and sustainability. It aims to achieve this through the fulfilment of targets in balanced economic growth, efficient fiscal policy, the development of key sectors and small and medium-sized enterprises (SMEs), the reduction of poverty and inequalities, and reforms of labour markets and education and healthcare systems. Growth rates are strong and investment rates exceed targeted levels, but there is still room for making the productivity improvements that will be needed for Malaysia to become a high-income country. SMEs have a greater role to play in this transition, as do new industries that will need to develop further, such as ICT. At the same time, fiscal stability can be improved through reduced reliance on oil and gas revenue and the introduction of new revenue-raising tools, such as a goods and services tax (GST).

Table 2. **Policy challenges in implementing national plans in Emerging Asia**

Country	Policy focus
ASEAN countries	
Indonesia	The widest gaps are found in the area of health. Improving access to and the quality of health services, especially for mothers and children, is crucial. Coverage of the newly implemented health insurance scheme should also be expanded.
	Further efforts are required in order to improve the education system, particularly in access to secondary and tertiary education for students from low-income households.
	The national plan is not addressing growing inequality adequately.
Malaysia	Further improvements in productivity are needed to support sustainable economic growth and transform Malaysia into a high-income, developed nation.
	Further development of ICT, which is particularly important for supporting growth, is required.
	Fiscal stability should also be enhanced and dependence on oil reduced. The successful introduction of GST is important for improved tax performance.
Myanmar	Reliable indicators, quantifiable goals and measurements of government performance are necessary for effective planning and monitoring, particularly in the areas of regulatory reform and public finance.
	Policy planning and budgeting – including appropriate financial support in agriculture and education – should be developed.
	Co-operation with the private sector through public-private partnerships (PPPs) and setting up new businesses, and with civil society is an important part of Myanmar's on-going transition.
Philippines	To sustain economic growth, the Philippines needs to step up its competitiveness through quality employment and increase value added through innovation.
	A responsive, inclusive, development-oriented financial system must be built as a platform for the efficient management and mobilisation of resources.
	Social development must be further improved to ensure equal opportunity so that Filipinos may find decent jobs, acquire assets and lift their living standards.
Thailand	To ensure sustainable economic growth and enhance competitiveness, Thailand must accelerate its progress towards meeting certain targets and improve its productivity.
	The country should, in particular, make further efforts in environmental management in order to support green growth.
	Improving good governance – with particular emphasis on corruption and transparency – needs more effort to reduce obstacles to growth.
Viet Nam	Maintaining stability in key economic and social indicators is a priority for implementing socio-economic strategies.
	Addressing implementation gaps in the development of high-tech industries and skills training is essential not only to meeting the goals of the medium-term plan, but also to realising the 2020 vision of a modern, industrialised Viet Nam.
The two large economies in Emerging Asia	
China	Environmental degradation remains a major issue despite the country's efforts in reducing pollution. Further efforts are needed to increase consumers' access to clean energy.
	Rural and agriculture development could help promote urban-rural social equality.
	Continued improvements in education are required. Reforms are also needed to support the development of the services sector, which has the potential to help drive future growth.
India	De-industrialisation needs to be addressed. Manufacturing has been slowing down in the last few years and even showed negative growth in 2013-14.
	Access to secondary education needs to be widened to achieve the goal of universal secondary education by 2017.
	The public health system needs to be strengthened. Access to both curative and preventive healthcare facilities needs to improve.
	Accelerating the development of infrastructure is crucial, especially in rural areas.

Source: OECD Development Centre.

Figure 4. **Inequality in Indonesia and selected provinces, 2008-13**

Gini coefficient

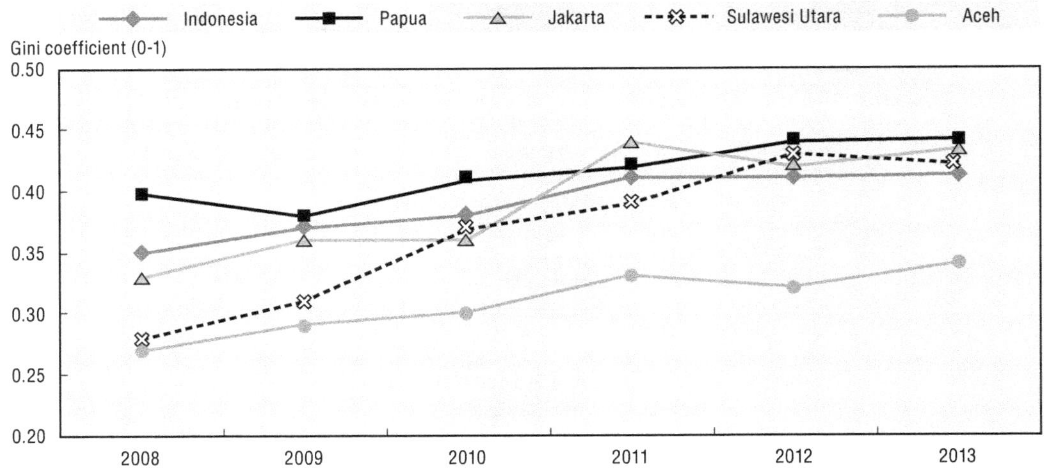

Source: Statistics Indonesia, Badan Pusat Statistik (BPS).

StatLink http://dx.doi.org/10.1787/888933179319

Myanmar's *Framework for Social and Economic Reforms* outlines transitional priorities for 2012-15 to help act as a bridge for the new government from the previous five-year plan. It prioritises necessary and achievable reforms in economic development, regulation and governance, the provision of public services and infrastructure development. These targets are less clearly defined than in other countries and more challenging to track, as reliable indicators are often not available in Myanmar. However, progress is being made in economic reforms to open space for the private sector and developing infrastructure. Progress is also being made in implementing programmes to assist agriculture and improve access to education, though it is unclear whether these projects target the areas of greatest need. The regulation of the financial sector and transparency of public finances are in particular need of more attention, as is the development of better government relationships with the private sector and civil society.

The ***Philippine** Development Plan*, 2011-16 aims to foster inclusive and sustainable growth through progress toward targets on macroeconomic stability, sectoral competitiveness, financial system resiliency and inclusiveness, social development (i.e. improved health, education, housing and social programmes and outcomes), crime reduction, and environmental protection. Overall, economic performance during the plan's period has been strong, though the same progress has not been made in improving inclusiveness.

Increased competitiveness is critical for the Philippines' continued growth and job creation, but more effort is needed to bring about change in the key sectors for this transformation. Tourism and SMEs hold great potential for driving future growth, but appear to be under-performing. A resilient and accessible financial system is also critical, but has been slow to improve its inclusiveness. While the services sector is expanding, further innovation here and in manufacturing will lay the basis for a high-tech economy. Serious barriers in access to education and health hinder human capital development and fail to address the root causes of inequality (Figure 5).

Figure 5. **Elementary and secondary enrolment rates in the Philippines, 2008-09 to 2012-13**

Number of students and annual growth rates

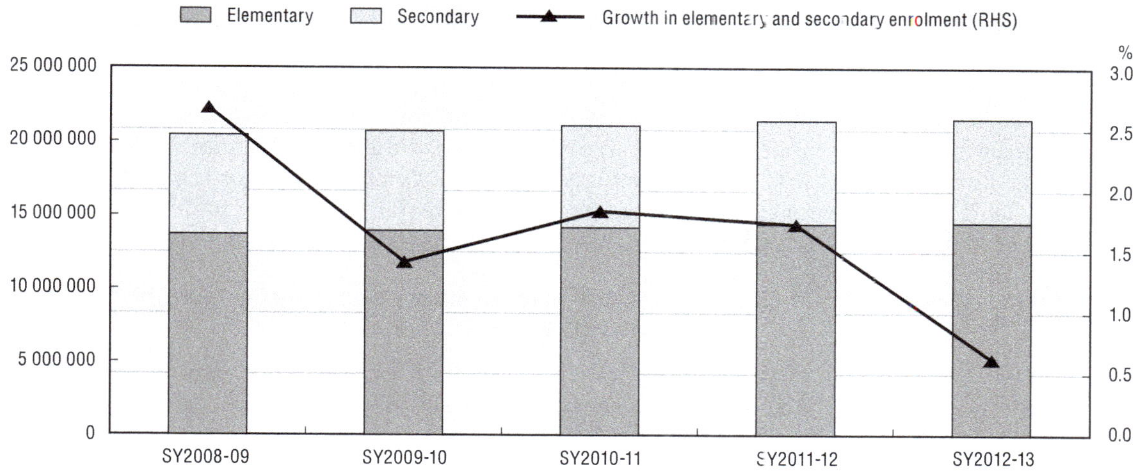

Source: National Statistics Office, Department of Education, Philippines.
StatLink http://dx.doi.org/10.1787/888933179328

Thailand's *Eleventh National Economic and Social Development Plan* (2012-16) is intended to support inclusiveness and innovation-led growth in the country. The plan's targets focus on inclusive and broad-based growth, education and other areas of human development, food and energy security, increased innovation and growth, trade and investment, and environmental protection. Thailand is on track to meet or exceed macroeconomic targets for growth and inflation, even if other economic performance targets are unlikely to be met. While alternative and renewable energy production is increasing, fast-rising energy demand has left the country's dependence on fossil fuels unchanged or worse than before the plan began (Figure 6). New strategies are needed to meet these challenges, foster creative and research-based industries, and reduce corruption to facilitate innovation-led growth in Thailand.

Figure 6. **Final energy consumption expenditure by energy source in Thailand, 2008-12**

THB million

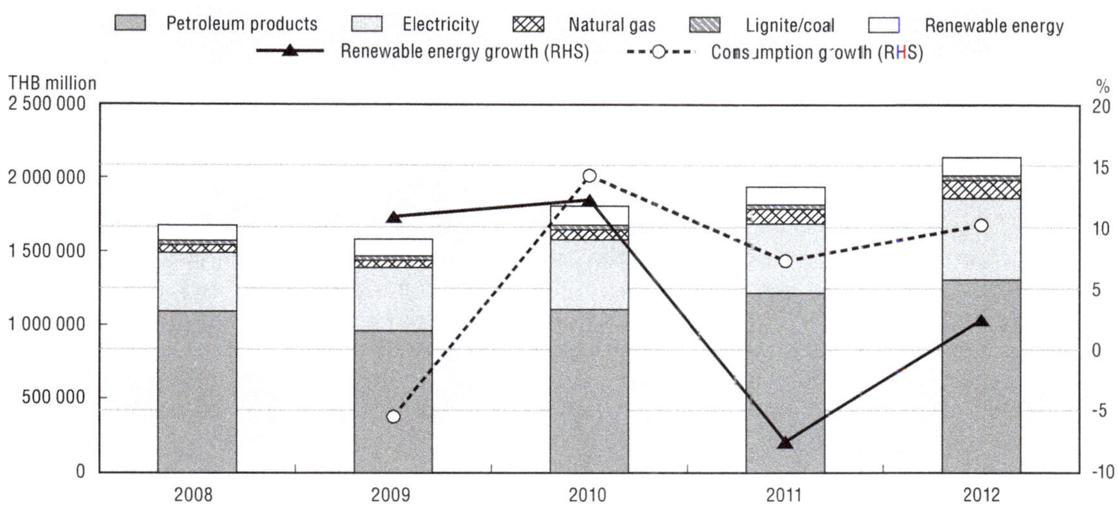

Source: PTT, EGAT, DOEB and DEDE, compiled by Energy Policy and Planning Office (EPPO).
StatLink http://dx.doi.org/10.1787/888933179332

Viet Nam's *Socio-economic Development Plan* (2011-15) emphasises development through upgrading and improvements in efficiency and competitiveness through targets for overall and sectoral economic performance, social targets (e.g. regarding job creation and poverty reduction) and the implementation of environmental protections. GDP growth has been lower than targeted, but other economic targets, such as those regarding unemployment and social investment, are near or above target levels. Insufficient progress is being made by current approaches to a wide range of social challenges, such as alleviating rural poverty and expanding access to technical training and education. The need for improved banking governance amid rising levels of bad debt is another serious challenge that needs to be addressed to support continued development (Figure 7).

Figure 7. **Domestic credit to the private sector and non-performing loans in Viet Nam, 2004-13**

Domestic credit as percentage of GDP and non-performing loans as percentages of total loans

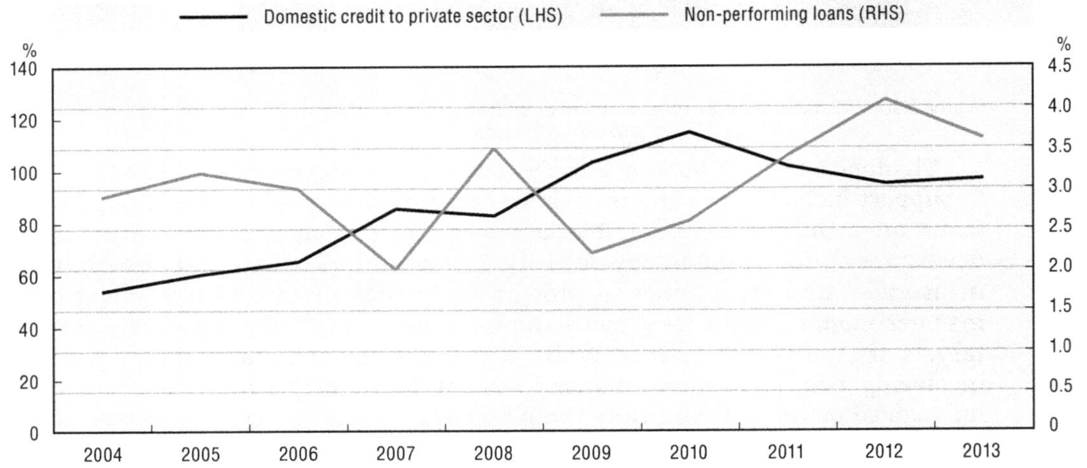

Note: Domestic credit figures represent annual averages, while NPL ratios represent monthly averages from December in the respective year.
Sources: World Bank (2014), *World Development Indicators*, World Bank, Washington, DC; State Bank of Vietnam (2014), *Statistics on the Performance of Credit Institutions*, State Bank of Vietnam, Hanoi, www.sbv.gov.vn.
StatLink http://dx.doi.org/10.1787/888933179346

The **Chinese** *Twelfth Five-Year Plan* (2011-15) addresses a range of issues related to rebalancing and promoting continued growth while ensuring inclusiveness and sustainability. It therefore targets progress in macroeconomic performance, economic restructuring, innovation, protecting the environment and reducing pollution, agriculture, and livelihoods and well-being. GDP growth is lower than that seen in China's recent past and greater effort is needed to address the quality of growth by improving environmental and social outcomes and fostering broad-based growth. While pollution is declining, it remains a major issue to address and more could be done on energy efficiency. The urban-rural divide comprises a large component of Chinese inequalities, necessitating improved rural and agricultural development. Generally, the services sector also has the potential to expand to improve the stability of growth and potential for continued innovation and productivity growth. The continued improvement of education systems will play an important role in supporting this expansion.

India's *Twelfth Five-Year Plan* (2012-17) sets out targets with the intention of improving sustainability and inclusiveness and quality of life in the country. Included targets focus on growth, poverty reduction and job creation, education, health, infrastructure development, and reduced emissions and improved environmental protection. Currently, well-being and the improvement in human capital are restrained by low levels of access to education and healthcare. Access to financial services is also low, particularly in rural areas. Infrastructure development and the expansion of renewable energy production are gradually progressing, suggesting that greater and alternative means of investment may be needed.

Lessons from experiences with public sector reforms in Emerging Asia

Emerging Asian countries have been actively engaged for several decades in reforms to improve the quality of their public sectors. These public sector reforms (PSRs) encompass public financial management (PFM) reforms to improve budgeting, expenditure implementation, and tax administration, as well as administrative reforms to streamline the organisation of government activities, decentralise functions to sub-national governments, strengthen the civil service and combat corruption.

Public sector reforms are motivated by the recognition that the effectiveness and efficiency of the public sector in managing its finances, implementing government programmes and delivering public services are critical to the success of overall development and the achievement of key development objectives. The rapid growth and profound transformation that Emerging Asia has undergone have made PSRs of special importance to the region. Public sector reforms can contribute to economic and social development in a number of ways, including by:

- improving the capacity of governments to effectively and efficiently carry out their policies;
- reducing costs and improving the overall efficiency of the business sector;
- improving the business climate through greater certainty about government policies and greater macroeconomic stability;
- increasing international competitiveness, particularly for FDI;
- strengthening the effectiveness of policies to reduce poverty and to achieve inclusive and green growth; and
- improving the credibility of the government and political processes and overall social cohesion.

Public sector reform has made significant progress in the region but much remains to be done

The experiences of developing countries, including those in Emerging Asia, underscore that public sector reforms are complex, long-term processes whose ultimate success is determined by broader institutional capacities and political economy factors. A recent study of PSR in developing countries found that civil service reforms and anti-corruption reforms improved performance in less than half and barely more than half, respectively, of World Bank-supported programmes in these areas. Outcomes were somewhat better for public financial management reforms but even in these cases major improvements occurred in only one-third of the programmes. These mixed outcomes demonstrate that PSRs are difficult processes and raise the question: what makes them more or less successful?

PSRs have made substantial progress in Southeast Asia, China and India, but a range of indicators of public sector performance highlight the need for further efforts. These countries rank noticeably below OECD countries on the *Government Effectiveness Index* produced by the World Bank – a composite measure of public perceptions from a wide range of sources of the quality of public services and the civil service, the effectiveness of policy formulation and implementation, and the credibility of the government in carrying out its policies (Figure 8). Higher-income countries usually, although not always, outperform their lower-income neighbours. This pattern reflects a broader tendency for the overall quality of public governance to be positively correlated with countries' level of development.

Figure 8. **Indicators of overall governance in selected countries, 2012**

Government Effectiveness Index percentile rankings

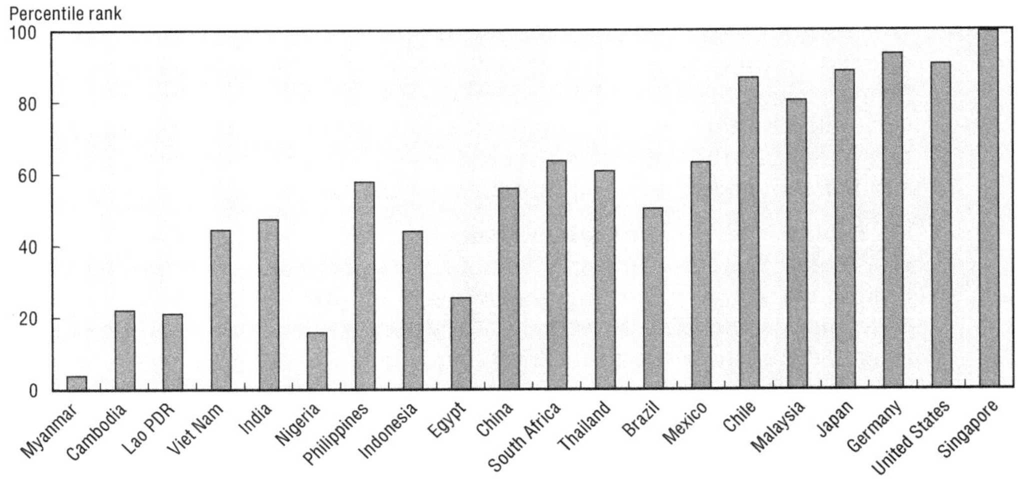

Notes: The figure shows percentile rankings among all countries (ranging from 0 [lowest] to 100 [highest]). Countries are arranged from lowest to highest *per capita* income at purchasing power parities. Ranking reflects perceptions of the quality of public services, the quality of the civil service and the degree of its independence from political pressures, the quality of policy formulation and implementation, and the credibility of the government's commitment to such policies.

Source: World Bank (2014), *World Governance Indicators* (database), World Bank, Washington, DC.

StatLink http://dx.doi.org/10.1787/888933179354

Indicators for specific aspects of public sector performance show a similar pattern. Public expenditure management systems and tax administrations are more advanced in middle-income countries like China and India than in the lower-income countries in ASEAN, but still less advanced than in OECD countries. Except for Malaysia, results-based budgeting has either not yet been instituted or is at a very early stage of development. Tax administrations in the majority of countries are at least partially organised along functional lines but only about half have instituted separate units for large taxpayers. The cost to businesses and time required to comply with tax obligations is significantly higher in the region compared to more advanced countries.

Corruption remains a significant concern. International surveys indicate that corruption in the region is both rampant and extensive. Both the Transparency International Corruption Perceptions Index, based on extensive surveys of members of the public in the individual countries, and the corruption components of the World Economic Forum's *Global Competiveness Indicators*, drawn from surveys of business executives, place most Emerging Asian countries in the bottom half of their rankings. Corruption is overall most severe in the CLM countries but still bad in the other countries, although somewhat less so in China and Malaysia. Moreover, there has been at best limited improvement in corruption perceptions since the mid-1990s, although somewhat more in China and Indonesia. Corruption in most Emerging Asian countries extends beyond the core government actors of civil service and politicians (Table 3).

Table 3. **Corruption perceptions by sector in Emerging Asia**

Percentage of survey respondents who think of national institutions as "corrupt" or "extremely corrupt", 2013

Percentage of those surveyed believing sector is corrupt or highly corrupt	Political parties	Parliament/legislature	Judiciary	Police	Public officials/ civil servants
Cambodia	28	16	30	37	30
Indonesia	86	89	36	91	79
Malaysia	69	44	35	76	46
Philippines	58	52	56	69	64
Thailand	68	45	18	71	58
Viet Nam	27	28	53	72	55
India	86	65	45	75	65

Source: Transparency International (2013), *Global Corruption Barometer 2013*, Transparency International, Berlin, http://www.transparency.org/research/gcb/overview.

Country experiences reveal that public sector reform is a complex and long-term evolutionary process

Emerging Asia has undertaken numerous public sector reforms since the 1970s in all major areas. The reforms have been driven and shaped by both domestic and external factors: globalisation and international agreements on trade and investment, the Asian financial crisis, and major political shifts have been particularly important drivers of the reforms. Overall, PSRs in Emerging Asia can be said to have made significant but uneven progress, with more success in some areas of reform and in some aspects of specific reforms than in others.

The experiences show that PSRs are best viewed as long-term evolutionary processes whose payoffs are usually limited in the near term. PSRs are complex undertakings whose design needs to be carefully tailored to and sequenced in line with institutional capacities in the government, the economy and society. Design matters greatly, although it is not sufficient for success by itself. Sustaining reforms until their main objectives have been achieved has proved to be much more difficult than initiating them. The benefits of PSR generally take a long time to be fully manifest and reforms need to be adapted as institutional capacities develop. Thus, reforms are best viewed as a series of measures over a longer period rather than as measures that are done once and then left alone.

A review of the experiences with PSR in Southeast Asia, China and India leads to a number of observations that provide insights into the circumstances under which they are likely to be most successful.

- First, sustained commitment by high-level political authorities and senior civil servants is very important, indeed often critical, to the success of PSRs. Sustained commitment is critical to gain the support of the public and stakeholders who may perceive threats to their interests and to ensure that the government bureaucracy effectively implements the reforms. This commitment is particularly essential for civil service and anti-corruption reforms to overcome the opposition of stakeholders within and outside the government who perceive threats to their interests.
- Second, PSRs seem to have been most successful and durable when they have become embedded in an institutional culture of reform where the long-term objectives are accepted among the political elite and the public and early stage reforms provide lessons and impetus for further action. In Malaysia, the on-going commitment to developing and refining results-oriented public sector management since the 1970s has helped to ensure continuity and focus in overall PSR efforts across successive

government administrations. Conversely, although economic and political upheavals in the region have often triggered PSRs by galvanising government, the public and outside actors to address the need for fundamental change, the window of opportunity they have created does not guarantee that reforms are sustained. In the Philippines, for example, successive attempts to reform the tax administration from the 1970s through the 1990s had very limited long-term benefits in large part because high level political support was uneven and not sustained.

- Third, strong constituencies for PSR outside the government have been a major force for the initiation of PSRs and, even more importantly, in ensuring that PSR is sustained. Foreign-invested businesses have been a major driver of PSRs throughout the region, especially of reforms to improve tax administration and to reduce corruption. Civil society and the general public can and often have been important in sustaining PSR initiatives. However, they are most likely to be actively engaged in supporting PSR when government policies are reasonably transparent and the legal/regulatory framework promotes strong accountability of the government to its citizens.
- Fourth, there are both advantages and disadvantages to incremental or partial reform as opposed to comprehensive change. Incremental reforms often gain acceptance more easily and do not have the high costs of failure associated with more comprehensive reforms, as they can also be adapted to unexpected changes in circumstances. However, incremental reforms do run the risk of being overtaken by rapid economic and social change. In China, the incremental approach has proven beneficial in some areas but it has led to recurring problems in fiscal decentralisation reform. Although consensus on the need for comprehensive reform may be harder to achieve and its implementation more challenging, it can bring longer-lasting and ultimately more effective solutions, at least in some areas.
- Finally, reforms that address the root causes of the problems are more likely to be effective and have durable benefits than those that do not. For example, opaque and excessive regulations, inadequate pay for civil servants, and poorly defined rules governing relations between government agencies and businesses create numerous opportunities and incentives for corrupt behaviour and have been an important factor behind the pervasive corruption in many developing countries. Anti-corruption reforms that focus only on legal and administrative enforcement are likely to meet with incomplete success until these root causes are addressed. Similarly, tax administration reforms to improve tax collection need to address not only outright evasion and avoidance but also the inadequate knowledge of tax obligations that is often common in developing countries.

A number of guidelines would help to improve the effectiveness of public sector reform

Experiences in Emerging Asia do not provide any magic bullets for ensuring that public sector reforms are effective but they do suggest some guidelines for designing and implementing reforms that should help to increase the prospects of their success.

- PSR measures need to be carefully adapted to existing institutional capacities. While there are useful models and best practices for PSR in some areas, these need to be adapted to local circumstances and to evolve as those circumstances change. For example, there are several kinds of medium-term budget frameworks, ranging from frameworks emphasising definition of and imposition of aggregate resource constraints in budgeting that are most suitable for countries in an early stage of development to more sophisticated frameworks, including results-oriented budgeting techniques.

- Where feasible, beginning a PSR programme with a few relatively easy to implement measures with high short-term payoffs can help to improve the credibility of the overall programme and provide lessons for implementation of subsequent and often more difficult steps. For example, the Indonesian tax administration reforms beginning in 1971 were divided into short-term and long-term phases, with the short-term phase focused on using existing capacities to improve tax collection and compliance in order to provide a near-term boost in revenues. The successes of these initial steps provided a foundation for subsequent reforms.
- On-going commitment to PSR from the highest level of political leadership is essential. Top leaders need to lead not only in instituting reforms but also to maintain pressure for their effective implementation. Unlike Indonesia's tax administration reforms, which benefitted from sustained political support, this was weaker for reforms in the Philippines, which contributed to a series of disappointing results.
- PSR implementation is likely to make more rapid and ultimately greater progress when the concerns of key stakeholders are taken into account. Active efforts by senior political leaders and civil servants to inform government staff about the need for and content of reforms can go a long way toward overcoming bureaucratic inertia and obstruction.

Strong and effective public support can make it much easier to initiate PSR measures and increase the likelihood for their success. Government transparency and accountability and a legal and regulatory environment allowing active participation by civil society are, however, likely to be necessary for such support.

Institutions and informality in Emerging Asia

Informal economic activity tends to be very important in the Emerging Asian economies

Informal firms and workers are found in all economies. The sheer extent of informality makes it a critical issue for policy makers to understand and address – particularly in economies like those found in Emerging Asia that are undergoing significant structural transformation. Informal activities are more likely to develop in such countries, with serious effects on growth and inclusiveness.

Institutions and institutional capacity are central to understanding the causes and consequences of informality and to developing formal alternatives. While informality may be difficult to define and has multiple overlapping causes, institutional factors are fundamental determinants of how prevalent informal output and employment are. Weak institutional capacity may, in turn, also be exacerbated by informality, as hidden activity lowers government revenue, its regulatory reach and its credibility. And although informality ensures the livelihoods of many, it harms growth and development when it replaces dynamic formal activities. Policies to address informality – which include strengthening institutional and enforcement capacities – are therefore needed to support resilient and inclusive growth.

Informal employment and output by informal firms are relatively common in a number of Emerging Asian economies, particularly the region's lower-income countries and those where institutional capacities are most seriously underdeveloped (Figures 9 and 10). Conversely, more developed Singapore and Malaysia tend to have much lower levels of informality. Indirect measures of informal employment and output over time also suggest that the shares of each in total economic activity are gradually declining across the region as these economies continue to grow and develop and as governance and institutional capacities are improved upon.

Figure 9. **Much of employment is informal across Emerging Asia**

Shares of total non-agricultural employment, by employment type

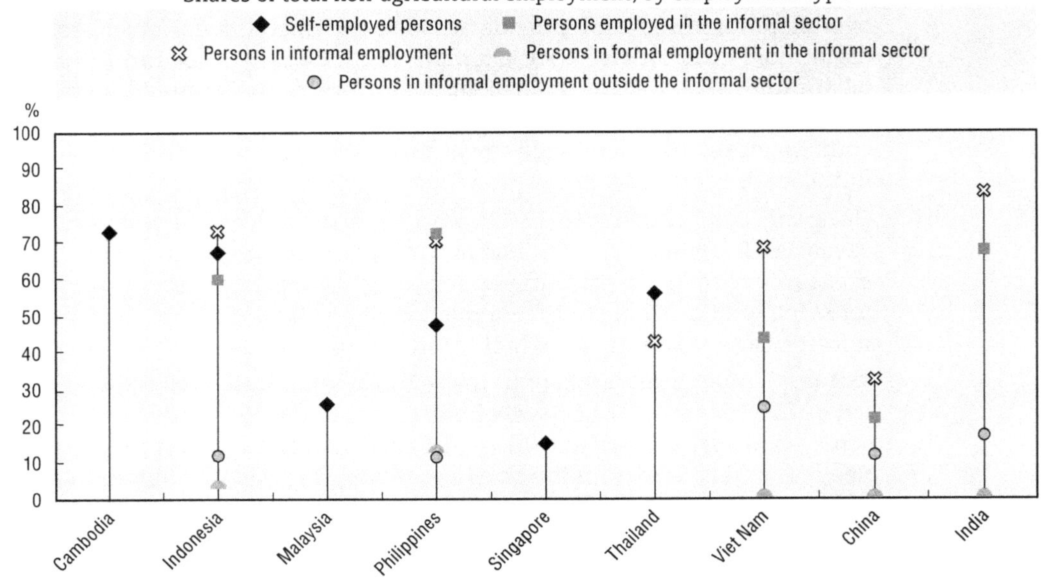

Note: All data from various years in 2008-10.

Sources: International Labour Organization (2010a), *LABORSTA* (database), ILO, Geneva, http://laborsta.ilo.org/.

StatLink http://dx.doi.org/10.1787/888933179369

Figure 10. **Estimates of informal output show some similar patterns**

Informal sectors' shares of total output, by type of estimation

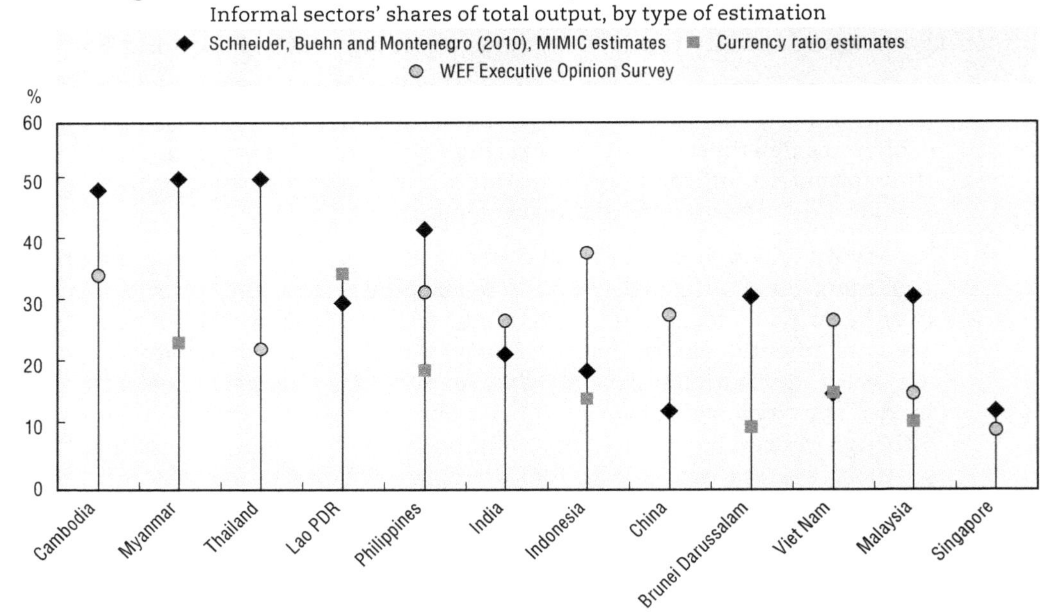

Note: Averages of 2000-07 values from MIMIC and currency ratio estimations and 2006 survey results.

Sources: Schneider, F., A. Buehn and C.E. Montenegro (2010), "Shadow economies all over the world: New estimates for 162 countries from 1999 to 2007", *World Bank Policy Research Working Paper*, No. 5356, World Bank, Washington, DC; World Economic Forum (2006), *The Global Competitiveness Report 2006-2007*, World Economic Forum, New York; OECD Development Centre calculations.

StatLink http://dx.doi.org/10.1787/888933179379

The region's experiences regarding informality have multiple interconnected proximate and deep-lying causes. High levels of informality are often blamed on excessive tax and regulatory burdens on firms, though these are not always significantly more restrictive where higher rates of informality are found. Factors beyond governments' market interventions also affect informality, as it tends to be higher in underdeveloped and industrialising economies and where social and cultural pressures to comply with laws are weaker. Government capacities remain relevant here as well, however, as social norms in Emerging Asia supporting tax compliance appear to be stronger where opinions on governments' effective use of the collected revenue in providing public goods and services are higher.

At a more fundamental level, institutions are responsible for determining levels of informality over the long term. Effective institutions encourage formality both through push factors – tax and regulatory enforcement and penalties for non-compliance – and pull factors – access to market-supporting public goods and institutions such as the rule of law, the protection of property rights and contract enforcement, as well as closer interaction with formal sector financers, suppliers and customers. Informality tends to be less prevalent in Emerging Asian economies with strong, effective and impartial legal systems, for example (Figure 11).

Figure 11. **Weaker rule of law is associated with higher informality**

Rule of law and estimated informal share of total output in selected countries, 2011

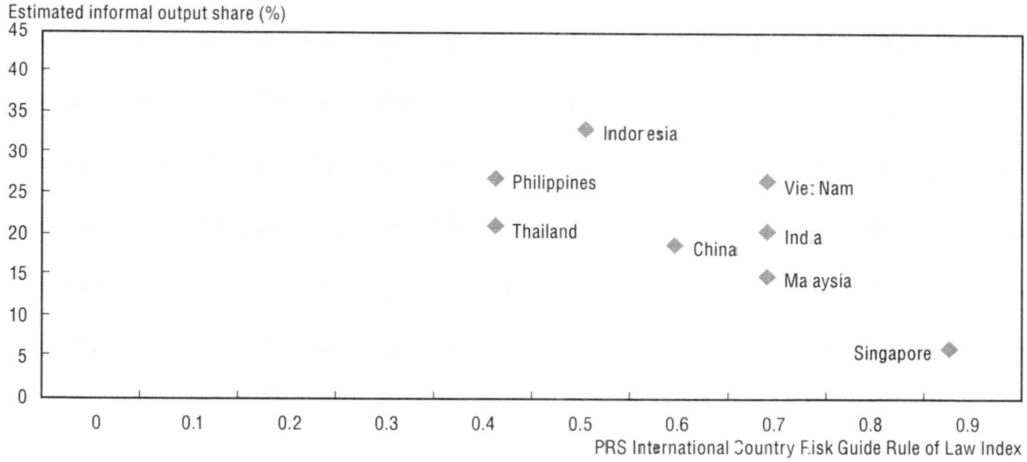

Notes: The PRS Rule of Law Index, which varies from 0 to 1, gives higher scores to countries where the legal system is strong and impartial and the law is popularly observed. Informal output shares estimated using WEF Executive Opinion Survey values for 2006, extended with growth rates estimated using the electricity consumption method.

Sources: Political Risk Services (2014), *International Country Risk Guide* (database), PRS, Syracuse; OECD Development Centre calculations.

StatLink http://dx.doi.org/10.1787/888933179389

Despite some benefits, informality often impedes growth

The consequences of informality can be for the good in emerging economies where they facilitate economic flexibility. Informal firms create jobs for workers excluded from the formal economy, particularly during downturns, which has a buffering effect. Estimates of informal shares of total output, for example, rose considerably in 1998 in Indonesia, Malaysia, the Philippines, Singapore and Thailand, which were among the Emerging Asian economies worst affected by the 1997 Asian Financial Crisis. Informality also creates employment for poor, marginalised and excluded workers. However, these benefits are outweighed by downsides if better formal jobs could have instead been created in their place.

In addition, there are numerous negative consequences of informality. Most directly, it stunts government capacity by lowering tax revenues and limiting the reach of its influence on the private sector through product and labour market regulation. Informality also typically constrains growth, as it lowers productivity. Operating informally limits the productivity potential of firms, as they cannot easily access the efficiency-raising institutions available to the formal sector. Because they lack collateral and do not enjoy a legal status, informal firms tend not to borrow through the formal financial system. Instead, they use alternatives that increase costs or provide lower funding, which limits their ability to invest in productivity-enhancing machinery, equipment and technology.

The informal sector constrains productivity not only directly, but indirectly, too. In part, indirect effects are manifest in the greater relative tax burden on compliant formal firms, as noted above, while a related impact is to be found where formal firms share markets with informal producers. They may well find themselves at a disadvantage – even when they are more productive – because of the lower production costs of informal firms which avoid taxes and compliance with other laws and regulations.

Comprehensive strategies are needed to address informality

As a result, strategies are needed to further discourage informal employment and output. Economic growth and industrialisation alone cannot be relied upon to reduce informality, particularly as informality itself already slows growth. Apart from low income levels, institutional and other factors are conducive to the rise of informality. What is needed are comprehensive policy responses that deter disruptive informality without affecting the livelihoods of the poor and marginalised workers who depend on informal income sources. These may include elements of reform that address four policy areas: judicial institutional capacities, investment in formal sector productivity and assistance for SMEs, the tax and regulatory environment, and targeted enforcement and concessions.

Reforming legal and judicial institutions

Informal activities can be curbed if formality is a more attractive proposition. To that end, policy makers should improve governance and administration, particularly with respect to the rule of law and the judicial system as a whole, contract enforcement, and the protection of property rights. These fundamental institutions are relatively underdeveloped among a number of countries in Emerging Asia that rank poorly in international comparisons of the ease of dispute settlement and of property registration, among other issues. Even countries that perform fairly well overall in the World Bank report, *Doing Business 2014*, are ranked low in areas of critical importance when it comes to addressing informality. Brunei Darussalam, for instance, is ranked 59th overall out of 189 countries, but 161st on enforcing contracts. Cambodia, India and Myanmar also perform poorly on contract enforcement, coming 162nd, 186th and 188th, respectively.

The strengthening of fundamental institutions may, in turn, require legislative and organisational change. Broad-based reforms may also help to boost tax morale, as an improved image of effective, credible government is more likely to coax individuals and firms into paying their taxes. Addressing corruption at all levels through strengthened government oversight bodies and civil service reforms is also important to ensuring the rule of law and improving the public image of government.

Supporting SMEs

At the same time, governments can help more dynamic formal sectors to emerge. Since informal firms often tend to be small and SMEs offer considerable potential for growth in Emerging Asia, policies encouraging formalisation and supporting productivity growth among SMEs should also help to reduce informality. Expanded access to training and finance is particularly important for SMEs. Broadly speaking, they thrive where there are strong financial and education systems, though they may also benefit from additional SME-specific schemes like targeted programmes and indirect financial support such as loan guarantees. At the same time, efforts to increase SME awareness of the costs of informality and opportunities to formalise through public information campaigns complement broader policy reforms.

Rethinking tax regulation and administration

As part of efforts to discourage informality, some countries should give thought to the direct costs, levels of taxation, and regulations that weigh on the private sector. They may well have to reform the nature and administration of companies' legal obligations in order to encourage the growth of the formal sector. For the same average tax rate, changes in the structure of taxation and reforms benefitting smaller firms – such as tax exemptions on reinvested earnings or tax credits for investment and job creation – could be part of a comprehensive strategy to reduce informality.

Regulatory and administrative barriers – including those related to tax administration – are high in several Emerging Asian economies. Administrative barriers in starting new firms – a very important factor behind informality – are often relatively high in the region and in need of reform. The problem of low-level corruption among public officials is related to and often a result of complex administrative barriers. This is a particularly large challenge in the CLM countries; in Myanmar in 2014, for example, 35% of formal firms reported being asked for a bribe by tax inspectors.

Additional measures targeting informality

In addition to these broad policy reforms, targeted enforcement and, possibly, concessions for non-compliant firms and industries prone to informality may be useful. Informality in the region tends to be concentrated in smaller firms operating away from the modern, international sectors of the economy – sectors that may be useful targets of anti-informality policy reforms. Targeted strategies should also seek to simultaneously formalise firms, their competitors, suppliers, customers and even lenders from the informal financial sector. Such a broad approach would help to alleviate concerns over lost cost competitiveness and offer opportunities to formalise business-to-business and financial relationships. In many cases, stepped-up enforcement and legal deterrents will still be needed alongside these targeted approaches. Recent investments in Indonesia in expanding the number of tax office employees and reforms in Viet Nam to amend the statute of limitations on firms' and individuals' tax procedure violations and increase the size of maximum fines, for example, should help to encourage greater levels of compliance.

Chapter 1

Medium-term economic outlook and assessment in Emerging Asia

The growth prospects of Emerging Asia (Southeast Asia, China and India) look favourable overall in the medium term. Growth in the ASEAN-5 countries (Indonesia, Malaysia, the Philippines, Thailand and Viet Nam) remains robust and the CLM countries (Cambodia, Lao PDR and Myanmar) are emerging as an engine of regional growth, while there will be slowing in China. The region also remains exposed to several other external risks (including those stemming from the normalisation of US monetary policy, economic reform in Japan and euro area uncertainty) and internal risks (including political uncertainty and instability in a few countries). While most countries are well positioned to manage these risks, further efforts will be needed to improve the conditions for growth. Fiscal balances are, in general, not expected to change significantly but fiscal reforms still need to be strengthened further. Deeper regional integration in implementing the ASEAN Economic Community by 2015 is also critical for Southeast Asia.

Introduction

Emerging Asia is facing several challenges from both its external economic environment and domestic sources. The main external challenges stem from monetary policy normalisation in the United States, the slowing of growth in China, continued moderate growth in OECD countries, and the impacts from "Abenomics" structural reforms in Japan. Domestically, uncertainties arising from recent elections and political upheavals along with the implementation of structural reforms also pose important challenges for economic management.

In the face of these challenges, growth in Emerging Asia – Southeast Asia, China and India – should remain resilient over the medium term due to generally sound policies and economic fundamentals. Inflationary pressures and volatility in financial markets have generally been subdued. Fiscal challenges still remain and structural reforms will be critical in sustaining robust economic growth in the region. China, the largest country in the region, faces challenges in coping with slower growth as it seeks to adjust to its changing demographic landscape, switch to consumption-led growth, and cope with agricultural, environmental and educational issues. At the regional level, ASEAN faces challenges in meeting its objective to create a common market by 2015. Expedited efforts on priority initiatives are needed to reach this goal. Disparities within ASEAN member countries remain substantial and efforts to address them need to be intensified if the benefits of integration are to be realised.

This chapter provides an overview of the regional landscape over 2015-19 and discusses the potential risks and policy challenges in Emerging Asia.

Overview and main findings: The economic outlook for 2015-19

While the growth prospects of OECD countries continue to moderate, they look favourable overall in Emerging Asia for 2015-19, averaging 6.5% per year, according to this Outlook's Medium-term Projection Framework (MPF-2015) (Table 1.1). Although growth in Emerging Asia will moderate gradually due to the slowdown in China, for the ten ASEAN countries as a whole, growth momentum remains robust and broadly similar to that of the past ten years, averaging 5.6% in 2015-19. The year 2014 saw major transformations in the region's political landscape that will affect growth rates in the future, though these impacts will differ across the region. Indonesia's presidential election brought Joko Widodo to power and India's general election ushered in Narendra Modi as the new Prime Minister. The electoral processes in both countries were widely regarded as successful, peaceful changes of government. However, territorial disputes over the sovereignty of the South China Sea affected tourism and exports in some countries and political unrest in Thailand has had relatively strong economic impacts.

Individual countries' growth paths point in different directions. The large **ASEAN-5** economies – Indonesia, Malaysia, the Philippines, Thailand and Viet Nam – will sustain their growth momentum in the medium term, led by **Indonesia** and **the Philippines**. Indonesia's economy will be supported by robust domestic demand and expectations of reform, with the Widodo administration possibly reforming the fuel subsidy. Another economy driven by domestic demand, strongly supported by remittances from overseas and political stability, is the Philippines, where growth is expected to be favourable in the medium term. The success of measures to create jobs, reduce unemployment and improve infrastructure will be key to sustained growth.

Table 1.1. **Real GDP growth of Southeast Asia, China and India**

Country	2013	2019	2003-07	2011-13	2015-19
ASEAN 10 countries					
ASEAN-5 countries					
Indonesia	5.8	6.3	5.5	6.2	6.0
Malaysia	4.7	5.6	6.0	5.2	5.6
Philippines	7.2	6.3	5.7	5.9	6.2
Thailand	2.9	4.6	5.6	3.2	4.1
Viet Nam	5.4	5.8	7.2	5.6	5.7
Brunei Darussalam	-1.8	1.9	1.7	0.9	1.6
Cambodia	7.5	7.3	10.6	7.3	7.1
Lao PDR	8.0	7.7	7.1	8.1	7.6
Myanmar	7.5	7.8	-	6.9	7.8
Singapore	3.9	3.6	7.9	4.1	3.5
Two large economies in the region					
China	7.7	6.6	11.7	8.2	6.8
India	5.0	6.8	8.8	5.5	6.7
Average of ASEAN 10 countries	5.2	5.8	5.9	5.4	5.6
Average of Emerging Asia	6.5	6.5	9.5	7.0	6.5

Notes: The cut-off date of data is 6 October 2014. Emerging Asia denotes ASEAN-10 countries plus China and India. ASEAN-5 includes Indonesia, Malaysia, the Philippines, Thailand and Viet Nam.

Source: OECD Development Centre, MPF-2015 (Medium-term projection framework). For more information on MPF, please see www.oecd.org/dev/asiapacific/mpf.

Malaysia's vigorous domestic demand, supported by the rise of the middle class and the growing export-oriented sector, will remain resilient despite the still weak demand in OECD economies. Political unrest in **Thailand** adversely affects growth prospects relatively seriously in the near term, as consumer and investor confidence and the country's trade performance weaken amid uncertainty over the effectiveness of the military government's successors and their economic roadmap. With declining although long lasting high inflationary pressures, **Viet Nam** could enjoy stable economic growth in the medium term, although risks remain in the banking sector.

Economic growth prospects are stable for **Brunei Darussalam** and **Singapore**. Brunei's growth performance will depend on the energy sector and the volatility of oil and gas prices. Meanwhile, ensuring smooth economic transformation in healthcare and social services and effective land use will be challenges for the Singaporean economy.

More rapid growth is expected for the **CLM** countries (Cambodia, Lao PDR and Myanmar) than for the ASEAN-5. Their growth is slated to exceed 7% over the next five years. Improvement in the agriculture sector and the business environment will be engines of the growth of **Cambodia** and **Lao PDR**. As for **Myanmar**, it has seen remarkably rapid progress in many areas, which will maintain it on a favourable path in the medium term. The performance of the new growth CLM engine in Emerging Asia will also affect the speed of the ASEAN integration initiative.

The region's two largest economies, **China** and **India**, face significant challenges. China's growth is slowing as it seeks to adjust to its changing demographic landscape, switch its hub of growth from investment to consumption, and cope with environmental, agricultural and educational issues. Growth is forecast to average 6.8% over 2015-19. India's growth should be stable over the medium term (averaging 6.7%), but its prospects could change as the new Modi government carries out its intended reforms. These plans include promoting domestic and foreign investment, creating jobs, improving food security, raising the standards of education and skills development, building new key infrastructure, enhancing water governance, and increasing India's overall competitiveness, particularly in the manufacturing sector.

The key points of the medium-term economic outlook are as follows.

- Despite slight moderation in the first quarter of this year, growth in Emerging Asia is still robust, averaging 6.5% annually over 2015-19. The Chinese economy is slowing, but the large ASEAN economies are showing resilience and growth momentum remains broadly similar to that of the past ten years (5.6% over 2015-19). The CLM countries are expected to become the new centres of growth in ASEAN, with average annual growth in each exceeding 7%.
- Overall, current account imbalances are gradually improving – particularly in the ASEAN-5. The CLM countries will continue to show a deficit in the medium term. There are signs that foreign direct investment (FDI) is slowing in the region. Additional efforts to attract and retain investors will be required.
- Generally speaking, there will be no dramatic changes in fiscal conditions, though trends will differ by country. While fiscal balances in Malaysia and the Philippines may improve, those in Thailand and Viet Nam will worsen in the medium term. Overall, fiscal reforms need to be strengthened further in the region.
- Emerging Asian countries may have to contend with external risks. For instance, the normalisation of US monetary policy, the slowdown in the Chinese economy, the implementation of structural policies related to "Abenomics" in Japan, and uncertainties concerning the growth prospects of the Euro area. However, the impact of these factors on the region will be moderate, since markets have already factored these changes into their expectations (as of November 2014). Transformations in the political landscape will affect different countries in different ways. There are particularly worries over the current political unrest in Thailand. Overall, effective capital flow management (of both inflows and outflows) will remain a challenge in the region in the medium term.
- Further acceleration of regional integration by 2015, towards the goal of the ASEAN Economic Community, by 2015 will be necessary – particularly to narrow disparities within the region.

Recent macroeconomic developments and near-term prospects

Growth in the OECD economies is expected to improve moderately over the next two years, though performances are likely to be uneven and exposed to several uncertainties. Growth will continue to be driven by a combination of accommodative monetary policy, gradual improvement in employment and a slowing pace of fiscal consolidation. International trade has not been making the same contribution to global growth as it did before the financial crisis, and is expected to continue growing at roughly the same pace as overall economic activity. This reduced contribution is a result of the sluggish trade performance in Europe and rising levels of trade restrictions across the advanced economies. The improvements in growth recently seen in the United States and United Kingdom are expected to continue. However, stagnation is expected to persist in the euro area – as a result of geopolitical tensions affecting confidence – and in Japan – due to an increase in the consumption tax. The overall outlook for the OECD is subject to some downside risks.

Against this background, growth in the Emerging Asia region appeared to moderate in the first quarter of 2014 but recovered momentum in the second quarter (Table 1.2). The increased momentum after Q2 of 2014 is reflected in trade and financial indicators for the region. Growth should continue at a steady pace through 2015, though growth paths will differ across countries (Figure 1.1).

Figure 1.1. **Real GDP growth of Southeast Asia, China and India**

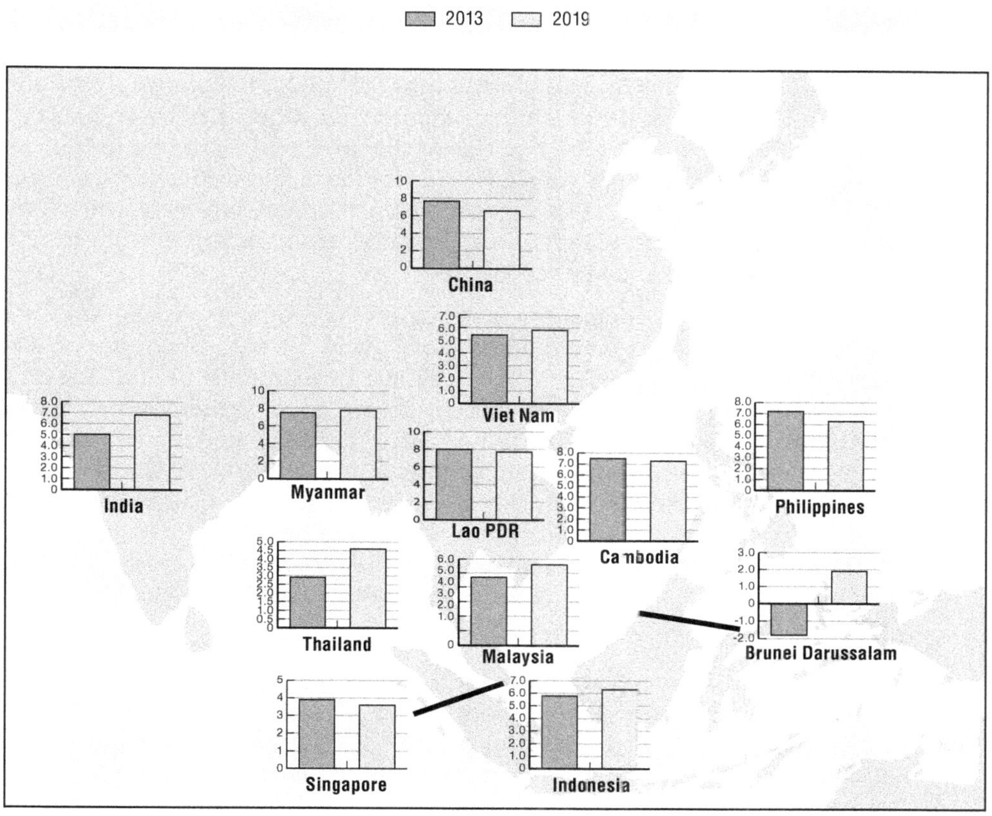

Source: OECD Development Centre, MPF 2015.

StatLink http://dx.doi.org/10.1787/888933179392

Table 1.2. **Real GDP growth of Q1 and Q2, 2014 in Emerging Asia**

Percentage change from previous year

Country	2013	2014 Q1	2014 Q2
Brunei Darussalam	-1.8%	-3.3%	-
Cambodia	7.9%	-	-
Indonesia	5.8%	5.2%	5.1%
Lao PDR	8.0%	-	-
Malaysia	4.7%	6.2%	6.4%
Myanmar	7.5%	-	-
Philippines	7.2%	5.6%	6.4%
Singapore	3.9%	4.8%	2.4%
Thailand	2.9%	-0.5%	0.4%
Viet Nam	5.4%	5.1%	5.3%
China	7.7%	7.4%	7.5%
India	5.0%	6.0%	5.9%

Source: CEIC and national sources. 2013 data for Myanmar is from the ADB.

Most ASEAN-5 economies showed stronger growth performances in the second quarter, bolstered by a recovery in exports (Figure 1.2). **Indonesia**, ASEAN's largest economy, has shown robust growth following the global financial crisis. The country's growth, however, decelerated in the first quarter of 2014 to 5.2% (yoy), the lowest rate since 2009. Weak exports contributed to the slowdown, while private consumption, the biggest contributor to the country's growth, has remained robust. Indonesia's current account balance has been a concern in recent years as the deficit continues to widen. Merchandise exports dropped in the first half of 2014. However, the trade balance still recorded a surplus of USD 2.9 billion, since imports declined by even more than exports. Slowing GDP growth has led to a rise of the unemployment rate in Indonesia from 6.1% in 2012 to 6.2% in 2013 (Figure 1.3). This increase followed a drop in the rate from 7.1% in 2010 to 6.6% in 2011. The highest unemployment rate is in the segment of people between the ages of 15 and 24, particularly fresh graduates from vocational schools, universities and secondary schools.

The Philippines – one of the fastest growing economies in the ASEAN-5 countries in recent years – grew at an annual rate of 6.4% in the second quarter of 2014, faster than the revised 5.6% expansion in the previous three-month period. Buoyant remittances have helped to support the country's private consumption, which accounts for more than half of the country's overall growth. Increased employment also contributed to higher private consumption. Remittances increased by 6.2%, while employment rose by 2.8% (1.1 million new jobs) in the 12 months to July 2014, although the unemployment rate in Philippines, at 6.7% in the second quarter of 2014, is the highest among ASEAN countries. Growth was also supported by the recovery in exports of goods and services due to improved external demand. There are also continuing challenges to the recovery arising from Typhoon Yolanda (Box 1.1).

Viet Nam is projected to grow at a robust pace over the medium term. Weak macroeconomic management policies could also pose downside risks to growth. The annual GDP growth rate dropped to 5.1% (yoy) in 2014 Q1, but rose to 5.3% in the second quarter. This performance reflects a robust growth potential, based on the export manufacturing sector. Viet Nam has turned its large merchandise trade and current account deficits into surpluses since 2012. The external accounts showed solid growth in exports and imports in the first half of 2014. The average unemployment rate (around 2% in 2013) is very low, but vulnerable jobs (including home businesses and self-employment), which do not offer pensions or unemployment insurance, account for three-quarters of employment. The unemployment rate among young people (between 15 and 24 years of age) is also high.

Malaysia and **Thailand** have experienced contrasting economic performances. **Malaysia**'s GDP showed a steady increase of 6.3% (yoy) through the first half of 2014. A strong labour market has supported Malaysia's economy by boosting private consumption, the main driver of the country's overall growth. Malaysia's exports of goods and services increased in volume terms by 8.3%, following a contraction of 3.9% in the same period last year. Imports of goods and services also improved. A large increase in exports has supported the country's buoyant current account surplus. The unemployment rate in Malaysia was 2.8% in June and July 2014, 0.2% below the rate in July 2013. In **Thailand,** political unrest has had a negative impact on consumption and investment, depressing overall near-term growth. Indeed, private consumption decreased by 1.4% in the first months of 2014 (yoy), while private and government investment dropped by 7.2% and 11.3%, respectively. There was some improvement in the second quarter, with GDP expanding by 0.4% (yoy) compared to a revised 0.5% contraction in the previous quarter, due in part to better than expected domestic consumption. Thai exports dropped by 7.4% (yoy) in August 2014. The steep decline in imports contributed to a turnaround in the trade balance and generated a large current account surplus in the first half of 2014.

Figure 1.2. **Contributions to growth in Emerging Asia in the first half of 2014**

Percentage of GDP

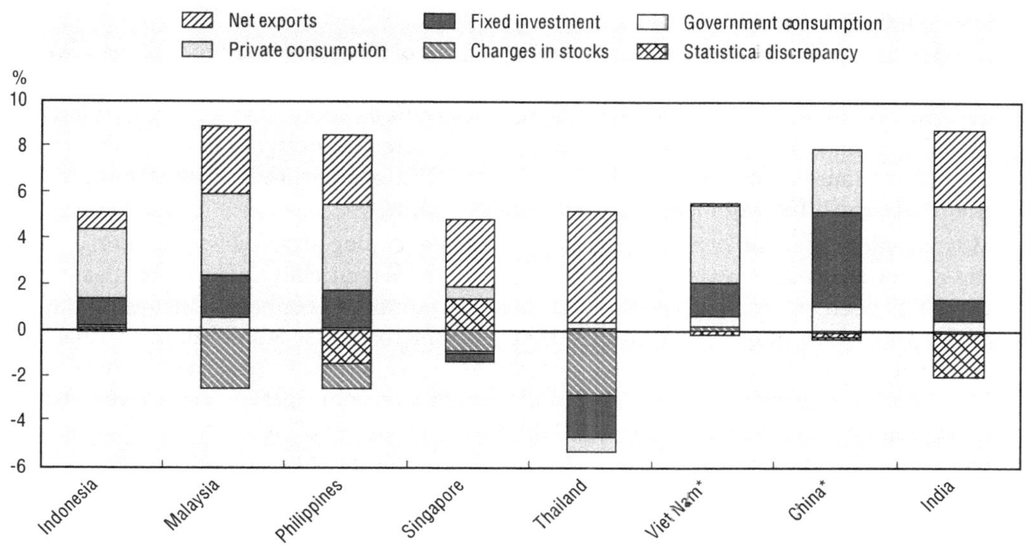

Note: *Data for Viet Nam and China refer to 2013.
Source: CEIC.
StatLink http://dx.doi.org/10.1787/888933179404

Figure 1.3. **Unemployment rate in Emerging Asia**

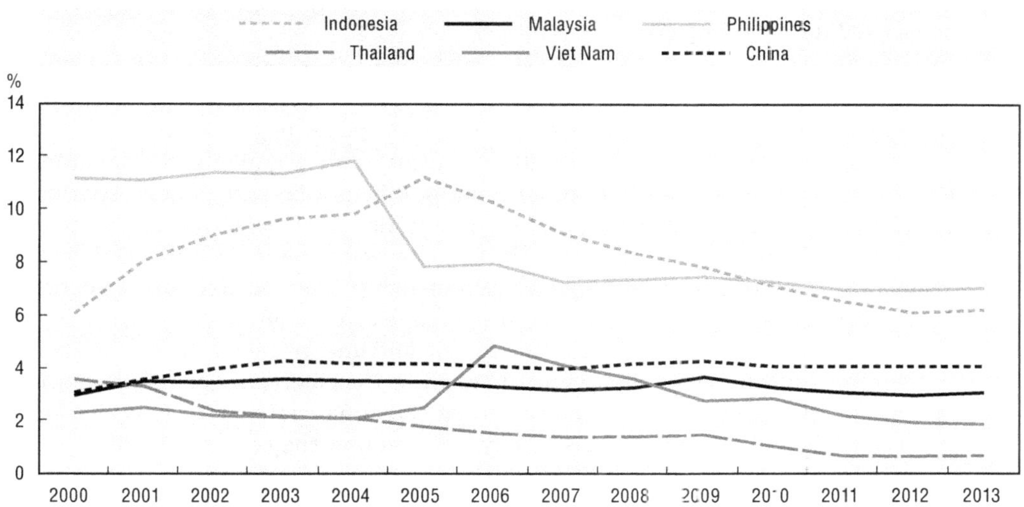

Source: Asian Development Bank's Statistical Database System (SDBS).
StatLink http://dx.doi.org/10.1787/888933179419

Box 1.1. The Philippines: The challenges of recovery from Typhoon Yolanda

In November 2013, Typhoon Yolanda caused catastrophic damage in the Philippines, a country whose geographic location exposes it to severe natural disasters. Despite Typhoon Yolanda and other natural disasters throughout 2013, the Philippines' economic growth reached 7.2% that year. The immediate economic impact of Yolanda was less severe than initially projected and showed that a rapidly executed reconstruction programme can, in the short term, even boost economic growth (World Bank, 2014b). However, the vulnerabilities that are inherent to the development level of the Philippines, which are amplified by natural disasters, pose risks to medium-term growth prospects that are illustrated by the growth slowdown expected in 2014. These vulnerabilities include still high poverty rates as well as a lack of inclusive growth and of productive employment.

In response to the increasingly devastating effects of disasters, the Philippines government had strengthened the risk management framework long before Typhoon Yolanda. More recently, after Typhoon Yolanda, *Reconstruction Assistance on Yolanda* was adopted as a strategic plan for recovery. Globally, a focus has increasingly been put on ex-ante risk mitigation strategies (rather than on ex-post measures) and on risk financing capacity in order to reduce underlying vulnerabilities that make the effects of disasters persistent over time.

Most developing-country disaster policy consists of coping after the fact and ex-ante policies, to the extent that they have existed, were usually not specifically targeted to disasters. However, there has been an emphasis since the 2000s in a number of countries, including the Philippines, on ex-ante risk-mitigation strategies that attempt to reduce vulnerability to natural hazards and that can be less costly than ex-post measures. (For example, the US Federal Emergency Management Agency calculated that a dollar spent on risk mitigation could save two dollars spent on coping ex-post, see World Bank, 2014b). However, to be efficient, ex-ante measures should be well designed, and their design is more complex than that of ex-post measures.

There are also important differences in the issues that need to be taken into account when designing policies regarding risk financing capacity.

- One important issue is how the domestic resources and the aid provided by donors can be made complementary. In this connection, Paul K. Freeman calculates "resource gaps" for disaster-prone countries as a function of *per capita* income, geographic variation in risk, and the frequency of hazard events (Freeman, 2003). The evidence shows that aid is often not sufficient, so that countries need to complement aid by mobilising domestic resources. Regarding domestic resources, it is therefore key to assess the opportunity cost of having a certain amount of reserve funds to help reduce risks or that can be mobilised quickly in case of disasters, but which can also be used for other purposes.
- In the Philippines, the National Disaster Risk Reduction and Management Fund provides a calamity fund for ex-post disaster relief and rehabilitation and has recently been made more flexible for ex-ante disaster risk reduction purposes (e.g. preparedness and mitigation programmes, construction of evacuation centres, and payments for insurance policies) (OECD, 2013a). However, the level of its funding may not be sufficient to bear optimally the risks of disasters (OECD, 2015). It can be efficient to also develop private insurance mechanisms to insure risks that can be individualised: The risk assessment systems needed to make such private insurance efficient are, however, challenging, even in developed economies where insurance markets are mature. For instance, escape clauses often imply that the public sector bears all risks of heavy losses in case of extreme and unexpected disasters. In the Philippines, it is therefore crucial to improve regulation to allow the emergence of an insurance sector that can improve risk assessment. On the consumer side, financial education is also key to helping citizens understand the potential risks they face and how they can be insured against them.

Sources: "Reconstruction Assistance on Yolanda, Building Back Better", report of the Government of the Philippines, 2013, available at: http://reliefweb.int/report/philippines/reconstruction-assistance-yolanda-ray
OECD (2015), *Multi-Dimensional Country Review of the Philippines*, phase 2, forthcoming
OECD (2013a), "Disaster Risk Financing in APEC Economies, Practices and Challenges", OECD Publishing, Paris.
World Bank (2014b), "Philippine economic update pursuing inclusive growth through sustainable reconstruction and job creation", *Report No. 83315-PH*, March.

The two smallest ASEAN countries in terms of geographic area and population are subject to comparatively volatile near-term growth. **Brunei's** economy is highly dependent on the oil and gas sector, which accounts for more than 60% of GDP. Dependence on oil and gas has made the economy vulnerable to fluctuations in oil and gas production and prices. Brunei's real GDP contracted by 1.8% in 2013 due to a sharp decline in oil and gas output. A further decline in the energy sector led to a contraction of 3.3% (yoy) in 2014 Q1. Natural gas and crude petroleum are the biggest contributors to Brunei's exports, accounting for 95% of the country's total exports in 2010. Brunei's export destinations are mainly other Asian countries, such as Japan (especially for natural gas), Korea, Indonesia and India. In 2014 Q1, Brunei's exports of oil, natural gas and methanol dropped by 9.1%. At the same time, imports fell even more, by 18.4%. This has led to a decline of the country's trade surplus and a narrowing of the current account surplus. The unemployment rate in Brunei was 3.7% in 2013, lower than the 3.8% recorded in 2012 but still higher than the 3.5% and 3.2% rates in 2009 and 2008, respectively.

Singapore's GDP grew at 4.8% annual rate in the first quarter of 2014, but slowed to 2.4% in the second quarter due to a slowdown in manufacturing growth and a decline in non-oil domestic exports. Singapore merchandise exports, led by non-oil domestic exports, fell by 6.6% (yoy) in May 2014, and by 4.6% in June. Singapore's strong economy has supported a stable unemployment rate. The annual average unemployment rate in 2013 was 1.9%, lower than 2% in 2012. Singapore is widely considered to have an environment supportive of business; with a few exceptions, tariffs are mostly zero. Singapore's priorities are to boost skills across job categories and to strengthen the abilities of its companies to seize business opportunities in Asia.

Cambodia, Lao PDR and **Myanmar** have been experiencing high growth rates in the 2000s, with annual average GDP growth of around 8%. These countries are projected to continue growing at a robust pace over the medium term, led by Lao PDR at 7.6% per annum, while Cambodia and Myanmar are projected to grow at 7.1% and 7.8% respectively per annum during 2015-19. The Cambodian economy grew at 7.5% in 2013 aided by rapid expansion in exports and growth in supply from the service sector. High GDP growth is expected to continue in 2014 despite labour unrest and uncertainty stemming from wage negotiations in the garment industry, the main driver of recent economic growth. The garment industry is still the key engine of Cambodia's growth, followed by construction. The garment industry contributes around 80% of the country's exports and is Cambodia's main source of foreign currency. The government's ability to solve the issues underlying labour unrest in the garment industry is thus crucial for the economy since the uncertainty threatens the industry's growth potential and investor's confidence.

Growth in Lao PDR's economy increased to 8.0% in 2013 from 7.9% in 2012. However, rising inflation due to accommodative monetary policy and a widened fiscal deficit will hamper economic growth in the medium term. Despite the modest slowdown, Lao PDR still has one of the highest growth rates in the region. The country's growth is mainly supported by the resource sector, hydropower industry (a major recipient of FDI), and massive road and railway infrastructure projects. The mining and hydropower sectors' contribution to the economy, however, appears to be vulnerable to lower output growth. The cancellation and suspension of some investment projects, including a hydropower dam project and some infrastructure loans from China might also lead to some slowing in the country's growth. The Myanmar economy grew at 7.5% in 2013 and is expected to grow even faster in 2014, benefitting from an improved investment climate. The high growth is driven by private investment, notably externally-financed large projects, which are also boosting commodity exports. Myanmar's economic growth has been strongly supported by foreign investment inflows. FDI inflows to Myanmar increased by 17% in 2013 over 2012 (UNCTAD, 2014). Energy and infrastructure are the main industries receiving large foreign investment. The recent liberalisation of the telecommunications sector has also helped to attract foreign investment into the country. The Central Bank of Myanmar recently announced that the country has taken steps to open its banking sector to foreign participation for the first time in nearly 50 years: nine foreign banks have been given licenses to operate in Myanmar. Although they still provide limited services due to remaining restrictions, foreign banks will benefit foreign investors in Myanmar. Exports of natural resources, such as natural gas and mining products, will also support Myanmar's accelerating growth.

Furthermore, progressive economic opening and integration in the ASEAN market provides CLM countries with opportunities to benefit from the comparative advantages associated with their relatively low labour costs and energy wealth. ASEAN integration will also help CLM countries to start tapping global markets. Driven by continued intra-regional restructuring in manufacturing, Cambodia and Myanmar are attractive FDI locations for labour-intensive manufacturing, whereas Lao PDR is more specialised in natural resources (UNCTAD, 2013) (Box 1.2).

Box 1.2. **Risks to the CLM countries, the engines of growth in the region**

Within the generally favourable economic landscape, there are some macroeconomic risks which are common among the three countries (Cambodia, Lao PDR and Myanmar) and which are linked to common structural characteristics.

- Dependency on external demand is still high, as witnessed by the high share of exports to GDP compared with other low-income countries, or even with other developing Asian economies. The limited development of internal markets poses risks, given the volatility of external demand, especially when exports are concentrated in terms of products or destination. For instance, in Cambodia, the stability and competitiveness of the garment industry, which accounts for about 70% of total exports, is crucial. The vulnerability of the sector is illustrated by the dramatic fall in garment exports to Europe in 2008, which led to a deep economic slowdown in the country. The government has been trying to promote rice exports to reduce the risks associated with over-specialisation in garments. Similarly, Lao PDR is overly concentrated in terms of its trading partners, with Thailand accounting for 65% of its imports and 40% of its exports. Therefore, a prolonged economic downturn in Thailand may deeply affect Lao PDR.
- In general, there is a trade-off between economic specialisation to take advantage of comparative advantages and economic diversification. While specialisation at early levels of development may facilitate reaping low-hanging fruits of globalisation, economic diversification at later stages of development fosters technology upgrading and capacity to adapt the production structure to an evolving economic environment. Cambodia, Lao PDR and Myanmar are indeed benefitting now from specialisation in labour-intensive activities. They can, however, seek to avoid a too high dependency on a small number of activities and trade partners. However, they also need to start preparing for future diversification, for instance by enhancing access to quality education.
- While overall, ASEAN-5 countries remain in current account surplus, Cambodia, Lao PDR and Myanmar are projected to continue to run significant current account deficits through 2019, although they should narrow. High current account deficits are normal at early stages of development but they may pose some risks from over-reliance on external funding. In particular, current account deficits for these countries are mainly financed by FDI and ODA (Figure 1.4). While significant ODA may continue in the future, due to growing relations with diverse partners, attracting huge FDI inflows over the medium term may pose more challenges. Indeed, high operation costs, in particular from poor infrastructure and expensive electricity may become key constraints. In addition, although the business climate should improve gradually, many challenges remain. The three countries have some time to tackle these challenges, since in the short run, due to low GDP *per capita* and a demographic dividend, cheap labour costs underpinning comparative advantages in labour intensive industries will likely persist in the foreseeable future, helping to attract further FDI inflows.

Box 1.2. **Risks to the CLM countries, the engines of growth in the region** *(cont.)*

Figure 1.4. **FDI and ODA are significant in Cambodia and Lao PDR**

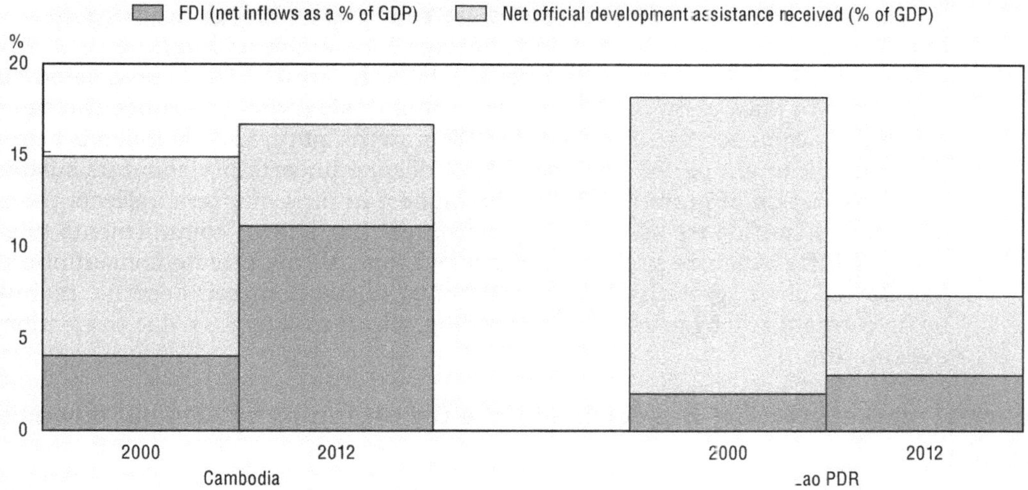

Notes: Data unavailable for Myanmar.

Source: World Bank (2014a), *World Development Indicators* (database).

StatLink http://dx.doi.org/10.1787/888933179422

- Inflation pressures are currently subdued, but rapid credit growth without financial deepening poses inflationary risks over the medium term. In particular, in Myanmar, inflation has decreased compared to the 2000s, but over-heating remains a risk. In Cambodia and Lao PDR, credit growth has also been strong in the past several years. Large state ownership currently limits competition and market mechanisms in the banking sector. A more commercially-driven banking sector and financial markets would help to strengthen macroeconomic management and to improve the allocation of resources by giving a greater role to market forces in determining interest rates and allocating credit.

To sum up, Cambodia, Lao PDR and Myanmar are well placed to reap the benefits of their comparative advantages in the next years, but they should already tackle risks that could slow growth over the medium run.

In the two largest economies in the region, growth has slowed somewhat due to external and internal factors but has remained reasonably robust. While much slower than the last five-year average growth rates, 9.2%, real GDP growth in **China** is still high at around 7.5% in the first two quarters of 2014, aided by a "mini stimulus" by the government. The stimulus measures, including an acceleration of spending on infrastructure and social housing, have to sustain real growth. While the investment contribution to GDP growth decreased in the first half of 2014, strong real household income growth of 9.8% (yoy) has led to a higher contribution of consumption to the country's GDP. The reduced dependence on investment also reflects the government effort to rein in credit growth, particularly that from off-budget financing by local government. Private consumption has been underpinned by a steady rise in household incomes, which is also leading to expansion in the services sector. China's exports in the first quarter of 2014 faced some constraints from weakening external demand. In the second quarter, however, export growth rebounded to 4.9%, as compared to the same period last year. Import growth slowed to 1.3% in 2014 Q2, from 2% in Q1. The combined result has been a rise in the trade surplus from USD 16.6 billion in the first quarter of 2014 to USD 85.9 billion in the second. In the medium and longer term, China's export sector is likely to face new pressures from increased international integration, ageing populations and relatively faster growth in other emerging economies. These global trends may provide opportunities for diversification beyond the advanced economies and in China's neighbours, although rising incomes in the emerging Asian economies may also provide larger markets for exporters targeting middle-class consumers. Unemployment in China stood at 4.08% in June 2014. China's labour markets are tightening, which is contributing to increases in wages that are currently outpacing those in the advanced economies.

In **India**, effective policy measures are calming the turbulence triggered by the QE tapering announcement by the United States Federal Reserve in June 2013. The Indian rupee, which traded at 61.9 rupee per US dollar in April of 2013 appreciated by 20% to 53.8 rupee in May, upon the announcement and is back to 60.2 rupee the same as the pre-announcement level. The 2014 Q2 GDP growth figure, 5.7%, is much better than the pre-announcement period average of 5.4% despite uncertainty about its sustainability. The acceleration of growth to 5.7%, the highest in nine quarters, reflects the recovery of business confidence as the new government has shown commitments to speed up pending infrastructure projects and cut red tape. While private consumption growth has slowed down, growth is still supported by higher domestic demand, mainly driven by investment and by government spending, which rose by 8.8% due to election-related expenditure.

Financial market volatility has declined since the beginning of 2014 but downside risks have increased

After a period of heightened volatility in the financial markets from May 2013, triggered by the prospects of a tapering of quantitative easing (QE) in the US, market conditions stabilised and then improved after the beginning of 2014 (Figure 1.5). Indeed, stock indices have increased in 2014 in most countries, following large decreases between May 2013 and December 2013 in some countries, in particular the Philippines, Thailand and Indonesia. In India, stock indices surged after the May 2014 election victory of the BJP, which was generally welcomed by the business community.

Similarly, credit default swap (CDS) premiums decreased significantly from the beginning of 2014 in most emerging Asian countries, and dramatically in Viet Nam and Indonesia (Figure 1.6). In June 2014, CDS premiums reached levels close to their lows of May 2013, but have increased again slightly since. The decrease in global bond yields since the beginning of 2014 contributed to lower financing costs and went along with a slowdown in capital outflows in most countries compared with the second half of 2013.

Globally, stock indices and CDS rates since 2011 reflect comparatively good resilience in the economies of Emerging Asia. Nevertheless, some downside risks have either not diminished or have increased since 2013, despite the relative stabilisation of financial markets. Emerging Asian economies with relatively large current account deficits and comparative vulnerability to capital outflows, such as India and Indonesia, remain vulnerable. In both India and Indonesia, the share of portfolio liabilities in total capital inflows remains high, exposing them to the risks of sudden withdrawals (Figure 1.7), and the overall net international indebtedness position (NIIP) has increased significantly since 2009. While the current level of the NIIP does not point to significant near-term risks, the dynamics could become worrying over time and weigh on future growth. The political situation in Thailand also threatens to prolong the economic slowdown and may be worrying in the medium term. The slowdown could spill over to Cambodia, whose main trading partner is Thailand. Finally, in the Philippines, the NIIP has improved considerably due to a build-up of foreign assets by the private sector and the public sector. However, there are uncertainties about the recovery following Typhoon Yolanda, which may explain the decline in portfolio liabilities in the first half of 2014. International reserves across Emerging Asian economies have generally increased since 2000, which will help to provide a buffer against external shocks, in particular when compared with the reserve levels before the crisis of the end of the 1990s. However, external reserves decreased since 2012 in some countries, in particular Indonesia, Thailand and Malaysia, and increased only slightly in other countries such as India and Viet Nam.

Figure 1.5. **Stock indices in Emerging Asia**

Index, January 2011=100

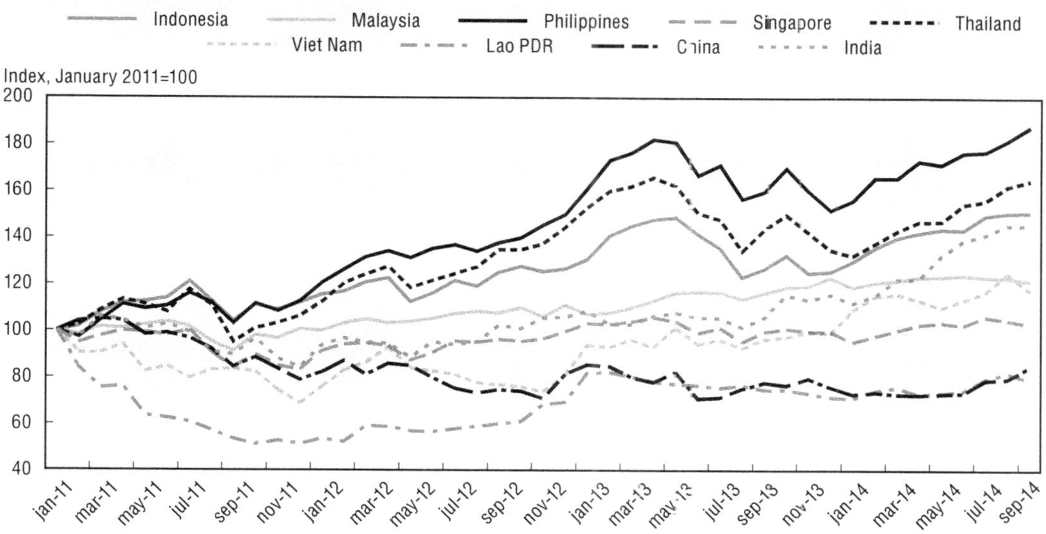

Source: CEIC

StatLink http://dx.doi.org/10.1787/888933179433

Figure 1.6. **Credit default swap premiums in Emerging Asia**

Premium mid spread

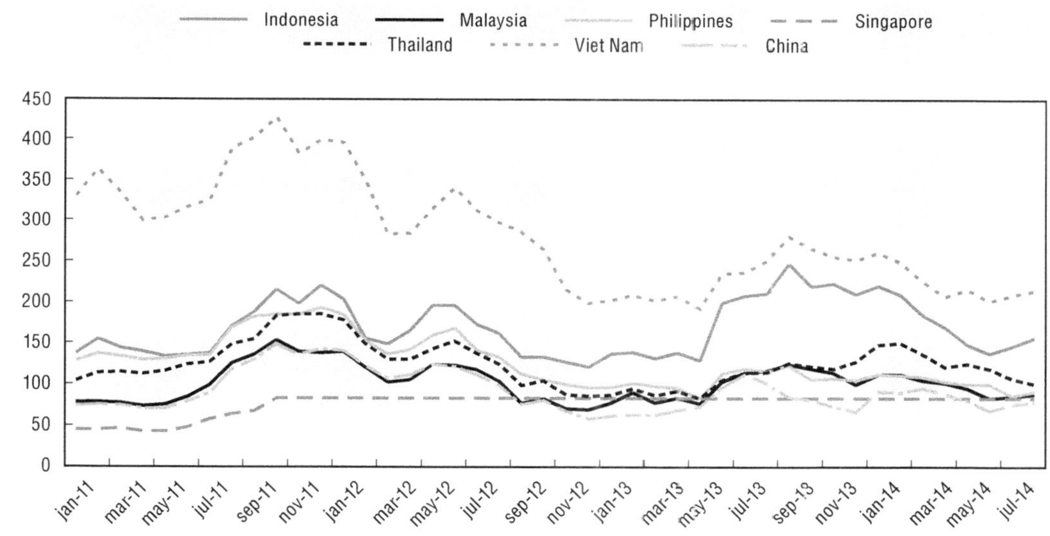

Source: Datastream.

StatLink http://dx.doi.org/10.1787/888933179445

Overall, effective capital flow management (of both inflows and outflows) remains a challenge in the region in the medium term. Since 1997, Emerging Asian economies have implemented macro-prudential and capital flow management (CFM) measures, in addition to greater exchange rate flexibility, in order to deal with the effects of capital inflow surges and reversals. In a context of rising housing prices and the associated prudential concerns, credit-related measures such as loan-to-value (LTV) and debt-to-income (DTI) caps, property-related taxes and capital-related measures have been commonly used across Emerging Asian economies.

There is, however, considerable heterogeneity among Emerging Asian countries in the CFM measures put in place, reflecting differences in domestic risks. For instance,

China and India maintain relatively extensive restrictions on capital flows and have a rather high number of capital-related measures. Viet Nam, to some extent, still maintains restrictions on capital flows, but has not strengthened its CFM measures to deal with inflows and has few measures in place. Countries like Malaysia, Thailand, China and India impose capital requirements based on risk weights, but not Indonesia or Viet Nam. In addition, few Emerging Asian countries have CFM measures (like caps) to deal with large credit growth or foreign currency lending.

While some ASEAN countries may have to undertake capital account liberalisation in order to meet the requirements of the ASEAN Economic Community (AEC), the great heterogeneity in prudential arrangements and domestic risks may be a barrier to deeper financial integration in the region. It also underlines that despite trade integration, the financial landscape within the region remains fragmented.

Figure 1.7. **Breakdown of capital inflows to Emerging Asia**

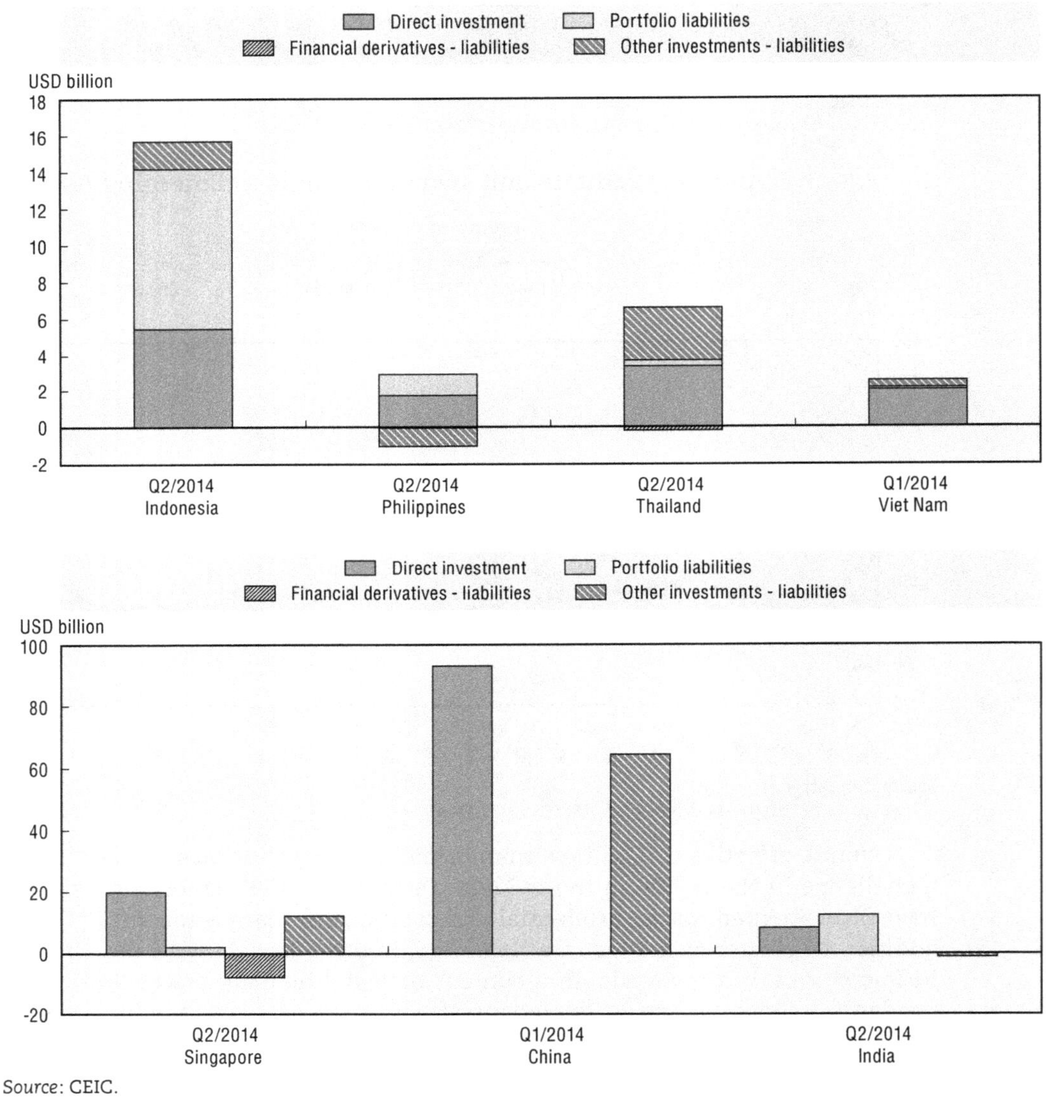

Source: CEIC.

StatLink http://dx.doi.org/10.1787/888933179457

Non-performing loans are improving though credit growth has slowed

The banking sector's performance in Southeast Asia countries, notably Indonesia, Malaysia, Singapore and Thailand, has generally been improving (Figure 1.8). Non-performing loans (NPL) have been gradually decreasing in the past few years. There was an uptick in NPL in the Philippines in 2013, when the rate rose to 3% from 2.2% in 2012 – but it remained below the 2010 level. More recently, NPL growth in Viet Nam has been more worrying; the rate risen from 3.74% in January 2014 to 4.03% by the end of April 2014, and independent rating agencies claim the real figure is even higher (see Chapter 2).

Figure 1.8. **Banking indicators in Southeast Asia**

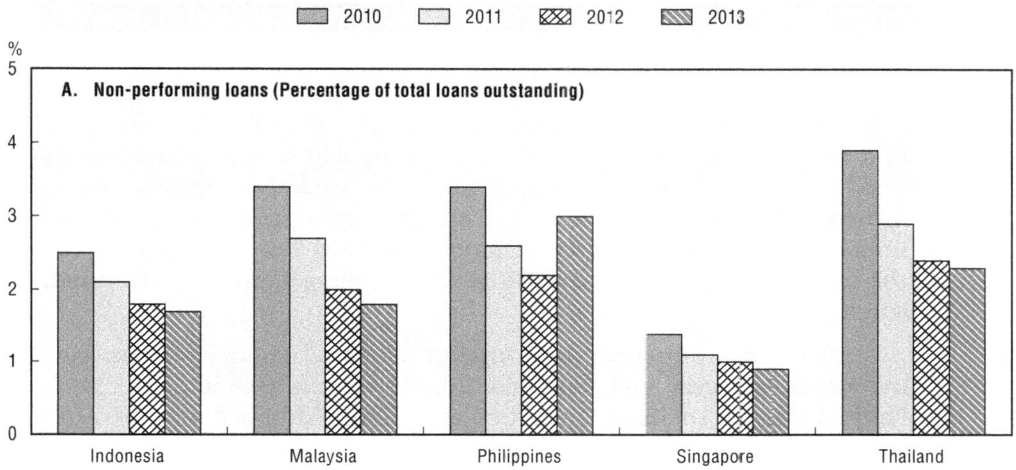

Source: World Bank (2014a).

StatLink http://dx.doi.org/10.1787/888933179465

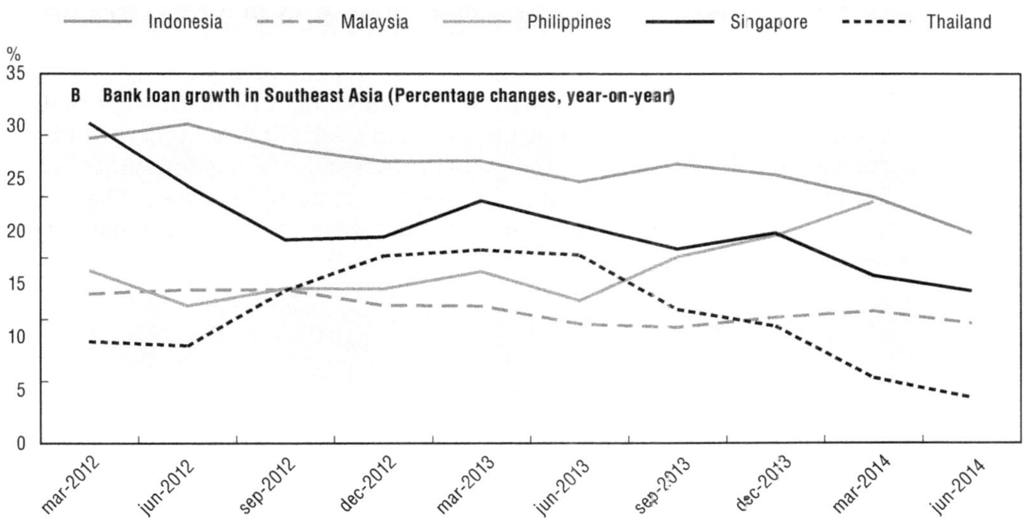

Note: In Malaysia, total loans do not include loans sold to Danaharta, the National Asset Management Company.
Source: CEIC.

StatLink http://dx.doi.org/10.1787/888933179465

Credit growth in Southeast Asia has generally slowed or remained stable in the past few years. Thailand bank loans year-on-year growth increased in 2012 and the first quarter of 2013, but slowed in 2013 Q2, and recorded the slowest growth in the Southeast Asia region in the first two quarters of 2014. This suggests that political turmoil has depressed credit growth in Thailand. Credit growth also decelerated in Indonesia, although its growth is still higher than elsewhere in the region. The series of monetary tightening steps in 2013 related to the QE tapering in the US has contributed to this moderation.

Inflationary pressures are generally subdued in the region

Both the level and volatility of inflation rates have generally been low in Emerging Asia recently (Figure 1.9). Generally, this moderating trend is expected to continue in the near future. The year-on-year change in headline consumer prices has been declining from a peak of 6.85% on average across ASEAN in May 2011 – largely driven by Viet Nam and, to a lesser extent, Lao PDR and Myanmar. Over the past year, the regional average has not risen above the 4.6% seen in July 2013, though Indian headline inflation rose to a high of 11.16% in November 2013, partly due to supply constraints in the face of rapid growth. Much of this moderation is due to relatively stable commodity prices; the differences between headline and core consumer price inflation have been relatively limited. Core consumer price inflation has been low and stable throughout most of the region, though it has recently been increasing sharply in Myanmar, from 3.53% in January 2014 to 7.4% by June.

Inflationary pressures were easing in many emerging Asian countries (notably Indonesia, Malaysia, Viet Nam and China) from the second half of 2013, except for the Philippines and Thailand. In particular, inflation dropped markedly in Indonesia from 8.38% in December 2013 to 4.53% in July 2014. Inflation in India has also eased, though the level is still relatively high compared to other countries in the region. Inflation has not increased greatly in these countries recently and remains relatively low. The year-on-year change in headline consumer prices over the preceding 12 months peaked at 8.3% in Indonesia in January 2014 before falling to 4% in August. It remained below 5% in both the Philippines and Malaysia. Nevertheless, risks are present in the near future due to developing economic conditions and recent policy changes. Domestic supply constraints in the Philippines may push up consumer prices there. Recent cuts to petrol subsidies in the Philippines and the planned continued reduction in fuel subsidies in Indonesia, while beneficial for these governments' fiscal sustainability, will temporarily contribute to a rise in inflationary pressures in both countries. The subsidy cuts are likely to eventually translate into price increases in energy-intensive sectors and in wages as well.

Figure 1.9. Consumer price inflation

Year-on-year percentage change

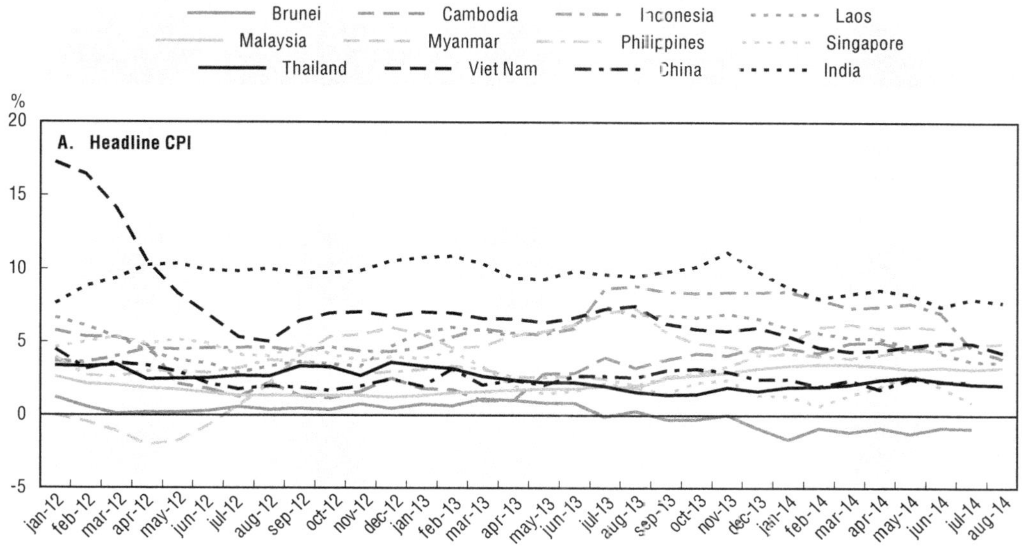

Notes: For Cambodia data refer to inflation as registered in Phnom Penh.

Sources: CEIC and Datastream.

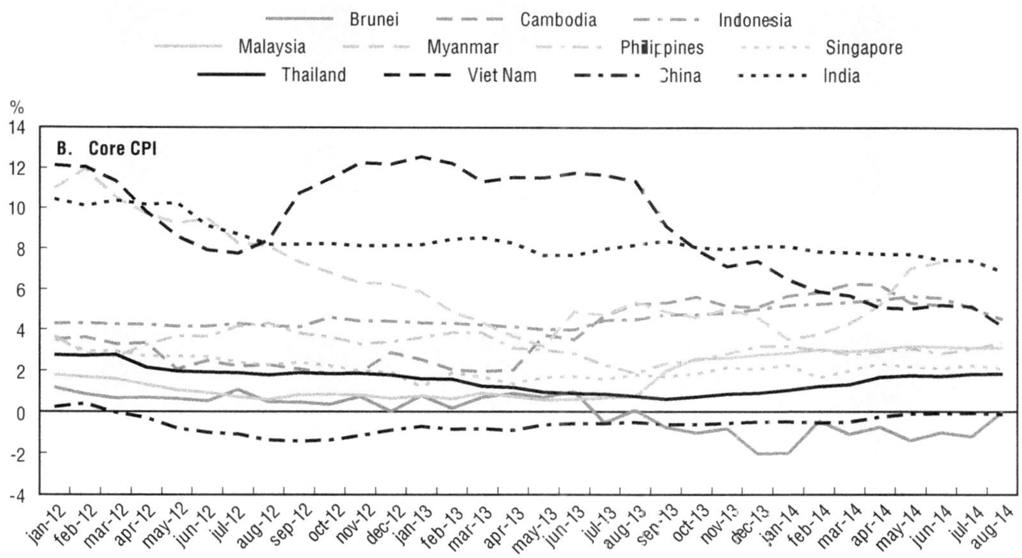

Notes: For Brunei core inflation refers to weighted average of Non-Food and Non-Housing, -Water, -Electricity, -Gas & -Other Fuels and Non-Transport consumer prices. For Cambodia core inflation refers to weighted average of Non-Food and Non-Housing & -Utilities and Non-Transportation consumer prices. For Malaysia core inflation refers to weighted average of Non-Food and Non-Housing, -Water, -Electricity, -Gas & -Other Fuels consumer prices. For Myanmar core inflation refers to simple average of Non-Food and Non-Fuel & -Light consumer prices. For Singapore the core inflation measure of the Monetary Authority of Singapore (MAS) monitors excludes the components of "Accommodation" and "Private Road Transport". For Viet Nam core inflation refers to weighted average of Non-Foods & -Foodstuffs and Non-Transportation consumer prices. For India core inflation refers to weighted average of Non-Food, -Beverages & -Tobacco and Non-Fuel & -Light consumer prices. For China the index of core inflation refers to same period of previous year=100 and it is the simple average of non-food consumer prices.

Source: CEIC.

StatLink http://dx.doi.org/10.1787/888933179478

Risks remain in real estate markets. Housing markets have been heating up in most of the Emerging Asian countries in recent years (Figure 1.10). Overall, housing price indexes have been increasing in Emerging Asia, particularly in India. Malaysia's housing prices have also shown rapid growth, especially over the past four years. Measures have been taken in some countries to prevent housing price bubbles. Malaysia has implemented some macro-prudential policy measures, including tightening the loan-to-value ratio for purchases of property. Thailand and Indonesia have also lowered their loan-to-value ratios, while the Philippines has announced stricter capital requirements for real estate lending.

Figure 1.10. **Housing price indices in Emerging Asia**

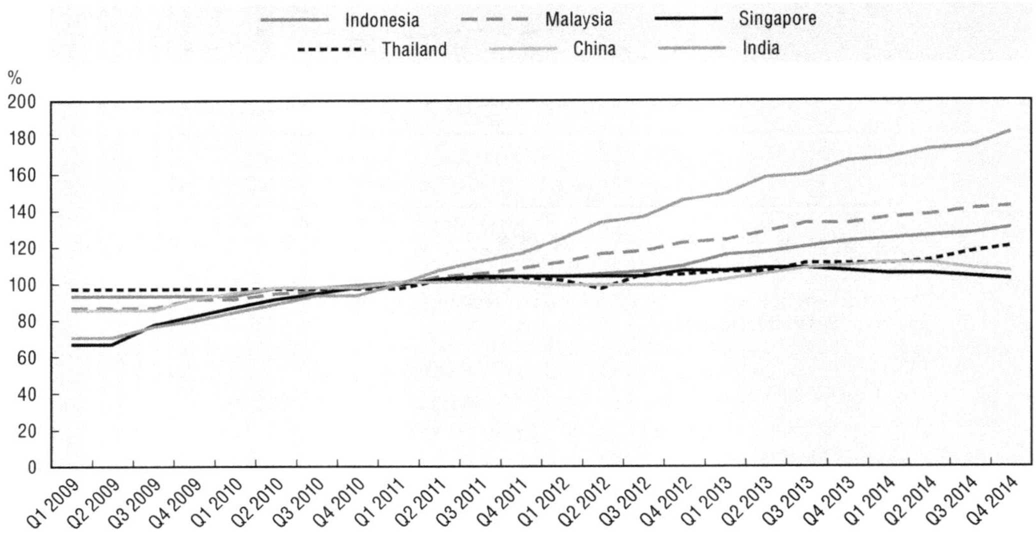

Source: Datastream

StatLink http://dx.doi.org/10.1787/888933179488

Oil and food prices need to be carefully monitored

External factors could have significant impacts in Emerging Asia through changing commodity prices, though the effects of these developments will differ significantly by country. While large swings in global oil prices are not anticipated in the medium term, if they were to occur the fluctuations could impact the exports and current account balances of countries in the region. An increase in fuel prices would be detrimental to the region's net oil importing countries but a boon to the net oil exporters, Brunei Darussalam and Malaysia, the former of which would be particularly impacted; liquefied natural gas accounted for 52% of Brunei Darussalam's exports in 2013 and crude petroleum for a further 45%. Similarly, an increase in food prices could have a particularly large impact on the region's agriculture-based economies. Agriculture is prominent in the CLM economies (as a share of GDP) and agricultural exports are very important in Viet Nam and Indonesia, where they accounted for 18% and 17%, respectively, of the total value of goods exports in 2012. They are also a large component of Myanmar's trade, making up 20% of the value of exports in 2010. Vegetables and seafood account for most of Myanmar's agriculture exports.

Overall, policy interest rates have been fairly stable in the region

The variation in monetary policy measures among the Emerging Asian economies reflects their differences in growth and other economic conditions. Overall, policy interest rate movements have been modest during 2013-14. There has been an upward movement for Malaysia, the Philippines and India, corresponding to tightening monetary policy, while Thailand has eased monetary policy by lowering its policy rate (Figure 1.11). Indonesia, Viet Nam and China have maintained their monetary policy stances, keeping constant policy rate roughly stable over the two years.

Figure 1.11. **Evolution of inflation and policy interest rates**

Annual percentage changes

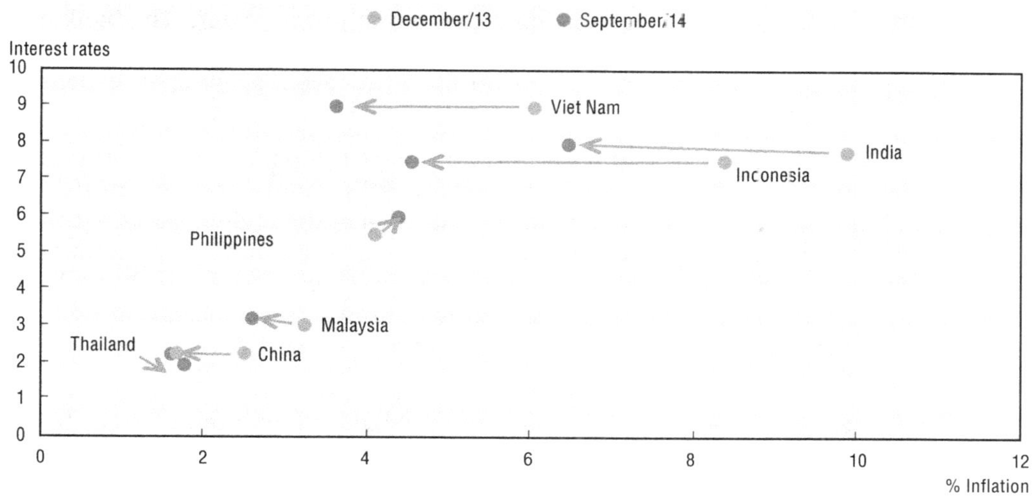

Notes: The figure above illustrates inflation on the horizontal axis and policy interest rates on the vertical axis. For each country, the figure plots inflation and interest rates in December 2013 and September 2014. As a consequence, a movement to the right in the figure means rising inflationary pressures, while a movement upwards corresponds to tightening monetary policy in the same period. Indonesia: Policy Rate: Month End: Reference rate (BI Rate); Malaysia: Policy Rate: Month End: Overnight Policy Rate; Philippines: Policy Rate: Month End: Repurchase Rate; Thailand: Policy Rate: Month End; Viet Nam: Policy Rate: Month End: Prime Lending Rate; China: Policy Rate: Month End: Rediscount Rate; India: Policy Rate: Month End: Repo Rate.

Sources: CEIC, Datastream and national sources.

StatLink http://dx.doi.org/10.1787/888933179495

Indonesia's policy rate remained unchanged over the two years despite falling inflation and slowing GDP growth. Although headline inflation, driven by lower food price inflation and controlled core inflation, eased to 4.53% in September 2014, Bank Indonesia has kept the country's policy rate unchanged since November 2013, following a series of tightening steps over the second half of 2013. At its last meeting in September 2014, the bank decided to continue holding the BI reference rate at 7.5% in order to help narrow the current account deficit to reach a more sustainable level. The central bank also kept the Lending Facility and Deposit Facility rates unchanged at 7.5% and 5.75%, respectively. The tight policy stance has been kept as a precaution against several remaining risks as the economy slows down. In addition, the bank appears to be waiting for a decision on the next fuel price adjustment that will likely be taken by the incoming government, which took office in October 2014.

The policy interest rate in Malaysia increased slightly in July 2014 by 25 basis points to 3.25%. This was the first change in the rate since May 2011 and suggests confidence that the economy is healthy enough for some tightening in policy. The decision was also intended to anticipate possible risks of financial and economic imbalances. No further changes have been made to the policy rate through September 2014.

The Philippines' Bangko Sentral ng Pilipinas (BSP) has also increased policy interest rates as a pre-emptive measure to restrain price pressures and contain inflationary expectations. Driven by higher food (due to tight domestic supply) and electricity prices, inflation increased in the Philippines from 4.1% in December 2013 to 4.9% in July 2014, near to the upper limit of the central bank's 3-5% target range. The inflation rate eased in September 2014 to 4.37%, although it was still above the December 2013 rate. The BSP's inflation targets for 2015 also remain at risk, since CPI inflation is forecasted to be above the official target.

The slowing down of the economy in Thailand has led to the easing of monetary policy. The Bank of Thailand cut the policy rate by 25 basis points from 2.25% in December 2013 to 2% in March 2014, making it the lowest in the region. The bank has, however, since maintained the rate at 2%. Monetary policy needs to remain accommodative to help the country's economy to recover from the recent slowing in response to political uncertainty.

The State Bank of Viet Nam (SBV) has kept the policy interest rate constant since November 2010. The SBV base interest rate of 9% remains, however, relatively restrictive and the highest as compared to other countries in the region. Many critics have argued that the high interest rates have burdened businesses and made Vietnamese products less competitive with those of its neighbouring countries which apply lower rates. The high interest rate policy has been maintained, nevertheless, in part to encourage depositors and to bolster profits for the banks.

The policy rate has also remained unchanged at 2.25% in China from December 2013 to September 2014. This 2.25% rate has actually been maintained since December 2010, after rising from 1.8% in November 2010. The policy rate has fallen slightly in real terms due to the decline in inflation from 2.5% in December 2013 to 1.6% in September 2014, the lowest rate since January 2010. Weak food price increases were the main driver of the decline.

Facing a high level of inflation, the Reserve Bank of India raised its policy rate to 8% in January 2014. The increase followed a series of increases over the second half of 2013 cumulating to 75 basis points taken in response to high consumer price inflation. The benchmark rate has, however, been kept unchanged since then. This levelling off reflects the fact that inflation has been falling and is expected to continue to ease thanks to the recent strengthening of the rupee and expected measures by the new government to increase food supplies.

In most cases, currency pressures have been neutral or upward

Financial market stabilisation and recovery of net inward investments have triggered a relative stabilisation of exchange rates or in some cases renewed exchange rate appreciation. Indeed, after significant depreciation and volatility of exchange rates in most countries in 2013, nominal exchange rates have since stabilised or appreciated (Figure 1.12). A nominal appreciation of the domestic currency against the US dollar was particularly marked in Thailand, Malaysia and the Philippines. The path followed in the first half of 2014 is more consistent with the long-term trend of currency appreciation for most Emerging Asian countries. Exceptions are India and Indonesia, which have witnessed depreciation of their nominal exchange rates. However, the nominal depreciation has been accompanied by comparatively high inflation, so that the depreciation is less marked in real exchange rates.

Downside risk in currency markets exists, particularly in the short run. The risk of sluggish global growth in advanced economies and emerging markets has come to the fore (IMF, 2014). Even if investors are less concerned than in 2013 regarding the exit from the QE policy in the United States, a disorderly reaction could lead to a spike in global interest rates and sharp reversals in capital inflows into Emerging Asia. In this context, a number of regional currencies face risks of significant depreciation in the near term.

Figure 1.12. **Nominal exchange rates**

USD per national currency (2010 average = 100)

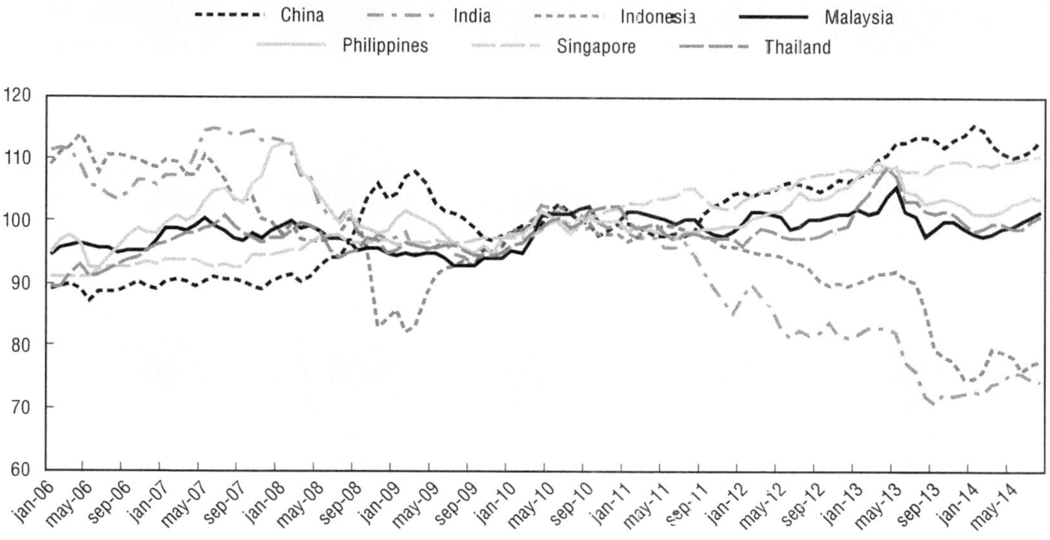

Source: International Financial Statistics.

StatLink http://dx.doi.org/10.1787/888933179509

The long-term trend towards currency appreciation associated with short-term depreciation risks may lead, as in 2013, to relatively high exchange rate volatility in the short and medium run that has to be managed.

Indeed, while exchange rate flexibility helped macroeconomic adjustment in 2013 and should remain a shock absorber in the event of capital flow reversals, monetary policy that provides for some smoothing of large exchange rate movements can be beneficial for Emerging Asian economies. Structural changes in low and middle-income economies require investment in new sectors whose conditions are likely to be less familiar to investors. Low exchange rate volatility may be important to investment in those new sectors, as currency volatility puts off investors who fear uncertainty in the returns on their investments. Wide fluctuations in real effective exchange rates, for example, can undermine foreign and export investors' incentives to invest in non-traditional sectors (Williamson, 2000; McKinsey, 2009). In this sense, long-term economic transformation requires smoothing out sharp currency fluctuations, as China did in the 2000s.

In the same vein, large exchange rate fluctuations can also have an impact that is more pronounced in developing economies than in developed ones. This calls for a management of large fluctuations. For example, most sustained large exchange rate appreciations may have little negative effect on developed economies because their industries have the resilience to adapt and gain in competitiveness (e.g. by importing more modern techniques when these become less expensive due to a higher exchange rate), whereas this resilience appears significantly lower for developing economies (Kappler et al., 2013). In the case of large sustained appreciations, the resilience of developing economies is likely to be higher when resources can be shifted from exports towards domestic sources of growth. In a number of Emerging Asian economies, however, the domestic market will take time to develop, which underlines the need to avoid high volatility of exchange rates.

Expedited efforts on priority initiatives are needed for attainment of the AEC by the end of 2015

The *ASEAN Economic Community Blueprint* identifies 4 key characteristics, 17 core elements and 176 priority actions needed to achieve the goal of the ASEAN Economic Community (AEC) by the end of 2015. The Blueprint envisages four inter-related key pillars of: (I) a single market and production base; (II) a highly competitive economic region; (III) a region of equitable economic development; and (IV) a region fully integrated into the global economy. The AEC Blueprint serves as a detailed outline for the ASEAN member countries to co-operate in implementing the initiatives required to deepen economic integration within the Southeast Asian region.

Progress in implementing the initiatives specified in the Blueprint is monitored through the *AEC Scorecard*.[1] According to the latest AEC Scorecard report, 67.5% of the measures set for Phase I (2008-2009) and Phase II (2010-2011), had been achieved. For Pillar (I) of a single market and production base, 65.9% of mandated measures are reported to have been implemented. Significant improvement can be seen in the free flow of skilled labour, the free flow of capital and in the priority integration sectors, with the respective measures fully implemented by 2011. Measures to implement initiatives for the free flow of goods and services seem to be at a standstill. In terms of Pillar (II) of a competitive economic region, 67.9% of measures have been fully implemented. Progress in implementing the measures can be seen in the areas of competition policy, intellectual property rights, and information and communication technology (ICT). Pillar (III) of Equitable Economic Development has achieved 66.7% of its targeted measures. For this pillar, 100% of the measures for phase I were attained but only 55.5% attainment has occurred during Phase II. Pillar (IV) of integration into the global economy reached the highest attainment among the four pillars, with 85.7% of measures achieved by the end of 2011.

Notable achievements up to now in implementing measures include success in **tariff reduction**, with the current Common Effective Preferential Tariffs (CEPT) rates now at essentially 0% for the ASEAN-6 (Brunei Darussalam, Indonesia, Malaysia, the Philippines, Singapore and Thailand) and 2.6% for Cambodia, Myanmar, Lao PDR and Viet Nam (CMLV) (Figure 1.13). **Trade facilitation** is being strengthened with Indonesia, Malaysia, the Philippines, Singapore, Thailand, Brunei Darussalam and Viet Nam in advanced stages of implementation of their National Single Windows (NSW) as part of the ASEAN Single Window and in streamlining and integrating the NSW of all ASEAN Member Countries (AMC) toward a single platform for electronic trade. However, there is still a wide disparity within ASEAN in the state of trade facilitation initiatives. For example, according to the World Bank *Trading Across Borders* database, a wide gap exists across the region in the number of days needed to comply with all procedures required to export and import goods. Where Singapore requires 6 days to export and 4 days to import goods, Myanmar requires 11 and 27 days for exports and imports, respectively.

Further progress in implementing measures of **ASEAN free trade agreements (FTA)** with other countries can be seen in the past year, with the ASEAN free trade agreement with India in services and investment currently in its final stages of being officially implemented. The past ASEAN-India FTA operationalised in 2010 was restricted to trade in goods, while the new FTA will cement the economic partnership between India and ASEAN. ASEAN currently has six FTA partners: China, Japan, Korea, India, Australia and New Zealand. Current integration efforts seem to have affected trading patterns as well. China is now the largest trading partner of ASEAN, displacing the past dominance of the EU, the US and Japan. ASEAN's trading with China accounted for 14% of total ASEAN trade in 2013, 12% of the region's exports and 16% of its imports. Tasked with eliminating all tariff and non-tariff barriers and narrowing the development gap with less developed ASEAN countries, negotiations for the inauguration of the *Regional Comprehensive Economic Partnership* (RCEP) between ASEAN and its six dialogue partners are currently ongoing. Aligned with the expected formation of the ASEAN Economic Community, the target year to sign the final RCEP agreement is currently set at 2015. Setting a framework for the free flow of **investment** is also an area where there has been progress. For instance, the *ASEAN Comprehensive Investment Agreement* (ACIA), that came into effect in 2012 lays out rules for investment with the purpose of enhancing the investment environment to attract more domestic and international investment throughout the ASEAN region and beyond. The ACIA is built from the past two ASEAN investment frameworks – the *ASEAN Investment Area Agreement* (AIA) and the *Investment Guarantee Agreement* (IGA)

Figure 1.13. **Regional integration in trade in Emerging Asia**

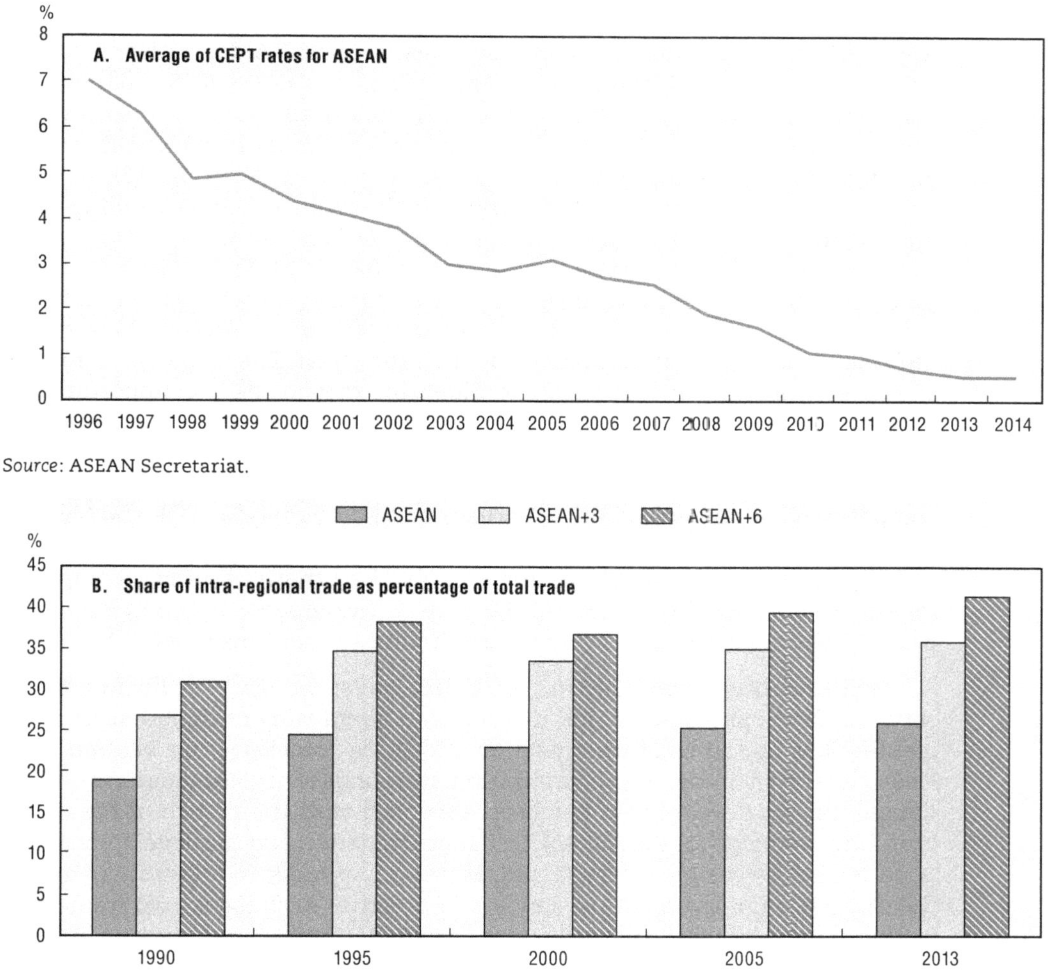

Note: ASEAN+3 includes ASEAN 10 countries plus China, Japan and Korea. ASEAN+6 includes ASEAN+3 plus Australia, India and New Zealand.

Source: CEIC, OECD Development Centre calculations.

StatLink http://dx.doi.org/10.1787/888933179511

Positive progress can be seen in terms of performance in investment liberalisation. In the goods sector in the AMSs, the overall foreign investment liberalisation rates reflect a region that has a fairly open investment environment in the goods sector. The *Mid-term Review of the Implementation of AEC Blueprint* undertaken by the ERIA reports that 3 AMSs (the Philippines, Malaysia and Cambodia) have liberalisation rates of at least 90% out of 100%, five AMSs (Lao PDR, Brunei Darussalam, Myanmar, Singapore and Thailand) are between 85% and 89%, with the Indonesia and Viet Nam rating around 80%. Positive changes, such as the surge in foreign direct investment to the ASEAN region in recent years, may be attributed to the various measures taken to implement initiatives for AEC. For example, the value of total FDI inflow from ten source countries increased steadily, from USD 97.56 billion in 2011 to USD 122.4 billion in 2013 (ASEAN Statistics). The extra-ASEAN net inflow in foreign direct investment is higher than that of intra-ASEAN FDI inflows. However, the net inflow of intra-ASEAN FDI is rising, from USD 15 228.4 in 2011 to USD 21.3 billion in 2013.

Improvements have been made in the areas of **infrastructure**. Adopted in 2010, the *Master Plan on ASEAN Connectivity* strives to enhance physical, institutional and people-to-people connections as a vital process in realising AEC. Along with energy co-operation outlined in the *ASEAN Plan of Action for Energy Cooperation 2010-2015* and the ASEAN Energy Management System, the transport sector, including air transport liberalisation, is a key component in the path towards AEC, especially to boost trade and tourism. Designed in conjunction with the AEC Blueprint and the Master Plan on ASEAN Connectivity, the *ASEAN Strategic Transport Plan* serves as the main reference guiding land, air, and marine transport and transport facilitation. Various air transport agreements, such as the *Multilateral Agreement on the Full Liberalization of Air Freight Services*, the *Multilateral Agreement on Air Services* and the *Multilateral Agreement on the Full Liberalization of Passenger Air Services* have been made under the ASEAN-X formula, toward the establishment of the ASEAN Single Aviation Market (dubbed the Open Skies Policy). To foster a culture of fair competition in the AEC, the Blueprint recognises the importance of putting **competition laws and policies** into place as an integral part of achieving the goal of a competitive economic region. Noticeable development progress within the AMC has been made with the Philippines currently in the process of adopting a comprehensive competition law, and with Brunei Darussalam, Cambodia, Lao PDR and Myanmar still to finalise their national competition laws. With 2015 fast approaching, ASEAN is forging ahead to develop an effective framework for the construction of a competition-aware region by 2025. The formulation of the post-2015 Competition Action Plan for the period of 2016-25 is presently on its way toward finalisation in November 2014.

Financial integration is also a crucial area under the AEC. The liberalising of financial services, development of capital markets and liberalising of capital accounts have been identified as key areas of prioritisation under *The Roadmap for the Integration of ASEAN in Finance*. On financial services liberalisation, six rounds of negotiations have been completed. Capital market development has been advanced with the launch of the marketing and branding campaign for the ASEAN Exchanges initiative, and the development of an ASEAN Bond Market Development Scorecard. Moreover, in order to attain financial integration, the integration of the banking sector is imperative. At present, two frameworks for the banking sector integration are in place: The *ASEAN Framework Agreement on Services* (AFAS) and the complementary *ASEAN Banking Integration Framework*. The multilateral currency swap arrangement among ASEAN+3 members (ASEAN, China, Japan and Korea) has been strengthened through the recently amended *Chiang Mai Initiative on Multilateralisation* (CMIM), which enlarges the total size to USD 240 billion, with the IMF de-linked portion raised from 20% to 30%. The amended facility will strengthen the region's ability to respond to liquidity difficulties in times of crisis. In relation to this initiative, the ASEAN+3

Macroeconomic Research Office (AMRO) is effective in monitoring and analysing regional economies as well as to support the decision-making of CMIM. Competition policies will play a large part in the formation of the AEC.

The implementation of initiatives toward the AEC has indeed progressed since its affirmation in 2003. But intensified efforts will be needed for the AEC to become a reality by the end of 2015, as recognised in the *Nay Pyi Taw Declaration on Realisation of the ASEAN Community by 2015*. Remaining issues such as the removal of non-tariff barriers along with improvements in trade and investment facilitation are urgent matters that need to be addressed with priority. In addition, integration should also continue with a broader range of issues addressed, including topics like the environment and green growth that have so far been mostly left aside.

Medium-term growth prospects: 2015-19

The results of MPF-2015 indicate that overall, Emerging Asia is projected to sustain stable growth in the period to 2019 (Box 1.3). Although growth in the largest economies, notably China, will moderate somewhat, the robust growth momentum of the ASEAN region will continue. Indonesia and the Philippines will lead the growth in the ASEAN-5, underpinned by strong domestic demand supported by the growing middle class that will enhance the economies' resilience to changes in the external environment. Less developed countries in the region (e.g. Cambodia, Lao PDR and Myanmar) will grow faster than 7% annually – a somewhat faster pace than for the ASEAN-5 economies.

Box 1.3. **Key assumptions of the medium-term outlook to 2019**

- Output gaps – the gap between actual and potential GDP – will converge to zero by 2019.
- Inflation targeting countries will continue to pursue price stability and adjust monetary policies to support their targets.
- Regional economic integration initiatives and projects will remain on track.
- The five-year plans of Emerging Asian countries will largely be implemented, subject to budgetary and other policy considerations (see Chapter 2 for reference).
- Unanticipated economic events and other external factors will not significantly alter the situation beyond the cut-off date.
- The cut-off date of data for the projections is 6 October 2014. For more detailed information on MPF, see www.oecd.org/dev/asiapacific/mpf.

Consumption is likely to account for a larger share of future domestic demand

Sound macroeconomic conditions will underpin the projected upward trend in consumption and consumer confidence over the next five years (Figure 1.14). The rising demand for skilled workers in many of the region's countries, together with improved skills, have seen wage levels rise. That trend will persist, with workers' growing disposable incomes supporting buoyant domestic demand during the 2015-19 projection period. The mounting numbers of middle-class households will further drive consumption, as will population ageing and wider access to loans, although there is plenty of room for improvement in banking in the less developed countries. Policy, too, has played and will play a part in rising domestic demand. Extensive social assistance schemes across the region will ease the need for precautionary savings and help to boost consumption.

Figure 1.14. **Private consumption in Southeast Asia, China and India**

Percentage changes

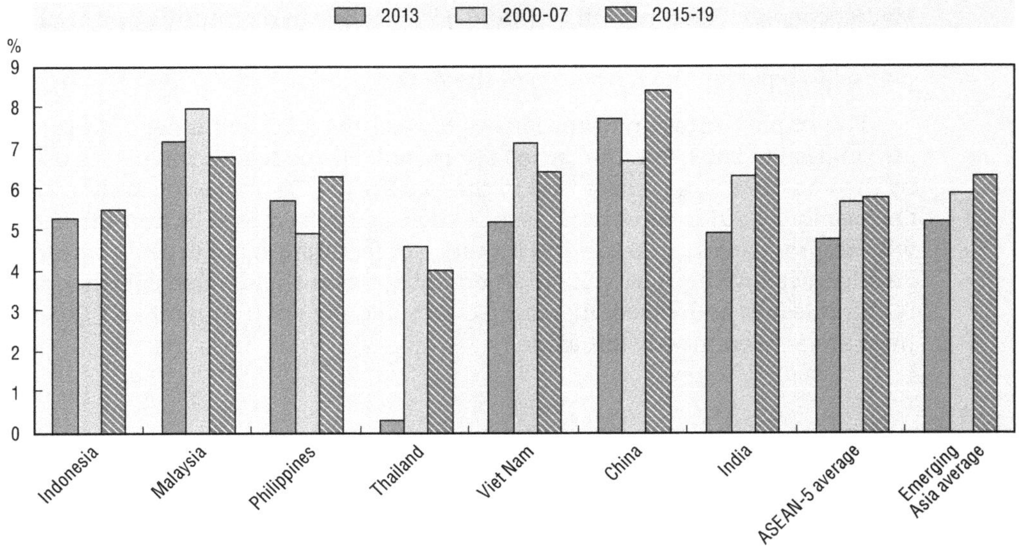

Source: OECD Development Centre, MPF-2015.

StatLink http://dx.doi.org/10.1787/888933179524

Household consumption accounted for a large share of total demand in most Emerging Asian economies in 2013, particularly the Philippines, Viet Nam and India and generally grew steadily in absolute terms, particularly in China and Malaysia.[2] While cyclical factors, including the on-going global recovery, are partly responsible for the upward trend, it is also the result of a number of longer-term structural and policy factors that can be expected to foster consumption over the medium term and beyond. In many countries, output per worker is gradually increasing along with physical and human capital. Industrial upgrading and the expansion of modern services sectors are raising demand for skilled workers, which is being supplied by expanding education systems. This upgrading has often translated into higher wages – for instance, wages in China grew at an average annual rate of 11.89% per year over 2006 to 2010. In contrast, wages decreased by an average of 1.28% in India over the same period, although this is partly a reflection of the growth slowdown following the global financial crisis. Middle classes throughout Emerging Asia can be expected to continue to expand. The increasing disposable incomes of workers will continue to further support domestic demand over the longer term, particularly for consumer goods, including consumer durables, and for health, education and personal financial services. While demographic factors continue to help keep savings rates high and to depress consumption somewhat, over the longer term, ageing populations throughout Asia will gradually lead to a reversal in this trend.

In addition to these structural trends, sound macroeconomic conditions will contribute to strong growth in consumption. Sound macroeconomic conditions should generally prevail over the medium term despite some current short-term inflationary pressures in the region that have accompanied depreciating currencies over the past year (see the prior section). Central banks remain broadly committed to and capable of handling these pressures, however, and low and stable inflation rates can be expected to prevail over the longer term and to underpin consumer confidence.

Government policies to provide social safety nets and other social assistance programmes will help to reduce households' precautionary savings and thereby support consumption. These programmes are already very large in some countries in the region; Thailand has one of the highest coverage rates in the world for its poor population (82.6% of the poorest 20% of the population) and India's National Rural Employment Guarantee Scheme is the world's largest public works-based social safety net programme, covering

193 million people, or 16% of the total population (Gentilini, Honorati and Yemtsov, 2014). These programmes are also undergoing significant change. In July 2014, China's State Council outlined plans to gradually reform its *hukou* system of household registration, which denies rural migrants to cities access to government services such as education, health care, housing and state pensions. While these reforms will be limited to medium-sized and, later, large cities, they will help to encourage further urbanisation and increased consumption among migrants. Although fuel subsidies inefficiently help to prop up household consumption in some countries in the region (government spending on these supports significantly exceeds that on social safety nets in Indonesia, India and Malaysia), reform is starting here as well. Indonesia's new president, Joko Widodo, has announced plans to cut the fuel subsidy in that country. Cuts in the fuel subsidy need not necessarily depress consumption if, for instance, the savings are directed to assistance programmes that better target the poor, as the plans envisage.

At the same time, the on-going expansion and modernisation of financial services in Emerging Asia – access to credit and insurance in particular – can be expected to further reduce precautionary savings over time. Significant progress remains to be made in most of the region's less-developed countries, however; while there were 1 076.16 borrowers from Singapore's banks for every 10 000 people in the country in 2012, the equivalent number in Myanmar was only 0.87.

Domestic investment remains important to Emerging Asia's growth

Projections of both public and private domestic investment across Emerging Asia point to a steadily upward trend over the next five years (Figure 1.15). Investment will rise faster than in 2013 in most countries, then often at a similar or lower rate than in the years prior to the global financial crisis – although it will start from generally higher shares of GDP. Slowing investment will be particularly noticeable in China and India, where 2015-19 growth will be significantly lower than that of 2000-07. Compared with growth in 2013, the pace of capital investment growth will speed up in Indonesia, Thailand and Viet Nam, though these countries will also see slower growth than in the pre-crisis years. Only the Philippines can expect to see a significant jump in investment in 2015-19 compared to 2000-07, with a minor increase in Malaysia as well.

Figure 1.15. **Gross fixed capital formation in ASEAN-5, China and India**

Percentage changes

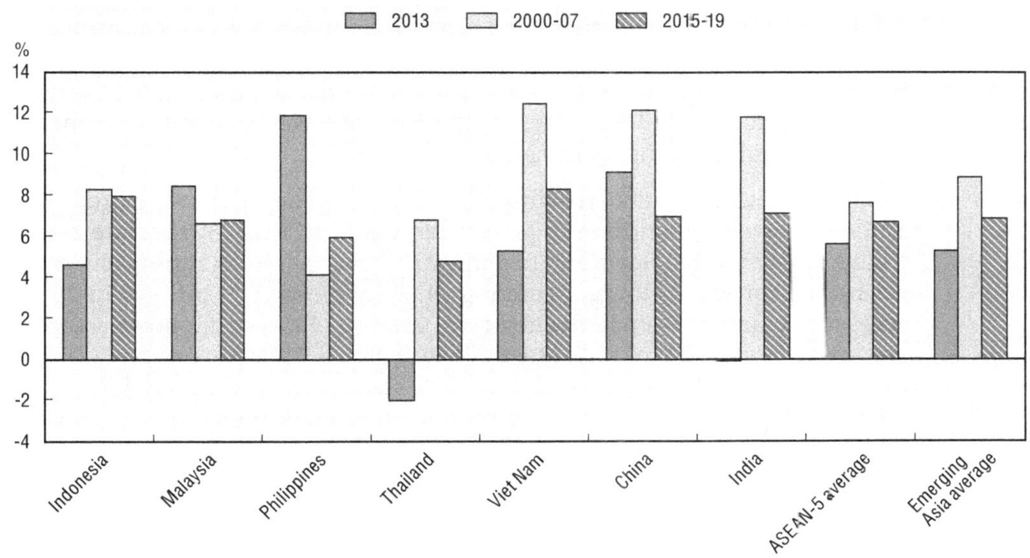

Source: OECD Development Centre, MPF-2015.

StatLink http://dx.doi.org/10.1787/888933179530

Clearly, then, public and private investment will remain major sources of demand even as the importance of consumption as an engine of growth in Emerging Asia increases. Gross capital formation has continued to make large contributions to output, particularly in China, where it accounted for 49.29% of GDP in 2013. This share represented a high for China and an increase of 9.2% over gross fixed capital formation in 2012. In several other countries in the region, however, investment growth has slowed relative to recent years, and declined from 2012 levels in India, Singapore and Thailand.

Much of public investment in Emerging Asia is likely to be made in infrastructure, as significant growth is needed to alleviate existing bottlenecks and to accommodate further economic development and urbanisation. In 2012, the ADB estimated that ASEAN member countries would need to spend approximately USD 60 billion per year over the next decade to address infrastructure needs in the region (ADB, 2012). Recognising this need, infrastructure investment is featured heavily in the longer-term development plans of the region, including Indonesia's Master Plan for Acceleration and Expansion of Indonesia's Economic Development (MP3EI) and Malaysia's Economic Transformation Programme (ETP). In July 2014, Thailand's military-led government approved a USD 75 billion master plan to improve transportation infrastructure over the next eight years. Multilateral development banks and regional initiatives are helping to support public investment in infrastructure. In May 2014, Myanmar announced that it would join the ASEAN Infrastructure Fund (AIF), a move that would bring all ten ASEAN members into the regional fund administered and co-financed by the ADB for the first time since its launch in 2012.

Private investment is also making a sizeable contribution to GDP, accounting for over 20% of GDP in Lao PDR, Thailand and India in 2012.[3] Though they have been used infrequently in the past, public-private partnerships (PPPs) in infrastructure investment are expected to make important contributions in the future, particularly where the scale of needed investment is too great for the public sector to bear alone. India has been active in implementing PPP projects and has set the goal in its Twelfth Five Year Plan of private funds providing around half of infrastructure financing. PPPs are also central to Indonesia's MP3EI. As a result, the PPP Book released by BAPPENAS, Indonesia's national planning agency, in November 2013, identified 27 projects with a combined value of USD 47.3 billion that were to be made available to private investors in 2014. The legal and financial frameworks needed to effectively balance public and private risks and to help facilitate these partnerships are not yet in place in all countries in the region, however. Only Indonesia, the Philippines, Thailand and Viet Nam have established or are planning to establish project development funds. Meanwhile, the barriers to PPPs are at a more basic level in Myanmar, which does not have a specific law concerning PPPs or a dedicated unit working on the issue.

The region's large and growing markets and generally strong productive potential can be expected to continue to attract large FDI inflows, in absolute terms as well as relative to total global flows and to domestic investment. Emerging Asia remains a major destination for FDI inflows, attracting 24.8% of global FDI inflows in 2013. This share represents a first and small decline from 25.9% in 2012, and follows steady increases in every year from 2007 to 2011. Most of the region's FDI has gone to China (8.53% of the global total) and to Singapore (4.39%). FDI also made a relatively large contribution to GDP in Singapore (21.40%) and in Cambodia (8.82%). While manufacturing and financial services are the most popular sectors for inflows into ASEAN countries, accounting for 32% and 21% of the region's FDI stock over 2000-12, respectively, the sector composition of FDI varies greatly by country. The power and fuel industries attract most of Myanmar's FDI, for example, and agriculture is relatively popular for FDI in Cambodia.

The region as a whole will record a current account surplus but country positions will vary

Taken as a whole, Emerging Asia looks set to be a net lender by 2019, but current account positions will differ across countries (Figure 1.16). As a rule, the more highly developed countries – with oil and gas exporter Brunei Darussalam and high-income Singapore leading the way – will show surpluses, while the less developed ones – Cambodia, Lao PDR and Myanmar – will struggle to limit their current account deficits. The current account surpluses of most of the ASEAN-5 economies will remain positive. Only Indonesia will still be a net borrower, but its deficit will have narrowed slightly. China's surplus will expand slightly, while India's deficit will widen.

Figure 1.16. **Current account balances of Southeast Asia, China and India**

Percentage of GDP

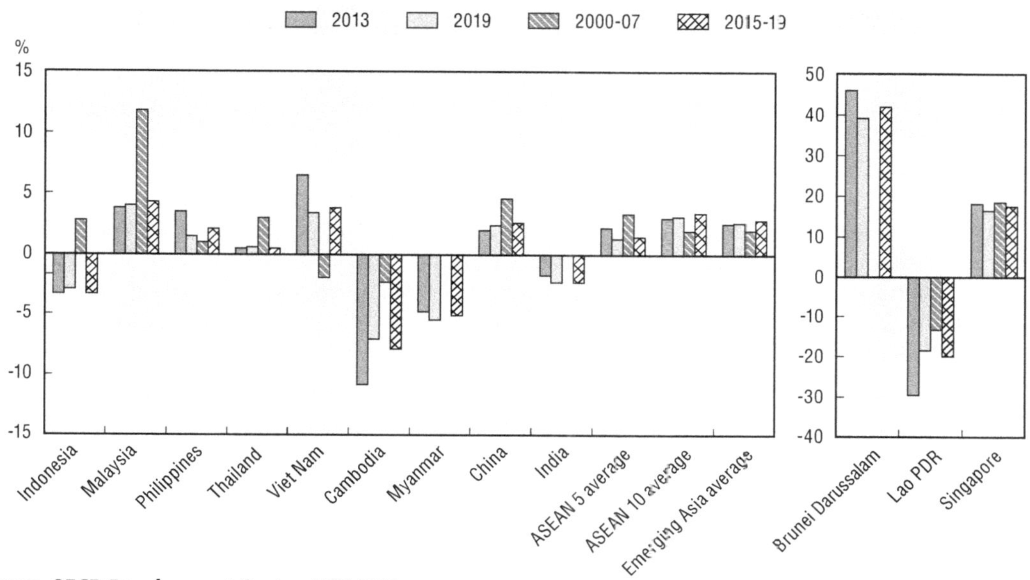

Source: OECD Development Centre, MPF-2015.

StatLink http://dx.doi.org/10.1787/888933179547

Trade balances remained buoyant in some Emerging Asian countries but weakened in others. In the first half of 2014, merchandise exports dropped in Brunei Darussalam, particularly in oil, natural gas and methanol, leading to a decline of its trade surplus. Merchandise exports also fell in Indonesia and Thailand. Singapore's exports, notably non-oil domestic exports also fell. Malaysia and the Philippines, on the contrary, had a rebound in exports. Myanmar's foreign trade also performed well, driven by exports of oil and gas spurred by large investments from China and Thailand in natural gas.

The two largest Emerging Asian economies showed different current account trends. China's current account surplus stood at 1.8% of its GDP in the first half of 2014. Although weakening external demand has weighed on exports in the first six months of 2014, import growth also slowed due to weakness in construction and regulations restricting the use of metals as collateral, which have weighed on imports of industrial commodities. This has led to a widening of China's trade surplus. However, the widening deficit on services and transfers led to decline in both the current account surplus and the overall balance of payments. India's current account recorded a deficit of 1.7% of GDP in 2014 Q1. This represents a narrowing compared to the 4.8% deficit in 2013 Q1, as the trade balance strengthened with measures to curtail gold imports. However, the deficit was still larger than in the three last quarters of 2013.

Among the Southeast Asian countries, current account balance trends are also diverse. Some countries have sustained persistently large surpluses, while others continue to be in deficit. Brunei Darussalam maintained huge current account surpluses, although they have narrowed due to a decline of the trade surplus. The higher global energy prices led to the country's large trade surplus in 2011. However, the surplus in both the trade and current accounts, declined sharply in 2012 and 2013. Singapore's current account surplus has also remained large. A rising trade surplus led to an increase in the current account surplus in 2013 to around 18% of GDP from 17% in 2012. Malaysia's current account surplus continues to be buoyed by export growth supported by strong demand from the Asia Pacific region. A larger trade surplus along with narrower deficits in services, income and transfers has led to a strong performance in the current account balance, which recorded a surplus of 6.9% of GDP. The Philippines' current account surplus also remained resilient, supported by a rebound in exports, in particular rising surpluses on services and income thanks to its rapidly growing business process outsourcing (BPO) sector and strong remittance inflows from overseas Filipinos. Viet Nam's external accounts have shown solid growth in exports and imports in the first half of 2014.

In contrast, current account deficits in some other Emerging Asian countries have remained a concern. Indonesia has been struggling with its current account deficit. A rise in the trade surplus due to a sharper fall in imports than in exports was more than offset by an increase in the services and income deficits. As a result, the country's current account recorded a deficit of 3.3% of GDP in 2013. In Thailand, merchandise exports fell slightly due to lower demand from major markets, including China and Japan, but merchandise imports dropped even more sharply, by 13.3% in the first quarter of 2014. The drop has brought the current account back into surplus following the deficit recorded in 2013.

Current accounts in Cambodia, Lao PDR and Myanmar have remained in deficit. Cambodia's growth in total merchandise exports weakened in the first half of 2014 as compared with the same period of 2013. Lao PDR's current account has recorded persistent deficits. In 2012, the current account deficit accounted for 28.5% of the country's GDP, and widened to 29.5% in 2013 due to a larger trade deficit. Myanmar also continues to record current account deficits, despite strong exports driven by the energy sector. The rising flows of foreign direct investment in recent years, together with strong consumer demand, have led to a surge in demand for imports, particularly of capital goods. Myanmar's merchandise trade deficit continues to widen, with imports easily outpacing exports. In Q1 2014, imports rose by 32.5% while exports continued lagging behind, with an increase of 18.1% as compared to the same period last year. The sharp widening of trade deficit increases will lead to a further deterioration of the current account balance.

Some signs of slowing in FDI have appeared in Emerging Asia

FDI flows remain strong in Emerging Asia. Despite a slight fall in 2013, Emerging Asia's share of global FDI inflows has, overall, shown steady increases, from 15.4% in 2008 to 24.8% in 2013 (Figure 1.17). Since 2012, FDI inflows to the region have been significantly above the inflows into the EU. Buoyant macroeconomic fundamentals have helped in attracting and sustaining strong investment flows to the region. China's FDI inflows have continued to slow recently in 2014. Overall, inward FDI into Emerging Asia remains relatively stable, although there are some signs of slowing in Indonesia and Thailand. FDI inflows to ASEAN rose by 6.7% to USD 125 billion in 2013. Singapore, which attracts half of the total Southeast Asia FDI inflows, was still among the world's top 10 recipients, while India and Indonesia were among the top 20.

Figure 1.17. **FDI inflows in Emerging Asia**

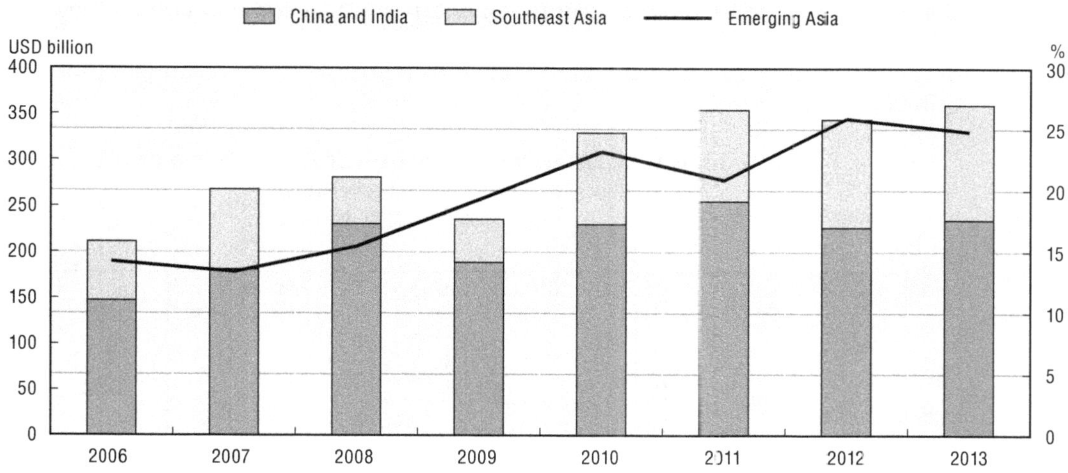

Note: China includes Mainland, Chinese Taipei, Macao and Hong Kong. Southeast Asia does not include Timor-Leste.

Source: UNCTAD World Investment Report 2014.

StatLink http://dx.doi.org/10.1787/888933179556

FDI flows to Indonesia have been slowing from 2012 – partly due to weakness of the mining sector, which is the largest recipient of FDI. The weak record of the first half of 2014 is related to uncertainty during the presidential election period. Malaysia recorded 22% growth of FDI inflows in 2013, the highest in the region. Although manufacturing was still the main recipient with a 37.6% share, the services sector recorded the highest rise from the previous year. The Philippines has also kept investors' confidence despite the devastation caused by Typhoon Yolanda. FDI inflows to the Philippines reached a record level in 2013, rising by 20% from the previous year to USD 3.9 billion. Thailand's political instability has discouraged some foreign investors. According to UNCTAD, 400 FDI projects have been cancelled or postponed due to political uncertainty. Despite the problems, FDI into Thailand increased to USD 12.9 billion in 2013, thanks to the rising Japanese investment in manufacturing. Inflows to the region's lower-income countries have shown mixed performances. FDI into Myanmar surged by 17% in 2013 over 2012, due to investment in the energy sector, garment industry, information technology, and food and beverage industries (World Bank Myanmar Economic Monitor, 2013). Viet Nam recorded a 6.4% increase in FDI over the same period. The level of FDI inflows stayed almost at the same for Lao PDR in 2013, and slightly decreased in Cambodia.

The rising importance of intra-regional FDI driven by regional integration efforts in East and Southeast Asia has contributed to the region's strong FDI flows. Intra-regional FDI flows among ASEAN member countries have risen significantly over the past decade. Intra-regional flows are now the biggest source of overall FDI inflows for the region, and have risen from around 10% in 2004 to about 24% in 2011. The intra-regional FDI flows, particularly in infrastructure and manufacturing industries, have been bringing development opportunities for lower-income countries such as Myanmar and Lao PDR (UNCTAD, 2014).

Public finance will continue to gradually improve in many of the region's countries

Overall, fiscal balances in countries in the region are unchanged, though trends will differ by country and there will be a lot of room for improvement (Figure 1.18). In Indonesia, the success of the reforms to cut fuel subsidies could be critical to strengthen fiscal soundness. In Malaysia, more subsidy rationalisation and introduction of a 6% goods and services tax (GST) in April 2015 will be critical. Fiscal reforms in Thailand at the moment are stalled but an improvement in political stability could allow them to be restarted. In the Philippines, many infrastructure projects are required and the success of the on-going fiscal reforms (to the tax administration and the budget process) will be critical.

Figure 1.18. **Public finances of Southeast Asia, China and India**

Fiscal balances (central government)

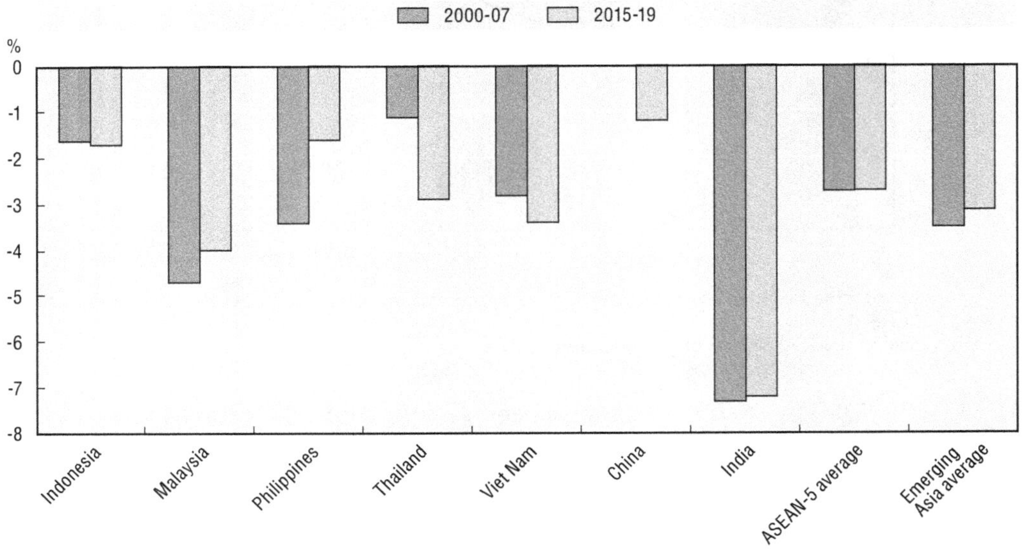

Source: OECD Development Centre, MPF-2015.

StatLink http://dx.doi.org/10.1787/888933179564

Underlying this overall picture are considerable differences in individual country circumstances and the resulting prospects for their public finances.

Public finance prospects are mixed in the ASEAN-5 …

In Indonesia, the country's fiscal position has improved drastically since 2000, with a low debt level of less than 30% of GDP partly attributable to a fiscal rule that limits the deficit to less than 3% of GDP.

In 2013, the deficit rose slightly to 2.3% of GDP. The main reason was an increase in social spending and in the energy subsidy due to currency depreciation, while tax revenues dropped as a result of slow growth domestically and in foreign trade. The same fiscal deficit level is projected for 2014. Contributory factors to the increased deficits were the high election-related expenditure, higher subsidy costs due to the weak rupiah (including the fuel subsidy), and lower tax revenues that may be ascribed to lacklustre international commodity markets and declining oil production. In the 2015-19 period, however, the fiscal position will be more or less unchanged for various reasons: GDP is expected to recover from the recession following the tapering of the quantitative easing policy in 2013; on-going tax reforms will improve tax collection; and subsidies, particularly for fuel, will be reduced gradually.

Malaysia has seen a worsening in its fiscal position and public debt due to the recession triggered in 2008 by the collapse of the Lehman Brothers investment bank. The government has run a deficit of more than 4% every year since 2008 and public debt has mounted steeply to over 50% of GDP from around 40% in the early 2000s. In 2013, the government began to tackle the fiscal deficit by rationalising subsidies for public services such as electricity and by lowering development expenditure. As a consequence, the country's fiscal position has slightly improved despite sluggish commodity market conditions. The fiscal position is projected to improve further as Malaysia diversifies away from a heavy reliance on oil revenues – which account for nearly 30% of total government income – and a scheduled 6% goods and service tax comes into effect in 2015. The newly established Fiscal Policy Committee will also help in reducing the deficit to around 3% of GDP over the 2015-19 period, with the public debt ratio shrinking by a moderate amount.

In the Philippines, thanks to rapid economic growth and policy measures to improve tax collection, the fiscal position has dramatically improved – even in the adverse post-2008 economic environment. In 2013, the consolidated public sector account ran a 1.4% deficit, a slight improvement on the 2.4% for 2012. The improvement is attributable to higher alcohol and tobacco duties that helped offset increases in infrastructure and social service expenditure. The fiscal consolidation of the last five years has also brought the debt-to-GDP ratio down from 63.5% in 2009 to 50.1% in 2013. From 2014, however, it is projected that the fiscal deficit will narrow although there is uncertainty about post-hurricane reconstruction.

In Thailand, the fiscal deficit widened in response to the 2008 global financial crisis and in the wake of the 2011 floods. Then, in 2013, political unrest halted fiscal consolidation. Throughout that year, revenues declined as growth stagnated but the fall was partly offset by delays in disbursements for large infrastructure projects. As a consequence, the fiscal position slipped only moderately to 2.4% of GDP. From 2014 onward, further fiscal shortfalls are projected, but are expected to be moderate. As for total debt, it is projected to stay flat throughout the 2015-19 projection period.

In Viet Nam, the fiscal deficit has been on the rise in recent years to support economic growth. It widened further in 2013 with increases in spending on infrastructure and social welfare. The fiscal position is projected to continue worsening in 2014 and onward, with tax revenues dwindling as a share of GDP due to sluggish economic growth, tax concessions, and reductions in import tariffs. However, the deficit will gradually narrow again in the later stages of the 2015-19 projection period, aided by a pick-up in growth. Total debt will decline marginally.

... and are subject to some uncertainties in the two big economies

In China, official data paint a moderately healthy budget picture with a deficit-to-GDP ratio of less than 2%. However, the data do not include the off-budget and quasi-fiscal activities of local governments. These have swollen in the last few years and are significant contingent impediments to financial stabilisation. The central government is currently endeavouring to limit local government off-budget borrowing. It is expected to tolerate some local expenditure hikes during the transition and to obtain a clearer view of fiscal workings at local government level. As a consequence, the budget deficit is projected first to widen slightly and then gradually narrow in the later stages of 2015-19.

Historically, India runs a large fiscal deficit – sometimes over 10% of GDP. It has sought to cut the deficit to less than 5% of GDP with fiscal measures like the Fiscal Responsibility and Budget Management Act enacted in 2003. However, with the onset of the global financial crisis in 2008, the deficit immediately widened again. Since then it has slowly improved. The budget deficit is expected to increase temporarily in 2014 as the depreciation of the rupee pushes up fertiliser and petroleum prices and swells the amount of subsidies. Over the 2015-19 period, the deficit is projected to slowly narrow in the wake of the introduction of a goods and service tax. Nevertheless, it will remain at a high level – over 3% of GDP – and the government's medium-term goal of fiscal consolidation, which includes moves such as cutting subsidies, is expected to advance only gradually. There is further uncertainty over the speed and quality of fiscal consolidation with the advent of the newly elected administration.

Risks and policy challenges to sustain healthier growth in the medium-term

While basically favourable, the medium-term economic outlook is subject to some risks. Realisation of the region's potential will require the overcoming of some important challenges.

- US monetary normalisation, the implementation of Abenomics in Japan, and the slowdown of the Chinese economy will pose moderate risks for the region.
- Political uncertainties in the region could undermine growth for Emerging Asia, in particular in Thailand.
- Structural policy reforms will need to be effectively but skilfully implemented.
- Expedited efforts will be required to attain ASEAN economic integration (by 2015) with narrowing development gaps within the region a key regional challenge.

US monetary policy normalisation continues to pose moderate risks for the region

The US Federal Reserve began QE1, its first bond-buying programme, in 2008, which was followed by QE2 in 2012 and QE3 in 2012. It announced in June 2013 that a tapering of the programme would begin as the economy improved, and that interest rates would rise at some point in the future. Although a subsequent announcement stated that the tapering would be delayed, the anticipated end of the programme nevertheless prepared investors for a return to higher interest rates. While India and Indonesia were relatively more exposed to these risks in the second half of 2013 – and saw their exchange rates depreciate in the wake of the tapering announcement – US monetary normalisation does not pose major threats to the region in general. The normalisation process of ending the programme of quantitative easing and gradually raising interest rates from the very low levels kept since the beginning of the global financial crisis is expected to have some effects on the Emerging Asian economies but they should be limited (as of November 2014).

The shift in US monetary policy will continue to affect the Emerging Asian economies negatively through two channels – current and future capital flows and global interest rates. However normalisation is likely to coincide with improving conditions that will create upside risks. In particular, the continued recovery of the US economy may help to support growth in the Emerging Asian region through increased demand for exports.

Investors have already factored their future expectations of the effects of US monetary policy normalisation into their positions and macroeconomic conditions in the Emerging Asian economies that received capital inflows stimulated by the QE programme make them well positioned for managing upcoming pressures when they are reversed. Effective prudential measures will help to dampen the effects on growth of countries facing capital outflows. Appropriate macroeconomic management in general, as evidenced by low and stable inflation and sound fiscal and current account positions should also help to slow and limit sudden capital flow reversals.

Empirical results from a DSGE approach to examine the impact of a US interest rate increase on the domestic economy of the ASEAN-5 suggest that the adverse impact of US normalisation on growth – moderation of domestic consumption and investment – will be at most a decline of 0.3% in quarter-on-quarter GDP growth (as of November 2014) (See Technical Appendix 2).

Over the medium term, rising interest rates in the United States and other advanced economies as their recoveries continue will create pressures on Emerging Asia currencies and domestic interest rates. Increased interest rates in the region could slow investment and growth but the extent of any hikes in the near future is expected to be limited. As noted in a recent IMF study, additional factors keeping real interest rates low are likely to remain in place – in particular, continued high savings rates in emerging economies including those in Asia, demand for safe assets and low investment rates in advanced economies (IMF, 2014).

The implementation of structural policy reforms in Japan will pose additional challenges to the region

Two other developments – structural reforms (Abenomics) in Japan and slowing growth in China – pose challenges for the Emerging Asian region. Abenomics refers to a set of economic policies implemented by the administration of Prime Minister Shinzo Abe aimed at reviving the Japanese economy and ending deflation. Abenomics consists of three "arrows": an aggressive monetary policy easing, a flexible fiscal policy, and a growth strategy to stimulate private investment (Table 1.3). Under the first arrow, the government and the Bank of Japan (BOJ) have set a target of 2% inflation. To attain this target and boost real growth, the BOJ has eased monetary policy by expanding the monetary base from JPY 138 trillion in 2012 to JPY 270 trillion in 2014, and by doubling the average lifespan of long-term government bonds. Under the fiscal policy arrow, the Japanese government introduced an economic stimulus package in January 2013 with JPY 10.3 trillion of additional spending.

The measures have so far affected the economy through a depreciation of the Japanese yen and a rise in the stock market. Significant improvements have also been seen in some of the country's economic indicators, including increased real GDP growth in 2013 and a lower unemployment rate. GDP growth has, however, contracted in the second quarter of 2014, following the consumption tax hike in April 2014.

Table 1.3. **Summary of Abenomics**

Arrows	Objectives	Measures
Aggressive monetary policy	Eliminate deflation and reduce real interest rates	Price stability target of a 2% inflation rate Monetary (qualitative and quantitative) easing
Flexible fiscal policy	Revive economic growth immediately through increased government consumption and public works investment	Economic stimulus package of JPY 10.3 trillion
Growth strategy	Strengthen competitiveness and raise investment	Japan revitalisation strategy: - Restoring Japan's "earning power" - Cultivating human resources - Reviving long-idle industries and promoting entry of new participants

While the first two arrows were implemented according to schedule, the third one started somewhat later. The growth strategy encompasses structural reforms to strengthen the competitiveness of the economy, while at the same time accelerating the removal of domestic institutional obstacles, including some regulations. The strategy has set some targets which include increasing real GDP growth to 2% per annum and doubling foreign direct investment and agricultural exports. Many of the measures have been implemented over the past year, including private sector investment revitalisation, labour market reform, innovation encouragement, agriculture development, and healthcare services improvement.

Box 1.4. Structural reforms under Abenomics

The corporate tax reform was implemented by reducing the effective corporate tax rate by 2.4 percentage points in April 2014, with a view to further reducing the rate to below 30% by FY2015. Other initiatives include enhancing corporate governance and accelerating industrial regeneration and venture businesses in order to restore Japan's earning power. To address the ageing population, initiatives have been taken to attract skilled workers and professionals from overseas, in part by relaxing requirements for skilled overseas professionals to work in Japan, revising standards for salary levels and research achievements, accepting employees of overseas subsidiaries in the manufacturing industry, and shortening the requirement for permanent residency from five to three years. To enhance female labour force participation, measures have been taken to improve childcare capacity, expand childcare leave benefits, and to encourage promotion and advancement of women in companies. A target has been set to increase the proportion of women in management positions to 30% by 2020. Measures to improve "working styles" are also being taken, including initiatives to prevent overwork, create systems for rewarding performance rather than hours worked, and development of conflict resolution systems. The strategy also includes creation of several special economic zones with liberalised business regulation. The first six special zones were selected in May 2014, covering areas of healthcare, employment, education, urban revitalisation, agriculture, and utilisation of historical buildings. With these and other measures, the strategy is also intended to prepare for further challenges in the future: to improve productivity, encourage innovation, stabilise the population at the 100 million level in 50 years' time, and to continue economic recovery with fiscal soundness.

In June 2014, the growth strategy was revised with expanded and strengthened measures. These include reforms to the corporate income tax to enhance Japan's international competitiveness; encouraging women's participation in the labour force, attracting skilled workers and professionals from overseas; stimulating innovation through science, technology and a "Robotics Revolution" to secure sustainable growth amid the declining birth-rate and ageing population; reforms to address inefficiencies in agriculture and to help revive long-idle industries strategy; as well as reforms of the health care and medical sectors. Consideration is also being given to raising the retirement age (Box 1.4).

More recently, on 31 October 2014, the BOJ announced an expanding programme of its quantitative easing, contrasting the US Federal reserve announcement to end its QE two days earlier. This monetary stimulus, unexpected by the market, has been taken as an additional measure to drive inflation upwards. The monetary policy announcement was followed by the Government Pension Investment Fund, another key element of the Abenomics, announcing its plan to cut its holdings of local bonds from 60% to 35% and boost investment in domestic and foreign stocks.

The impacts of the implementation of Abenomics have been estimated by a multi-country VAR model (see Technical Appendix 3 for details) (Figure 1.19). Overall, the impact of Abenomics is relatively small, although it is somewhat higher for Thailand. In most countries, the impact is predicted to be short-lived (as of November 2014).

Figure 1.19. **Impact of Abenomics on GDP trends in ASEAN countries**

Percentage change

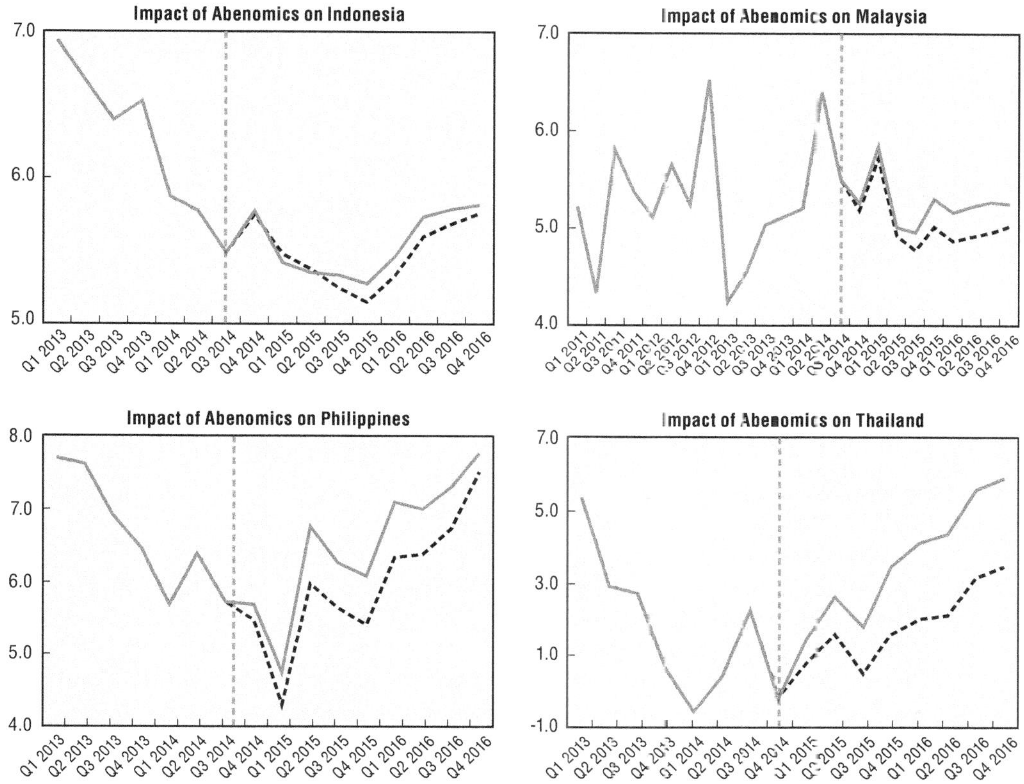

Notes: Blue line above is result projections. Black dotted line shows the downside impact of Abenomics on GDP of ASEAN economies.

Source: OECD Development Centre's estimation.

China's slowing growth will be felt throughout the region …

China and the ASEAN member countries are becoming more integrated and these relationships are expected to continue to deepen even as China's growth slows. The strong trade links that have grown between China and ASEAN mean that Southeast Asian exporters are likely to feel the effects of the anticipated future slowdown in Chinese demand.

China and ASEAN member countries are very important trading partners for each other. Since 2009, China has been ASEAN's largest trading partner and, since 2010, ASEAN has been China's third largest partner, behind the European Union and the United States (Figure 1.20). While the value of trade in services is increasing (particularly between China and Singapore, which accounted for 44% of trade in services between China and ASEAN in 2013), trade in goods still accounts for the vast majority of total trade. Much of this trade is in intermediate manufactured goods, and this may continue even as trading patterns change. Rising wages in China are pushing some manufacturers – particularly those operating in labour-intensive industries and production segments – to lower-cost countries in ASEAN, changing the geography of regional production.

Figure 1.20. **Increase of China's share of total ASEAN exports and imports**

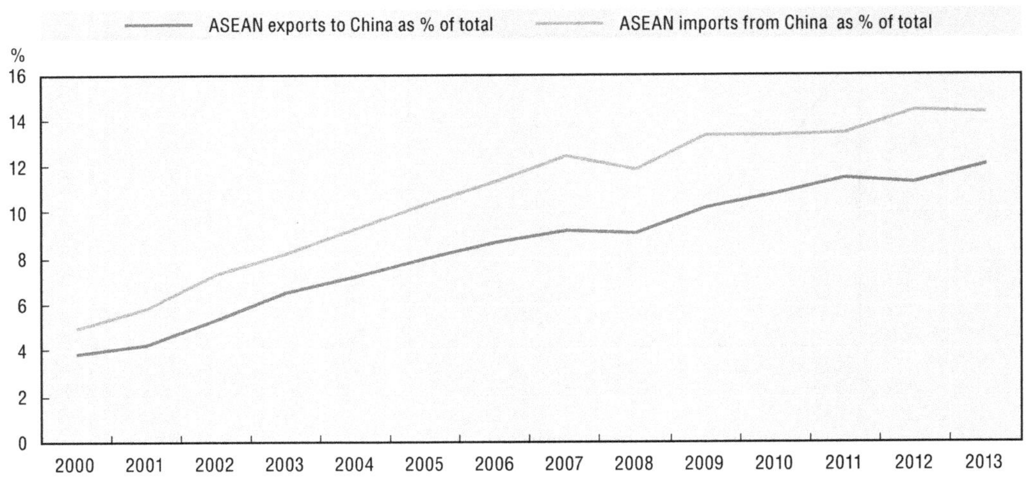

Source: UN Comtrade.
StatLink http://dx.doi.org/10.1787/888933179588

Investment flows within the region are relatively small when compared with trade flows or measured against the size of these economies. In fact, FDI flows to China from most ASEAN member countries are larger than their inflows originating in China. Singapore is a major exception to this pattern – in 2012, for example, it received USD 6.3 billion in FDI from China, more than four times Singapore's FDI outflows to China, ranking Singapore among the most popular destinations for Chinese FDI. The region's share of China's total FDI outflows has not changed considerably in the recent past, though the structure of these flows is evolving along with the development of Chinese firms and of the ASEAN economies. While previously concentrated in commodities, in particular energy resources, Chinese investments in the region are increasingly focused on higher-value-added sectors, such as real estate development, manufacturing, and a range of business and other services. These investments are being made by both privately- and state-owned firms looking for access to resources, low-cost production and new markets.

The room for expanded FDI flows and increased interest by Chinese firms in investing in new industries are examples of the ways in which ties between China and Southeast Asia can continue to be strengthened in the future. Increased and broader-based trade and FDI are likely to be a part of the continued development of regionally-based global value chains. At the same time, rising consumption and domestic demand across Emerging Asia will create new opportunities for trade and investment. In light of these trends, there appears to be growing recognition of the benefits of integration and increased momentum to put it in place.

At the same time, China's structural slowdown will pose challenges to this integration and reduce an external source of demand that has been a major driver of growth in the ASEAN region. Exposure to China's slowing growth varies among ASEAN member countries. Over the medium term, the impact is expected to be felt relatively more heavily by Thailand and Malaysia, and relatively less in Indonesia and the Philippines.

Simulation of the impact of the slowdown of the Chinese economy with the multi-country VAR model indicates that it will continue to weigh on the current account balance positions in Emerging Asia. The slowdown depresses export performances of Emerging Asian economies both directly and indirectly through its impacts on regional global value chains. The softening of the Chinese economy is already felt by tepid international commodity market prices and exchange rates in natural resource exporting countries. Further slow-down in the Chinese economy will have a considerable impact on the Emerging Asian economies (as of November 2014) (Figure 1.21).

Figure 1.21. **Impact of slowdown of Chinese economies on GDP trends in ASEAN countries**

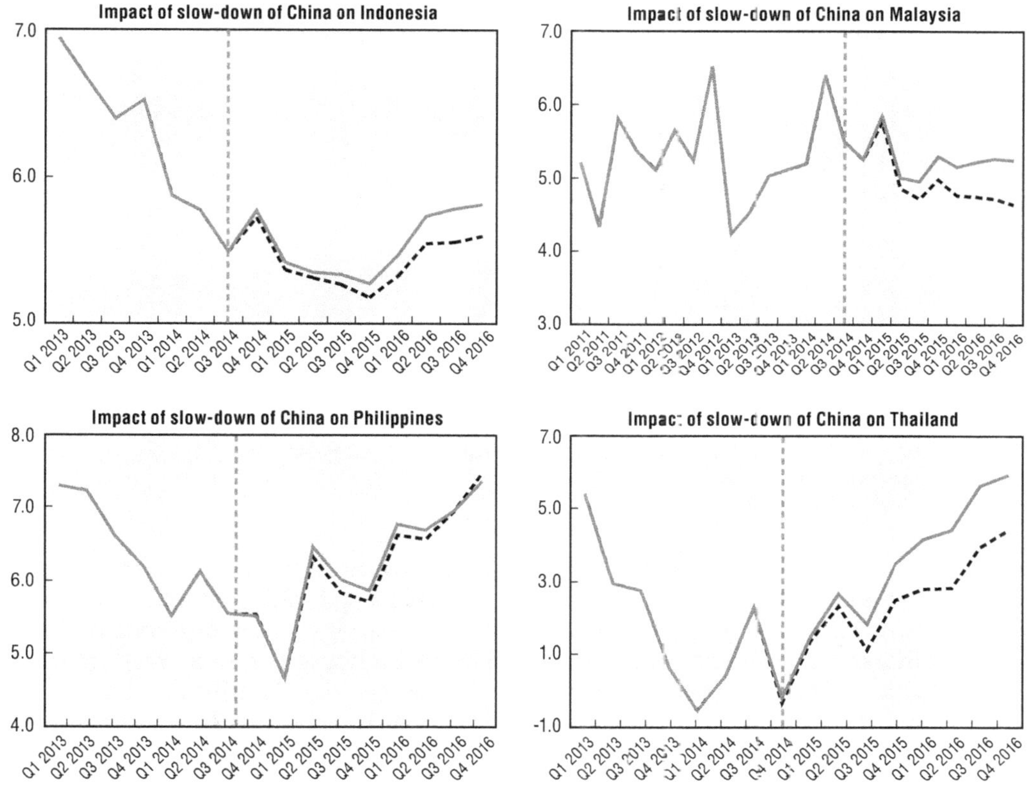

Note: Blue line above is result projections. Black dotted line shows the downside impact on GDP of ASEAN economies.
Source: OECD Development Centre's calculations.

The impact is relatively large in Thailand, Malaysia and to a lesser extent in Indonesia, as indicated by the Chinese share of their exports. Indonesia is a natural resource exporting country and has a comparatively large exposure to the Chinese economy. While Thailand and Malaysia both have a well-developed manufacturing sector, Thailand is more connected with Japan in global supply chains than is Malaysia, which has rubber and palm oil as major export items. Limited impact of the Chinese slowdown is expected for the Philippines economy, given its strong domestic demand.

... but the slowdown in the European Union will have limited impact

Growth prospects of the European Union appear relatively weak over the medium term. The main direct effects of a slowdown in the European Union on emerging Asia are determined by trade linkages, since financial flows from European countries are comparatively limited. Emerging Asian economies are differently exposed by their trade to a slowdown in demand from the European Union. While many Asian economies are export oriented, some countries such as India are less so, which gives them some insulation from a slowdown of demand in other countries. However, Cambodia, India and Viet Nam have a relatively high share of their exports to the European Union market – and hence may be exposed – while countries like Indonesia, Malaysia or Myanmar export much less to European countries (Figure 1.22).

Figure 1.22. **Share of EU-27 in total exports of selected products* of Asian countries in 2013**

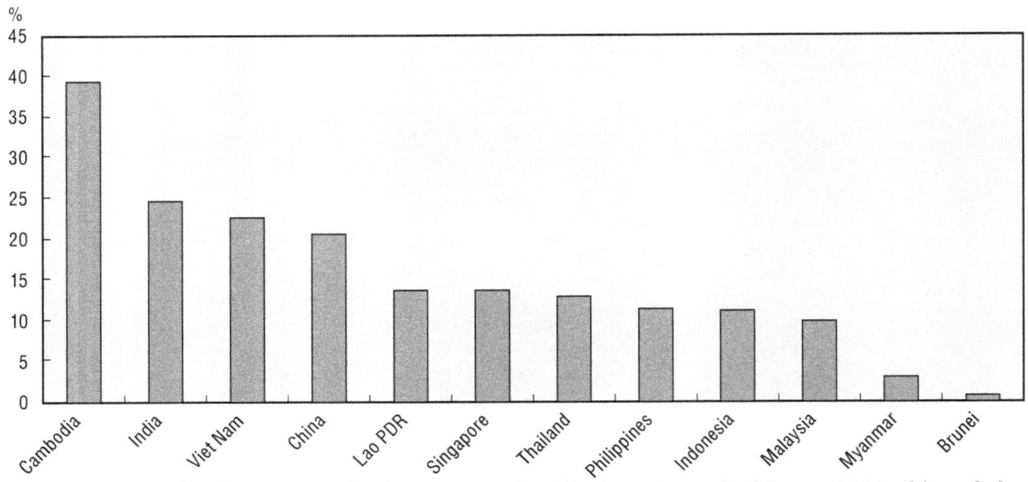

Note: (*) Categories of products 1-36 under the ISIC rev 3 classification, Harmonized System 2007 – this excludes services, in particular.
Source: UN Comtrade.
StatLink http://dx.doi.org/10.1787/888933179597

Furthermore, the exposure of Emerging Asia to shocks in the European Union depends not only on the share of its exports going to this market, but also on the sectors in which those exports are concentrated, the elasticities of demand in the European markets and the size of those sectors in the economy. For instance, Cambodia has a high share of merchandise exports to the EU that are heavily linked to the garment industry, which is a crucial driver of Cambodia's growth (Figure 1.23). This potentially implies a high exposure of Cambodia to a slowdown in the European market, as was witnessed in 2008. However, the income elasticity of demand for garments is rather low, which could help to mitigate these high risks, provided that other low-cost competitors such as Bangladesh don't massively gain market share in Europe. The same can be said of Viet Nam, which has a lower share of merchandise exports to the European Union than Cambodia but which are also concentrated in garments (followed by communication equipment). In India, which has a significant share of merchandise exports to the European Union, the main sectors linked to Europe are associated with the manufacture of coke and of chemicals products, whose income elasticities of demands are somewhat higher than for garments. However, Indian manufacturing exports to the European Union are more diversified than those of Cambodia and Viet Nam, which may reduce the impact of a sudden decrease in the demand in one sector. Furthermore, manufacturing exports are not a main driver of growth in India, which again limits the overall spill-overs of a European slowdown on the Indian economy.

Figure 1.23. **Share of exports to the EU by product categories* in Cambodia**, India and Viet Nam**

A. Cambodian exports to the EU are highly concentrated in garments

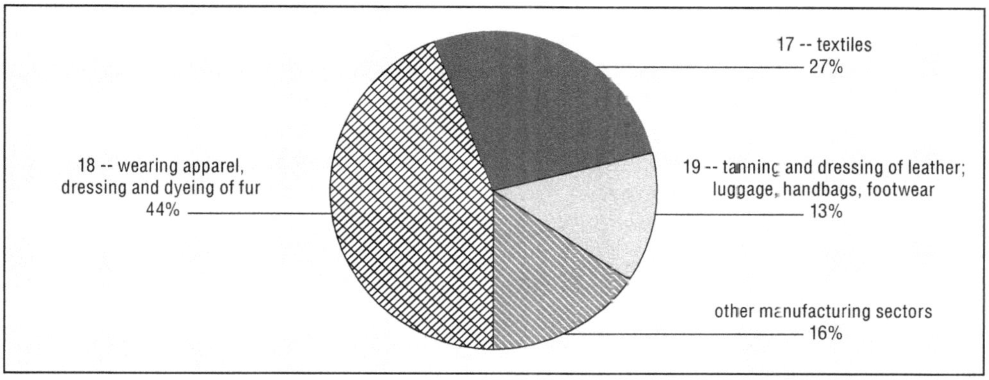

B. Vietnamese exports to the EU are concentrated in garment and communication equipment

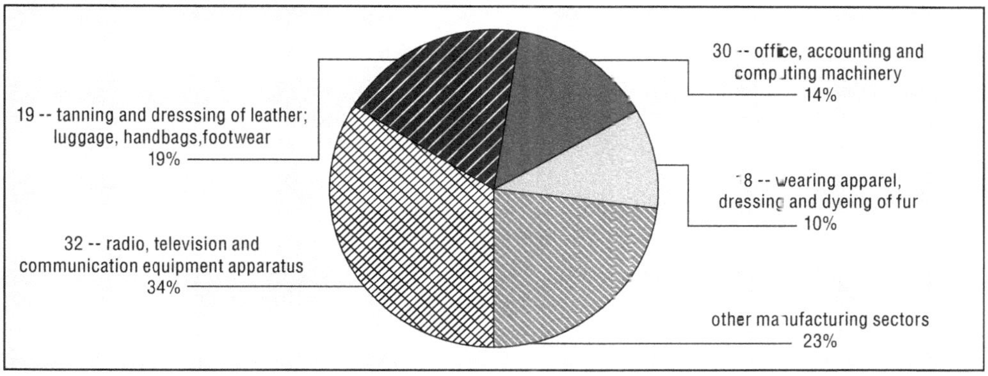

C. Indian exports to the EU show a much more diversified structure

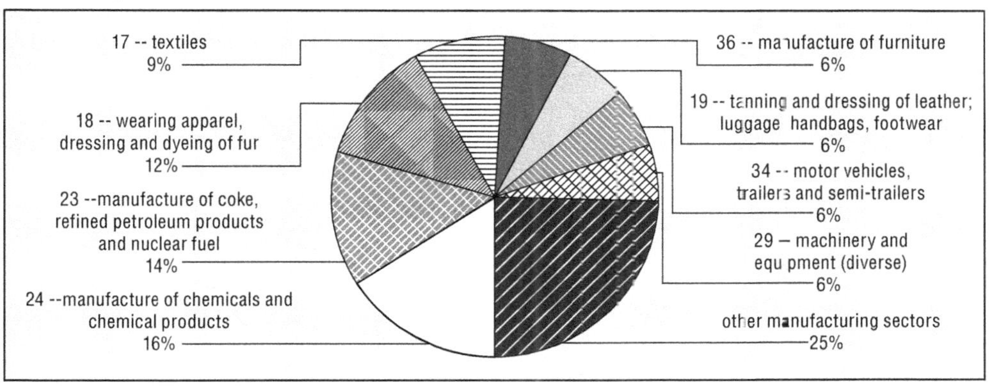

Notes: (*) Categories of products 15-36 under the ISIC rev 3 classification, Harmonized System 2007 – this excludes in particular the services and natural resources. (**) For Cambodia. Data excludes sector 23 – manufacture of coke, refined petroleum products and nuclear fuel, due to the unavailability of data.
Source: UN Comtrade.
StatLink http://dx.doi.org/10.1787/888933179600

To sum up, the direct spill-overs through trade and investment flows may be limited, and in any case lower than those from a growth shock from Japan or the United States (as of November 2014).

The indirect effects of an EU slowdown are more complex to assess, as they may depend on many factors, including characteristics of global value chains, increasing competition that may arise among producers if some markets slow down, or changes in consumer tastes. The 2013 IMF spill-over report builds an equilibrium model that assesses some of these indirect channels in the short run, in particular by including interest rates, exchange rates and progressive propagation of impacts across countries, and finds that the impact of a slowdown in the European Union may be lower than the impact of shocks in the US or Japan. However, a limit of those essentially medium-term models is that they cannot fully take into account the evolving comparative advantages and the ability of countries to adapt their production structure to the changing economic environment over the longer term.

Narrowing development gaps within ASEAN is an important regional challenge

The implementation of the Initiative for ASEAN Integration (IAI) (see Box 1.5) shows slow progress. By 2012, only 53 out of 182 actions (29% of the total number of IAI actions) had been implemented, along with only 32% of the AEC-related, 22% of the ASCC-related and 33% of the APSC-related actions (ASEAN, 2012). With 2015 approaching, further acceleration is needed to achieve the goals. To further promote development gap initiatives in ASEAN, the Master Plan on ASEAN Connectivity (MPAC) has also been developed and adopted since 2010. The MPAC objective is to narrow development gaps among member countries by enhancing physical, institutional and people-to-people connectivity through 19 key strategies and 84 key actions. Physical connectivity will be improved by developing national and regional infrastructure. The MPAC has prioritised land, maritime and air infrastructure development. It also includes ICT and energy infrastructure. Institutional connectivity focuses on connecting international and regional agreements and protocols to facilitate international transactions and the free flow of goods, services and investment. It includes trade, investment, and services liberalisation and facilitation, mutual recognition agreements/arrangements, cross-border procedures as well as transport facilitation. People-to-people connectivity will be improved by empowering people and increasing linkages among the member countries in education, culture and tourism.

Nevertheless, progress has been slow in most of the policy areas. Slow progress can be seen especially in people-to-people connectivity (ASEAN, 2013a). The efforts have been so far focused on improving skilled labour mobility. This actually increases risks of expanding the development gaps rather than narrowing them. More efforts will still, therefore, be needed in this area, especially to move beyond the skilled labour movement strategy of the Master Plan to include the movement of semi-skilled and unskilled workers (ASEAN, 2013b).

To improve human resource development, the ASEAN initiatives have been particularly focused on higher education. The MPAC has given priority to four areas: promoting ASEAN awareness among its citizens, especially youth, strengthening the ASEAN identity through education, building ASEAN human resources in the field of education, and strengthening the ASEAN University Network (AUN). The IAI has been concentrated on advancing and prioritising education, especially on conducting programmes for training in the management of higher education for CLMV countries. In addition, the Southeast Asian Ministers of Education Organisation (SEAMEO) Regional Centre for Higher Education and Development (RIHED) has been established to improve efficiency, effectiveness and harmonisation of higher education in the region. Nevertheless, gaps in tertiary education enrolment are still large between the two groups (Figure 1.24). This suggests that education has not been adequately addressed by the regional initiatives. There should be greater attention to policies to enhance the equitable access to education in CLMV and to improve education quality.

Box 1.5. Initiative for ASEAN Integration (IAI)

Narrowing social disparities and economic development gaps among member countries is one of the key challenges faced by ASEAN in achieving its end-goal of the ASEAN Community by 2015. Development gaps can be seen especially between the ASEAN-6 and the CLMV countries. CLMV countries have relatively low development achievements as compared to their ASEAN-6 counterparts. GDP per capita in the CLMV, especially Myanmar and Cambodia with around USD 1 600 and USD 2 300 respectively in 2012, is lagging behind the USD 4 300 and USD 4 900 of the Philippines and Indonesia, the poorest members of ASEAN-6.* Three of the CLMV: Cambodia, Lao PDR and Myanmar are classified as Least Developed Countries (LDCs) as defined by the United Nations Committee for Development Policy.** Graduating all ASEAN member states from LDC classification is an intermediate goal towards achieving the goal of closing the development gap, not only in income but also non-income dimensions, between the two groups.

To address the development gaps, the ASEAN member countries have adopted a number of initiatives, one of which is the Initiative for ASEAN Integration (IAI). The IAI, launched in 2000, is aimed at giving direction and sharpening the focus of collective efforts to narrow the development gap within ASEAN. It assists the member countries which are lagging behind to catch up with the others. The IAI is currently in the second phase of the work plan (IAI Work Plan II 2009-2015) consisting of 182 actions, which support the CLMV countries in addressing the gaps and disparities, based on three ASEAN Community Blueprints and Pillars (Table 1.4). The work plan covers infrastructure, human resource development, ICT, tourism, poverty and the quality of life, and regional economic integration, including trade and investment, as priority areas.

Notes: *Source: Gross domestic product (GDP) based on purchasing-power-parity (PPP) per capita GDP, International Monetary Fund: World Economic Outlook Database. ** Source: ASEAN Secretariat, 'Initiative for ASEAN Integration: Graduation of all ASEAN Member States from Less Developed Country Status", Policy Brief 4.

Table 1.4. ASEAN Community Blueprints and Pillars

Blueprints	Pillars
ASEAN Economic Community (AEC)	A. Single Market and Production Base B. Competitive Economic Region C. Equitable Economic Development D. Integration into Global Economy
ASEAN Socio-Cultural Community (ASCC)	A. Human Development B. Social Welfare and Protection C. Social Justice and Rights D. Ensuring Environmental Sustainability E. Building ASEAN Identity F. Narrowing the Development Gap
ASEAN Political-Security Community (APSC)	A. A Rules-Based Community of Shared Values and Norms (Political Cooperation) B. A Cohesive, Peaceful and Resilient Region with Shared Responsibility for Comprehensive Security (Security Cooperation) C. A Dynamic and Outward-Looking Region in an Increasingly Integrated and Interdependent World (External Relations)

Source: ASEAN Secretariat (2009), "Roadmap for ASEAN Community (2009-2015)".

IAI initiatives on human capital do not yet sufficiently address health. Significant gaps persist between the two groups in this area. For instance, the difference in average mortality rates for those under the age of five years between CLMV and ASEAN-6 is still large: at 54.9 in 2008 and 46.7 per 1 000 live births on average in 2012 in the CLMV as compared to 17.4 and 15.6, respectively, on average in ASEAN-6 in the same years. Despite this fact, the IAI work plan includes only very few actions related to access to health care and promotion of healthy lifestyles. Improvement in health sectors, especially in access to and quality of health care services to reduce maternal and infant mortality, should be given more attention considering their importance and their contribution to reducing poverty, for which considerable gaps persist despite the IAI initiatives in poverty alleviation. The poverty headcount ratio was 33.9% (2008) in Lao PDR, 25.6% (2010) in Myanmar, and 22.8% (2008) in Cambodia, much higher than that of Thailand and Malaysia.[4]

Table 1.5. **Infrastructure projects in ASEAN**

Project	Description	Country
Projects for ASEAN physical connectivity:		
ASEAN Highway Network	Complete 227 km of missing road links of AHN	Myanmar
	Upgrade more than 5,300 km of roads with below Class III quality	Lao PDR, Myanmar, Viet Nam, Philippines, Indonesia and Malaysia
	Upgrade the extension of AHN to China and India, particularly sections from Hanoi - northern Lao PDR - Myanmar - border of India	
	Build Mekong Bridge in Neak Loung	Cambodia
	Upgrade "Class II or III" sections with high traffic volume to "Class I"	
	Build highway Kanchanaburi - Dawei	Thailand and Myanmar
	Build missing link in the East West Economic Corridor (EWEC)	Myanmar
Singapore Kunming Rail Link (SKRL)	Construct the missing link sections:	
	2013: 48 km	Cambodia: Poipet - Sisophon
	2014: 6 km	Thailand: Aranyaprathet - Klongluk
	2015: 254 km	Cambodia: Phnom Penh - Loc
	2020: 153 km	Thailand : Three Pagoda Pass - Nam Tok
	110 km	Myanmar: Thanbyuzayat - Three Pagoda Pass
	466 km	Lao PDR: Vientiane - Thakek - Mu Gia
	129 km	Viet Nam: Loc Ninh - Ho Chi Minh City
	119 km	Mu Gia – Tan Ap – Vung Ang
ASEAN Broadband Corridor (ABC)	Provide the infrastructure backbones to enable ICT services to all communities in ASEAN; and put in place the required enabling policies and legislation to attract businesses and investments to the region.	
Maritime and port infrastructure	Accomplish an integrated, efficient and competitive maritime transport system	
	Enhance the performance and capacity of the 47 designated ports by 2015	
	Establish efficient and reliable shipping routes, including Roll-on/Roll-off (RoRo) services connecting mainland and islands	
	Strengthen linkages between global and regional routes and domestic shipping routes	
	Study on the RoRo network and short sea shipping	
ASEAN Power Grid	Link the electricity grids in the region to optimise the utilisation of energy resources among the member countries.	
	Melaka-Pekan Baru Interconnection: 600 MW high voltage direct current (HVDC) interconnection between Peninsular Malaysia and Sumatra, Indonesia consisting of: (i) Submarine cable (52 km) through the Straits of Malacca from Telok Gong in Malaysia to the Island of Rupat in Indonesia; (ii) Overhead transmission lines (30 km) crossing the Rupat Island; (iii) Submarine cable (5 km) crossing the Rupat Straits up to Dumai; (iv) 275 kV overhead transmission lines (200 km) from Dumai to Garuda Sakti in Central Sumatra to be built by Indonesia's state electricity firm - Perusahaan Listrik Negara (PLN); (v) Converter stations in Telok Gong and Garuda Sakti including harmonic filters and other necessary transmission facilities.	Indonesia, Malaysia and Thailand
	West Kalimantan-Sarawak Interconnection: 120 km high voltage 275kV AC interconnection (West Kalimantan-Sarawak Interconnection and Bengkayang substation). PLN will build an 82 km line in West Kalimantan side while the length of line in Sarawak side will be around 38 km. To allow the power to reach the load centre in West Kalimantan, PLN will build 60 km of 150 kV AC line from Bengkayang substation to Singkawang substation.	Brunei Darussalam, Indonesia, Malaysia and the Philippines.
Trans-ASEAN Gas Pipeline	Interconnect the gas pipeline infrastructure of ASEAN Member States and to enable gas to be transported across the borders of the Member States	

Table 1.5. **Infrastructure projects in ASEAN** (*cont.*)

Sub regional initiatives:		
The Greater Mekong Sub-region (GMS)	Achieve a well-integrated, prosperous and harmonious Mekong sub-region It covers projects in transport, energy, and telecommunications	Cambodia, Lao PDR, Myanmar, Thailand, Viet Nam and China
The Brunei-Indonesia-Malaysia-Philippines East ASEAN Growth Area (BIMP-EAGA)	Address the economic and social development of the less developed and more remote areas of the Member States (except for Brunei Darussalam), with initial focus primarily through increased trade, investment, and tourism, and ultimately through economic diversification beyond resource extraction.	Brunei Darussalam, Indonesia, Malaysia and the Philippines
The Indonesia-Malaysia-Thailand Growth Triangle (IMT-GT)	Better connect the sub region through the construction of highways, ports and railways access.	Thailand, Malaysia and Indonesia
CLMV Sub-Regional Co-operation on Air Transport	Facilitate air transport connectivity between the countries in the sub region Contribute to the ASEAN open skies policy for liberalising air transport within the CLMV sub region replacing all existing bilateral air services agreements signed between member countries of the CLMV sub region.	Cambodia, Lao PDR, Myanmar and Viet Nam

Source: ASEAN (2010), "Master Plan on ASEAN Connectivity", ASEAN Secretariat, Jakarta.

Concerning people-to-people connectivity, ASEAN has made significant progress in facilitating the free flow of services in tourism through the implementation of the ASEAN Mutual Recognition Arrangement (MRA) on Tourism Professionals, and the ASEAN Tourism Qualifications Equivalent Matrix, which function as main references for the tourism industry. The implementation of the ASEAN Tourism Strategic Plan (ATSP) 2011-2015 has helped the tourism sector to improve in terms of number of tourists visiting the region. The region welcomed 99.2 million tourists in 2013, 11.7% higher than the number in 2012.

Other programmes in this area include jointly promoting and marketing ASEAN tourism activities among the ten member countries through social media and websites; developing comprehensive tourism standards and certification processes; and collaborating with other countries, for instance Japan, Korea and China, to improve the sector. Nonetheless, gaps between CLMV and ASEAN-6 persist in tourism. CLMV countries are especially lagging behind ASEAN-6 countries in the number of international tourists. In 2012, Thailand had 22.3 million international tourist arrivals and Malaysia had around 25 million; only 593 000 international tourists visited Myanmar (World Bank, 2014a). Further integration of the sector, including harmonisation of visa requirements and standardisation of tourism-related services, is needed to narrow the gaps. Upgrading in tourism-related infrastructure in CLMV could also help to improve the sector.

Progress has also been slow on infrastructure development. The ASEAN Highway Network (AHN) programme, one of the ASEAN physical connectivity flagship projects, is behind schedule. The project is expected to build 23 designated routes covering 38 400 kilometres by 2020, yet in 2010 only the inventory of all national route sections had been completed (OECD, 2013b). Another flagship land transport project, Singapore Kunming Rail Link (SKRL), has nonetheless shown steady progress (OECD, 2013b).

While the flagship projects of the infrastructure initiatives are mainly focused on transport, ICT and energy (Table 1.5), the efforts in addressing gaps between CLMV and ASEAN-6 should be widened to reach other areas of infrastructure, such as access to improved water sources and sanitation. Only around 80% of the population in CLMV countries (on average), for instance, has access to improved drinking water sources while more than 94% of population in ASEAN-6 countries did so in 2012. Addressing these issues is important since they are linked to other policy areas which show significant development gaps such as health and poverty.

Narrowing the gap in access to electricity also needs to be further accelerated. The ASEAN Power Grid initiative focuses on optimising utilisation of energy resources by linking electricity grids in the region. CLMV countries, however, still lag behind the other countries in the region in accessing electricity. Barriers to getting electricity are still high, both in terms of time and cost (Figure 1.25). Addressing this issue should thus be given priority.

Figure 1.24. **School enrolment, tertiary (% gross)**

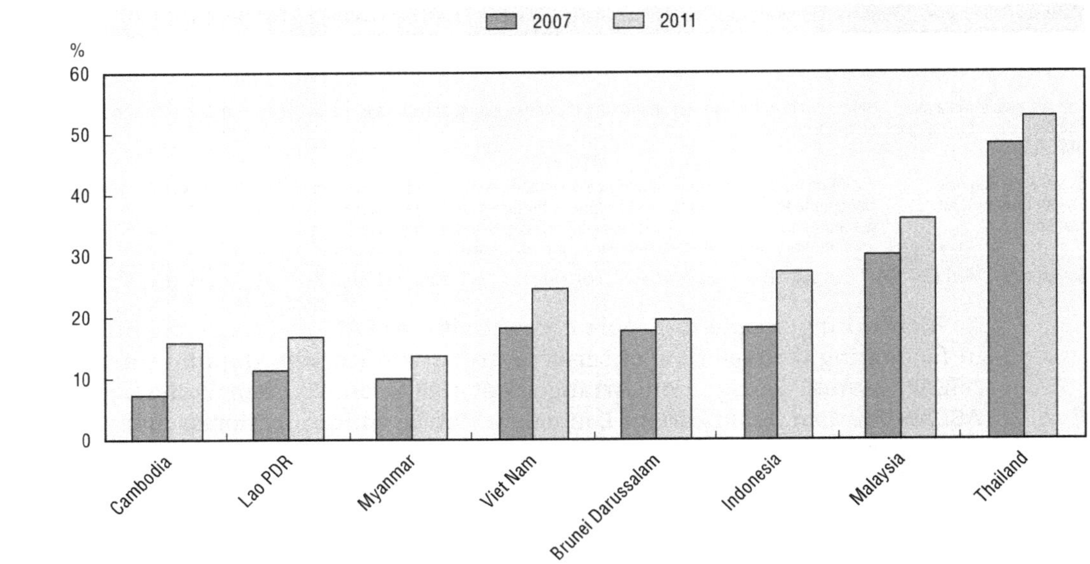

Source: World Bank (2014a).
StatLink http://dx.doi.org/10.1787/888933179613

Figure 1.25. **Getting electricity (2012)**

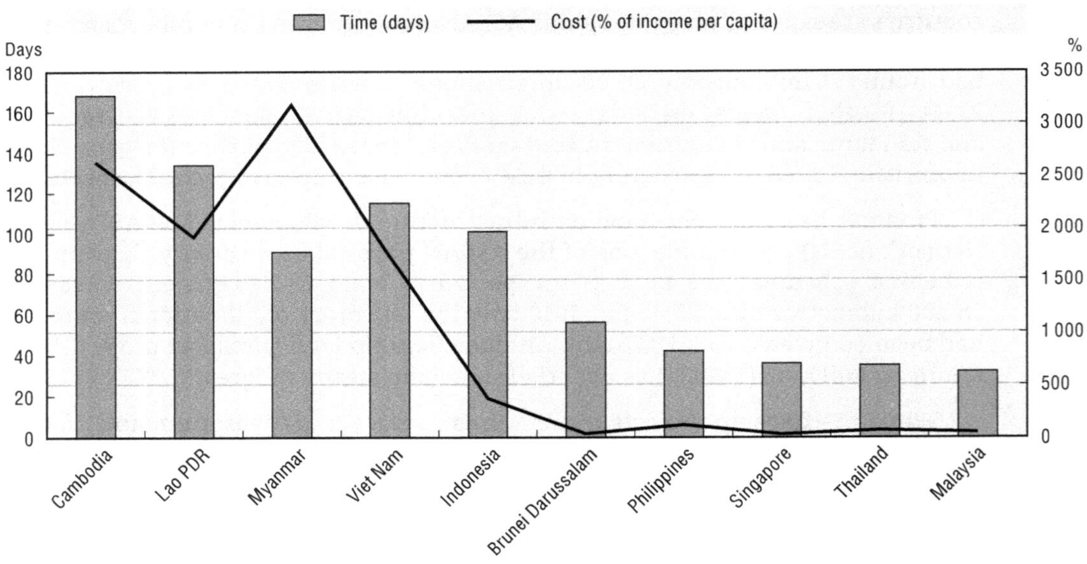

Source: World Bank (2014a).
StatLink http://dx.doi.org/10.1787/888933179623

CLMV countries are also still lagging behind in the area of ICT. Despite efforts such as the ASEAN Broadband Corridor (ABC), the ASEAN Internet Exchange Network, and capacity building programmes under the IAI, progress in this area has been slow and wide disparities persist between CLMV and ASEAN-6. There are significant gaps in internet access between the two groups. In 2008, the level of internet users per 100 people was 0.5 in Cambodia and 0.2 in Myanmar, compared to 69 in Singapore and 55.8 in Malaysia (World Bank, 2014).

The gap persists despite noticeable improvements in the CMLV in recent years: in 2013 the level was 6 in Cambodia and 1.2 in Myanmar, while it was 73 and 66.9 in Singapore and Malaysia respectively (World Bank, 2014a). To narrow the gap, better co-ordination to ensure connectivity among the member countries is needed, including harmonising ICT regulations for connectivity projects. In addition, commitment from each of the member countries to develop and improve their national ICT sectors is also necessary.

ICT infrastructure is fundamental to supporting trade and investment and expanding markets through its ability to facilitate information exchange, to connect people, to support delivery of services and to reduce the cost of business and trade-related transactions (ASEAN, 2010). This is important since significant gaps are found in the area of trade and investment. Wide disparities persist in the trade area between the CLMV and the ASEAN-6. Slow progress can be seen in improving international trade of the CLMV to achieve the goal of a free flow of goods. The issue of trade openness is especially important for Myanmar, since its exports and imports relative to GDP have shown a downward trend over the last decade (ASEAN, 2013c). Greater regional co-operation to further liberalise trade in the ASEAN region is needed, especially in improving trade facilitation initiatives, including the full implementation of National Single Windows, and measures to increase trade flows of CLMV, not only with the ASEAN-6 but also with other trade partners.

The ASEAN institutional connectivity strategy has been focused on trade and transport facilitation to support the free flow of goods, services and investment (Table 1.6). Nevertheless, to ensure that the strategy is well implemented, good institutional quality is crucial. ASEAN should pay more attention to addressing corruption and improving government effectiveness and regulatory quality. The region, on average, is not performing very well in many governance indicators, suggesting that there is still much room for improvement (McGillivray and Carpenter, 2013).

Table 1.6. **Progress of ASEAN Institutional Connectivity Projects**

Key Actions	Progress
ASEAN Framework Agreement on Facilitation of Goods in Transit (AFAFGIT):	
- Sign Protocol 2 (Designation of Frontier Posts)	Ongoing consultation between Member States
- Sign Protocol 7 (Customs Transit System)	Undergoing domestic processes
- Sign Protocol 6 (Railway Borders and Interchange Stations)	Signed by ASEAN Transport Ministers in 2011
ASEAN Single Aviation Market (ASAM):	
- Sign the ASEAN Multilateral Agreement on the Full Liberalisation of Passenger Air Services (MAFLPAS) by 2010 and ratify Protocol 1 by 30 June 2010	Pending ratification by several Member States
- Conclude the Air Transport Agreement with China by 2010.	Signed by ASEAN and China Transport Ministers in 2011
- Conclude the Air Transport Agreements with India and ROK.	Draft being discussed
- Formulate ASAM Roadmap	Implementation Framework of ASAM adopted
Develop strategies for an ASEAN Single Shipping Market (ASSM)	Strategy paper for ASSM adopted
Accelerate the liberalisation of services such as logistics and telecommunications	Being undertaken as part of 8th, 9th and 10th packages of services commitments
Implement National Single Windows (NSWs)	Member States are at various stages of NSW development. NSW of Singapore is already in operation
Improve regional – sub regional co-ordination of policies, programmes and projects	Ongoing efforts with a mapping exercise being undertaken
Investment liberalisation, facilitation, promotion and protection	The ASEAN Comprehensive Investment Agreement (ACIA) was finally ratified in March 2012, after being delayed since it was signed in 2009.

Source: ASEAN Secretariat, "Connecting ASEAN through the Master Plan on ASEAN Connectivity", presentation in workshop on "Enhancing Connectivity through Multi-layered Regional Frameworks: The Roles of Dialogue Partners", in Bangkok, Thailand on 19 July 2013.

To ensure effective implementation of the initiatives, regular assessments and monitoring of the projects' implementation are needed. It is important to track and monitor the changes in gaps between CLMV and ASEAN-6. Regular consultation with each of the CLMV countries is also necessary to ensure that the actions are well-targeted and able to meet their needs. Additionally, the effectiveness of the initiatives cannot be ensured without political will from the ASEAN member countries. Finally, capacity building is needed for the CLMV, the ASEAN Secretariat and other actors involved in implementation.

At the 24th ASEAN Summit in Nay Pyi Taw, Myanmar, on 11 May 2014, the ASEAN member countries made a declaration on the realisation of the ASEAN Economic Community by 2015. Through this declaration, the member countries have agreed to undertake necessary efforts to achieve the realisation of a community that is politically cohesive, economically integrated and socially responsible. The actions include further enhancement of co-operation in many areas such as trade; competitiveness; science, technology and innovation; environment and climate change; disaster management; empowerment of women, youth and other vulnerable groups; promotion of democracy; good governance and the rule of law in the region; strengthening unity, solidarity, peace and stability; and accelerating actions in realising regional connectivity initiatives. The Nay Pyi Taw declaration also calls for intensifying the efforts to realise the ASEAN Economic Community by 2015 by ensuring the implementation of the actions, programmes and activities under the Roadmap for an ASEAN Community (2009-15), implementing initiatives to achieve an ASEAN single market and production base, and ensuring the timely formulation of the ASEAN Community's Post-2015 Vision. It also calls for better implementation of the IAI Work Plan II by further enhancing technical and development co-operation to narrow development gaps and to alleviate poverty, and by initiating work on developing the Post-2015 work plan for the IAI.

Political uncertainties could undermine growth in Emerging Asia

2014 has brought about some major transformations in the political landscape within Southeast Asia. These transformations have had significant but somewhat different economic impacts in Indonesia, India, Thailand and Viet Nam. In India and Indonesia, the election of Narendra Modi as Prime Minister in the 2014 general election and the election of Joko Widodo as president of Indonesia has brought the instalment of two new leaders, as well as peaceful transitions toward a new government in each country. The outcomes demonstrate a willingness to break free from a governance culture of corruption and economic stagnation. The rising stock markets that preceded the two elections reflected national optimism and expectations of a new administration committed to economic change. However, as Widodo and Modi begin their respective terms in office, whether the new administrations will be able to live up to the public's rising expectations for rapid economic growth and reform remains yet to be determined.

Political unrest in Thailand and Viet Nam has led to stagnant growth in both countries. In Thailand, despite the military government's efforts to accelerate economic recovery in the aftermath of political turmoil, the downturn of tourism and production, delayed investment approvals and a downturn in domestic spending have resulted in a slow economic growth (as of November 2014). In Viet Nam, the territorial dispute with China over the sovereignty of the South China Sea has depressed tourism and trade with China and has exposed Viet Nam's economic dependency on China.

Strains on the Thai economy have followed the 2014 change in administration

Thailand has suffered from political unrest since 2013, largely due to repeated protests. Ever since taking over the government in May of 2014, the new leadership has made economic revival their priority and has carried out steps to bolster the economy as well as to increase public confidence. Revival efforts include approval of plans to upgrade the country's transport infrastructure that were stalled due to past political instability.

Prolonged political deadlock and administrative paralysis do have negative impacts, as recent developments in the Thai economy have shown. During the first quarter of 2014, Thai GDP contracted by 2.1%, compared with the previous three months. A survey by the University of the Thai Chamber of Commerce revealed that consumer confidence in September dropped for the first time in five months since May. The business sentiment index also indicates poor confidence among firms, retreating from 49.6 in July to 49.1 in August. Stronger consumer and business confidence will be needed for better economic growth. The tourism industry, which serves as a significant contributor to Thai GDP, has seen a large drop in foreign tourist arrivals and in the hotel occupancy rate. Foreign tourist arrivals fell from 2.07 million in August 2014 to 1.86 million people in September. Data from the Bank of Thailand show that the hotel occupancy decreased to 50.78% in September from 54.80% in August and was down nearly 10% from September of the previous year. In addition, 13 consecutive months of a slump in industrial output can also be seen in the data produced by the Office of Industrial Economics, which show that the average capacity utilisation rate was down from a revised 64.5% in March to 61.1% in September. Compared with the period before the change in administration in May, weaker domestic demand and the downtrend in spending resulted in a worrying decline of the manufacturing sector, with the MPI (manufacturing production index) falling from 178.5 in May to 166.0 in September, and contracting by 4.5% during September over August. Last but not least, the mass exodus of Cambodian workers returning to their country which, according to the International Labour Organization, amounts to more than 200 000 as of June 2014, is also an issue of concern. The loss of migrant workers is bound to have significant economic ramifications in both Thailand and Cambodia if it should persist.

Table 1.7. **Thailand's Roadmap to Democracy (three stages)**

Stage	Time	Focus Issue
1st Stage	From August 2014 (2-3 months)	Facilitation of reconciliation and peace through dialogues between all political sides, overseen by reconciliation centres set up by the NCPO. A temporary Constitution is created in July to legitimise the change of administration under the NCPO and allow the establishment of an interim government.
2nd Stage	September-October 2014	The 250-member National Reform Council, which will be tasked with recommending reforms as well as approving the new charter that will take effect from July 2015, is formed.
3rd Stage	October 2015 (Expected)	General election will take place under a democratic system.

Source: National source.

Political uncertainty affected growth performance in Viet Nam

China's decision to plant an oil rig in the ongoing disputed territory in May 2014 has provoked fervent bouts of protests across Viet Nam. The significance of claiming territorial ownership lies in the fact that the areas surrounding the contested islands in the South China Sea are thought to be not only rich in natural resources of oil and gas but also serve as an integral waterway for trade.

The turbulent political situation has not only affected the peace and stability of the region, but has exacerbated economic repercussions for both countries. Viet Nam's tourism industry has been greatly impacted with a decline in the number of international visitors in September 2014 to an estimated 590 881 arrivals, down 3.89% over the same month last year, as well as down 4.48% compared to August. Revenue from exports to China has also fallen during the period of August and September 2014, from USD 1.31 billion to USD 1.27 billion. However, significant and negative broader economic impacts seem to be lacking for the moment. According to the General Statistics Office of Vietnam, export turnover for the first ten months in 2014 reached an estimated USD 123.1 billion, which is a 13.4% increase compared with the same period in 2013. Meanwhile, import turnover is reported to have reached USD 121.2 billion, an 11.2% increase during the ten months of 2014 compared with the same period in the previous year. China remained Viet Nam's top export destination during the ten months of 2014, with an estimated turnover of USD 35.6 billion and an increase of 17.1% compared to the same period in 2013.

Tackling structural reform awaits the newly elected presidents in Indonesia and India

Almost a week after taking office in October, 2014, President Widodo of Indonesia announced his "working" cabinet, consisting of 34 ministers who will work under his administration for the period of 2014-19. The announcement was delayed for several days as Widodo ensured that all the candidates for ministers were first examined by the Corruption Eradication Commission (KPK) and the Financial Transaction Reports and Analysis Centre (PPATK), reflecting his commitment to addressing corruption and forming a clean cabinet.

There have been mixed reactions from markets and the public to Indonesia's new cabinet. The reaction has been positive to the Widodo administration's choice of several professionals for key positions, including the economic ministries (i.e. the Coordinating Ministry for Economics and the Finance Ministry). The choice of a professional for the position of transport minister has also been greeted positively as it will be the key to the country's transport infrastructure improvement. Some critics have, however, questioned the choices for some other positions. The choices have led to speculation about the strong influence of the former Indonesian President on Widodo's decisions. However, the new President can also be expected to seek support from key political parties in order to implement his programmes smoothly, particularly as the opposition has a majority in the parliament.

The high hopes and expectations for the first Indonesian president coming from outside the political and military elite have led to some disappointment. While market reactions post-election have been favourable, the Jakarta Composite Index dropped by 0.96% on 27 October, the day after Widodo announced his new cabinet. The Indonesian rupiah, according to the Bloomberg composite index, showed little change, closing at 12 109 per US dollar, following earlier gains. Widodo is expected to face a range of crucial challenges in implementing meaningful reform in the near future, including the fuel subsidy cut to ease the country's deficit.

India's general election of 2014 to constitute the 16th Lok Sabha (Lower House of Parliament) ended with a landmark achievement of the formation of a new government led by the National Democratic Alliance (NDA) on 12 May, after a month-long election running from 7 April. Securing an absolute majority of 282 parliamentary seats out of 543, the historic landslide victory of the Bharatiya Janata Party (BJP) and Prime Minister-elect Narendra Modi implies a fundamental changing of the political landscape in India, where the Indian National Congress of the Nehru-Gandhi dynasty has been the ruling party for most of India's political history. The defeat of the Congress Party may well be the outcome of strong anti-incumbent sentiments due to the persistently high inflation, continuous allegations of corruption in the Party, and the hopes of the 814 million voters' for a break out of the flailing economy into new economic opportunities under the leadership of pro-business Modi.

The outcome of the 2014 general election seems to hold positive promise for India's future economic growth and stability. Data from the Ministry of Statistics and Programme Implementation (MOSPI) shows the CPI steadily increasing from 138.1 in March to 141.0 in June. The insurance and defence sector is expected to grow with increased FDI inflows expected once the proposed increase in the FDI ownership limit to 49% from the current level of 26% takes effect. The BJP's parliamentary majority will enable the new government to overcome legislative barriers without interference from coalition politics and thereby meet the public's rising expectations for faster economic reform, which has fallen to its lowest level of less than 5% these past years. Having a sole party with the majority is expected to speed up tax reforms, thus renewing investors' confidence in the Indian market. According to BJP's annual budget presented to Parliament on 10 July, boosting the manufacturing sector, expansion of foreign investments and improving infrastructure are some of the key agendas the new government will be tackling as part of its efforts to revive India's economic growth.

Box 1.6. Challenges for Modi's reforms in India's federal system

The victory of Bharatiya Janata Party and its allies (National Democratic Alliance) in the May elections has given the new Prime Minister a clear majority which should help reforms to be passed and implemented swiftly. The new government's economic policy agenda has set out ambitious plans, which include, among others, domestic and foreign investment promotion, job creation, food security, improvement of the quality of education and skills development, creation of new key infrastructure, enhancement of water governance, and an overall increase in India's competitiveness, in particular in manufacturing sectors. The first policy announcements have been well received by the markets. However, in areas where local governments have strong power, reforms may be more difficult. These areas concern in particular the tax system, the management of infrastructure, land and water issues, as well as product and labour market regulation. Difficulties in implementing reforms in these areas may have deep impacts on most other priorities of the new government.

Tax system

A priority of the new government is to reform the tax system to make it simpler and more rationalised, so that it is more conducive to investment and growth. The current indirect taxation system is complex and involves cascading taxes that bias production decisions and hinder inter-state trade. There is now a clear principle of separation regarding the assignment of tax powers: tax categories are exclusively assigned either to the federal level or to the states. However, there are complexities that lead to overlaps. For instance, although taxes on production (federal excise levies) and sales (state sales taxes) are separate, they tax the same base, causing cascading of rates and crowding out of taxes. The states have also been allowed to levy taxes on the sale and purchase of goods but not services. The introduction of a long-awaited general sales tax across the country could rationalise indirect taxes while preserving states' financial autonomy. Ideally, a single tax rate should apply in each state and where differential rates apply they should be kept as low as possible and confined to a limited range of products. However, a major effort is required to define implementation details and to measure the gains or losses for each State and at the Federal level.

Beyond, there is the need to simplify the arrangements between the federal level and individual states, as fiscal arrangements have led to the existence of multiple and sometimes overlapping channels for federal-state transfers. India's assignments and implementation of tax and expenditure authorities lead to a vertical fiscal imbalance, with over a third of state expenditures having to be covered by transfers from the Federal level. The Finance Commission determines the tax shares between the federal level and of each state and recommends grants to states as needed. However, there is criticism that the use of grants to fill revenue-expenditure gaps claimed by the states creates disincentives for the states to maintain fiscal discipline. There is a need to clarify the frameworks, as India often faces general government deficits, and as there are plans to improve the efficiency of subsidies such as those in energy, transport and agriculture.

Infrastructure and land management and water governance

In order to develop infrastructure – in particular the road network and the electricity system – the new government has so far cleared several infrastructure projects worth more than USD 10 billion. The aim in this domain is also to attract private investment through enhanced PPP schemes. The issue of expropriation of land is, however, sensitive, as India is mostly rural and land rights are not the same across states – and sometimes are not even fixed. The government has employed its political capital to reach out to state governments run by its political allies to ensure resolution of land acquisition issues related to large projects. However, differences across states in land rights make the situation more complex, and some state authorities may be not willing to fully co-operate with the federal government on such a sensitive issue.

Box 1.6. **Challenges for Modi's reforms in India's federal system** (*cont.*)

Water governance is also an increasingly urgent issue in India, in particular as fast urbanisation has just started, but also in rural areas. The institutional organisation limits the role of the central government to interstate projects in this domain. But in practice, as all major rivers flow through more than one state, and because almost half of the 604 districts are affected by drought, the central government is a key actor in the decision-making process and intervenes beyond its official prerogatives. Through the Planning Commission, it decides the allocation of funds to state governments and has substantial influence on state water policies Policy coherence and multi-level governance are challenging, especially when it comes to delivering positive outcomes of public policies.

Product and labour market regulation

Product and labour market rules need to be reformed, as excessive regulation is a barrier to growth and job creation in India. There are in particular rising concerns that India has recently experienced jobless growth, and that many firms or employees are in the informal sector. The situation is even more worrying since large waves of youth will enter the labour market over the next few years (around 1 million each month until 2020, according to some studies) and will need to find decent jobs.

The situation is complex, however, as there are wide differences in the extent of regulation across states and as competencies in these areas are shared. This heterogeneity affects the overall clarity of regulation and makes India a fragmented market. This can hamper domestic and foreign investment, and productivity growth and job creation. Regarding product market regulation, while the Indian Central Government and some individual State Governments have enhanced regulatory frameworks for a better environment for businesses (in terms of investment, starting-up and conducting business) in the last years, this has not happened in a concerted manner. Similarly, the scope to reform labour market laws at the level of the federal government is generally limited due to the absence of consensus amongst the social partners. A number of states have made reforms to the extent allowed by federal laws and the Constitution, but these reforms have varied considerably across states, leading to a lack of clarity among investors.

While all levels of government should ease product and labour market regulations, the Indian Central and state governments need to adopt a "whole of government" regulatory policy to ensure a clearer framework and a more unified market across India.

There are also other key domains in which greater harmonisation is needed. For instance, a range of funding and management models apply in the education sector, which leads to difficulties in co-ordinating policies for skills development. An overall simplified system may help to enhance the quality of education and reduce inequality of opportunity in the labour market.

To sum up, the political economy in India may complicate reforms that are priorities of the new government. Better co-ordination between levels of government is key, but it is a big challenge in such a large and diverse country.

Sources: Ministry of Labour and Employment (2010), Planning Commission (2010), Tooley and Dixon (2007), Economic Survey of India (2011).

Conclusion

Growth in Emerging Asia will remain resilient in the medium term but future development is likely to be uneven across economies. In addition, economic reforms within the region present both upside and downside risks. The robust growth projections for much of the region are predicted on the success of macroeconomic and structural policies. For instance, delay of key infrastructure projects could lead to lower growth than now projected. However, timely implementation of planned reforms will bring significant benefits for productivity and real growth. With the economic landscape changing rapidly, effective management of several key downside risks will be critical to the region.

- **Financial market volatility and inflationary pressures are subdued overall in the region but risks remain.** Although their exports benefit from the relatively high level of oil and gas prices, volatility in these prices will present challenges for Indonesia, Malaysia and Brunei Darussalam as well as the net oil importing countries in the region. Rising real estate prices and the risks of property market bubbles will require careful monitoring and management, particularly in India but also in many other countries in the region. Capital flows (both inflows and outflows) need to be carefully monitored – particularly as US monetary policy normalisation proceeds-and prudential and other measures to deal with capital inflow surges and reversals should be bolstered. Liquidity provision schemes at the regional level such as the Chiang Mai Initiatives should also be strengthened.
- **Fiscal reforms need to be strengthened.** Overall, fiscal balances in countries in the region are unchanged, though trends will differ by country and there will be much room for improvement. In Indonesia, the success of the reforms to cut fuel subsidies could be critical to strengthening fiscal soundness. In Malaysia, more subsidy rationalisation and the introduction of a 6% GST in April 2015 will be critical. Fiscal reforms in Thailand are stalled at the moment but an improvement in political stability could allow them to be restarted. In the Philippines, many infrastructure projects are required and the success of the on-going fiscal reforms (to the tax administration and the budget process) will be critical.
- **There are signs of FDI slowing in some countries.** FDI flows remain strong in Emerging Asia but have been decreasing recently in some countries, notably Indonesia and Thailand. Improvement in investors' perceptions of regulatory frameworks (particularly those related to resource-based sectors in Indonesia) and macroeconomic and political stability (especially for Thailand) will be critical factors.
- **Managing political transformations arising from leadership changes (for instance, Indonesia and India) will be critical.** So far, reactions from markets to the new administrations in Indonesia and India have generally been positive but whether this continues beyond the near term will depend on how faithfully and effectively promised policy reforms are implemented. Successful implementation of reforms contributes to political stability. Prolonging political uncertainty in Thailand will create large negative economic impacts. Effective exploitation of the opportunities created by political transformation will be critical for healthy growth.

- **Further acceleration of regional integration towards the goal of the ASEAN Economic Community by 2015 will be necessary.** Continued healthy growth depends on the success of key regional initiatives, including improvement of trade facilitation, acceleration of the development of institutional arrangements for investment, financial integration, education and infrastructure and greater progress on narrowing regional disparities. The integration agenda should also be extended to a broader range of issues, including topics such as the environment and green growth that have so far been mostly left aside.

Annex 1.A1: Modelling framework and estimation of the impact of external factors on growth

Technical Appendix 1

Major revision of Medium-term Projection Framework for 2015 edition of the Outlook

The Medium-term Projection Framework (MPF), constructed in 2010 is an analytical tool for the *Economic Outlook for Southeast Asia, China and India* (see OECD (2012), Technical Appendix). The MPF evolves each year to reflect the changing economic situation. A major revision for the 2015 edition of the Outlook (MPF-2015) in the Baseline model, based on the DSGE (Dynamic stochastic general equilibrium) approach, is the following:

Theoretical framework

The measure of the potential output is the stochastic trend level of output expected to prevail in the long run without any other temporary shocks. The potential output A_t evolves according to the following law of motion:

$$\log A_t = \log \gamma + \log A_{t-1} + z_t^a,$$

where γ represents the long-run growth rate and z_t^a is the permanent technology shock that affects the potential output growth rate. According to this definition, the output gap is defined as the deviation of output from its stochastic trend:

$$GAP_t = \log(Y_t / A_t),$$

where Y_t is the actual output.

The baseline model of MPF-2015 is derived from the optimising behaviour of a) **households** and b) **monopolistically** competitive firms that face price stickiness. c) **Monetary policy** follows an interest-rate feedback rule. For empirical validity, the model features stochastic trend for real variables and gradual adjustment in consumption, inflation and the interest rate. The equations presented below are the linear approximation of the model, and the variables are denoted as deviations from the balanced growth path.

a) **Households** derive utility from consumption goods and disutility from labour supply. The optimality conditions for utility maximisation are given by: ,

$$\left(1-\frac{\beta b}{\gamma^{\sigma}}\right)\left(1-\frac{b}{\gamma}\right)\lambda_t = -\sigma\left(c_t - \frac{b}{\gamma}c_{t-1} + \frac{b}{\gamma}z_t^a\right) + \frac{\beta b}{\gamma^{\sigma}}\sigma\left(Ec_{t+1} - \frac{b}{\gamma}c_t - z_{t+1}^a\right)$$

$$\lambda_t = E_t\lambda_{t+1} + r_t^n - E\pi_{t+1} - \sigma z_{t+1}^a.$$

where β is the subjective discount factor, b represents habit persistence in consumption preferences, σ measures the risk aversion. λ_t is the Lagrange multiplier interpreted as the marginal utility of consumption and c_t is private consumption, r_t^n is the nominal interest rate, and π_t is inflation.

According to these equations, consumption increases (decreases) when the real interest declines (rises). As observed in the data, however, the adjustment of consumption is gradual because of the habit persistence in consumption.

The market clearing condition for final-goods is:

$$y_t = \frac{c}{y} c_t + \frac{g}{y} z_t^g ,$$

where $\frac{c}{y}$ and $\frac{g}{y}$ are the steady-state share of private consumption and the other demand components. z_t^g is the external demand shock that captures government expenditure and net export.

Combining these three equations above, a dynamic IS equation is obtained that characterises the demand side of the economy.

b) **Monopolistically competitive firms** maximise their profits by setting the prices of their product. It is assumed that not all firms adjust prices every period. In each period, a fraction $1-\theta$ of firms reoptimises prices, while the remaining fraction θ keeps prices unchanged or indexes prices to past inflation.

The profit maximisation gives a dynamic AS equation called the New Keynesian Phillips curve:

$$\pi_t - \omega\pi_{t-1} = \beta\gamma^{1-\sigma}\left(E\pi_{t+1} - \omega\pi_t\right) + \frac{(1-\theta)(1-\theta\beta\gamma^{1-\sigma})}{\theta}\left(\eta y_t - \lambda_t\right) + z_t^p ,$$

where ω is the weight of price indexation to past inflation and η is the inverse of the labour supply elasticity in the households' utility function. The term $\eta y_t - \lambda_t$ represents the real marginal cost that is equivalent to real wage derived from households' maximisation problem. z_t^p is the marginal cost shock that captures an exogenous cost push to the firms' price setting such as the changes in oil price and taxes.

This equation means that the current inflation is determined by past and expected future inflation, the real marginal cost, and the exogenous cost shock. Both backward- and forward-looking features of the equation enable the model to replicate realistic inflation dynamics.

c) The monetary authority follows the Taylor-type inflation targeting rule:

$$r_t^n = \rho_r r_{t-1}^n + (1-\rho_r)\left(\psi_\pi \frac{1}{4}\sum_{j=0}^{3}\pi_{t-j} + \psi_y y_t\right) + \varepsilon_t^r ,$$

where ρ_r determines the degree of policy smoothing, and ψ_π and ψ_y measure the responsiveness of the interest rate against inflation and the output gap respectively. ε_t^r is the monetary policy shock interpreted as an unsystematic component of the monetary policy.

This means that the monetary authority gradually adjusts the short-term nominal interest rate in response to the deviation of annual inflation from its target and the output gap.

Empirical framework

The data used for estimation is the real GDP growth rate ($\Delta \log GDP_t$), the CPI inflation rate ($\Delta \log CPI_t$), and the short-term interest rate (SR_t). These data are related to model variables by the following measurement equations:

$$\begin{bmatrix} \Delta \log GDP_t \\ \Delta \log CPI_t \\ SR_t \end{bmatrix} = \begin{bmatrix} 100(\gamma - 1) \\ \bar{\pi} \\ \bar{\pi} + \left(\dfrac{\beta b}{\gamma^{\sigma}} - 1 \right) \end{bmatrix} + \begin{bmatrix} y_t - y_{t-1} + z_t^a \\ \pi_t \\ r_t^n \end{bmatrix},$$

where $100(\gamma - 1)$, $\bar{\pi}$ and $\bar{\pi} + \left(\dfrac{\beta b}{\gamma^{\sigma}} - 1 \right)$ are the GDP growth rate, inflation rate and nominal interest rate that prevail in the long run respectively.

Baseline models of MPF-2015 apply Bayesian methods to estimate model parameters. Given the estimated parameters, series of potential output and output gaps are estimated so that the estimates are consistent with both the model and data.

Technical Appendix 2

Simulation by DSGE approach for the effect of US monetary normalisation on ASEAN

Model setting

Based on the model of Aguiar and Gopinath (2007)[5], a modified version to analyse the impact of the US monetary normalisation (i.e. interest rate increase) on ASEAN-5 economies was applied. ASEAN-5 economies in this model will receive permanent shocks on productivity growth. In addition, frequent regime switches motivated by the dramatic reversals in fiscal, monetary and trade policies are commonplace. Aguiar and Gopinath (2007) modeled this feature by introducing the stochastic trend in the growth rate. Specifically, the production is modeled as follows:

$$\begin{aligned} Y_t &= e^{z_t} K_t^{1-\alpha} (\Gamma_t L_t)^{\alpha} \\ z_t &= \rho_z z_{t-1} + \varepsilon_t^z \\ \Gamma_t &= g_t \Gamma_{t-1} \\ ln(g_t) &= (1-\rho_g) ln(\mu_g) + \rho_g ln(g_{t-1}) + \varepsilon_t^g \end{aligned}$$

where Y_t is production, z_t is total factor productivity, K_t is capital, L_t is labour and Γ_t is the cumulative product of "growth" shock, g_t.

In this model, the domestic interest rate is not determined by the domestic market only under the open economy. Moreover, domestic bond price is determined by the following Schmitt-Grohe and Uribe(2003) style equation:

$$\frac{1}{q_t} = 1 + r_t^* + \psi\left(e^{\frac{B_t}{\Gamma_t} - b} - 1\right)$$

where q_t is a bond price, r_t is the world interest rate, B_t is the level of debt due, and Γ_t is the cumulative product of "growth" shocks. This equation says that domestic real interest rate increases when the world interest increases or the domestic debt increases. In this model, the world interest rate follows AR(1) process with mean to incoporate the dynamics of global financial conditions, different from Aguiar and Gopinath (2007). Agents have perfect foresight for the path of interest rate.

Calibration and assumptions

The steady state value for the interest rate is the average of the US real interest rate[6] for the 2009Q4-2014Q2 period.[7] In 2014 Q2, the difference between the steady state real interest rate and current interest rate is 1%. The assumption on US monetary normalisation is, therefore, that the real interest rate increases by 1% in three years, goes back to the steady state level and remains at the same level thereafter.

Technical Appendix 3

Impact of Abenomics and slowdown of Chinese economy on the region by Multi-country VAR approach

Methodology:[8]

For the analysis on the impact of GDP growth rates in one country on another, Multi-country Vector Auto-Regression (MVAR) is built and estimated with four lagged own variable and other country GDP growth rates and rates of inflation and exchange rates as exogenous variables. In general, when many countries are involved in the models, the models tend to be large and complicated. MVAR can handle the estimation in a simple way while still incorporating the GDP growth rates of many other countries. MVAR is also handy in projections and capturing the impact of the shock to GDP growth rates in one country on another country's GDP growth rates while maintaining high explanatory power.

In terms of variable selection, to measure the impact of (the failure of) Abenomics and slowdown of the Chinese economy, both Japan and China's GDP growth rates are included in the model. In addition, US growth rates are added to the model if they are statistically significant. Moreover, since a number of country variables and lags used in the regression totals to eight, the use of more variables is likely to result only in worsening Akaike Information Criterion. Therefore, after a number of trials on many variables, only rates of inflation and exchange rates are used if they are in fact statistically significant.

The regression outcomes are presented below. The criterion for selecting variables is Adjusted R^2 rather than t-values since the purpose of this exercise lies in subsequent simulation rather than in identifying determinants. Rates of inflation and exchange rates are regressed one by one with lagged variables from -1 to -4 for each country and the one which generates highest t-values are employed. Different sample periods are regressed with different sets of rates of inflation and exchange rates. Their outcomes are simulated each time with shocks. The one which has converging forecast values and fits lowest standard deviation in the forecast period is adopted.

Some of the lagged country GDP growth rates are not statistically significant, e.g. PHL(-1) to PHL(-4) and CHN(-1) to CHN(-4) for the Philippine VAR and USA(-1) to USA(-4) and CHN(-1) to CHN(-4) for Thailand VAR. These variables are used in the model because the VAR will lose considerable explanatory power without them. In the Filipino VAR, the explanatory power for CHN is lower than 67%. However, this set of the variables fits best and does not explode in the forecast period. That is why it is selected.

VAR Analysis

The table below is the sum of parameter values of lagged own variables, Japan, USA and China for Malaysia, Indonesia, the Philippines and Thailand. From the table, the US GDP growth rates have the largest impact among three repressor countries and sometimes even rather than own country lagged GDP growth rates. For Malaysia and the Philippines, Chinese GDP growth rates have a greater impact than Japan while for Thailand, the impact of Japanese GDP growth rates is larger. The impacts of both country GDP growth rates are the same in Indonesia.

	Lagged own variables	JPN	USA	CHN
MLS	0.22	0.13	0.21	0.17
IDN	-0.72	0.06	n. a.	0.06
PHL	0.08	-0.08	0.54	0.15
THA	-0.21	0.37	0.83	0.22

Simulation: Abenomics

Each of the VAR models identified in the above is simulated with shocks. Various shocks are tested and one standard deviation is selected as a shock. The failure and upside risk of Abenomics is incorporated as one standard deviation minus and plus Japanese GDP growth rates during eight quarters from 2014Q3 to 2016Q2. The shocks are 12.5% in annual terms.

Simulation: China slowdown

The shocks are given as the same way as the Abenomics case. However, the size of the shock, one standard deviation, is 2.3% smaller than that used in the Abenomics. This is to apply the shocks which has the same probability of happening rather than the same significance in size.

Notes

1. AEC score card was established by ASEAN, as well as reviewed by the Mid-term Review of the Implementation of AEC Blueprint published in 2012 and produced by the Economic Research Institute for ASEAN and East Asia (ERIA).
2. 2013 data were not available for Cambodia, Lao PDR and Myanmar, though older data from Cambodia and Lao PDR household consumption would likely account for a large share of GDP in these countries as well.
3. 2012 data were not available for Brunei Darussalam, Cambodia, China, Indonesia, Myanmar, Philippines, Singapore or Viet Nam.
4. Poverty headcount ratio at USD1.25 a day (PPP) (percentage of population living on less than USD 1.25 a day at 2005 international prices), ADB Key Indicators for Asia and Pacific 2012.
5. Their model is a standard small open economy DSGE model for emerging markets. The model at its core is a simple RBC model. Monetary aspect and inflation dynamics is not captured in the model from the assumption of no rigidity and perfect competition. No exchange rate dynamics exists because there is only one good and no trade frictions. Law of one-price holds globally in this model.
6. Using market yield on U.S. Treasury securities at ten-year constant maturity, quoted on investment basis, inflation-indexed from FED.
7. Parameter values of the model is mostly from the Aguiar and Gopinath (2007). The capital adjustment cost was changed to 10, following Peter N. Ireland (2001).
8. Country Abbreviations all indicate quarterly GDP growth rates year-on-year. IDN: Indonesia, MYS: Malaysia, PHL: the Philippines, THA: Thailand JPN: Japan and CHN: China. Variable abbreviations are EX: exchange rates, INF: rate of inflation, D_EA: dummy for Currency Crisis and D_THA: dummy for floods and political unrests in Thailand.

References

ADB (Asian Development Bank) (2012), *Facts and Data about Southeast Asian Infrastructure*, Asian Development Bank, May.

Aguiar, M. and Gopinath, G.(2007), *Emerging Market Business Cycles: The Cycle Is the Trend Journal of Political Economy*, 2007, 115, 69-102.

ASEAN (2013a), "Initiative for ASEAN Integration: Enhancing Connectivity to Narrow the Development Gap in ASEAN", *Policy Brief 2*, Association of Southeast Asian Nations (ASEAN) Secretariat, Jakarta, www.aadcp2.org/home/technical.php.

ASEAN (2013b), "Initiative for ASEAN Integration: Policy Recommendations for Narrowing the Development Gap in ASEAN", *Policy Brief 3*, ASEAN Secretariat, Jakarta, www.aadcp2.org/home/technical.php.

ASEAN (2013c), "Initiative for ASEAN Integration: Graduation of all ASEAN Member States from Less Developed Country Status", *Policy Brief 4*, ASEAN Secretariat, Jakarta, www.aadcp2.org/home/technical.php.

ASEAN (2012), "Initiative for ASEAN Integration: An Update", ASEAN Secretariat, Jakarta, October.

ASEAN (2010), "Master Plan on ASEAN Connectivity", ASEAN Secretariat, Jakarta.

ASEAN (2009), "Roadmap for ASEAN Community (2009-2015), ASEAN Secretariat, Jakarta.

IMF (2013), "Spillover report", *IMF Policy Paper.*

IMF (2014), *Asia and Pacific Economic Outlook: October 2014 Update.*

Ireland, P.N. (2001), Sticky-price models of the business cycle: Specification and stability, *Journal of Monetary Economics*, 47, pgs. 3-18.

Gentilini, U., M. Honorati and R. Yemtsov (2014), *The state of social safety nets 2014*, World Bank Group, Washington, DC.

Kappler, M., Reisen, H., Schularick, M. and E. Turkisch (2013), "The Macroeconomic Effects of Large Exchange Rate Appreciations," Open Economies Review, Springer, vol. 24(3), pages 471-494, July.

McGillivray, M. and D. B. Carpenter (2013), "Narrowing the Development Gap in ASEAN: Drivers and Policy Options", Routledge, London.

McKinsey (2009), McKinsey Global Survey, quoted in: "An Exorbitant Privilege? Implications of Reserve Currencies for Competitiveness", McKinsey Global Institute Discussion Paper, December.

Ministry of Labour and Employment (2010), *Annual Report, India.*

OECD (2015), *Multi-dimensional Country Review of the Philippines, Vol. 2*, OECD Publishing, Paris, forthcoming.

OECD (2013a), "Disaster Risk Financing in APEC Economies, Practices and Challenges", OECD Publishing, Paris, http://www.oecd.org/daf/fin/insurance/OECD_APEC_DisasterRiskFinancing.pdf

OECD (2013b), *Southeast Asian Economic Outlook 2013: With Perspectives on China and India*, OECD Publishing, Paris, http://dx.doi.org/10.1787/saeo-2013-en

OECD (2011), *OECD Economic Surveys: India 2011*, OECD Publishing, Paris, http://dx.doi.org/10.1787/eco_surveys-ind-2011-en

Planning Commission (2010), *Annual Report, India.*

Schmitt-Grohe, S., Uribe, M.(2003), "Closing Small Open Economy Models", *Journal of International Economics*, 61, 163-185.

Tooley, J. and P. Dixon (2007), "Private Education for Low Income Families: Results from a Global Research Project". In: Srivastava, P; Walford, G, ed. *Private Schooling in Less Economically Developed Countries: Asian and African Perspectives*, Symposium Books, Didcot, pp. 15–39.

UNCTAD (2014), *World Investment Report 2014.*

UNCTAD (2013), *Global Value Chains and Development: Investment and Value-Added Trade in the Global Economy*, United Nations Conference on Trade and Development, Geneva, http://unctad.org/en/PublicationsLibrary/diae2013d1_en.pdf

Williamson, J. (2000), "Exchange Rate Regimes for Emerging Markets: Reviving the Intermediate Option", Policy Analyses in International Economics 60, Peterson Institute for International Economics. Available at: www.piie.com/publications/chapters_preview/320/iie2938.pdf.

World Bank (2014a), *World Development Indicators* (database), World Bank, Washington, DC.

World Bank (2014b), "Philippine economic update pursuing inclusive growth through sustainable reconstruction and job creation", Report no. 83315-PH, March 2014.

World Bank (2013), *World Bank Myanmar Economic Monitor.*

Chapter 2

Institutions for effective implementation of national medium-term plans in Emerging Asia

Medium-term development plans, which are used to co-ordinate government economic, social and environmental policies, can be used as benchmarks against which to measure performance and institutional capacities. This chapter includes country case studies on planning and plan implementation in the ASEAN-5 countries (Indonesia, Malaysia, Philippines, Thailand and Viet Nam), together with Myanmar, China and India. Although these countries have generally identified priority areas for growth well, they have uneven track records when it comes to meeting the targets they set. The recognition of areas of relative weakness should therefore be used to help identify targets that require rethinking or more effective implementation efforts. In general, greater attention could be paid to target setting and co-ordinating activities within government. Broad reforms to medium-term budgeting, supervision of line ministries and agencies, data collection, and staffing selection and incentivising can all help support effective implementation.

Introduction

Medium-term development plans (MTDPs) provide opportunities for governments to organise and publicly state their policy priorities and intended strategies for reform. As such, these plans offer unique insights into the intentions of policy makers. By comparing targeted and actual results with each other, this chapter gauges the capacities of governments to marshal available resources for implementing their plans. Such an approach is particularly relevant to the analysis of Emerging Asia.

Countries in the region have enthusiastically adopted and applied development planning in pursuit of their economic, institutional, social and environmental goals. Although they generally identify priority growth areas well, they have uneven track records when it comes to meeting the targets they set. Greater attention needs to be paid to target setting and co-ordinating activities within government.

Institutional capacities and meeting plans' targets

Governments use MTDPs as valuable tools for co-ordinating and steering their policies towards strategic goals and for signalling their intentions to domestic and international actors. Although MTDPs are widely used in Emerging Asia and around the world and need to be credible, they often fail to meet their targets. While contextual and political factors may be part of the reason, institutional weaknesses in design and implementation are important factors. Indeed, the degree to which plans meet their targets is a useful way of measuring countries' institutional capacities.

The concept of development planning spread quickly among developing countries as they gained independence. Despite its origins in central planning, it has been embraced by governments with a wide range of policy objectives seeking to pursue a coherent set of economic goals. It has proved particularly popular in Asia, where it was adopted beginning in the mid-twentieth century with widely varying approaches.

India was an early starter of planning in mixed economies, with a dedicated department established under the colonial government and unofficial plans produced by the Indian National Congress Party even before independence in 1947. The country's early plans emphasised investment targets by sector, though markets and price mechanisms played more prominent roles from the 1970s and 80s. A similar trend was seen in Bangladesh, while Japan, Korea and Singapore developed a distinct approach to develop consistent long- and short-term strategies. China, India, and many of the ten ASEAN member countries now have some form of development plan.

Many developing countries use medium-term plans to set out key government objectives, usually over consecutive five-year periods. The goals and means to which they commit vary greatly and some have included targets for the implementation of free market reforms. Many countries' plans no longer set only macroeconomic goals like stable growth. They also have more specific ones – such as output, employment and productivity targets for particular sectors – and non-economic goals like social inclusion, environmental protection and institutional development. In fact, most MTDPs in Emerging Asia make such issues part of their main themes.

Credible MTDPs can help to define policy objectives, strategies for meeting targets and internally consistent frameworks for day-to-day decision making. Regular failures to meet targets, though, can make plans little more than policy wish lists. Even early analyses questioned to what degree developing countries were capable of implementing plans. In a review of planning across more than 100 countries, Waterston (1966) concluded that "only one or two" economies with a sizeable private sector were successful in reaching their targets for sectoral and macroeconomic performance. Later, looking back on several largely disappointing decades of development planning, Turner and Hulme (1997) placed the blame for its shortcomings on over-ambitiousness, poor data, unscientific or misappropriate methods, a lack of flexibility in the face of the oil price shocks of the 1970s, weak institutional capacities in the public sector and political interference.

A more analytical categorisation of the factors behind plans' failures came from Agarwala (1983), who described sets of contextual factors associated with government capacity and deeper-seated problems inherent to the planning process. The capacity-related factors include insufficient or unreliable data, skilled staff shortages, barriers to inter-ministry co-operation and disconnects between planning and budgeting. The deeper-lying problems include technical limitations in forecasting, changing political conditions and the limits to the civil service's ability to influence the actions of the private sector.

While multiple factors shape the success of governments in meeting their planning goals, the discrepancy between targeted and actual achievements offers an easily measured, highly visible indicator of government capacity and credibility, regardless of political intentions or plans' ultimate suitability. Evaluating to what extent plans meet their targets does not produce quantified or comparable indicators of institutional capacity, unlike measures that are subjective (e.g. opinion surveys of the prevalence of corruption) or narrowly defined (e.g. the time it takes to register new businesses). It does, however, enable comparison of performance across different sectors

The importance of institutional capacity – i.e. data availability, staffing, intra-governmental co-ordination and budgeting – is evident throughout the process of design, implementation and evaluation that is repeated with successive plans (Figure 2.0.1). The complex sets of tasks required to set targets across sectors and to implement plans draw on a wide range of human and organisational resources within government.

Figure 2.0.1 **The planning process comprises design, implementation and evaluation**

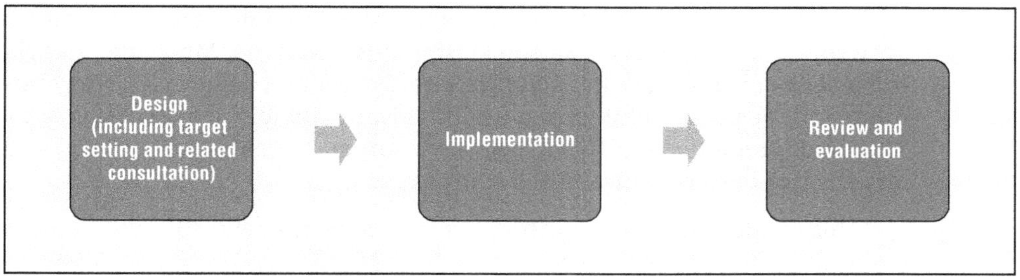

Plans in Emerging Asia identify important development issues, but shortcomings remain in design and implementation

Medium-term plans in Emerging Asia demonstrate how well countries identify priority development targets when designing their plans. How well they meet them, though, varies across countries and across policy areas within countries. The recognition of areas of relative weakness may be used to help identify targets that require rethinking or more effective implementation efforts.

The overarching visions or themes behind Emerging Asia's MTDPs and the specific targets that countries set within them reflect their circumstances reasonably accurately

(Table 2.0.1). The region's wealthier economies, which seek to pull themselves clear of the middle-income trap and move into the high-income bracket, place emphasis on the productivity growth needed to make that transition. Targets in these countries include greater educational access and quality and increased investment in innovative activities. China, Thailand and Malaysia, for example, all spell out explicit R&D-related targets.

As for the region's less developed countries, they tend to accord greater importance to fundamental development factors, such as the provision of basic education and healthcare and the creation of jobs.

Table 2.0.1. **Medium-term development plans in Southeast Asia, China and India**

Country	Period	Theme / Vision
ASEAN 10 countries		
Brunei Darussalam	2013-17	Knowledge and innovation to enhance productivity and economic growth
Cambodia	2014-18	To move out of least developed country status and to become an upper middle income country in 2030
Indonesia*	2010-14	Realisation of an Indonesia that is prosperous, democratic and just
Lao PDR	2011-15	Socio-economic development, industrialisation and modernisation towards the year 2020
Malaysia	2011-15	Charting development towards a high-income nation
Myanmar	2012-15	Development of industry, balanced development, improvements in education, health and living standards, and improved statistical capacities
Philippines	2011-16	Pursuit of inclusive growth
Singapore	2010-20	High skilled people, innovative economy, distinctive global city
Thailand**	2012-16	A happy society with equity, fairness and resilience under the vision of the philosophy of a Sufficiency Economy
Viet Nam	2011-20	A modern, industrialised country by 2020
Two large economies in Emerging Asia		
China	2011-15	Rebalancing the economy, ameliorating social inequality and protecting the environment
India***	2012-17	Faster, more inclusive and sustainable growth

Notes: *Indonesia's new president, Joko Widodo, began his five-year term in October 2014 following presidential elections in July. He will serve for the third phase (2015-19) of Indonesia's national long-term development plan (RPJPN 2005-25).**The Thai military took administrative control in May 2014. ***A new Indian government assumed office under Prime Minister Narenda Modi in May 2014, following the general election in April and May. This government will serve during the latter half of India's current medium-term plan.
Source: OECD Development Centre based on national sources.

Several countries of different income levels emphasise goals that go beyond income growth. Indonesia, Myanmar, the Philippines, Thailand, Malaysia, Viet Nam, China and India seek social goals like inclusiveness. Targets for reduced poverty rates were set by India, Indonesia, the Philippines and Viet Nam and for income equality by Malaysia and Thailand. Some plans also include environmental goals, particularly energy efficiency and the use of renewable energy sources.

This chapter includes country case studies on how the ASEAN-5 countries (Indonesia, Malaysia, Philippines, Thailand and Viet Nam), together with Myanmar, China and India, have targeted and implemented their medium-term development plans. These studies address the key policy focuses in each country's current plan, the shortcomings in development that warrant them and where governments should further concentrate their efforts (Table 2.0.2).

Indonesia is nearing the end of its 2010-14 *National Medium-Term Development Plan* (as of November 2014). It seeks to create a prosperous, just and democratic society through reforms in the areas of macroeconomic growth and stability, poverty reduction, education, health, food production, energy production and distribution, infrastructure development, and good governance. Overall, the country is making sound progress towards its targets, particularly in macroeconomic performance and junior high school enrolment. A number of important gaps remain, however.

Table 2.0.2. **Policy challenges in implementing national plans in Emerging Asia**

Country	Policy focus
ASEAN countries	
Indonesia	The widest gaps are found in the area of health. Improving access to and the quality of health services, especially for mothers and children, is crucial. Coverage of the newly implemented health insurance scheme should also be expanded.
	Further efforts are required in order to improve the education system, particularly in access to secondary and tertiary education for students from low-income households.
	The national plan is not addressing growing inequality adequately.
Malaysia	Further improvements in productivity are needed to support sustainable economic growth and transform Malaysia into a high-income, developed nation.
	Further development of ICT, which is particularly important for supporting growth, is required.
	Fiscal stability should also be enhanced and dependence on oil reduced. The successful introduction of GST is important for improved tax performance.
Myanmar	Reliable indicators, quantifiable goals and measurements of government performance are necessary for effective planning and monitoring, particularly in the areas of regulatory reform and public finance.
	Policy planning and budgeting – including appropriate financial support in agriculture and education – should be developed.
	Co-operation with the private sector through PPPs and setting up new businesses and with civil society is an important part of Myanmar's on-going transition.
Philippines	To sustain economic growth, the Philippines needs to step up its competitiveness through quality employment and increase value added through innovation.
	A responsive, inclusive, development-oriented financial system must be built as a platform for the efficient management and mobilisation of resources.
	Social development must be further improved to ensure equal opportunity so that Filipinos may find decent jobs, acquire assets and lift their living standards.
Thailand	To ensure sustainable economic growth and enhance competitiveness, Thailand must accelerate its progress towards meeting certain targets and improve its productivity.
	The country should, in particular, make further efforts in environmental management in order to support green growth.
	Improving good governance – with particular emphasis on corruption and transparency – needs more effort to reduce obstacles to growth.
Viet Nam	Maintaining stability in key economic and social indicators is a priority for implementing socio-economic strategies.
	Addressing implementation gaps in the development of high-tech industries and skills training is essential not only to meeting the goals of the medium-term plan, but also to realising the 2020 vision of a modern, industrialised Viet Nam.
The two large economies in Emerging Asia	
China	Environmental degradation remains a major issue despite the country's efforts in reducing pollution. Further efforts are needed to increase consumers' access to clean energy.
	Rural and agriculture development could help promote urban-rural social equality.
	Services have the potential to help drive future growth, but their development requires continued economic reform and improvements in education.
India	De-industrialisation needs to be addressed. Manufacturing has been slowing down in the last few years and even showed negative growth in 2013-14.
	Access to secondary education needs to be widened to achieve the goal of universal secondary education by 2017.
	The public health system needs to be strengthened. Access to both curative and preventive healthcare facilities needs to improve.
	Accelerating the development of infrastructure is crucial, especially in rural areas.

Source: Compiled by OECD Development Centre.

Progress in improving health outcomes in Indonesia has been particularly weak and has even worsened by some measures. High poverty rates persist in some parts of the country and it has failed to adequately address inequalities. While continued growth requires the expansion of knowledge-based industries, access to advanced education is still low. Greater investment and attention to infrastructure development and corruption are also required if Indonesia is to continue to attract investment and encourage the growth of new businesses.

The *Tenth Malaysia Plan* (2011-15) focuses on growing the country to high-income status while ensuring inclusiveness and sustainability. It aims to achieve this end by meeting the targets of balanced economic growth and efficient fiscal policy, further developing key sectors and SMEs, reducing poverty and inequalities, and reforming the labour market and education and healthcare systems.

Growth rates are strong and investment rates exceed targeted levels, but there is still room for making the productivity improvements needed for Malaysia to become a high-income country. SMEs have a greater role to play in this transition, as do new industries – such as information and communication technology (ICT) – that will need to develop further. At the same time, fiscal stability can be improved through reduced reliance on oil and gas revenues and the introduction of new revenue-raising tools, such as a goods and services tax (GST).

Myanmar's *Framework for Social and Economic Reforms* outlines transitional priorities for 2012-15 to help the new government bridge the gap with the previous five-year plan. It prioritises necessary, achievable reforms in economic development, regulation and governance, the provision of public services, and infrastructure development. Those targets are, however, less clearly defined than in other countries and more challenging to track, as reliable indicators are often not available in Myanmar. Still, progress is being made in economic reform to create space for the private sector and develop infrastructure. The country is also making headway in implementing programmes to assist agriculture and improve access to education, though it is unclear whether these projects target the areas of greatest need. The regulation of the financial sector and transparency of public finances are sorely in need of greater attention.

The ***Philippine*** *Development Plan* 2011-16 aims to foster inclusive, sustainable growth by meeting targets related to macroeconomic stability, sectoral competitiveness, financial system resilience and inclusiveness, social development (i.e. improved health, education, housing, and social programmes), crime and environmental protection. Overall, the plan's economic performance has been strong, although it has not made the same gains in inclusiveness.

Increased competitiveness is critical for the Philippines' continued growth, but the country needs to step up efforts to bring about change in sectors that are key to achieving that growth. Tourism and SMEs offer great potential for driving future growth, but appear to be under-performing. A resilient and accessible financial system is also critical, but it has been slow to improve its inclusiveness. Although the services sector is expanding, it requires further innovation – as does manufacturing – to lay the foundations of a high-tech economy. Serious barriers in access to education and health slow human capital development and fail to address the root causes of inequality.

Thailand's *Eleventh National Economic and Social Development Plan* (2012-16) is intended to support the concept of a "Sufficiency Economy" in the country. The plan targets inclusive, broad-based growth, education and other areas of human development, food and energy security, increased innovation and growth, trade, investment, and environmental protection. Thailand is on track for meeting, or even exceeding, its macroeconomic targets for growth and inflation, although it looks as if it will fall short of other economic performance targets, such as boosting regional trade. While alternative and renewable energy production is increasing, fast-rising energy demand has left the country's dependence on fossil fuels unchanged or greater than before the plan. If it is to facilitate innovation-led growth, Thailand needs new strategies to meet its challenges, foster creative and research-based industries, and reduce corruption.

Viet Nam's *Socio-economic Development Plan* (2011-15) emphasises development through upgrading, improving efficiency and competitiveness through targets for overall and sectoral economic performance, meeting social targets (e.g. job creation and poverty reduction), and implementing environmental protection.

Although GDP growth has been lower than targeted, the country is close to, or has even improved on, other economic targets like unemployment and social investment. However, it is not making enough ground with its current approaches to a wide range of social challenges, such as alleviating rural poverty, and expanding access to vocational education and training. The need for improved banking governance amid rising levels of bad debt is another serious challenge that needs to be addressed to support continued development.

The **Chinese** *Twelfth Five-Year Plan* (2011-15) addresses a range of issues related to rebalancing and promoting continued growth, while ensuring inclusiveness and sustainability. It therefore targets progress in macroeconomic performance, economic restructuring, innovation, protecting the environment and reducing pollution, agriculture, and livelihoods and well-being. Greater effort is needed to address the quality of growth by making it more broadly based and improving environmental and social outcomes. While pollution is declining, it remains a major issue and more could be done on energy efficiency. The urban-rural divide is a major component in Chinese inequalities, necessitating improved rural and agricultural development. Generally, the services sector could also be expanded to improve the stability of growth and support continued improvements in innovation and productivity.

India's *Twelfth Five-Year Plan* (2012-17) sets out targets for improving sustainability, inclusiveness and the quality of life in the country. They incorporate improvements in growth, poverty reduction and job creation, education, health, infrastructure development, emissions reduction and improved environmental protection. The plan's highly ambitious target for GDP growth looks unlikely to be realised, particularly given the slow pace at which India has implemented structural reforms. Improvements in well-being and human capital are held back by low levels of access to education and healthcare. Access to financial services is also restricted, particularly in rural areas. Infrastructure development and the expansion of renewable energy production are progressing only gradually, which suggests a need for greater, and alternative approaches to, investment.

Reshaping medium-term development plans in Emerging Asia

Clearly, then, it is important to set targets that are relevant, reasonable and ambitious as otherwise they risk being mere distractions or likely failures. Targets should be the outcomes of governance and the planning process – particularly who is involved, within what arrangements they work together to arrive at a single planning document, how budgetary constraints are accommodated and what data limitations they face. Once medium-term plans have been implemented, another process in the planning cycle kicks in; review and evaluation. It considers examples of where and how successful plans were designed and implemented and supplies lessons as to what should be done differently in the future. Rethinking the approaches taken to the design and implementation of MTDPs could help meet targets and make planning more generally useful.

Well targeted and well designed national plans are critical

While the lead responsibility for co-ordinating the design of the development plan typically lies with a national planning agency or ministry, other central government bodies, such as the executive or ministry of finance, may play major roles. The planning body should consult closely with line ministries – offering them guidance and harnessing their inputs. The purpose is to collect information on the current state of the sectors for which line ministries are responsible and the programmes they are running, as well as on their potential goals and the resources needed to meet them. Beyond internal government discussions, the consultation process may examine submissions from lawmakers, civil society and the public at large. Inclusiveness can help to create development plans that are widely perceived as legitimate and that strive towards goals in the public interest. It also offers opportunities for assembling an attainable set of targets, even as it throws up new challenges. It is consequently important to strike a balance between the consultative and technocratic processes of designing MTDPs.

One central challenge in designing coherent, feasible plans is identifying priorities and choosing between actions that compete for government resources or conflict directly, as may happen when simultaneously pursuing certain economic and environmental goals. The process of planning itself can be a means of developing policies that factor in interdependencies and potential trade-offs by facilitating and institutionalising the exchange of information within government (Kornai, 1970). Inclusive consultation processes can help to highlight where contradictions may arise and yield additional information about the associated costs and benefits of alternative options. At the same time, however, increasing the number of stakeholders (and so expanding the scope of planning) can increase the likelihood of such challenges arising.

As a result, trade-offs may create limits to inclusiveness. The leadership and expertise of officials in agencies in charge of producing plans may be needed to weigh competing costs and benefits against each other when trying to determine what constitutes the public good. Planning requires these agencies to have – or have access to – strong technical capacities. Budgeting strategies may also be needed to manage multiple projects, as successfully implementing development plans is largely dependent on matching programmes of work with appropriate funding. As line ministries tend to be less concerned about their overall budget impacts, budgeting strategies can offset their tendency to propose too many projects and make large expenditure requests that could otherwise lead to unsustainable deficits, poor resource allocation, and inefficient spending on public goods and services.

The targets established by medium-term plans may often be unfeasible because they are disconnected from annual budgets, which, unlike development plans, are binding on government. Reconciling planning and budgeting over annual and medium-term timeframes may be facilitated through medium-term budgetary frameworks (MTBFs) which use projected expenditure for guidance in preparing annual budgets. Most Emerging Asian economies use MTBFs – or the related medium-term fiscal framework (MTFF) and medium-term performance framework (MTPF).

Under MTBFs, line ministries prepare annual budgets and forward estimates of expected needs for new and anticipated costs over the coming years. The framework enables better-informed decision making in budgeting by showing the full cost of multi-year programmes and committing line ministries to future spending plans (subject, perhaps, to adjustment should changing conditions so require).

In most cases, targets must be quantified and measurable by some objective criteria to be meaningful. Consequently, regular, reliable statistics are needed to establish baselines and historical trends and, as the plan is put in place, to monitor on-going and final progress. The planning process is made more effective with a detailed, comprehensive, and reliable set of economic and social indicators, in addition to full information on government finances and the programmes themselves. Korea's development planning has relied on a sound statistical basis, as it uses industry information on output, employment, exporting and technology absorption to set targets and monitor progress. Governments can develop such resources through investment in regular surveys and censuses of poverty, labour force participation and industry. Indeed, planning may also contribute indirectly to the improvement of data and national statistics systems by publicly highlighting areas of weaknesses.

Skilled and knowledgeable staff are, of course, also needed to make proper use of data and determine appropriate targets. Planners should be able to frame their ultimate goals as targets for either government inputs and activities (e.g. resources committed to childhood education), direct outputs (e.g. student enrolment) or desired outcomes (e.g. improved literacy or student achievement).

Co-ordination and management are essential to implementing development plans

Assuming that it is committed to its own plan, a government is responsible for implementing the final plan and striving to meet its targets. However, this process is complicated by the multiple actors involved and the limited resources available to them. There must consequently be effective co-ordination between central agencies and line ministries, between ministries, and within ministries. Capable and motivated staff and flexible institutions are then needed to implement plans.

While a medium-term budgetary framework helps to map out a longer-term budgetary perspective, it does not necessarily enable the government improve its management of line ministries, which may have separate policy interests and priorities. Government budgets provide for the switching of budget appropriations to line ministries for the output of public goods and services, while finance ministries tend to favour the pursuit of broad, balanced development goals at the lowest cost. As for implementing ministries and agencies, they may prefer to pad their budgets and retain autonomy in their operations.

Along with such divergent interests, the inter-ministerial relationship is complicated by an information asymmetry – namely, that line ministries have better knowledge of the costs of programme implementation and their own efforts, but that they may conceal that knowledge. Where this occurs, even if the ministry of finance were to pursue planned targets and line ministries could implement the policies for achieving them, outcomes may actually be successful only at higher than necessary expense – if at all – if line ministries divert resources to other projects.

To reduce such costs and improve the supervision of line ministries, public expenditure management (PEM) systems are a useful tool. Supervision may be carried out directly by the ministry of finance, either *ex ante* or *ex post*. Under the so-called "Francophone system", ministry of finance employees work within line ministries to watch whether funds are used appropriately. Under the "Anglophone system", by contrast, the finance ministry supervises line ministry performance through *ex post* evaluations. Controls may also be institutionalised through automatic budget control systems. Whatever the approach, mismanagement may be dealt with through internal disciplinary action or, in cases of corruption, through the courts. As Chapter 3 points out, Emerging Asia has a mixed track record when it comes to the implementation of PEMs.

Co-ordination and management in plan implementation are not only the responsibilities of the ministry of finance and other central agencies; these organisational responsibilities are also needed to direct cross-ministry co-operation and within-ministry operations. As plans come to embrace more targets addressing complex and cross-cutting issues – like those related to inclusive and sustainable growth – line ministries can be expected to share implementation responsibilities. The development of shared strategies then becomes necessary to avoid inefficient overlap and the neglect of necessary tasks. Institutionalised information-sharing and the identification of focal points among co-operating ministries may therefore help facilitate work on cross-cutting issues.

Finally, even when implementing ministries and agencies firmly intend to meet the goals that they have been set, and even when they enjoy the resources and external support for doing so, they may fall short as a result of their own limited capacities. As with inter-ministerial work, ministries are at their most effective when they define tasks clearly, assign suitable workers the responsibility for completing them and develop cohesive organisational cultures. Human resources are perhaps the greatest potential constraint on operations. Managers face challenges in identifying and attracting skilled workers, keeping them motivated and retaining those with experience. Ministries are very likely to be limited in what they can accomplish if they cannot offer competitive, incentive-oriented pay. Assuming that workers are properly motivated, the availability of training and skills development also helps to improve human capital and institutional capacities.

Skilled staff and supportive institutions enable countries to respond to challenges that may encounter when conducting their MTDPs, as it may sometimes be appropriate to pursue alternative goals. Japan, for example, grew quickly even though it took a flexible approach in implementing its plans, dictated by changing conditions. Governments may improve the flexibility and management of their plans by incorporating ICT in the public sector. Already the focus of a number of programmes throughout Emerging Asia, ICT improves organisation, data collection and service delivery.

Indonesia

A. Medium-term economic outlook (forecast, 2015-19 average)

GDP growth (percentage change):	6.0
Current account balance (% of GDP):	-3.3
Fiscal balance (% of GDP):	-1.7

B. Medium-term plan

Period:	2010-14
Theme:	Realisation of an Indonesia that is prosperous, democratic and just

C. Basic data (in 2013)

Total population:	248 million*
Population of DKI Jakarta:	9.76 million (in 2011)
GDP per capita at PPP:	5 214 (current USD)**

Note: * Total population data for 2013 are estimates.
** IMF estimate.
Sources: OECD Development Centre, MPF-2015, national sources and IMF.

GDP growth rates (percentage change)

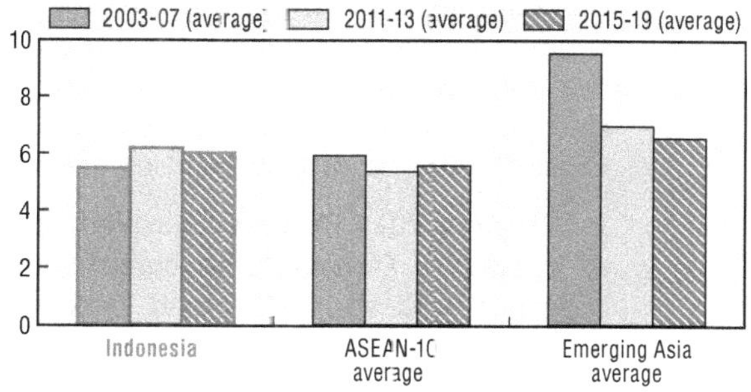

Source: OECD Development Centre, MPF-2015.

GDP per capita, 2013 (PPP, current USD)

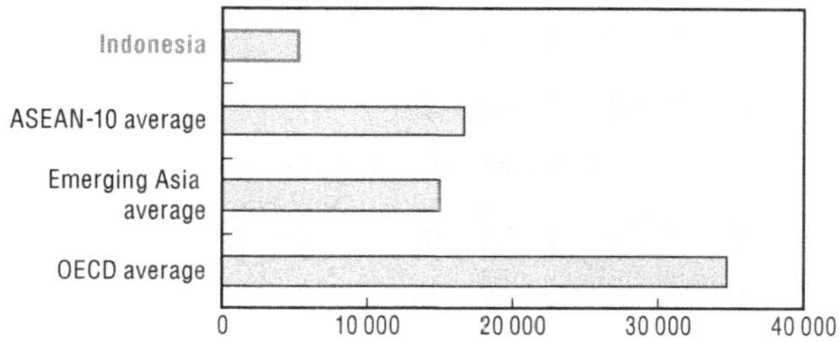

Source: IMF.

Composition of exports, 2013
(percentage of total exports)

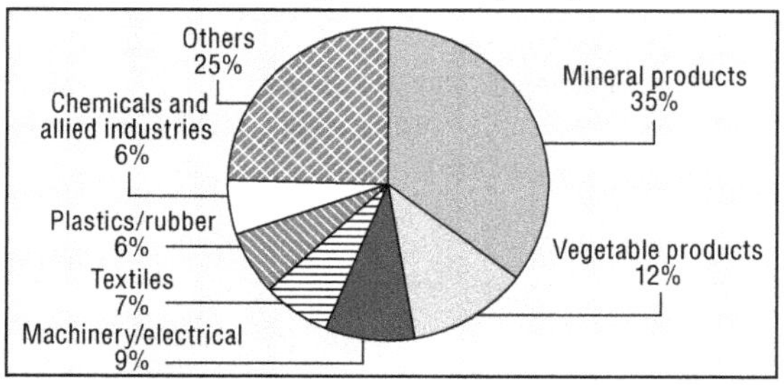

Source: Trademap.

Composition of imports, 2013
(percentage of total imports)

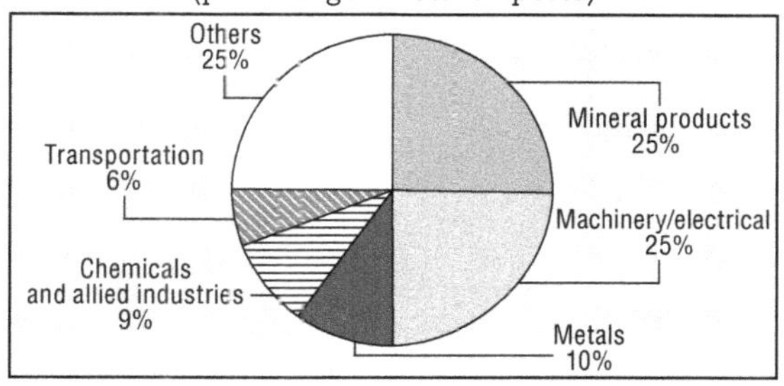

Source: Trademap.

Summary of the medium-term development plan: Towards a prosperous, just and democratic Indonesia

Indonesia's 2010-14 *National Medium-term Development Plan* (RPJMN 2010-14) is the second phase in the country's *National Long-term Development Plan* (RPJPN 2005-25). Now coming to an end (as of November 2014), its objective is to bring about a prosperous, just and democratic Indonesia across five socio-economic policy areas: economic development and increased prosperity; improved governance; strengthened pillars of democracy; law enforcement and corruption eradication; and inclusive, equitable development.

The long-term and medium-term plans' targets are based on the main thrusts of the RPJPN 2005-25, evaluation of the previous medium-term plan and background studies on strategic issues. The Ministry of Development Planning (BAPPENAS) co-ordinates the process of determining the plan and setting targets. It factors in the government's priority programmes and consultations with citizens. The plan identifies 11 sectors as development priorities: bureaucracy and governance reform; education; health; poverty reduction; food production; infrastructure; investment and the business climate; energy; environment and natural disaster management; least developed, frontier, outer and post-conflict areas; and culture, technology and innovation. There are also three cross-cutting priorities: politics, law and security; the economy; and people's welfare.

In May 2011, Indonesia rolled out its *Master Plan for the Acceleration and Expansion of Indonesia's Economic Development* (MP3EI) 2011-25. It is both a complement to and – together with the RPJPN and RPJMN – an integral part of the country's development strategy. Through the MP3EI, Indonesia plans to step up the pace of its development. Its aim is to increase income *per capita* to USD 14 250 - USD 15 500 and total GDP to USD 4 trillion to USD 4.5 trillion by 2025. To that end, the country has targeted 6.4% to 7.5% economic growth for the period 2011-14. It is implementing the MP3EI through three main strategies: increasing the potential of regional economic corridors (Sumatra, Kalimantan, Java, Sulawesi, Bali and Nusa Tenggara, and Papua-Maluku), strengthening national connectivity, and strengthening human capital and national science and technology capacities.

Following his victory in Indonesia's July 2014 presidential election, Joko Widodo assumed office in October, replacing former President Yudhoyono. The change of office may usher in changes in policy priorities, including those that are part of MP3EI.

Table 2.1.1. **Indonesia's key medium-term development targets, 2010-14**

Indicators	Initial status (2009)	Current status (2013)	Target (2014)
Macroeconomics			
GDP growth rate (%)	5.6, per year (2005-09, average)	6.2 (2010-13, average)	6.3-6.8 (2010-14, average)
Inflation rate (%)	9.0 per year (2005-09, average)	5.9 per year (2010-13, average)	4-6 per year (2010-14, average)
Unemployment rate (%)	7.87	6.25	5-6
Poverty			
Poverty rate (%)	14.15	11.47 (September 2013)	8-10
Education			
Average school stay of people of 15 years and older (years)	7.72	8.1	8.25
Illiteracy rate of population aged 15 years and over (%)	5.3	4.01	4.18
Net enrolment rate in elementary school education (%)	95.23	95.8	96
Net enrolment rate in junior high school education (%)	74.52	79.4	76 (81.9)
Gross enrolment rate in senior high school education (%)	69.6	82	85
Gross enrolment rate at universities of those in the 19-23 years age bracket (%)	21.57	28.7	30
Health			
Life expectancy (years)	70.7	71.1 (2012)	72
Maternal mortality rate per 100 000 live births	228	359 (2012)	118
Infant mortality per 1 000 live births	34	32 (2012)	24
Child deficient nutrition and malnutrition prevalence (%)	18.4	19.6	<15

Table 2.1.1. **Indonesia's key medium-term development targets, 2010-14** *(cont.)*

Food production			
Paddy production growth (%)	6.75	3.22	10.53
Maize production growth (%)	8.04	-4.51	10.02
Soybean production growth (%)	25.63	-7.49	20.05
Sugar production growth (%)	-2.96	-1.77	12.55
Cow meat production growth (%)	16.15	2.44	7.3
Energy			
Crude oil production (thousand barrel, per day)	945 (2010)	900	1 010
Capacity of electricity generating stations (MW)	31 959	42 339 (2012)	46 959 (Additional of 3000 MW per year)
Electrification ratio (%)	65.8	80.2	80
Utilisation of PLTP (geothermal power station) (MW)	1 189 (2010)	1 341	5 000
Infrastructure			
Highway/road construction (Trans Sumatra, Java, Kalimantan, Sulawesi, East and West Nusa Tenggara, Papua (km)	2 443	13 219 (in 2012)	19 370
Railway construction (km)	135.2	873.65	954
Democracy and governance			
Indonesian Democracy Index	67.3	65.48 (2011)	73
Transparency International Corruption Perception Index (1-10 scale)	2.8	3.0 (in 2011) 32* (in 2012)	5

Note: * In 2012 the methodology changed and the scale became 1-100.
Source: OECD Development Centre's compilation based on national sources.

Indonesia's development plan and implementation

Policy challenges of implementing the national plan in Indonesia

- Improve access to and the quality of health services – especially for mothers and children – as large gaps between targets and achievements are to be found in healthcare. Expand the coverage of the newly implemented health insurance scheme.
- Further improve the education system, particularly in access to secondary and tertiary education for students from low-income households.
- Address rising inequality adequately.

There is improvement in some policy areas, but more work is required in others

Overall, Indonesia's performance improved in many of the medium-term plan's priority areas. In fact, the country is on track to meet a number of its targets. Inflation, for instance, fell in the last decade from an average of 9% in 2005-09 to 5.9% in 2010-13 – within the average of 4-6% targeted in the 2010-14 RPJMN. Pro-job measures helped to bring the unemployment rate down from 7.9% in 2009 to 6.3% in 2013. The net enrolment rate at the junior high school level reached 77.7% in 2011 and 79.4% in 2013, higher than the 2014 target of 76% originally set in the RPJMN. Accordingly, the target has been revised up to 81.9%. Nevertheless, progress in meeting education targets has been slow, particularly in the tertiary level enrolment rate. Other targets also appear more difficult to achieve.

The 6.4%-7.5% GDP growth target set out in the MP3EI for 2011-14 is above the 6.2% average growth rate for 2011-13 and the 6.0% rate for 2015-19 forecast in Chapter 1 of this edition. Health indicators also appear to fall well short of targets despite increased public health spending in the last few years. While life expectancy has improved and is closer to the targeted level, the maternal mortality rate rose from 228 per 100 000 live births in 2009 to 359 in 2012 – even wider of the target of 118 by 2014. As for infant mortality, it has fallen even though it also still exceeds the targeted rate. Uncertainty stemming from the change of government may have some adverse effects on progress in reaching targets.

Although the poverty rate is down, targets have not yet been reached

The country has shown progress in reducing poverty thanks to the poverty alleviation instruments co-ordinated by the National Team for the Acceleration of Poverty Reduction (TNP2K). However, the MTDP has not yet reached its target poverty rate of 8% to 10%. Poverty reduction programmes – such as the National Programme for Community Empowerment (PNPM Mandiri) and the KUR loans programme – need to be strengthened.

Income inequality is on the rise

Rising income inequality and widening regional disparities are further challenges. Indonesia's Gini ratio climbed from 0.35 in 2008 to 0.41 in 2013 (Figure 2.1.1). Inequality is evidenced in regional poverty gaps, especially between the western and eastern provinces. For example, the poverty rate is 24.2% in Papua and Maluku, but only 6.7% in Kalimantan (Figure 2.1.2). To address the issue, Indonesia should seek to foster not only higher, but also more inclusive, growth so that the benefits of development can be more fairly shared. Access to better-quality education, healthcare and public facilities needs to be improved, especially in the least developed, frontier, outer and post-conflict areas.

Access to education, especially at the tertiary level, needs to be broadened

Access to secondary and tertiary education needs to be widened to accelerate the accumulation of human capital. One measure could be to strengthen the targeting of cash transfer schemes – such as the Poor Students' Assistance Programme (BSM) and the Family Hope Programme (PKH) – to ensure that they benefit the poor rather than middle-income households and reach remote areas, especially in the eastern provinces. The government should also widen coverage to save poor students from having to discontinue their studies due to a lack of funds. The PKH scheme for junior high school pupils, for example, covers only 43% of the total costs of education when transport costs are included (World Bank, 2012). Increasing the coverage of scholarships like the Bidik Misi grant for poor students in higher education is also important.

Improving the quality of teachers deserves greater attention since the higher education expenditure of recent years and the new curriculum introduced in 2013 have not automatically translated into higher teaching standards or better education outcomes. This is reflected in the country's PISA scores, which lag behind the OECD average.[1] Only 37% of teachers in 2006 and 58% in 2011 had the minimum four-year bachelor's degree stipulated in the 2005 Teacher Law (Suharyadi and Sambodho, 2013; BAPPENAS, 2013).

Serious challenges to reaching health targets remain

Health outcomes still lag far behind targets despite the increased public health spending of recent years, evidenced in the universal health insurance scheme, Jaminan Kesehatan Nasional (JKN), which was rolled out in early 2014.[2] However, it is crucial to further accelerate the expansion of JKN to achieve Indonesia's ambitious goal of universal health care by 2019.

In addition to access to healthcare, the standard of health services needs to be higher, especially for poor households, people living in remote and less developed areas, and mothers and children. There is also room for the improvement of programmes to improve nutrition and access to basic immunisations for children.

In general, efforts to achieve the development plan's goals require close co-ordination between different actors if programmes are to be successfully implemented. Several schemes are the joint responsibilities of multiple organisations. For example, the BSM is implemented by both the former Ministry of Education and Culture and the Ministry of Religious Affairs.[3] As for the JKN health insurance scheme, it brings together several different actors, including social security services, the government (the Ministries of Health, Labour, Home Affairs and People's Welfare), hospitals and other health service providers.

Infrastructure development and reduced corruption will help improve the investment climate

Infrastructure development is needed if Indonesia's investment climate is to be improved. While electricity provision has reached the level targeted in the medium-term plan, further efforts are still needed in other areas – particularly transport connecting Indonesia's regions. Although around 45% of total investment under MP3EI is earmarked for transport infrastructure projects (e.g. the Bali toll road, Sunda Strait Bridge, Jakarta MRT and the Soekarno-Hatta airport railway), together with energy, water and ICT, insufficient financing remains a considerable barrier. The involvement of the private sector through PPPs could help to address the funding issue.

The capacity of local government is a further challenge, as the implementation of MP3EI is based on economic corridors. Local authorities should have the power to define investment, allocate budgets and design and implement effective regulations. Also essential is efficient co-ordination and synergy between central and local governments.

Indonesia has demonstrated its commitment to combating corruption through the creation of the Corruption Eradication Commission (KPK) and the launch of the National Strategy to Prevent and Eradicate Corruption (Stranas PPK) 2012-25. As a result, its score on Transparency International's Corruption Perception Index rose from 2.8 in 2010 to 3.0 in 2011. Nevertheless, the score is low and below target, which suggests that the government still struggles to gain people's trust in its ability to provide high-quality public services. An efficient bureaucracy and good governance are also essential to improving the business and investment climate.

During the election campaign, President Widodo announced that he would gradually reduce fuel subsidies over his five-year term of office and reallocate funds to other sectors, including infrastructure. The direction of his infrastructure development policy, however, is likely to differ from that steered by the administration of his predecessor, former President Yudhoyono. The new president is expected to focus more on improving agriculture and strengthening the country's maritime sector. The result could well be changed priorities in infrastructure projects, which includes those set out in MP3EI.

Also thought to be high on President Widodo's agenda are civil service reform and the improvement of human resources through wider access to education and healthcare, seen as part of the new administration's commitment to creating an investment-friendly environment.

These policy directions, of course, are not without challenges. An especially daunting one is the politically sensitive issue of cuts in fuel subsidies. Previous such efforts sparked national street protests. Often considered as a new face on the country's political scene, Widodo enjoys popularity – a challenge in itself, since he has to live up to high expectations. Addressing corruption will also be a particularly stern test for his administration, especially when it comes up against resistance from the opposition and tackles deeply rooted local corruption.

Figure 2.1.1. **Inequality in Indonesia and selected provinces, 2008-13**

Gini coefficient

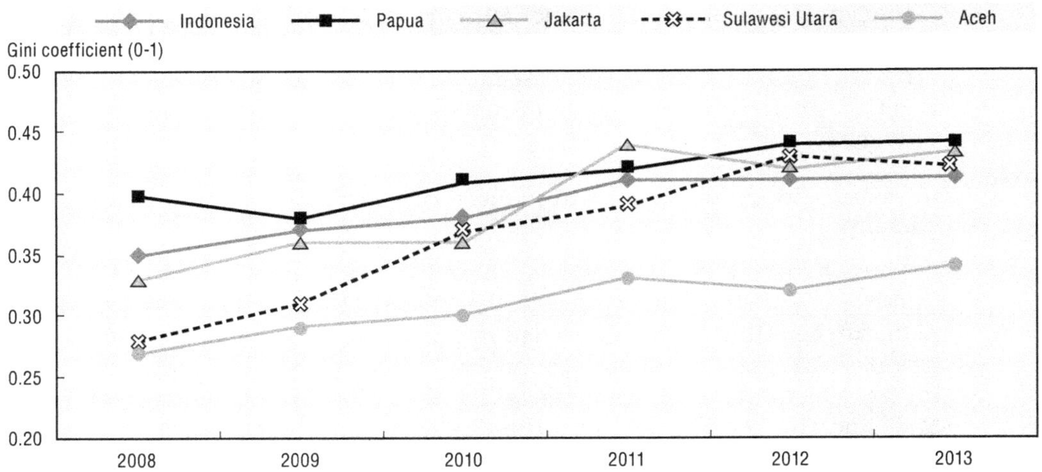

Source: Statistics Indonesia, Badan Pusat Statistik (BPS).

StatLink http://dx.doi.org/10.1787/888933179635

Figure 2.1.2. **Poverty rates by region, 2013**

Poverty rates as percentages of population in selected regions

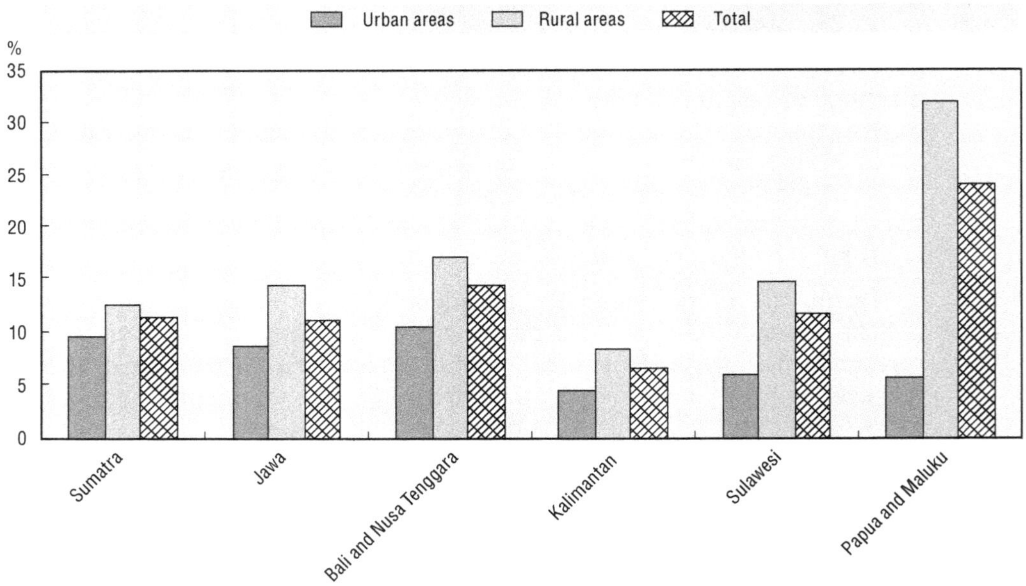

Note: Provinces' poverty lines range from IDR 217 547 to IDR 434 322 per month as of September 2013.

Source: Statistics Indonesia. Badan Pusat Statistik (BPS).

StatLink http://dx.doi.org/10.1787/888933179641

Notes

1. PISA stands for the Programme for International Student Assessment. It ranks 65 countries based on tests in reading, mathematics and science taken by 15 years-old students. In PISA 2012, Indonesia was ranked second-to-last, scoring 375 in mathematics, 396 in reading, and 382 in sciences, much lower than the OECD averages of 494, 496 and 501, respectively.
2. Jaminan Kesehatan Nasional (JKN) is managed by Badan Penyelenggara Jaminan Sosial (BPJS Health). BPJS is the social security administrative body. It includes BPJS Health (previously ASKES), which implements the JKN, and BPJS Employment (previously JAMSOSTEK), which covers work-related accidents, old-age benefits and life insurance. It will also cover pensions from 2015. Adequate provision of pension benefits needs to be ensured, taking into account the fiscal sustainability of the system.
3. Recently, Widodo announced that the Ministry of Education would be divided into two different ministries, the Ministry of Education and Culture and the Ministry of Research, Technology and Higher Education.

Malaysia

A. Medium-term economic outlook (forecast, 2015-19 average)

GDP growth (percentage change):	5.6
Current account balance (% of GDP):	4.3
Fiscal balance (% of GDP):	-4.0

B. Medium-term plan

Period: 2011-15

Theme: Charting development towards a high-income nation

C. Basic data (in 2013)

Total population:	30 million*
Population of Kuala Lumpur	1.69 million (in 2011)
GDP per capita at PPP:	17 748 (current USD)**

Note: * Total population data for 2013 are estimates.
** IMF estimate.
Sources: OECD Development Centre, MPF-2015, national sources and IMF.

GDP growth rates (percentage change)

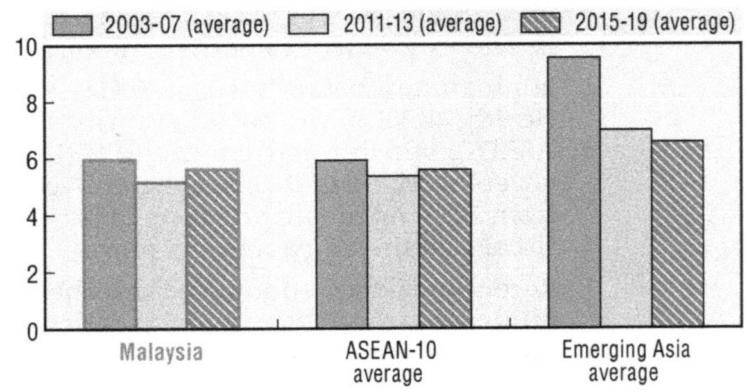

Source: OECD Development Centre, MPF-2015.

GDP per capita, 2013 (PPP, current USD)

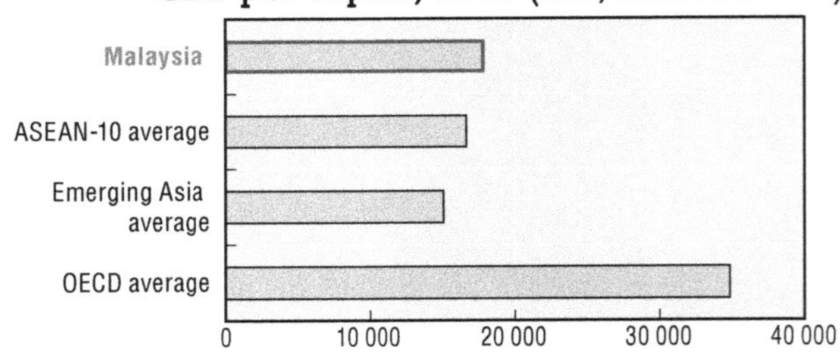

Source: IMF.

Composition of exports, 2013
(percentage of total exports)

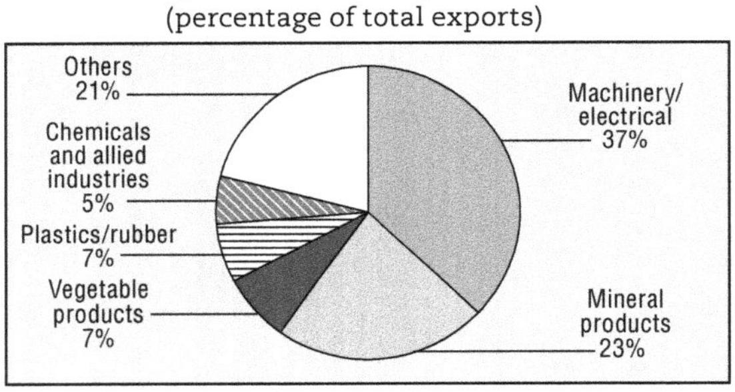

Source: Trademap.

Composition of imports, 2013
(percentage of total imports)

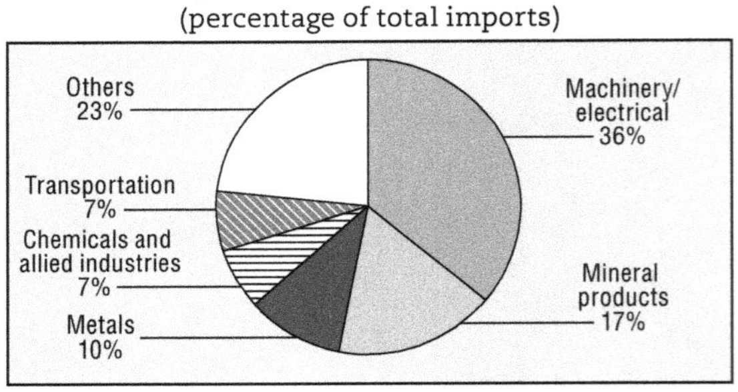

Source: Trademap.

Summary of the medium-term development plan: Charting development towards high-income status

The *Tenth Malaysia Plan* 2011-15 (10th MP) outlines medium-term strategies and approaches to meeting Malaysia's ultimate development objectives. The Tenth Plan identifies policy directions and programmes that are built into an operational framework for achieving greater growth. Key components of the framework are the Government Transformation Program (GTP), the National Key Economic Areas (NKEAs) of the Economic Transformation Programme (ETP) and the strategic economic reforms of the New Economic Model (NEM).

The NEM sets three goals for sustainable, inclusive growth: high-income status by 2020, a sustainable economy that meets present needs without compromising future generations and an inclusive-growth economy that enables all communities to benefit from the wealth of the nation.

The NEM is implemented through the GTP, itself driven by eight strategic reform initiatives that are directed towards strengthening national productivity and competitiveness.

The 12 NKEAs are economic sectors and Kuala Lumpur.[1] They are seen as drivers of strong, sustainable competitiveness that have the potential to generate high income and thus to power Malaysia's economic growth. At the same time, the 10th MP takes a new approach to boosting social justice which it anchors in two objectives: equal opportunity for all Malaysians and a social safety net for disadvantaged groups. The social justice objective also incorporates equal access to health, education and basic infrastructure as part of the thrust towards a more united, progressive society built on market-friendly, needs-based, meritocratic and transparent foundations.

Central to the Tenth Malaysia Plan are "10 Big Ideas" that will guide the country towards its 2020 development goal: (1) be internally driven and externally aware; (2) leverage Malaysia's diversity internationally; (3) transform the country to high-income status through specialisation; (4) unleash productivity-led growth and innovation; (5) nurture, attract and retain top talent; (6) ensure equality of opportunity and safeguard the vulnerable; (7) focus on concentrated growth and inclusive development; (8) support effective, smart partnerships; (9) value environmental assets; and (10) ensure that the government acts as a competitive corporation (Government of Malaysia, 2010).

The Malaysia National Development Planning Committee, with the Economic Planning Unit as its secretariat, is responsible for the formulation, implementation, progress evaluation and revision of the country's development plan. Preparing it is an interactive process which involves regular discussions and consultations with ministries and government agencies, academics, the private sector, and civil society.

Table 2.2.1. **Malaysia's key medium-term development targets, 2011-15**

Indicators	Initial status (2010)	Current status (2013)	Target (2015)
Economic performance			
GDP growth rate (%)	4.2, per year (2006-10, average)	5.2, per year (2011-13, average)	6, per year (2011-15, average)
Real GDP (RM billion)	552.1	787.6	740.3
GNI per capita (RM thousand)	27	31.8	38.8
Employment (million)	12 (0.9 million jobs created during the 9th Plan)	12.8	13.2
Unemployment rate (%)	3.3	3.1	3.1
Contribution of Total Factor Productivity to GDP (%)	34.7	31.5 (2012)	38.5 (10th Plan)
Private investment growth (%)	18.4	16.2	12.8 (10th Plan)
Private consumption growth (%)	6.9	7.4	7.7 (10th Plan)
Trade balance/surplus (RM billion)	110	70.7	142.4
Current account surplus percentage to GNI (%)	11.5	2.8	10.5
Fiscal policy			
Federal government fiscal deficits (% of GDP)	5.6	3.9	2.8
Federal government debt (% of GDP)	52.9	54.8	49.9
Sectoral targets (Share of GDP [%])			
Services	53.2	55.2	61.1
Manufacturing	24.2	24.5	26.3
Construction	3.1	3.8	2.9
Agriculture	8.0	7.1	6.6
Mining and quarrying	10.5	8.1	5.9

Table 2.2.1. **Malaysia's key medium-term development targets, 2011-15** (*cont.*)

Key growth engines (NKEAs)			
Oil and gas industry*, contribution to GDP (%)	12.7	10.7	11.1
Palm oil and related products, contribution to GDP (RM billion)	18.1	20.5	21.9
Finance and insurance sector, contribution to GDP (%)	9.1	9.1	12.7
Wholesale and retail, contribution to GDP (%)	14.0	14.4	15.1
Revenue from tourism (RM billion)	56.5	65.4	115
ICT, contribution to GDP (%)	10.5	12 (2012)	10.2
Business services, contribution to GDP (%)	3.8	4.1	3.3
Healthcare travel industry revenue growth (%)	31.5	15.8	10
Innovation-led growth and SMEs			
Increase GERD (Government Expenditure on R&D) (% of GDP)	1.01 (2009)	1.07 (2011)	1
Number of SMEs with 1-InnoCERT certification**	0	115 (2012)	500
Inclusive socio-economic development			
Reduce the incidence of poverty (%)	3.8 (2009)	1.7 (2012)	2
Mean income of the bottom 40% households (RM/month)	1 440 (2009)	1 847 (2012)	2 300
Income inequality (Gini coefficient)	0.441 (2009)	0.431 (2012)	0.420
Rural water coverage (%)	81 (Total), 90 (Peninsular), 59 (Sabah and Sarawak) (2009)	99 (Peninsular), 79 (Sabah), 90 (Sarawak) (2012)	99 (Peninsular), 98 (Sabah), 95 (Sarawak)
Rural electricity coverage (%)	92.3 (Total), 99.5 (Peninsular), 77 (Sabah), 67 (Sarawak) (2009)	99.8 (Peninsular), 88.7 (Sabah), 82.7 (Sarawak) (2012)	100 (Peninsular), 99 (Sabah and Sarawak)
Education system and labour market			
Pre-school enrolment rate for children aged 4+ and 5+ years (%)	67 (2009)	81.7	92
Percentage of graduate teachers in secondary schools (%)	89.4 (2009)	94 (as of 31 January 2014)	90
Percentage of graduate teachers in primary schools (%)	28 (2009)	48 (as of 31 January 2014)	60
Female labour force participation rate (%)	46.8	49.5 (2012)	55
Healthcare			
Doctor-population ratio	1:859	1:633	1:597
Nurse-population ratio	1:410	1:333	1:200
Dentists-population ratio	1:7437	1:5676	1:5040
Pharmacists-population ratio	1:3652	1:2949	1:2419

Note: *Includes crude oil and condensate, natural gas, and refined petroleum products. **1-InnoCERT was introduced to certify SMEs on the basis of innovation and commercialisation achievement. SMEs that receive 1-InnoCERT certification will receive benefits such as tax deduction for R&D activities and priority in government procurement.
Source: OECD Development Centre's compilation based on national sources.

Malaysia's development plan and implementation

Policy challenges of implementing the national plan in Malaysia

- Improve productivity to support sustainable economic growth and transform Malaysia into a high-income developed nation.
- Further develop ICT, which is particularly important in supporting growth.
- Enhance fiscal stability and reduce dependence on oil. The successful introduction of a goods and service tax (GST) is key to improving tax performance.

Despite much progress there is room for improvement, particularly in productivity

In furtherance of its goal of becoming a high-income nation, Malaysia has improved its national output. Real GDP rose to MYR 787.6 billion in 2013, exceeding the target set in the *Tenth Malaysia Plan*, while GNI *per capita* continued its climb from MYR 26 400 in

2009 to MYR 31 800 in 2013. Considerable improvements also come in the growth of private investment – higher, at 16.2%, than the 10th MP target of 12.8% – and increases in some targeted NKEAs, e.g. financial services, wholesale and retail, business services, and private healthcare (Table 2.2.1).

Nonetheless, further efforts are required. The country needs to address the problematic structural issues that still stand in its way. It must also boost productivity to improve growth. Although its average productivity level is on the rise, growth has actually slowed down over the decades – from 4.4 in the 1970s to 2.3 in 2011-12 (Figure 2.2.1). This suggests that there is still room for improvement.

If it is to become a high-income economy, Malaysia needs to further focus on maximising its potential. SMEs, which play a vital role in the economy, offer such potential. They make, for example, a major contribution as employers, accounting for 57.4% of total employment in 2012 (NSDC, 2013). Of all businesses in Malaysia, 97.3% were SMEs (DOSM, 2012). They accounted for 32.5% of the country's value added in 2011, compared to large firms' 67.5%. Clearly, they play a vital role in the economy and could provide strong foundations for the growth of new industries as well as strengthening existing ones for the country's future development (Munusamy, 2008).

Yet, although SMEs' economic contribution has grown over the years, there is still plenty of room for improvement. Their output is relatively smaller than that of their peers in Emerging Asia and in more developed countries (OECD, 2013a). In Japan and China, for example, their contribution to GDP is already more than 55% (NSDC, 2008).

Of all the SMEs in Malaysia, 90% operate in the services sector, 5.9% in manufacturing, 3% in construction, 1% in agriculture and 0.1% in mining and quarrying. While labour productivity is a determining factor in the performance of SMEs, it is lower than in Malaysia's large firms and lower than the performance of SMEs in other countries in the region and in more developed economies. In the USA, for example, SME productivity is seven times and in Singapore four times higher than in Malaysia (Sapie, 2014), the chief reason being the high numbers of unskilled workers employed in the country's labour-intensive industries (OECD, 2013a).

To improve workers' skills and so increase labour productivity, human capital development is a priority. To that end, the Malaysian government emphasises the role of education, training and talent recruitment. The Talent Corporation (TC) was established in 2013 in the Prime Minister's Department to lead Malaysia's campaign to attract, develop and retain the talent needed to create a high-income economy. Its remit includes:

- leading and driving innovative national talent management initiatives;
- facilitating recruiting processes in the private sector for attracting, creating and motivating a world class workforce; and
- delivering major national talent-fostering initiatives along the human capital development pipeline.

Human capital development, though, is not the only factor affecting the productivity of SMEs. They also need to improve capacity by investing in innovation and new technology. Yet many consider innovation to be a cost rather than an investment (Sapie, 2014). The result has been low technology adoption by Malaysian SMEs, with only 27% using ICT in their business operations (DOSM, 2012). The high cost of bandwidth and domain registration curbs SME access to the internet: registering a domain cost USD 143 in Malaysia in 2010, while it was only USD 64 in Chinese Taipei and USD 24 in the United States. Government encouragement for technology adoption and innovation could therefore help to improve SME performance.

Another problematic issue is financing. Whereas 51.7% of medium-sized firms and 33% of small ones rely on financial institutions, micro enterprises enjoy only very limited access to financing. Although they accounted for 77% of all Malaysia's SMEs according to the Economic Census 2011, just 17.4% sourced their finance from micro-credit organisations, banks or other financial institutions (DOSM, 2012). Further improving lending schemes to facilitate micro enterprises' access to financing is urgent.

Malaysia has fully recognised the issues and main challenges it should tackle to improve SME performance. Accordingly, the SME Masterplan 2012-20 (NSDC, 2012) incorporates the following focus areas: human capital development, innovation and technology adoption, access to financing, infrastructure, market access, and legal and regulatory environment.

Further development of ICT needed to support growth

Fostering enhanced technological innovation is one of the most important ways to improve competitiveness as it reduces operational and transaction costs. Against a background of global competitiveness, the Malaysian government has oriented policy towards productivity-led growth and an economy of innovation. To those ends, it seeks to create an environment that fosters innovation across the economy, supporting investment in science, technology, and human capital. The government has rolled out grants and funding schemes – such as Sciencefund, Technofund and Innofund – to encourage innovation and R&D projects. Greater efforts are, nevertheless, needed to further improve Malaysia's performance in innovation. Its position in the Global Innovation Index has remained largely stationary in recent years: in 2009 it was 25th out of 130 countries and 33rd out of 143 in 2014. (Cornell University, INSEAD and WIPO, 2014)

The Malaysian government has recognised the importance of ICT in boosting competitiveness. It has been identified as one of the key sectors in the country's economy and a significant amount of the government's budget has been allocated to ICT development over the years. ICT was included as one of the strategies for creating an industrialised economy. The ICT sector is expected to be a growth engine that will help the country to transform itself from an average producer of mainstream products and services into a niche provider of selected ones and climb the global value chain and drive the economy towards an advanced, high-income status.

As the largest sector in the Malaysian economy, services accounted for 54.6% of GDP, with a growth rate of 6.4% in 2012. Among service sub-sectors, ICT output grew 9.1%. Its contribution to the services sector output was still small, however. It accounted for 8.22%, compared to distributive trade with 30.6% and financial services with 20.2% (MPC, 2013b). In productivity performance, ICT grew 8% in 2012, with a 4.4% annual growth rate of capital productivity.

The evidence reveals considerable improvement in the ICT sector, although there is room for more. Its level of technological readiness is not yet satisfactory, for example. Furthermore, Malaysia needs new technologies able to improve the speed and efficiency of business transactions by cutting operating costs and making Internet access more equitable.[2]

The private sector makes great use of ICT products and services in Malaysia, and the role that it can play in creating an innovation economy must not be overlooked. It has invested significantly in ICT over time (Mudiarasan, Raman and Lee; 2009) and close public-private co-ordination would be a further boon. It is important to support private businesses, especially by increasing their access to financing for ICT-related investment and strengthening legal protection for intellectual property rights (IPRs) to encourage more innovation.

Improve fiscal stability and reduce over-reliance on oil and gas sector

Malaysia's dependence on the oil and gas sector is a concern for the country's fiscal stability. The tax base is narrow, the bulk of tax revenue coming from the oil and gas sector, with the state-owned oil company Petronas being the biggest single contributor. Malaysia's budget is thus over-exposed to the volatility of oil prices. To ensure fiscal stability and sustainability, the government should seek to reduce reliance on oil and gas – particularly as reserves are finite.

A successful GST could improve tax performance

There is scope for widening the tax base and improving tax administration and compliance. The decision to introduce a goods and services tax (GST) is a major step taken by the Malaysian government in its efforts to develop a sound tax system. The GST, due to be ushered in on 1 April 2015, will broaden the tax base as it is based on consumption rather than income, and could help make Malaysia's public finances sustainable. It is important, however, to ensure that the necessary support – e.g. infrastructure, training for tax officers, an information and communication plan – is available for the new tax to be phased in smoothly.

Improvements are also called for on the expenditure side. A better-targeted subsidy system is crucial to more efficient spending. According to its 2014 budget statement, the Ministry of Finance allocated almost MYR 47 billion to various types of subsidies, incentives and assistance for sectors including petroleum products, food, health, agriculture and fisheries, utilities, welfare, and education in 2013. The petroleum products subsidy of MYR 24.8 billion accounted for the lion's share – 53% – of all subsidies, which is higher than in other countries in the region as a percentage of GDP (Figure 2.2.2).

The petroleum products subsidy benefits not only the poor, but all other income brackets, too, including the highest. It is inefficiently targeted and should be reduced. The allocation would be more efficient if it went to the education and health sectors, where it would benefit the poor more than middle- and high-income groups. The government has started addressing the issue through a rationalisation plan, which involves gradually restructuring its subsidy scheme and reducing its share of the fuel bill. The move will require preparing businesses and individuals for the rise in prices and production costs that will result from the reduced fuel subsidy.

Figure 2.2.1. **Malaysia's average productivity levels and growth**

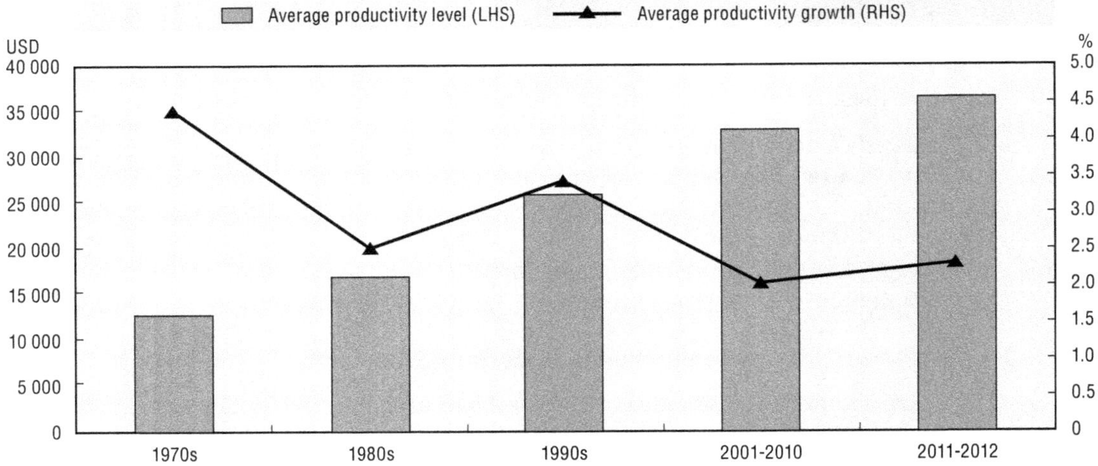

Source: MPC (2013a), *Productivity Watch*, Malaysia Productivity Corporation, Pataling Jaya, June, www.mpc.gov.my/Publication/ProductivityWatch1.pdf.
StatLink http://dx.doi.org/10.1787/888933179651

Figure 2.2.2. **Post-tax subsidies for petroleum products, 2011**
Percentage of GDP

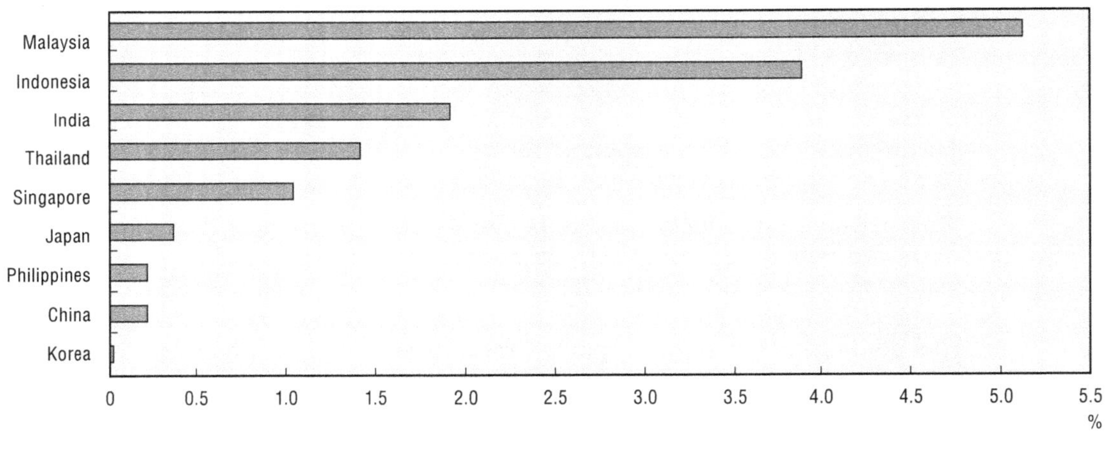

Source: IMF (2013a), *Energy Subsidy Reform: Lessons and Implications*, IMF, Washington, DC.
StatLink http://dx.doi.org/10.1787/888933179665

Notes:

1. The 12 NKEAs are: *(i)* oil and gas; *(ii)* palm oil and related products; *(iii)* financial services; *(iv)* wholesale and retail; *(v)* tourism; *(vi)* information and communications technology (ICT); *(vii)* education services; *(viii)* electrical and electronic; *(ix)* business services; *(x)* private healthcare; *(xi)* agriculture; and *(xii)* greater Kuala Lumpur.
2. Currently, the rate of high broadband subscription in urban areas is 60%, only 25% in suburban areas, 20% in rural areas and 15% in remote areas.

Myanmar

A. Medium-term economic outlook (forecast, 2015-19 average)

GDP growth (percentage change): 7.8
Current account balance (% of GDP): -5.1

B. Medium-term plan

Period: 2012-15
Theme: Development of industry, balanced development, improvements in education, health, living standards and statistical capacities

C. Basic data (in 2013)

Total population: 65 million*
Population of Nay Pyi Taw: 1 million (in 2009)**
GDP per capita at PPP: 1 740 (current USD)***

Note: * Total population data for 2013 are estimates.
**Provisional results of Census 2014: 1.16 million.
*** IMF estimate.
Sources: OECD Development Centre, MPF-2015, national sources and IMF.

GDP growth rates (percentage change)

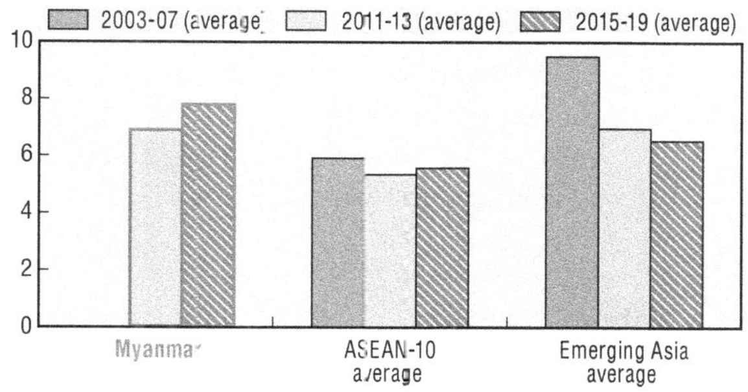

Source: OECD Development Centre, MPF-2015.

GDP per capita, 2013 (PPP, current USD)

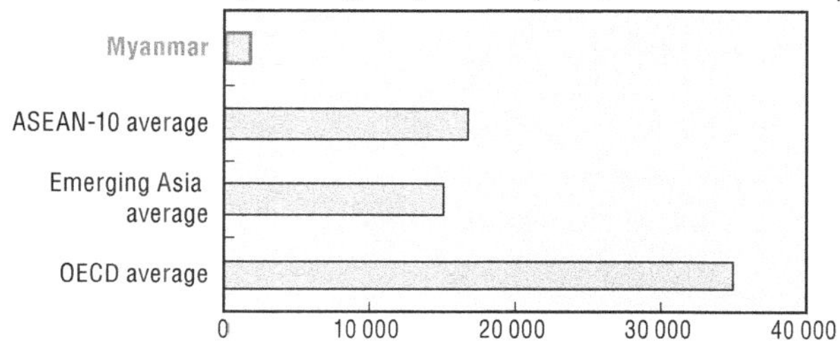

Source: IMF.

Composition of exports, 2013
(percentage of total exports)

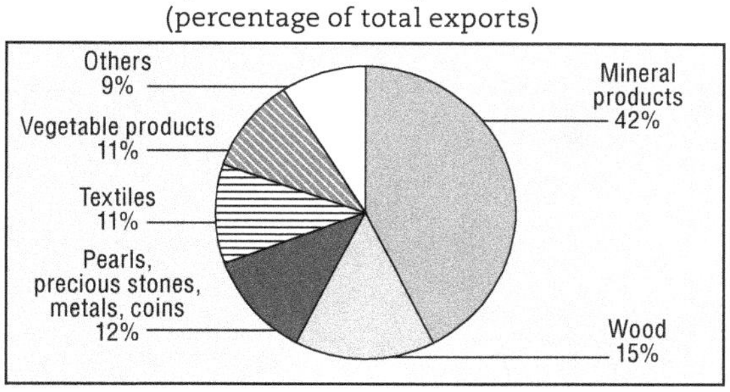

Source: Trademap.

Composition of imports, 2013
(percentage of total imports)

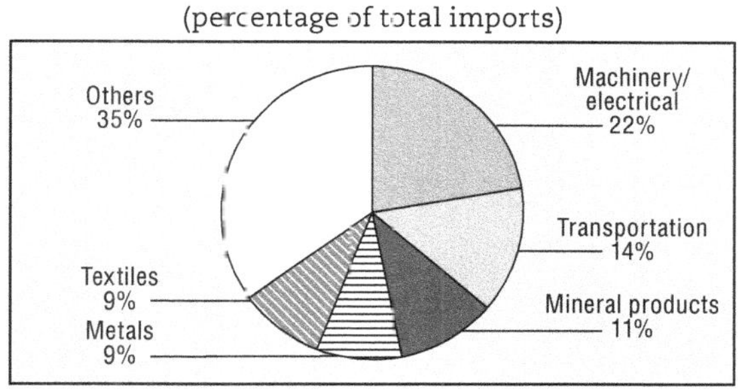

Source: Trademap.

Summary of the medium-term development plan: Balanced economic growth, social development and better statistics

Although Myanmar has a history of national and sector development plans, it has introduced new medium- and long-term planning tools with its liberalising reforms. The *Framework for Economic and Social Reforms* (FESR)[1] identifies policy priorities for the period 2012 to 2015. It acts as a bridge between the *Fifth Five-Year Plan* (2011-12 to 2015-16) on one hand and, on the other, the reform-oriented *National Comprehensive Development Plan* (2011-31) and the future five-year plans that will support it. The Ministry of National Planning and Economic Development co-ordinates and drafts the FESR after consulting with other ministries and departments.

The FESR reflects the progress that the new government has made since it was elected in March 2011 and its continuing commitment to the socio-economic reform goals in the near future in: tax and public finance, monetary policy and finance, trade and investment, private sector development, health and education, food security and agriculture, governance and transparency, mobile phones and the Internet, infrastructure, and government effectiveness and efficiency.

The proposed sequencing of reform gives priority to macroeconomic measures, followed by various quick wins in areas that do not need further analysis or consensus-building before they take action. Other high priorities are sectoral and institutional reform to improve competition and productivity, and long-term structural and governance reforms (Table 2.3.1).

Table 2.3.1. **Myanmar's key medium-term development targets 2011-12 to 2015-16**

	Initial status	Current status	Target (2015-16)
Economic performance			
Annual GDP growth (%)	6.4* (2012-13)	6.8** (2014-18, estimate)	7.7
Industry share of GDP	26% (2010)	32% (2012)	Increase
GDP per capita	USD 880 (2010)	n/a	30%-40% increase (USD 1 144 to USD 1 232)
Poverty	n/a	n/a	Reduce rate by half
Inflation	n/a	Recent increases	Maintain low inflationary pressures
Regulatory and governance reforms			
Data collection for GDP, revenue and other statistical purposes	n/a	Started	Revise and improve collection and make data publicly available
Public financial management	n/a	Little progress	Reform management and improve budget transparency
Tax system	n/a	Started	Simplification of tax system
Public-private partnerships	n/a	Started	Establish PPP legal framework
State-owned economic enterprises	n/a	Some privatisation	Privatise some SEE activities
Banking regulation	n/a	Some reform	Allow banks to lend for longer than one year and use moveable assets as collateral
Mobile phones	10.3% of population subscribed (2012)	Some reform, recent phone use by 50% of urban residents	Liberalise market and achieve 80% penetration
Extractive Industries Transparency Initiative (EITI)	n/a	Likely delayed	Adopt the EITI and establish supporting administration in the next two years
Yangon transportation	n/a	n/a	Allow Yangon bus fares to increase or reduce bus import duties
Public services			
Healthcare financing	n/a	n/a	Introduce innovative methods of health financing and improve resource allocation
Education financing	n/a	Started	Expand the scale and scope of school grants
Conditional cash transfers	n/a	Started	Consider introducing CCTs
ICT education	n/a	n/a	Support ICT training in schools and through worker training
Agriculture extension services	n/a	n/a	Increase services provided
Government loans to farmers	n/a	Large increase in seasonal loans, less in development loans	Increase loans
Infrastructure development			
Employment guarantee scheme	n/a	n/a	Consider establishing an employment guarantee scheme for public works
Electricity generation	Zero combine cycle plants	Multiple projects started	Replace all 14 gas turbine plants with combined-cycle plants
Transportation infrastructure	n/a	Started	Upgrade airports and transportation links to promote tourism

Notes: * IMF estimate for real GDP growth in 2012-13 (IMF, 2013b); **Taken from the OECD *Economic Outlook for Southeast Asia, China and India 2014: Beyond the Middle-Income Trap.*

Source: OECD Development Centre's compilation based on national sources.

Myanmar's development plan and implementation

Policy challenges of implementing the national plan in Myanmar

- Introduce reliable indicators, measurable goals and measurements of government performance to make planning and monitoring effective, particularly in regulatory reform and public finance.
- Develop policy planning and budgeting, which includes appropriate financial supports in agriculture and education.
- Ensure co-operation with the private sector through PPPs, enable business start-ups and foster civil society, because all are important to Myanmar's on-going transition.

The Framework for Economic and Social Reforms retains the optimistic macroeconomic outlook of past plans

The goal for average annual GDP growth remains the 7.7% originally set out in the *Fifth Five-Year Plan* – higher than the 6.8% for 2014-18 forecast by the OECD (2013a). As even acknowledged in the FESR itself, the government's estimations of Myanmar's growth have been considerably higher than those produced by other organisations in the recent past. Although Myanmar has recently been through a bout of high inflation after a period of moderation, the statutory independence of the Central Bank of Myanmar – enshrined in the Central Bank Law of 2013 – should enable it to better manage monetary policy and future inflationary pressure.

Better quality of data is needed for effective planning

While the FESR restates the government's commitment to the Millennium Development Goal (MDG) of cutting poverty to half of 2000 levels by 2015, no reliable information on the incidence of extreme poverty – the percentage of the population living on less than USD 1.25 per day – is available to determine what has been achieved. The government is, however, now seeking to improve estimates of GDP and other economic indicators by working with the UNDP to survey private-sector businesses as a first step in developing a System of National Accounts.

Financial regulation and public finances are still in need of much reform

Reform in financial sector regulation has been gradual. Loan terms are still limited to one year, for example, although some additional forms of collateral (such as machinery, gold and jewellery, deposits, and exportable crops) have been approved.

As for public finances, they are still opaque in Myanmar. Budgets have been criticised for the lack of accessibility and transparency shrouding allocations and sources of revenue, and for the insignificant reforms in the 2013 Budget. However, with the tax reform law coming into force in March 2014, the government is now working to make potentially significant changes to its tax system.

Support for agriculture is increasing, but not necessarily where it is needed

Agricultural lending has increased dramatically – most noticeably between 2011-12 and 2012-13, when seasonal loans from the Myanmar Agriculture Development Bank (MADB) rose from MMK 312 billion to over MMK 1 trillion (Figure 2.3.1). The value of longer-term development loans for the major purchases, like machinery, has also risen since 2011-12, although they are available only for restricted sets of investments and far less total funding is in fact available. Government support for development loans is inconsistent from one year to the next, however, and the MADB has occasionally used its own funds to make loans in years when the government has contributed only to seasonal lending.

Progress in infrastructure development is in its early stages

Work to meet the FESR infrastructure targets is still in its early stages and there is still a long way to go. While the public works employment guarantee scheme is still only a proposal, financing agreements are being developed to replace Myanmar's 14 gas turbine power plants with more efficient combined-cycle plants. As part of efforts to improve international transportation infrastructure, construction contracts have been awarded for expanding Yangon International Airport, building a new airport in nearby Pegu and refurbishing the airport that serves Myanmar's second-largest city, Mandalay.

While funding for education is increasing, it is not transforming schools as planned

The Ministry of Education is gradually rolling out schemes that offer grants to primary schools and stipends to primary pupils. Between 2012-13 and 2013-14, average grants increased from USD 50 to USD 250 for small schools, from USD 80 to USD 300 for medium-sized schools and from USD 100 to USD 400 for large schools. That trend will have to continue over the next three years to USD 900, USD 1 200 and USD 1 800 if the government's School Grants Programme is to meet its targets (Figure 2.3.2).

The government also plans to expand the Student Stipends Programme, which currently grants monthly stipends to about 11 000 students in 33 of Myanmar's 330 townships. The aim is to widen the programme to an estimated 200 000 students in 40 townships selected on the basis of drop-out rates and poverty indicators.

While the intention is to use grants and stipends to increase transparency and community participation in education, a preliminary assessment by external consultants warned that implementers did not always understand the programmes and that few community-based school-related organisations were participating.

Preliminary steps are opening up space for private enterprise and civil society

Myanmar could do more to engage with civil society. Its admission as a candidate to join the Extractive Industries Transparency Initiative (EITI) in 2014 was successful, though delayed. The EITI Cooperation Office (MEITI) suggested the Myanmar's difficulties in working with civil society groups – an essential component of the initiative – could further delay its becoming EITI-compliant until 2016 or 2017.

As for private enterprise, the government's plan to put in place a framework for PPPs is still in its early stages, with external partners facilitating discussions on opportunities and ways to improve relevant government capacities.

The government has announced plans to privatise all domestic airport management operations and some railway lines, and it has actually started to open up the mobile phone market. In June 2013 licenses were awarded to Singtel and Digicel, with the latter stating its intention to expand service to 96% of the population by 2016. While the results of a 2013 survey suggest that mobile phone use is greater than previously thought and spreading rapidly – at least in urban areas – it remains unclear whether the FESR target of 80% mobile phone penetration is achievable by 2015-16. The continued opening-up of the market should help, however.

Figure 2.3.1. **Myanmar Agriculture Development Bank's loans to farmers, 2000-01 to 2012-13**

The bank's annual seasonal and development lending

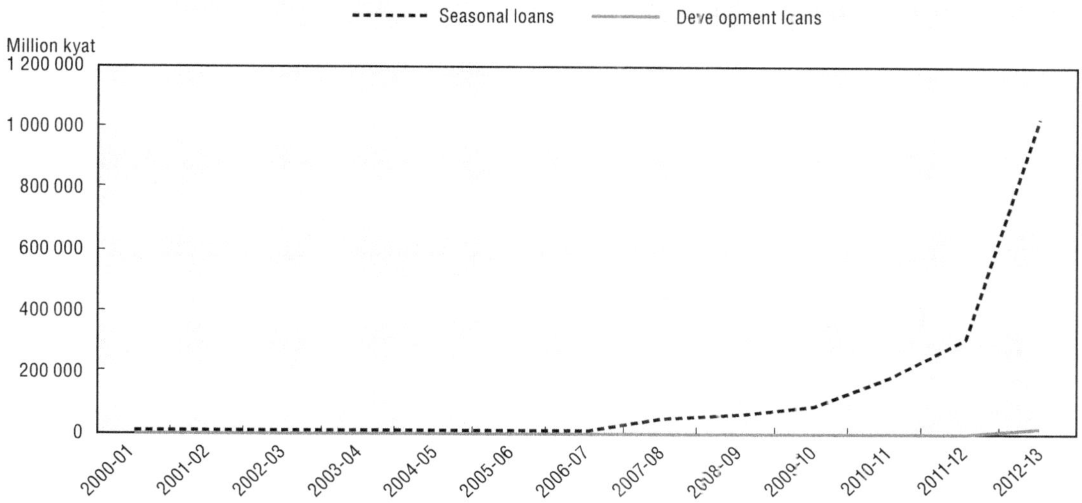

Source: MADB (Myanmar Agriculture Development Bank) (2013), Welcome to MADB (presentation), MADB, Yangon.

StatLink http://dx.doi.org/10.1787/888933179678

Figure 2.3.2. **School grants by size of establishment**

Average value of grant in USD

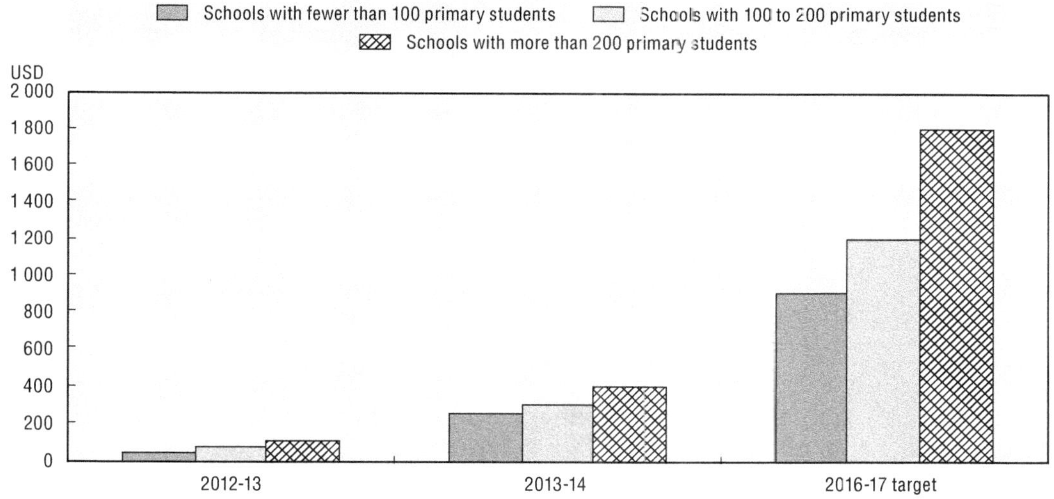

Source: Myanmar Development Research (2014), *Draft Preliminary Social Assessment: Myanmar Decentralizing Funding to Schools Programme*, World Bank, Washington DC.

StatLink http://dx.doi.org/10.1787/888933179682

Note:

1. This review is based on the Final Draft of the *Framework for Economic and Social Reforms – Policy Priorities for 2012-2015 towards the Long-Term Goals of the National Comprehensive Development Plan*, January 14, 2013 (MNPED, 2013).

Philippines

A. Medium-term economic outlook (forecast, 2015-19 average)

GDP growth (percentage change):	6.2
Current account balance (% of GDP):	2.1
Fiscal balance (% of GDP):	-1.6

B. Medium-term plan

Period: 2011-16

Theme: In pursuit of inclusive growth

C. Basic data (in 2013)

Total population:	97 million*
Population of Manila (NCR):	11.86 million (in 2010)
GDP per capita at PPP:	4 682 (current USD)**

Note: * Total population data for 2013 are estimates.
** IMF estimate.
Sources: OECD Development Centre, MPF-2015, national sources and IMF.

GDP growth rates (percentage change)

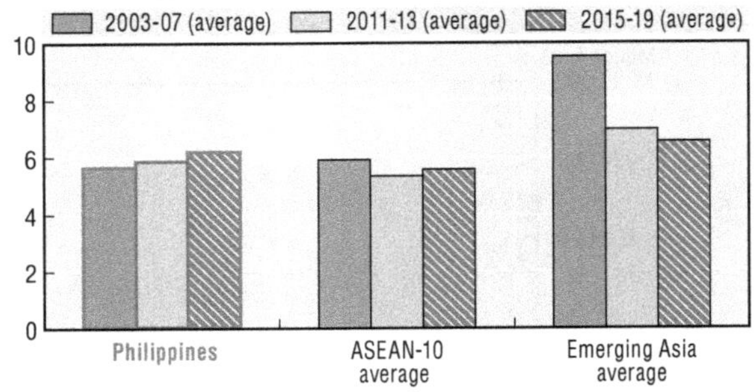

Source: OECD Development Centre, MPF-2015.

GDP per capita, 2013 (PPP, current USD)

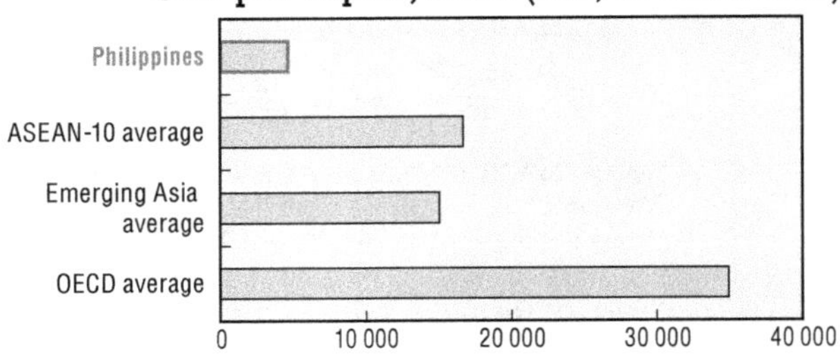

Source: IMF.

Composition of exports, 2013
(percentage of total exports)

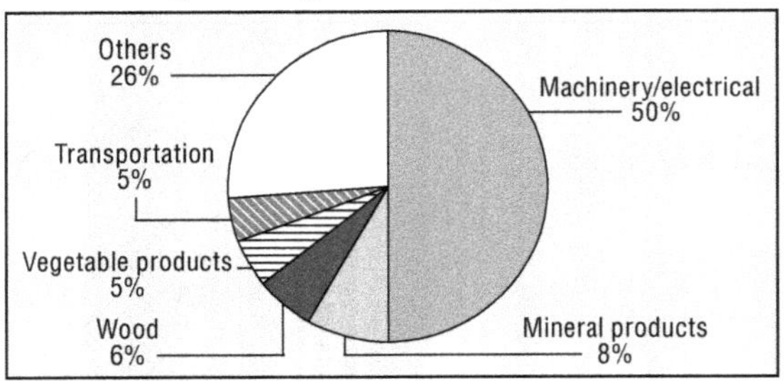

Source: Trademap.

Composition of imports, 2013
(percentage of total imports)

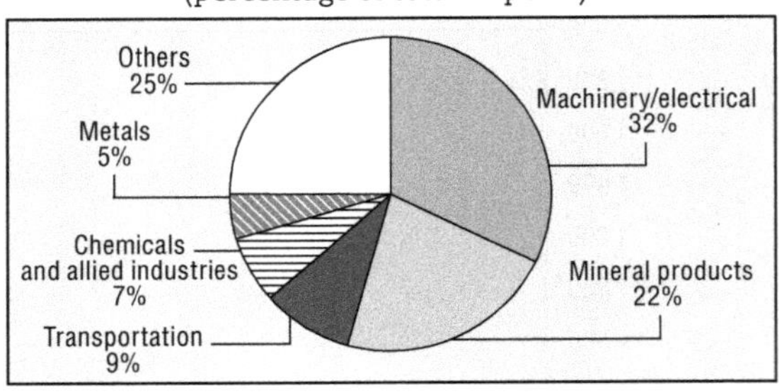

Source: Trademap.

Summary of the medium-term development plan: Inclusive growth with good governance, reduced poverty and high-quality jobs

The *Philippine Development Plan* 2011-16 (PDP) builds on a foundation of three broad strategies: sustained, inclusive economic growth; equal access to development opportunities; and effective, responsive social safety nets. The strategies are directed at improved national productivity, quality employment opportunities, poverty reduction and robust economic growth.

The National Economic and Development Authority (NEDA) of the Philippines is tasked with co-ordinating preparation of the Plan in ten focus areas that seek to achieve: inclusive growth; sound macroeconomic policy; competitive industry and services; competitive, sustainable agriculture and fisheries; infrastructure development; a dynamic, resilient financial sector; good governance and the rule of law; social development; peace and security; and conservation, protection, and rehabilitation of the environment and natural resources towards sustainable development.

Table 2.4.1. Philippines' key medium-term development targets, 2011-16

Indicator	Initial status (2010)	Current status (2013)	Target (2016)
Macroeconomics			
Real GDP annual growth rate (%)	7.6	7.2	7-8, per year (2011-16, average); 7.5-8.5 (2015-16)
Investment to GDP ratio, real (%)	18.2 (2004-10, average)	21.1	22
National Government fiscal deficit-to-GDP ratio	3.5	1.4	2
Inflation rate	3.8	3.0	2-4
Unemployment rate (%)	7.4	7.1	6.8-7.2
Poverty			
Poverty incidence based on population	26.3 (2009)	25.2 (2012)	16.6 (2015)
Industry and services			
Growth rate of gross value added in the industry sector (%)	5.2 (2004-10, average)	6.8 (2012)	9.3-10.3
Gross value added in services growth rate (%)	6.1 (2004-10, average)	7.6 (2012)	7.2-8.1
Labour productivity in I&S sectors increased (%)	n/a	4.9 (2012)	4.7-5.5
Employment generated from the I&S sectors (million)	1.07	2.20 (2011-13)	4.67 (2011-16)
Merchandise exports (USD billion)	51.39	52.1 (2012)	91
Services exports (USD billion)	12.27	18.6 (2012)	29
Agriculture and fisheries			
Agriculture and fishery gross value added (PHP million, at constant 2000 prices)	659 989	701 358	793 794-824 958
Labor productivity in A&F sector (in PhP)	n/a	57 797 (2012)	62 561-70 253
Rice self-sufficiency ratio	80	95 (2012)	100
Financial system			
National saving rate (Gross National Saving-to-GDP ratio) (%)	26.6	23 (2012)	>30
Number of deposit accounts per 1 000 population	499	454 (2012)	750
Microfinance services delivery (in PhP billion)	n/a	8.4 (2012)	>10
Social development			
Maternal mortality rate per 100 000 live-births	95	221 (2011)	50
Infant mortality rate per 1 000 live-births	25 (2008)	22 (2011)	19 (2015); 17 (2016)
Proportion of population with access to safe water (HH in %)	82.3 (2008); 82.5 (2010)	83 (2011)	88
National Health Insurance Program coverage (%)	53 (2008)	72 (2012)	95
Net enrolment rate – kindergarten (%)	57.2	77.4 (2012-13)	100
Net enrolment rate – elementary (%)	95.9	95.2 (2012-13)	99
Net enrolment rate – secondary (%)	64.7	64.6 (2012-13)	71
Completion rate – elementary (%)	72.1	73.7 (2012-13)	83
Completion rate – secondary (%)	75.1	74.8 (2012-13)	80
Achievement rate (NAT MPS) – elementary (%)	68.2	68.9 (2012-13)	77
Achievement rate (NAT MPS) – secondary (%)	47.9	51.4 (2012-13)	65
Number of TVET graduates	1 344 371	1 765 757	1 383 026
Number of higher education graduates	498 418	553 706	601 505
Percentage of poor families covered by PhilHealth as identified under the NHTS-PR and LGU sponsored program (%)	81.5 (2011)	88.7 (2012)	100
Number of poor households covered by conditional cash transfer (million)	1.04	3.94	2.9
OFW membership to OWWAs, disability and death benefits	1 355 311	1 304 197 (2012)	100%
Good governance and the rule of law, and peace and security			
Percentile rank in the WGI-Control of Corruption indicator improved	22.38	43.54	≥60
Percentile rank in the WGI-Rule of Law indicator improved	33.65	41.71	≥60
Percentile rank in the WGI-Regulatory Quality indicator improved	44.98	51.67	≥70
Crime volume*	Crime incidents: 296 059 (2010)	1 033 833	743 817
Crime solution efficiency rate (%)	18.4	28.6	38.3

Table 2.4.1. **Philippines' key medium-term development targets, 2011-16** (*cont.*)

Environment and natural resources			
Proportion of land area covered by forest (%)	23.8 (2003)	22.8	30
Area of degraded coral reefs within NIPAS (National Integrated Protected Areas Systems) MPAs (Marine Protected Areas) rehabilitated (in ha)	n/a	676 000 (2012)	510 012
Air pollution in Metro Manila and other urban centers reduced (ug/Ncm)	150 (in Manila NCR)	118 (in Manila NCR)	91.62 (in Manila NCR)
Gas emission reduced due to an increase in travel speed in Metro Manila (km/hr)	27.79	32.86	31.84
Gas emission reduced due to a decrease in travel time in Metro Manila (minute/km)	2.17	1.83	1.98
Solid waste diversion rate (%)	33	39.1 in Metro Manila, 30 outside Metro Manila (2012)	50
Number of provinces with all of its cities and majority of its municipalities having functional and empowered Local Disaster Risk Reduction and Management Office	n/a	20	80
Infrastructure development			
Load transported via the Central Roll-On/Roll-Off (RORO) Spine (tons per ship-hour)	n/a	189 (2012)	251
Passengers transported via air increased per annum	37 960 765	n/a	56 084 528
Irrigation service coverage (% of total potential irrigable area)	56.01	58.97 (2011)	73.8
Energy self-sufficiency (% of total energy)	58.5	56.32 (2012)	60

Note: *Data on crime volume and crime efficiency from 2010 to 2012 considered only crimes reported to the PNP. Starting in 2013, the PNP rectified these statistics to include those reported to the barangays and other law enforcement agencies.

Sources: National Economic and Development Authority (NEDA) (2011), *Philippines Development Plan 2011-2016, Results Matrices*; NEDA (2014), Philippines Development Plan Midterm Update with Revalidated Results Matrices, National Economic and Development Authority; Philippine National Statistical Co-ordination Board.

The *Philippine Development Plan 2011-16 Midterm Update* (Updated Plan) charts the achievements in 2012-13 measured against the indicators set out in the PDP. It also restates, in the form of annual plan targets, the desired outcomes, projections and realigned priorities for the rest of the PDP. The Updated Plan's overarching strategic framework identifies poverty reduction in its multiple dimensions, the massive creation of quality employment and sector-focused strategies to achieve the ultimate goal of inclusive growth. While it emphasises the government's facilitating role in promoting private sector business for the country's overall advancement, the Updated Plan also acknowledges the part the government plays in determining the policy and regulatory framework required to improve efficiency.

Since the PDP kicked in, the Philippines' economic performance has made impressive progress, with real GDP growing by 7.2% in 2013 and the investment-to-GDP ratio reaching 21.1% in 2013. By contrast, employment has not grown fast enough, with the unemployment rate remaining at 7.1%. The benefits of growth have not been widely shared and the population-based poverty incidence was still high – at 25.2% – at the end of 2012. The PDP's main challenge in the time it has left to run is to ensure sustained, inclusive growth. Other priorities are to address the infrastructure backlog, invest in human capital and foster social development.

Philippines' development plan and implementation

Policy challenges of implementing the national plan in the Philippines

- Sustain economic growth by stepping up the country's global competitiveness through quality employment and increase value added from innovation.
- Strive to put in place a responsive, development-oriented and inclusive financial system to serve as a platform for efficient management and the mobilisation of resources.
- Further improve social development to ensure all Filipinos benefit from equal opportunity when it comes to having a decent job, acquiring assets and enjoying higher living standards.

Despite macroeconomic progress, more effort is needed in the financial sector and education

The Philippines has made significant progress in macroeconomic performance and agriculture. GDP growth continued and the fiscal deficit steadily narrowed from 3.5% in 2010 to 1.4% in 2013, closing in on the 2016 target of 2%. Inflationary pressure gradually eased from 3.8% in 2010 to 3.0% in 2013. Agricultural output rose and the rice self-sufficiency ratio also improved considerably. In social development, there was gradual progress in national health system coverage and educational enrolment. However, there is scope for further effort.

Challenges persist in policy areas like financial systems, which need to be bolstered. And although the Philippines has climbed the industrial and services sector global competitiveness rankings (to 136th out of 189 in 2012), it is still well short of its targeted position of 62nd out of 189 in 2016 – all of which makes it harder to sustain its economic growth. In social development, the increase in health insurance coverage appears impressive – yet the maternal mortality rate shot up from 95 per 100 000 live births in 2010 to 221 in 2011. Similarly, net enrolment rates and completion rates in both elementary and secondary schools have not reached the targeted levels.

Tourism and SMEs are potential sources of employment

There is an on-going need for a more action-oriented job creation system in the Philippines. According to ILO modelled estimates, the Philippines had the second-lowest employment-to population ratio among ASEAN countries in 2012 at 60.7%, lagging far behind Cambodia's 81.2% and Lao PDR's 76.6%. Only Malaysia's 57.5% was worse. As the poor derive most of their income from work, employment opportunity and job quality are crucial factors in reducing poverty.

The tourism industry affords unskilled workers a chance to enter the workforce easily and earn an income. It thus has inclusive growth and job creation potential. Social tourism initiatives, of which the most recent is the so-called Bangon Tours Project, were put in place by the government with the support and co-ordination of the private sector. However, despite the government's efforts to make the tourism sector a strong engine of economic growth, the Philippines trails behind its neighbours as a major tourist destination because of its deficient infrastructure. For instance, the quality of its airports put it 113th of 143 countries in the World Economic Forum's *Global Competitiveness Report 2013-14* (World Economic Forum, 2013). To meet the Philippines Development Plan goal of 10 million foreign-tourist arrivals by 2016, additional efforts will be needed.

To create a greater number of jobs, the government must take further measures to foster small and medium-sized enterprises (SMEs), defined as enterprises with total assets (excluding land) of PHP 100 million or less. Of the 944 897 enterprises operating in the Philippines in 2012, 99.6% were SMEs and the remaining 0.4% were large companies. In the same year, SMEs generated a total of 4 930 851 – almost 65% of all jobs generated by businesses.

Access to finance remains critical to SME development, with government regulation bringing gradual progress. The Republic Act, passed in 2008, requires banks to allocate at least 8% of their loan portfolio to medium-sized, small, and micro enterprises (MSMEs) between 17 June of that year and 16 June 2018. The Bangko Sentral ng Pilipinas levies a fine of PHP 500 000 a year for non-compliance, yet international banks tend to pay the fine rather than set aside funds for MSMEs because of their lack of collateral and credit information. Ninety per cent of the fines collected are remitted to the MSME Development Fund. MSMEs may gain better access to finance by seeking funds from non-bank financial institutions, such as venture capitalists and partnerships with private enterprises, rather than relying on funding from banks.

One area with employment potential is the rapidly growing business process outsourcing (BPO) industry. With its large pool of qualified fluent English speakers and low-cost operation, it is particularly well suited to job creation, especially since Metro Manila edged out Mumbai to become the second largest BPO destination in 2014. From 2006 to 2011, the size of the market more than tripled, accounting for 9.5% of the global total. Last year's revenues exceeded the target of USD 9.9 billion and were about 18% higher than the USD 8.6 billion generated in 2012. Full-time employment in the industry was up too, reaching 586 000 compared to 502 000 at the end of 2012.

Emphasis on high-value manufacturing is key to long-term economic growth

The service sector's share of GDP has steadily climbed in recent years – from 53.5% in 2005 to 57.7% in 2013. Increased remittances from overseas Filipino workers and the rise of business process outsourcing are two critical driving forces behind those numbers. In contrast, the manufacturing sector accounts for only 23% of the Philippines' GDP and just 10% of employment, which locks the Philippines in a bind compared with other economies in the region.

The government should undertake measures specifically to strengthen the manufacturing sector and create a competitive environment that is conducive to long-term economic growth. Prioritising the manufacturing sector is crucial if the Philippines is to become a more productive actor in the global economy. Such a move would also create jobs for semi-skilled and unskilled workers. Indeed, in recent years the government has – under the auspices of several agencies – introduced the Manufacturing Resurgence Programme, designed to revive the manufacturing sector and make it more competitive. The Philippines should also seek to transition to high-value manufacturing and product diversification in its exports. A key measure would, for example, be to focus on strengthening the food processing industry, where the country enjoys a competitive advantage.

Other measures to boost the manufacturing sector's productivity include strict enforcement of the law and cutting business costs by providing low-cost electricity and transportation. It is also crucial that the government identify particular constraints that weigh on certain industries and address them with sound policies.

The manufacturing and services sectors have continued to be growth drivers. To ensure sustainable, inclusive growth and promote competitiveness, however, productivity and innovation must be further developed. While the gross value added accruing from innovation in the services sector reached 7.6% in 2012 – outstripping the targeted 7.2% – it was just 6.8% in manufacturing. There is a clear case for more improvement if the target of 9.3% by 2016 is to be met. Product diversification in manufacturing is also persistently low, as the sector is concentrated on relatively few products with particularly low value added.

In the *WEF Global Competitiveness Report 2013-14*, the Philippines recorded an improved showing in technological readiness and innovation. It moved from 95th out of 139 countries in 2010 to 77th out of 148 in 2013 in the Technological Readiness Index and climbed from 111th in 2010 to 69th out of 148 countries in 2013 in the Innovation Index (NEDA, 2014). In sum, the country plans to continue boosting productivity in its industry and services sectors, given their potential for innovation and adding value. The target for manufacturing growth is between 9.8% and 11% in 2014, 8.6% and 9.7% by 2015, and 9.3% and 10.3% by 2016. The services sector is projected to expand from 6% to 6.9% in 2014, from 6.8% to 7.8% by 2015, and from 7.2% to 8.1% by 2016.

There is room for improving equality of opportunity for all Filipinos

To improve opportunity and the accumulation of human capital, the Philippines needs to upgrade its health and educational performance. Although, there has been progress overall, the number of pregnancy-related deaths climbed steeply from 95 per 100 000 live-births in 2010 to 221 in 2011. The increase reflects failings in a health system that struggles to address the causes of maternal mortality and inequitable access to quality healthcare. In response to the poor health status of the population, the government has invested effort and funds in grappling with the challenges of access to and quality of healthcare. The Sin Tax Reform Act and the Responsible Parenthood and Reproductive Health Act of 2012 are two important instruments for promoting good health under the Philippines' Health-for-All programme (Kalusugan Pangkalahatan [KP]) that will eventually help improve healthcare. At the same time, the government has continued to increase the coverage and benefits of the Philippines health insurance system (PhilHealth).

The provision of education and skills training and affording people the chance to pursue economic opportunity are aspects of investment in human capital that help achieve inclusive development. The rate of the increase in overall enrolment rates – elementary and secondary – has slowed down (Figure 2.4.1).

There must also be improvement in enrolment rates in tertiary education and technical and vocational education and training (TVET) to enhance knowledge and skills. The government has responded by planning three strategic interventions:

- provide all Filipinos with access to full, high-quality basic education and prepare every graduate thereof for the workplace;
- give the labour force the competencies and life skills that enable them to pursue economic opportunities; and
- ensure that higher education graduates have the competencies and high-level skills that will contribute to national development and global competitiveness.

To promote access to basic education, the Department of Education (DepEd) has instituted critical reforms that align the country's basic education system with international standards and ensure children better learning opportunities. Reforms include the 2012 Kindergarten Act, which makes universal kindergarten compulsory, and the Enhanced Basic Education Act of 2013 which institutionalises the implementation of the kindergarten-to-12th-grade (K-12) education.

Another particularly important initiative is to develop workforce competencies and life skills through TVET skills development programmes. They have been incorporated into the National Technical Education and Skill Development Plan 2011-16 to enable current workers to develop their life skills and pursue economic opportunities. At the same time, enterprise-based training (EBT) schemes have been expanded to improve multiple skills and enhance productivity.

A clear guideline for K-12 implementation is necessary

After an extended period of being the last country in Asia to maintain a ten-year education system, the Department of Education (DepEd) recently implemented its K-12 Basic Education Programme. The purpose is to help Filipinos secure more gainful employment opportunities on completing their education. As universal kindergarten came into force only in the 2011-12 school year, it is still too early to evaluate the outcome and effectiveness of the newly imported system. However, it has met with a favourable reception from 72% of Filipino adults, who consider the 12-year education cycle preferable to the former system (Social Weather Stations, 2013).

Despite the positive public reaction, the transition to the new curriculum and system has not proven easy. The shortage of learning materials for both teachers and pupils and the insufficient time for training teachers have emerged as critical shortcomings. The average training time is said to have been between five and ten days. But if K-12 is to become an effective, sustainable education system, it requires a better-developed implementation plan that incorporates the distribution of appropriate teaching reference materials, up-to-date textbooks and ample teacher-training time. The government should also take action to ease the 36:1 average pupil-teacher ratio.

While the education reform reflects the vision of giving Filipinos the chance to earn higher incomes in the future, the cost of two extra years of schooling is a concern for families. Against that background, the elementary and secondary school dropout rates have risen. In the 2011-12 school year – when universal kindergarten was initiated – the dropout rate among elementary school pupils rose to 6.38% from 6.29% in 2009-10. Money is a critical factor that determines whether children and young people can continue their education. Schemes to help properly implement the new education cycle in the long run could therefore include partnerships with the private sector to raise funds for improving schooling conditions – e.g. the "Adopt a School" programme – as well as government subsidies.

Access to healthcare is improving, but target indicators will be difficult to achieve at this point

In recent years, the government has undertaken health sector reforms to improve access to healthcare for indigent Filipinos. It has, for example, re-established the benefit care package, Tamang Serbisyong Kalusugang Pampamilya (TSeKaP), and rolled out the Point of Care Program and the No Balance Billing Policy under the management of PhilHealth. Such measures are all aimed at the goal of universal healthcare coverage by 2016. The additional revenues generated by the Sin Tax Reform Act have also helped expand the health ministry's budget by 57.9%, with a total of PHP 83.7 billion in 2014 being channelled into the funding of healthcare coverage for 14.7 million families.

Although PhilHealth claims that it covers 80% of the 98 million population, there are weak points in the system that need to be addressed. One example is the obscure way in which beneficiaries are classified when they enrol. The identification of indigents has proven a challenge in many regions. There have been reported cases of people supplying the wrong information in order to become a sponsored member, for whom the government funds premiums. To ensure that people do not just pay into health insurance but actually receive the care they require, it is vital that both local and national governments allocate funding to healthcare facilities and management.

A particular effort should be made to bring down the persistently high maternal mortality rate by improving access to qualified reproductive health services, especially for women who live in remote rural areas and whose financial means are limited. Hopes have been placed in government initiatives to lower the maternal mortality rate to 52 per 100 000 live births by 2015 (in line with the poverty reduction Millennium Development Goal). Such a target seems unachievable, however, given the 221 maternal deaths per 100 000 live-births in 2011.

A more resilient, inclusive financial system is needed to support the national economy

The Philippines' banking system's overall physical network has continued to expand, with the number of domestic branches and ATMs increasing by 4% and 15%, respectively (Figure 2.4.2).

A number of financial sector targets in the PDP have either already been met or are on track. Access to banks and banking services is still inadequate in some municipalities, while national savings showed no progress, falling from 26.6% in 2010 to 23% in 2012 – even farther away from the 2016 target of 30%.

To improve financial inclusion, the Bangko Sentral ng Pilipinas (BSP) has adopted a three-prong strategy:

- boost public confidence in the health of the financial sector;
- educate the public on financial instruments and their rights; and
- encourage a varied offering of varied products to cater to different consumers.

The BSP continues to provide financial education and consumer protection in its bid to upgrade financial inclusion in the economy. Its Economic and Financial Learning Program seeks to keep households and businesses well informed so as to foster public awareness and enable people to make economic and financial decisions.

At the same time, the BSP's Credit Surety Program – a PPP initiative – continues to support the government's poverty alleviation effort. It also has a scheme in the pipeline for increasing SME access to finance so as to boost economic development, financial inclusion and job creation. The bank is also promoting a growing number of microfinance services designed to mobilise SMEs' financial resources. The number of microfinance borrowers rose by 191% to 1 137 813 in 2012 from 390 635 clients in 2002, while microfinance loans increased 223% – from PHP 2.6 billion in 2002 to PHP 8.4 billion in 2012 (BSP, 2012). From 2011 to 2012, there was a robust rise in the number of microfinance borrowers, the amount of microfinance loans outstanding and the savings of microfinance clients.

Nevertheless, there are still obstacles to financial inclusion. For example, a mere 26.6% of adults in the Philippines own an account in a formal financial institution (BSP, 2013). A greater effort is required to instil the culture and practice of using financial services and to evaluate the actual impact of the government's financial education schemes.

Fundamentally, though, the main task ahead of target year 2016 is to sustain a resilient, inclusive financial system underpinned by the discipline of credit standards. Steering that course also involves improving the financial system's asset base in order to serve the needs of a growing economy while expanding the coverage of financial services.

Figure 2.4.1. **Elementary and secondary enrolment rates, 2008-09 to 2012-13**

Students and annual growth rates

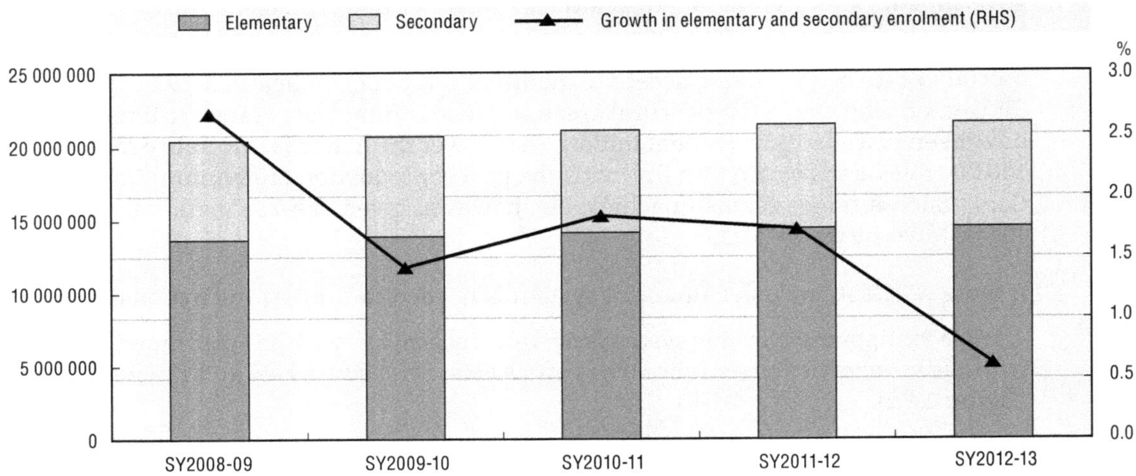

Source: National Statistics Office, Department of Education, Philippines.

StatLink http://dx.doi.org/10.1787/888933179695

Figure 2.4.2. **Numbers and growth of bank offices and ATMs, 2009-12**

Total numbers and growth rates

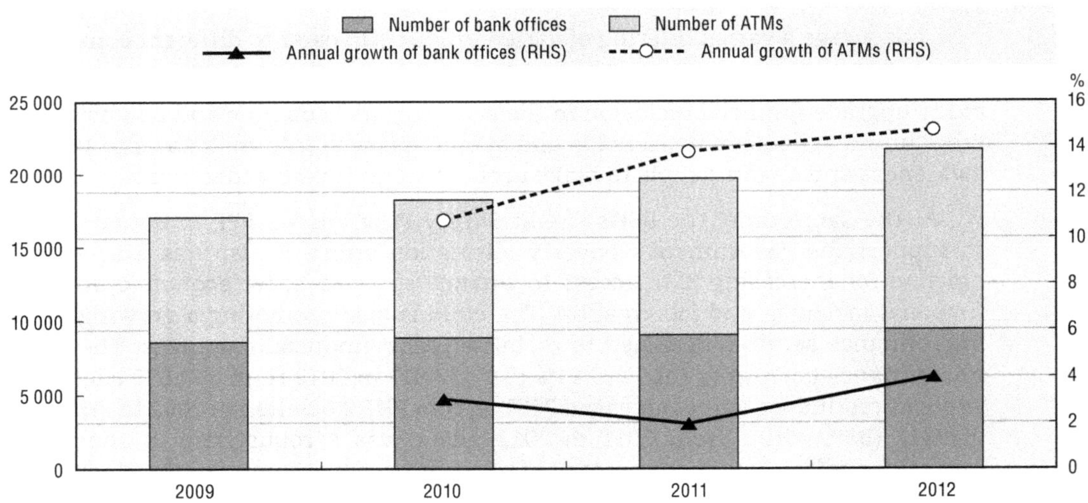

Source: BSP (Bankgo Sentral ng Pilipinas) (2013), *Report on the State of Financial Inclusion in the Philippines – 2013 Data Updates*, Inclusive Finance Advocacy Staff Supervision and Examination Sector, Bankgo Sentral ng Pilipinas, Manila.

StatLink http://dx.doi.org/10.1787/888933179709

Thailand

A. Medium-term economic outlook (forecast, 2015-19 average)

GDP growth (percentage change):	4.1
Current account balance (% of GDP):	0.5
Fiscal balance (% of GDP):	-2.9

B. Medium-term plan

Period: 2012-16

Theme: A happy society of equity, fairness and resilience - the vision of the Philosophy of a Sufficiency Economy

C. Basic data (in 2013)

Total population:	68 million*
Population of Bangkok:	5.67 million (in 2011)
GDP per capita at PPP:	9 875 (current USD)**

Note: *Total population data for 2013 are estimates.
**IMF estimate.

Sources: OECD Development Centre, MPF-2015, national sources and IMF.

GDP growth rates (percentage change)

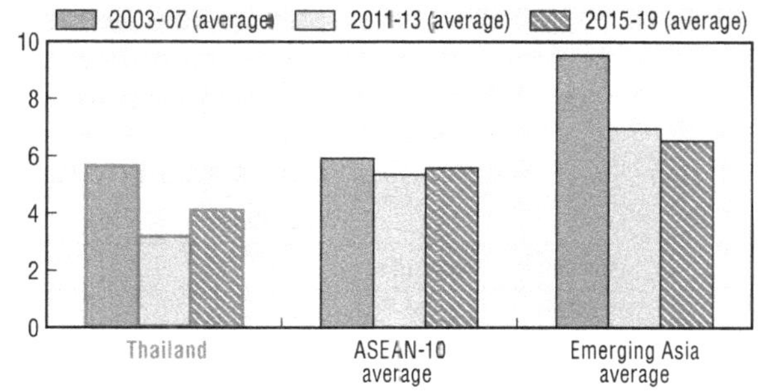

Source: OECD Development Centre, MPF-2015.

GDP per capita, 2013 (PPP, current USD)

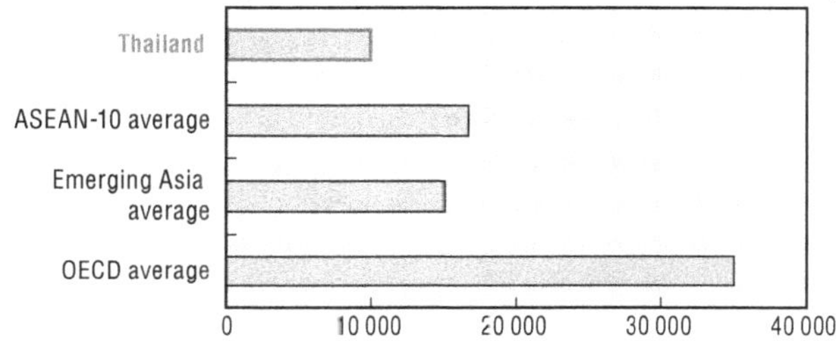

Source: IMF.

Composition of exports, 2013

(percentage of total exports)

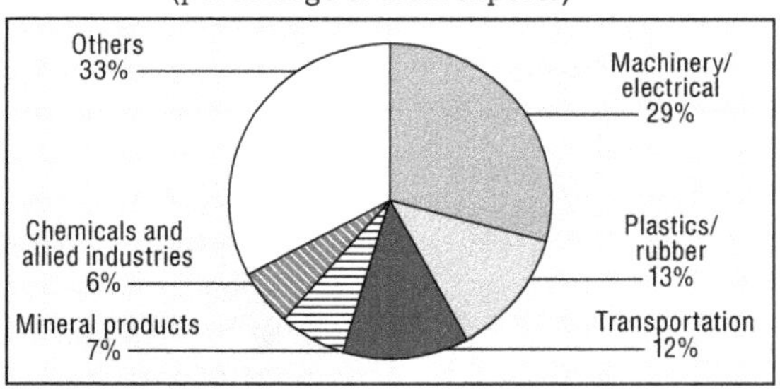

Source: Trademap.

Composition of imports, 2013

(percentage of total imports)

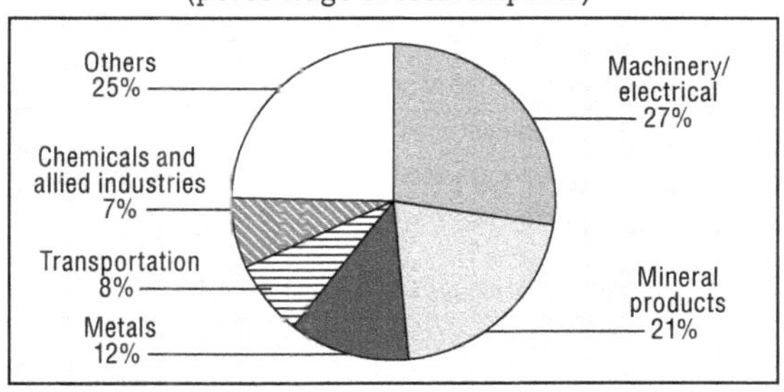

Source: Trademap.

Summary of the medium-term development plan: A happy society of equality, fairness, and resilience

Thailand's *Eleventh National Economic and Social Development Plan* (2012-16) was designed in pursuit of "a happy society with equality, fairness and resilience" (NESDB, 2011). The plan was formulated by the National Economic and Social Development Board (NESDB), the government's planning agency that operates under the aegis of the Prime Minister's Office, with the involvement of and contributions from a wide range of stakeholders. Under the King's vision of developing a "Sufficiency Economy", formally included in five-year plans since the ninth one, the current plan aims to help support balanced, inclusive and sustainable growth. Economic and social development has long been the focus of Thailand's development plans, but environmental considerations are a relatively recent addition.

The plan's main targets are to promote: growth and sustainability, human development, food and energy security, regional connectivity and stability, inclusiveness, and the management of natural resources and the environment.

Within these categories lies a wide range of specific targets for economic performance, human development and well-being, innovation, energy production and use, and environmental protection.

Table 2.5.1. **Thailand's key medium-term development targets, 2012-16**

Indicators	Initial status (2011)	Current status (2013)	Target (2016)
Economic performance			
GDP growth rate (%)	0.1	2.9	3.0
Average annual inflation rate (%)	3.8	2.2	3.5
Total factor productivity average growth (TFP) (% per annum)	-2.2	3.7 (2012)	3
Ratio of service sector to GDP (%)	52 (2010)	49.3	>50
Competitiveness by IMD ranking	27	29 (2014), 27 (2013)	16
Expenditure of R&D (% of GDP)	0.4	0.3 (2012)	2
Ratio of logistics costs to GDP (%)	15.2 (2010); 14.7 (2011)	14.3 (2012 estimates)	15
Ratio of renewable and alternative energy consumption to total energy consumption (%)	17 (2012); 18.4 (2010)	10.6 (Q2 2013)	19
Human development			
Total fertility rate (%)	1.427	1.412 (2012)	1.6
Labor productivity increases (%)	-0.8	5.2 (2012)	3 (per annum)
Thai Green and Happiness Index (GHI) (%)	66.8 (2010)	71.4 (2012)	improve
Number of people covered by health security system	98.1	99.9	100
Agriculture and food and energy security			
Share of agricultural commodities and agro-industrial products of GDP (%)	13.3	12	16
Ethanol Production (million litre/day)	1.4 (2012)	2.6	6.2
Bio-diesel production (million litre/day)	2.7 (2012)	2.9	3.6
Renewable Energy Production (Megawatt)	2786 (2012)	3788	3440
Justice and rule of law			
SME contribution to GDP (%)	36.6	37 (2012)	40
Transparency International Corruption Perception Index (1-10 scale)	3.4 (2011); 3.5 (2010)	35*	5
Institute for Economics and Peace (IEP) Global Peace Index	119 out of 153	130 out of 162 (2013); 126 out of 162 (2014)	improve
Natural resources and the environment			
Water resources of fair quality or higher (%)	85	82 (2012)	80
Proportion of conservation forest area to total land area (%)	37.2	37.3 (2012)	40
Municipal Disposal of Solid Waste (%)	40	37.1 (2012)	50
Garbage recycling rate (%)	26 (2010)	21.4 (2012)	30

Note: *Since 2012, the methodology has changed and the scale became 1-100.
Source: OECD Development Centre's compilation based on national sources, *World Bank WDI database*, and *Conference Board Total Economy Database*.

Thailand's development plan and its implementation

Policy challenges of implementing the national plan in Thailand

- Ensure sustainable economic growth and improve competitiveness through accelerated progress towards certain targets and enhanced productivity.
- Support green growth through further efforts to improve environmental management.
- Improve governance – particularly with regard to corruption and transparency – so as to reduce obstacles to growth.

Thai macroeconomic indicators have met expectations – GDP grew by 2.9% in 2013, on course for the 2016 target of 3%, and the inflation rate declined to 2.2% in 2013, an improvement over 2010 and below the 3.5% target. Yet economic progress in other areas has been mixed. Progress has been made towards some sector-based targets: agriculture contributed 12% to GDP, gradually homing in on the 16% goal, while the services sector contributed around 50%, already ahead of the 2016 target level of 50%.

Creative and knowledge-based development has not progressed as quickly as planned, however. Performance has also been weaker in regional connectivity. The benefits from free trade agreements (FTAs) slipped slightly and the growth of cross-border trade dropped from 2010, well shy of the target.

Thailand has nevertheless achieved sound progress in many aspects of human development, although some social issues, like security and education, need further improvement, as do energy and the environment. Such challenges, together with the Plan's broader goals, will therefore require further effort and new approaches.

Recent political turmoil has also complicated implementation of the medium-term plan (as of November 2014). New policy priorities which may diverge from the plan's targets are to be expected under the military administration that took power through the National Council for Peace and Order (NCPO) in May 2014.

Some social outcomes have improved, but concerns related to law and order appear to be worsening

Several targets in Thailand's development plan relate to such social issues as crime and well-being. Progress towards those targets has been mixed, however, with social cohesion indicators improving and measures of violence worsening. The Community Empowerment Index, Green and Happiness Index and Warm Family Index – composite measures designed to reflect how communities and families support their members and general well-being – are improving.

However, Thailand's ranking in the Institute for Economics and Peace's Global Peace Index slipped from 119th out of 153 in the world to 130th out of 162, with its relatively high levels of terrorist activity, political violence and crime. The inclusion of reduced domestic violence as one of the Plan's targets was an official recognition of the problem. Yet it has increased regardless. Such a worrying development suggests that ensuring safety and law and order deserve greater attention by, for example, addressing the root causes of violence and unrest.

Targeted policies and education will help further develop creative and knowledge-based sectors

Thailand has had uneven success in developing some new sectors, such as the creative and knowledge-based industries that would help it move up the global value chain (Figure 2.5.1). Stagnating innovation and the failure to develop new sectors are related to the decline in Thailand's international competitiveness ranking. Growth in creative products (culture- and knowledge-related outputs from both industry and services), which has fluctuated over the years and made little contribution to GDP growth, dropped from 2.1% in 2010 to 0.4% in 2012 – far below the target growth rate of 5% *per annum*.

Despite a promising start, recent progress in laying the groundwork for developing knowledge-based industries has been slow. The number of researchers working in R&D as a share of the total population increased dramatically between the late 1990s and 2000s. So did R&D expenditure as a share of GDP. Yet, at 0.26% of GDP, it now remains well below levels in Singapore (2.2%), China (1.7%), Malaysia (1.01%) and India (0.82%). The targeted R&D expenditure of 2% of GDP by 2016 looks unlikely to be reached.

The continued expansion of the services sector and development of the knowledge-based economy rely on improvements in the quality of and access to education – which is confirmed by the lack of progress made in reaching the medium-term plan target of 12 years of schooling on average. Although the share of the labour force with tertiary education increased quickly – from 14.9% in 2008 to 17.1% in 2012 – it remains considerably lower than in wealthier Singapore and Malaysia. Likewise, student performance, as measured by PISA 2012, is improving. Yet, although the mean score of 427 was above those of Malaysia and Indonesia, it was below the OECD average and those of Shanghai, Singapore and Viet Nam.

Agricultural productivity deserves greater attention

Agriculture remains important to the Thai economy, accounting for 12% of GDP and 39.6% of total employment. The sector is not sufficiently efficient, however. On-farm productivity needs to improve, effective irrigation systems implemented, the cost of production lowered and the broader agricultural food sector modernised. One of the main goals of Thailand's *Eleventh Economic and Social Development Plan* is to strengthen the agricultural sector and food security by boosting agriculture's share of GDP, a target where no headway has been made.

Agricultural modernisation and increased productivity should also help to raise rural incomes, which tend to lag behind those of urban dwellers. Compared with the other rice-producing ASEAN members as well as China and India, Thai paddy yields have grown slowly in past decades and remain relatively low. In 2013, Thai production averaged 31 348 hectograms per hectare, more than only Cambodia and Brunei Darussalam. Labour productivity in agriculture has grown at a lower rate than in the non-agricultural economy over recent decades, allowing rural-urban income gaps to persist. Further productivity improvements are necessary through investment in training and access to new technologies, including farming methods and ICT, which could help to improve efficiency on farms and deliver value added in the supply chain.

Renewable and alternative energy production is not increasing quickly enough

The government is also pursuing the idea of improving energy security to achieve its strategy of restructuring the economy toward quality growth and sustainability –

and to reduce dependence on imported energy. It is promoting biofuel (e.g. gasohol and biodiesel from biomass and solid waste), particularly for use in electricity production and transportation. While renewable energy production already exceeds the target of 3 440 Megawatt, energy demand is climbing fast. Renewable and alternative energy sources, which contributed to 18.4% of total energy consumption in 2010, had fallen to 17% in 2012 and away from the target of 19% by 2016. Petroleum products still account for the bulk of consumption (Figure 2.5.2).

In its 2012 energy policy, Thailand's Energy Policy and Planning Office (EPPO) emphasised the importance of renewable energy and conservation. EPPO established the Energy Conservation Promotion Fund to support biogas technology projects designed to increase biogas production from wastewater and agricultural, industrial and household waste (EPPO, 2013). From 2008-12, the target is to produce 761.8 million cubic meters per year of biogas.

An example of an EPPO project is the "Biogas Demonstration in Promotion Rubber Fund Co-operatives Phase 1", which aims to make biogas from the wastewater produced in smoked rubber production. It will help promote co-operatives' use of biogas technology in wastewater and biomass treatment. Since June 2013, ten rubber fund co-operatives have participated in the project, which is expected to produce an annual 105 000 cubic meters of biogas.

The achievement of environmental targets has been mixed

The management of natural resources and the environment to achieve sustainability is a central focus of the medium-term plan. Although Thailand has registered progress in the areas of forest conservation, water management and irrigation systems, it needs to put further work into several other facets of conservation and environmental management.

Coastal reforestation, for example, increased by only 1 797 *rai* (710 acres, 287 hectares) per year in 2012, a lot lower than the 2007-11 average of 4 026 *rai* (1 592 acres, 644 hectares) per year – and well short of the target level of 5 000 *rai* (1 977 acres, 808 hectares) set for 2016. Similarly, the solid waste disposal rate in municipal areas dropped from 40% in 2011 to 37% in 2012, again a long way from the 2016 target level of 50%. The rate of garbage recycling also declined in 2012 to 21% from 26% in 2010, although it was supposed to reach 30% in 2016. At the same time, greenhouse gas emissions have continued to rise since 2010, both per unit of GDP – from 1.02 in 2010 to 1.04 in 2012 – and *per capita* – from 2.95 in 2010 to 3.5 in 2012.

Thailand needs to improve its environmental development if it is to become a green growth economy in the near future. Community empowerment is a key factor for success in the management of resources and the environment. It involves people shouldering their responsibility towards society and making a commitment to the next generation as well as seeking to alleviate the impacts of climate change. Such commitment, combined with the King's philosophy of a "Sufficient Economy", could guide the community and the economy along a path relevant to their geographical and social context and help them make the transition to self-resilience and sustainability.

To promote green growth, Thailand introduced a green policy that addressed climate change more rigorously and moved towards a low-carbon economy and society. Thailand's Climate Change Master Plan (2012-50) was established with three key strategies in mind: mitigate GHG emissions and increase GHG sinks, strengthen human resources and institutions, and adapt to survive the negative impacts of climate change. Against that background, the government has launched a pioneering pilot project, "Thailand Low Carbon City Approach". Its goal is to cut *per capita* emissions by 100 kg of CO_2e annually (or 5%) within five years, and by 200 kg CO_2e annually (or 10%) within ten years. The initiative also seeks to create green spaces in the country's cities.

Ensure good governance and reduce corruption for better economic development

Corruption has been a barrier to Thailand's economic development, and to the efficiency and effectiveness of public policies and services. It not only obstructs economic development, but breeds distrust, segregation and conflict in society, and affects social institutions and the community. In Transparency International's Corruption Perception Index, Thailand has persistently scored low – between 3.2 and 3.5 – over the past decade. It rose slightly in 2012 to 3.7 – better than the Asian average of 3.6 – but still considerably shy of the target of 5 out of 10 in 2016. Thailand is ranked 102nd out of 177 countries in the index – far below regional leader Singapore, which is also ranked 5th in the world. Only 22.4% of citizens surveyed believed that the government was effective in the fight against corruption, while 23% reported having paid a bribe in the past 12 months.

The current plan identifies corruption as a major concern that needs to be resolved or, at least, alleviated. As part of the fight against corruption, a reform has been proposed for further empowering independent monitoring bodies as partners in scrutinising the government. Related rules and regulations should be amended to encourage effectiveness, fairness, transparency and sustainability in ending corruption.

Figure 2.5.1. **Contribution to GDP by sector and growth in GDP and creative products**

Percentage shares and annual growth in percentage

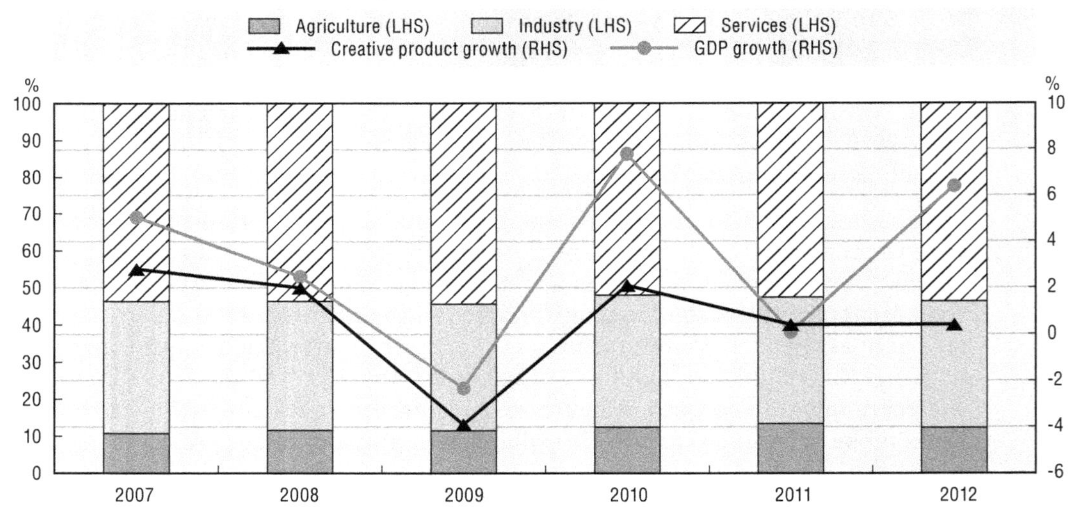

Source: NESDB (National Social and Economic Development Board) (2013), *First Year Progress Report*, National Economic and Social Development Board Office of the Prime Minister, Bangkok.

StatLink http://dx.doi.org/10.1787/888933179713

Figure 2.5.2. **Final energy consumption expenditure by energy source**
THB million

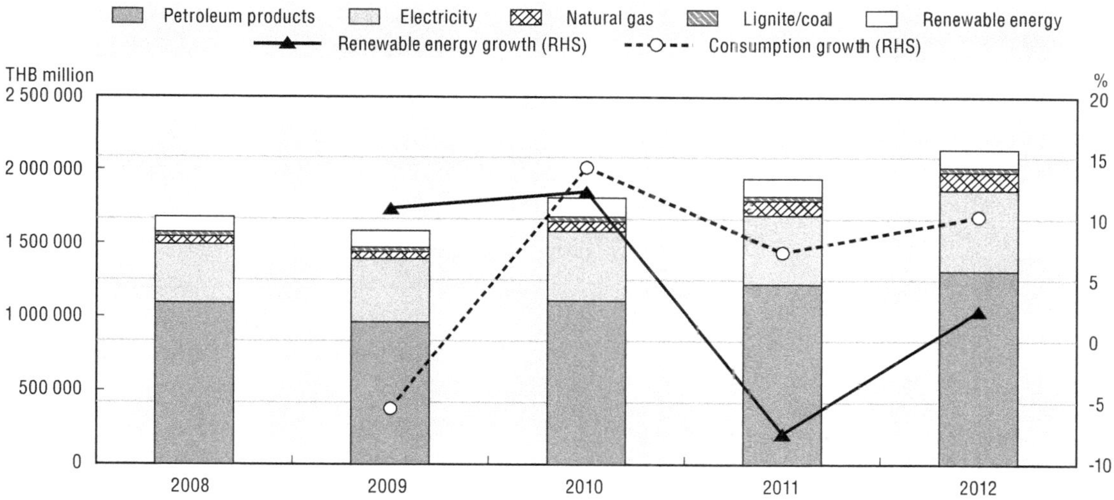

Source: PTT, EGAT, DOEB and DEDE, compiled by Energy Policy and Planning Office (EPPO).
StatLink http://dx.doi.org/10.1787/888933179725

Viet Nam

A. Medium-term economic outlook (forecast, 2015-19 average)

GDP growth (percentage change):	5.7
Current account balance (% of GDP):	3.8
Fiscal balance (% of GDP):	-3.4

B. Medium-term plan

Period: 2011-20

Theme: A modern, industrialised country by 2020

C. Basic data (in 2013)

Total population:	90 million*
Population of Ha Noi:	6.45 million (in 2009)
GDP per capita at PPP:	4 012 (current USD)**

Note: *Total population data for 2013 are estimates.
** IMF estimate.
Sources: OECD Development Centre, MPF-2015, national sources and IMF.

GDP growth rates (percentage change)

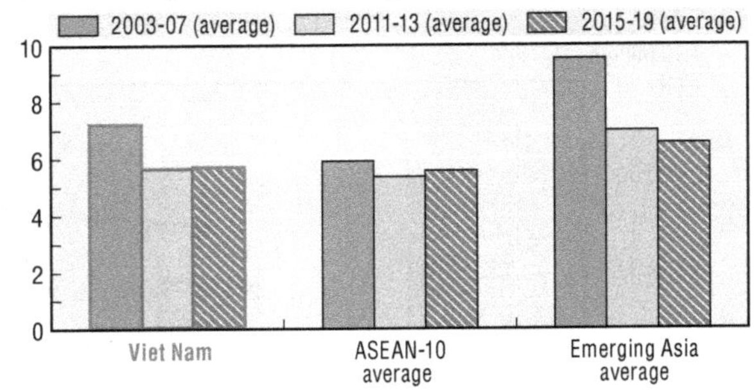

Source: OECD Development Centre, MPF-2015.

GDP per capita, 2013 (PPP, current USD)

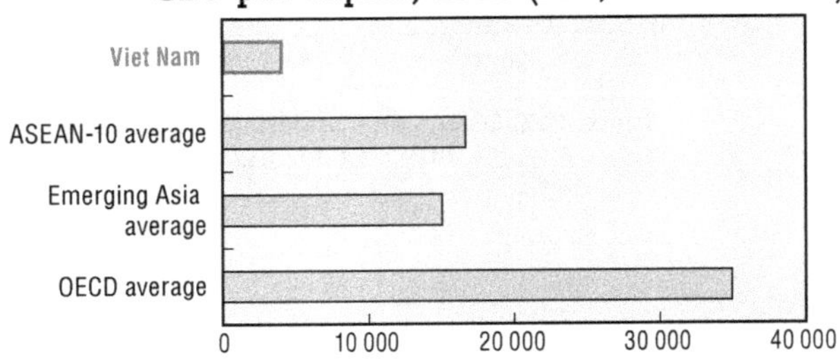

Source: IMF.

Composition of exports, 2013
(percentage of total exports)

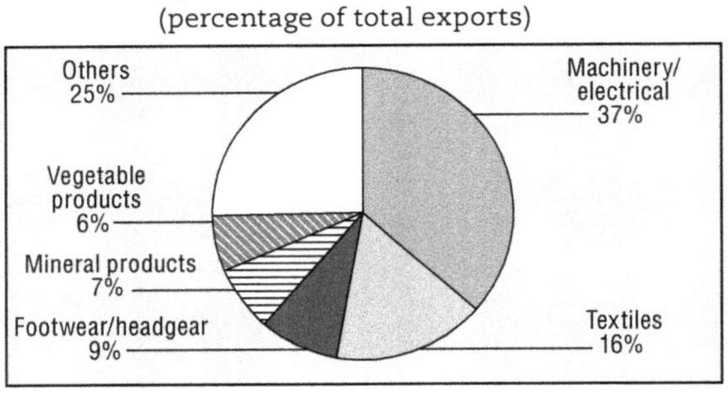

Source: Trademap.

Composition of imports, 2013
(percentage of total imports)

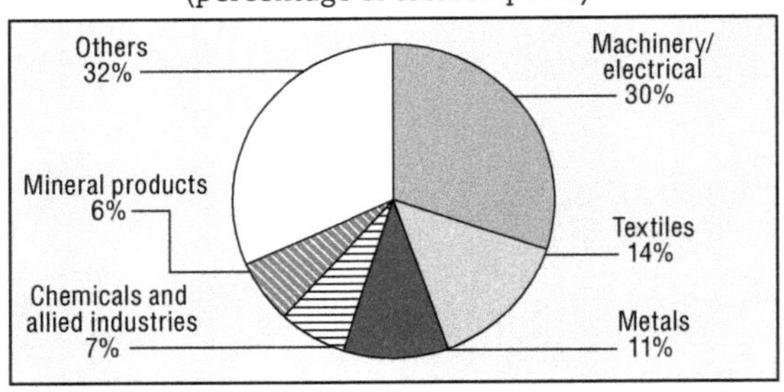

Source: Trademap.

Summary of the Socio-economic Development Plan: A modern industrialised economy by 2020

Approved by the 13th National Assembly in November 2011, Viet Nam's *Five-Year Socio-Economic Development Plan* (SEDP) 2011-15 is part of its long-term *Socio-Economic Development Strategy* (SEDS) that runs from 2011 to 2020. Formulated against the backdrop of the successful economic liberalisation brought about by the previous two SEDS (1991-2000 and 2001-10), the on-going SEDS is tasked with making Viet Nam into a modern, middle-income industrialised country by 2020. A strong commitment to a growth model of higher quality, efficiency and competitiveness is emphasised.

Whereas the SEDS outlines overall policy priorities and targets, the five-year SEDP identifies and details the specific measures required to meet them. The SEDP outlines a framework where its aims are not only innovative growth, but the reform of public investment and financial markets, trade, traffic infrastructure, healthcare and education, science and technology, judicial reform, and the environment. To this end, it sets out a mix of economic, social and environmental targets intended to support rapid and sustainable development.

The Ministry of Planning and Investment (MPI) of Viet Nam releases quarterly and annual reports on the implementation status of socio-economic indicators in the SEDP. It sets annual targets for meeting the 2015 end goals and monitors and adjusts them depending on conditions. Publicly-available reports give the public an easy-to-understand snapshot of the five-year plan's implementation status.

Table 2.6.1. **Viet Nam's key socio-economic development targets, 2011-15**

Indicators	Initial status (2010)	Current status (2013)	Target (2015)
Economic performance			
GDP growth rate (%)	6.8	5.4	6.5-7 per year (2011-15, average)
Budget deficit (% of GDP including government bonds)	4.4 (2011)	5.3	<4.5
Social investment (% of GDP)	41.9	30.4	33.5-35 per year (2011-15, average)
Trade deficit (% of total export)	17.3	2.3 (First half of 2013)	<10
Energy use and real GDP (% per year)	n/a	n/a	2.5-3 per year (2011-15, average)
Proportion of high-tech products of total industrial production value (%)	n/a	n/a	30
Rate of technological innovation (%)	n/a	n/a	13 per year (2011-15, average)
Social labour productivity (% increase from 2010)	0	42.7 (2012)	29-30
Collected tax and fee contributions to the State budget (% of GDP)	n/a	n/a	<22-23 per year (2011-15, average)
Public debt (% of GDP)	56.3	55.7 (2012)	<65
Government's (outstanding) debt (% of GDP)	44.6	43.3 (2012)	<50
National (external) debt (% of GDP)	42.2	41.1 (2012)	<50
Consumer price index (%, yoy)	9.2	6.6	5-7
Social development			
Job creation (number of new jobs)	n/a	n/a	8 million
Unemployment rate, urban (%)	4.3	3.2 (2012)	<4
Trained laborers (% of total workforce)	14.6	17.9	55
People's actual income (% increase from 2010)	0	44 (2012)	100-150
Poor households, national (decrease in % points)	1.6	1.5 (2011-12)	2 per year (2011-15, average)
Poor households, poverty-and extreme difficulties-stricken districts and communes (decrease in % points)	6.5	7.8 (2011-12)	4 per year (2011-15, average)
Population growth rate (%)	1.05	1.06 (2012)	1
Doctors per 10,000 people	n/a	n/a	8
Patient beds per 10,000 people	22	25	23
Housing floor space, national (sq.m. per capita)	n/a	n/a	22
Environment			
Forest coverage (%)	39.7 (2011)	40.7 (2012)	42-43
Heavy environmental polluters handled (%)	n/a	n/a	85

Source: OECD Development Centre's compilation based on national sources.

The development plan and implementation

Policy challenges of implementing the national plan in Viet Nam

- Maintain stability in key economic and social policy areas as a priority for implementing socio-economic strategies for the country.
- Address implementation gaps in developing high-tech industries and skills training in order not only to meet the medium-term plan's goals, but to make the 2020 vision of a modern, industrialised Viet Nam a reality.

Several targets have been met, yet significant improvement is needed in social development

Viet Nam has made progress towards a number of targets and met others. The urban unemployment rate declined from 4.3% in 2010 to 3.2% in 2012, and the 1.1% population growth was only fractionally over the target figure of 1%. Both targets were thus met. Social investment showed a slight increase from 29.5% in 2012 to 30.4% in 2013, so is still on course to meet the target of 33.5% to 35% by 2015.

However, there is still vast room for improvement if Viet Nam is to meet its targets and become a modern, industrialised country by 2020. More targets are yet to be met than have been fully or nearly met. Overall, improvements are needed to address the wide implementation gaps that still remain.

More must be done to boost the GDP growth rate and achieve the 6.5%-7% target, given that the 2013 growth rate of 5.4% was down from 5.9% in 2011. There also needs to be enormous progress in training skilled workers, the proportion of whom rose from 16.3% in 2011 to only 17.9% in 2013. Last, but not least, housing remains a challenge.

Priorities need to be carefully evaluated for efficient and sustainable rural poverty reduction

There has been considerable and rapid progress in poverty reduction. Efforts by the Vietnamese government to implement poverty alleviation programs, such as Program 135 and the National Targeted Program for Poverty Reduction have greatly contributed. According to the General Statistics Office of Viet Nam, the general poverty rate has declined steadily in the last ten years, falling from 28.9% in 2002 to 11.1% in 2012.

However, poverty reduction efforts have had uneven effects in different parts of the country. Figures from the General Statistics Office show there are still wide disparities in poverty rates among regions. For example, although poverty rates have fallen faster in rural than in urban areas, it is still higher in the former. As of 2011, the rural poverty rate was 14.4%, compared to 3.9% in urban areas. The worst poverty rates – as high as 42.8% – are concentrated in regions like the Northern Midlands, mountainous areas and the Central Highlands, where it persists, particularly among ethnic minority groups.

Although various ministries and government agencies have co-ordinated their efforts to put in place numerous programmes that specifically target rural poverty reduction, there have been issues of mismatch between the schemes and the priorities of the communities targeted. According to the results of an Oxfam survey conducted between 2012 and 2013, many beneficiaries of the state-funded Program 30A, designed to create rapid and sustainable poverty alleviation in Viet Nam's 64 poorest districts, reported failing to receive the appropriate benefits. It is vital to carefully evaluate and effectively address local needs.

Education and training reform should give labour market entrants with cognitive, behavioural and job-relevant technical skills

As one of the three main break-through policy thrusts in the country's socio-economic plan, the development of human resources is imperative to Viet Nam's sustainable growth. Reform in education and skills training is central to that purpose. Recent data from the *Report on Labour Force Survey 2013* produced by the General Statistics Office of Viet Nam show that only 17.9% of the employed population have technical qualifications (Figure 2.6.1). The inference is that few workers acquire the skills required by the labour market from their schooling. There appears to be a skills gap, where employers are unable to hire workers with the skills that match jobs. Reforming educational establishments and training organisations to make them more responsive to the labour market is vital to offsetting the prevailing mismatch between the supply and demand of skills.

According to the World Bank (2013), employers particularly prize job-relevant technical skills. However, when hiring, they also look for strong cognitive and interpersonal abilities. Such a mix of skills could be continuously fostered throughout education. TVET and higher education institutions should focus on equipping students with technical competencies by leveraging partnerships between universities and firms to link theory with practice. What is more, as Viet Nam shifts towards a more skill-conscious, non-manual labour market, it should seek to promote problem-solving skills and critical thinking in primary and secondary school, the period when children are most receptive. The *Report on Labour Force Survey 2013* shows that 30.7% of the employed population have completed lower secondary education, but only 11.8% completed upper secondary – down from 12.8% in 2012.

As a measure to enhance the development of cognitive and behavioural skills, the Ministry of Education and Training has incorporated the innovative education model Vietnam Escuela Nueva (VNEN). Viet Nam initiated the scheme in 2010 among 24 primary schools in six provinces. The move away from traditional to progressive, effective teaching methods illustrates its recognition of the need to enable children to learn in a creative, independent way and to develop the problem-solving skills they will need in the future. Nevertheless, if Viet Nam is to continue developing relevant skills that school-leavers can use upon entering the labour market, it should also introduce measures to increase the enrolment rate and improve the standard of teaching in secondary school.

Structural change toward improving banking governance is still a work in progress

The bad debt situation in Viet Nam is a priority issue. The accumulation of bad debt creates severe liquidity shortages and slows credit growth, preventing banks from operating as lenders to the economy. The Vietnamese government has been steadfast in its efforts to tackle the country's on-going bad debt problem, the result of escalating non-performing loans (NPLs) in the banking sector (Figure 2.6.2). To settle bad debt it has taken successive reform measures, such as consolidation among indebted banks and easing foreign ownership regulations to allow foreign strategic investors to take 20% stakes. Yet, progress has been slow. The bad debt rate appears to have risen from 3.74% in January 2014 to 4.03% by the end of April 2014, even though independent rating agencies like Moody's claim the real figure is much higher. In addition, the bad debt problem has curtailed bank lending which grew by a mere 3.5% in the first half of 2014.

In order to ensure a long-term healthy banking sector for an efficient economy, structural shortcomings in the sector needs to be addressed in parallel with bad debt. There is a dire need for access to high-quality, accurate information. To encourage transparency, Vietnamese banks should use international accounting standards instead of the Vietnamese Accounting Standard (VAS). The current dearth of accurate data makes it difficult to grasp the full magnitude of the bad debt ratio, and prompts fears that the path to resolving Viet Nam's unstable financial system will be a long one. Circular No. 2 issued by the State Bank of Vietnam (SBV) in 2013, is expected to contribute toward providing accurate loan data for each bank. It has not come into effect as yet, however.

Forestry reforms are progressing, but more systematic monitoring and evaluation may be required

The Forestry Development Strategy 2006-20, overseen by the Ministry of Agriculture and Rural Development (MARD), sets the long-term framework for sustainable forest management by 2020. To effectively achieve the strategy's targets and goals, the government put in place the Payments for Forest Environmental Services (PFES). PFES is to provide a financial incentive for individuals, communities and organisations to undertake environmental services, with central and provincial Forest Protection and Development Funds (FPDFs) playing a large part in the operation and organisation of the strategy. Revenues generated during 2009-13 amounted to nearly VND 2.85 trillion.

The operational aspect of PFES calls for improvement, however. Limited resources and poor monitoring and evaluation are still an impediment to effectively determining the results of forest preservation. The MARD needs to develop evaluation not only of forest coverage, but also of forest quality.

Figure 2.6.1. **Labour force structure in Viet Nam, by skill and educational attainment level, 2006-13**

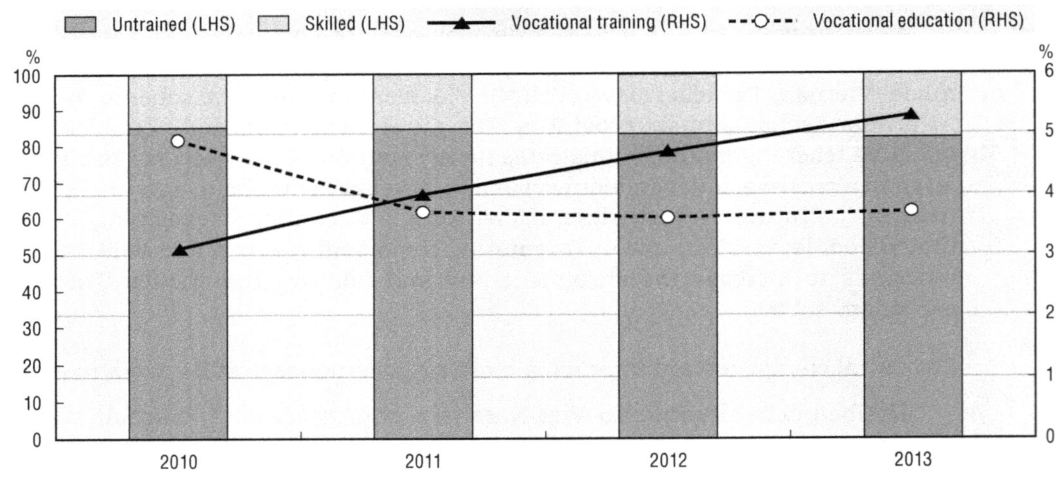

Source: General Statistics Office of Vietnam (2014), *Report on Labour Force Survey 2013*, Ministry of Planning and Investment, Ha Noi; OECD (2013a), *Economic Outlook for Southeast Asia, China and India 2014: Beyond the Middle-Income Trap*, OECD Publishing, Paris.

StatLink http://dx.doi.org/10.1787/888933179734

Figure 2.6.2. **Domestic credit to the private sector and non-performing loans, 2004-13**

Domestic credit as percentage of GDP and non-performing loans as percentages of total loans

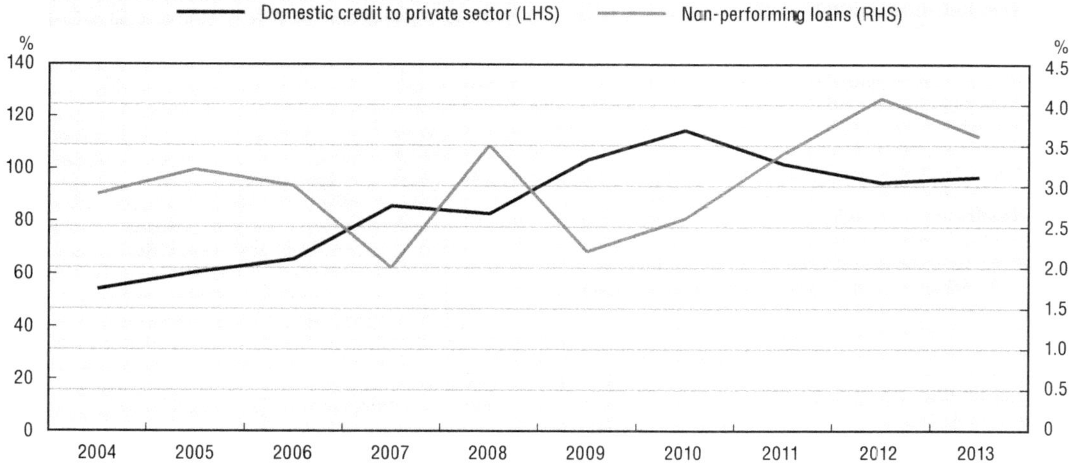

Note: Domestic credit figures represent annual averages, while NPL ratios represent monthly averages from December in the respective year.

Sources: World Bank (2014), *World Development Indicators*, World Bank, Washington, DC; State Bank of Vietnam (2014), *Statistics on the Performance of Credit Institutions*, State Bank of Vietnam, Hanoi, www.sbv.gov.vn.

StatLink http://dx.doi.org/10.1787/888933179745

China

A. Medium-term economic outlook (forecast, 2015-19 average)

GDP growth (percentage change):	6.8
Current account balance (% of GDP):	2.6
Fiscal balance (% of GDP):	-1.2

B. Medium-term plan

Period: 2011-15

Theme: Rebalancing the economy, ameliorating social inequality, and protecting the environment

C. Basic data (in 2013)

Total population:	1 361 million*
Population of Beijing:	19.6 million (in 2010)
GDP per capita at PPP:	9 844 (current USD)**

Note: * Total population data for 2013 are estimates.
** IMF estimate.
Sources: OECD Development Centre, MPF-2015, national sources and IMF.

GDP growth rates (percentage change)

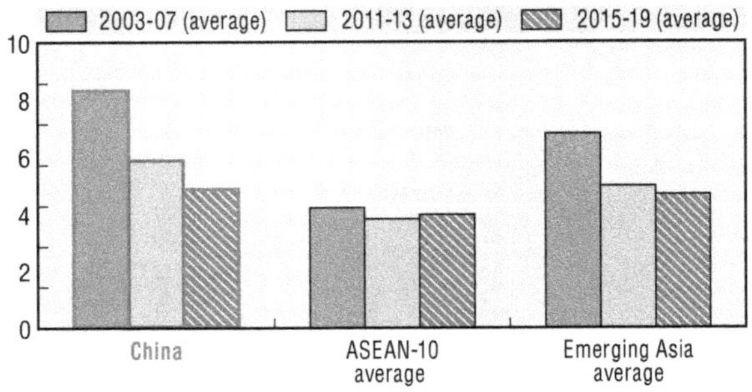

Source: OECD Development Centre, MPF-2015.

GDP per capita, 2013 (PPP, current USD)

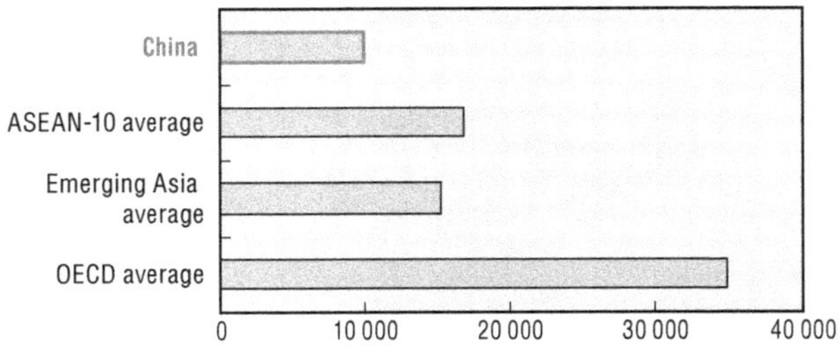

Source: IMF.

Composition of exports, 2013

(percentage of total exports)

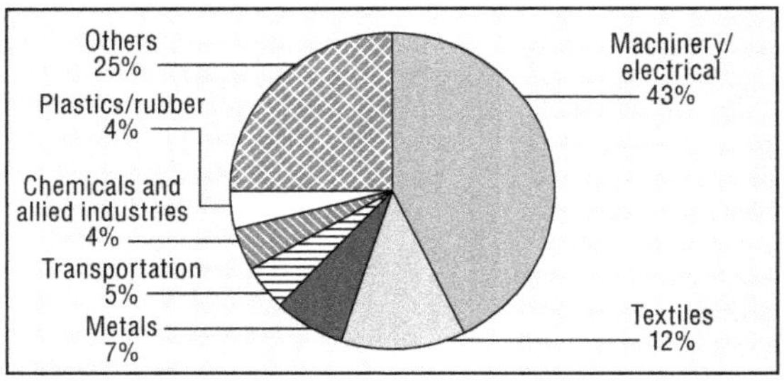

Source: Trademap.

Composition of imports, 2013

(percentage of total imports)

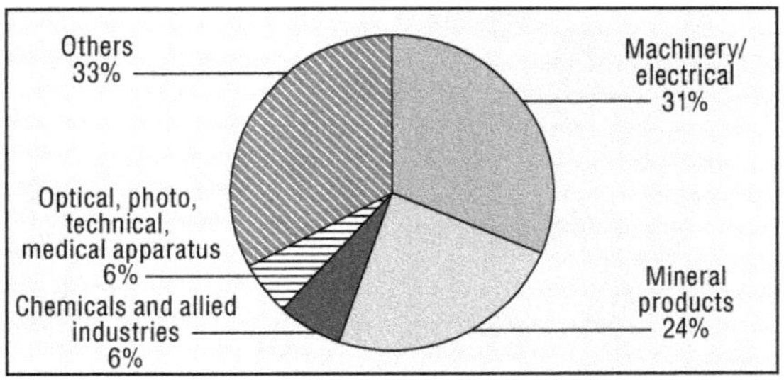

Source: Trademap.

Summary of the medium-term development plan

China's *12th Five-Year Plan* outlines the government's strategic policies and priorities over the period 2011-15. Its objective is to achieve high-quality, inclusive and sustainable growth. Promoting China's continued shift towards an economic development model driven by domestic consumption rather than exports and investment is therefore a central goal. The Plan also pays particular attention to issues of wealth disparity and inequality, and seeks a more equal distribution of economic benefits, while also addressing environmental concerns by aiming to reduce emissions of major pollutants, increase forest cover and improve energy efficiency.

Improvements in competitiveness are needed to support balanced growth. To that end, the government has identified seven strategic emerging areas as priorities for development over the Plan's five-year span. They are: new energy; energy conservation and environmental protection; clean energy vehicles, as part of the country's sustainable growth agenda; high-end equipment manufacturing; biotechnology; new information technologies; and moving up the value chain.

As the Eleventh Plan neared completion, China's National Development and Reform Commission (NDRC) started preparing the subsequent plan, determining its objectives and direction. The NDRC drafted proposals for the issues that the plan would address. The draft was then discussed in the Plenary Session of the Central Committee of the Communist Party of China (CPC). Meanwhile, municipal and provincial-level governments also prepared their policy proposals. The final draft of the Twelfth Plan was then drawn up from the CPC's proposal and inputs from provinces and ministries. The NDRC then consulted on the draft plan with a wide range of experts and stakeholders, including entrepreneurs, think tanks, research institutions, universities, local governments and ministries. The draft plan was then submitted to the annual session of the National People's Congress (NPC) to be reviewed and endorsed.

Table 2.7.1. **China's key medium-term development targets (2011-15)**

	Initial status (2010)	Current status (2013)	Target (2015)
Economic targets			
GDP (trillion Yuan)	39.8	56.9	55.8
GDP growth (%)	10.4	7.7	7 (annually, on average)
Number of new jobs in urban areas	0	38 (2011-13)	45 million
Registered urban unemployment (%)	4.1	4.1	< 5
Economic restructuring			
Service sector value added (% of GDP)	43.1	46.1	47
Urbanisation rate (%)	47.5	53.73	51.5
Innovation			
Expenditure on R&D (% of GDP)	1.8	2.1	2.2
Invention patents per 10,000 people	1.7	4.2 (March 2014)	3.3
Environment and clean energy			
Non-fossil fuel percentage of primary energy consumption (%)	8.3	9.8	11.4
Decrease in water consumption per unit of value-added Industrial output (%)	0	Decreased by 5.7% per 10 000 Yuan of value-added in 2013	30
Decrease in energy consumption per unit of GDP (%)	0	9.03	16
Decrease in carbon dioxide (CO_2) emission per unit of GDP (%)	0	10.68	17
Total decrease in emissions of major pollutants (% change):			
Chemical oxygen demand (COD)	0	7.8	8
Sulphur dioxide (SO_2)	0	9.9	8
Ammonia nitrogen	0	7.1	10
Nitrogen oxides	0	2	10
Forest coverage rate (%)	20.4	21.6	21.7
Forest stock volume (billion m^3)	13.7	15.1	14.3
Agriculture			
Annual grain production capacity (in million tonnes)	546	601.94	> 540
Farmland reserves (no less than 1.818 billion mu)	1.818	1.826 (February 2011)	> 1.818
Water efficiency coefficient in agricultural irrigation	0.4 (2009)	0.5 (2010)	0.5

Table 2.7.1. **China's key medium-term development targets (2011-15)** *(cont.)*

Livelihood			
Population (billion)	1.341	1.361	< 1.39
Life span per person to increase by 1 year	73.5	75.2 (2012)	74.5
Number of urban residents enrolled in basic pension scheme (million people)	257	322	357
Increase in rate of enrolment in basic medical insurance in urban and rural areas (%)	0	Medical insurance for non-working urban workers covers 90% of population; Rural cooperative medical care system 99%	3
Construction and renovation of apartments for low-income families (million units)	0	24.9 (2011-13)	36
Per capita disposable income of urban residents (Yuan)	19 109	26 955	> 26 810
Per capita net income of rural residents (Yuan)	5 919	8 896	> 8 310

Source: OECD Development Centre's compilation based on national sources.

China's development plan and implementation

The policy challenges of implementing the national plan in China

- Increase clean energy consumption in response to the serious environmental degradation that persists despite the country's efforts to reduce pollution.
- Increase rural and agricultural development to help improve urban-rural equality.
- Continue reforms and improve education in order to exploit the potential of the service sector to drive future growth.

Higher-quality growth, a better balanced economy, greater social equality and environmental protection

China has recorded impressive growth over the past decades. Although this has led to sharp reductions in poverty rates, inequality has increased. The country's Gini coefficient increased from about 0.38 in 1996 to 0.47 in 2013. Through its 12th Five-Year Plan, China aims to encourage more inclusive and sustainable growth. It has set a growth target of around 7% for 2015, much lower than the 11.2% average growth actually achieved under the 11th plan. Nonetheless, a number of challenges still need to be addressed to foster continued growth, particularly the improved quality of growth desired.

Rural and agriculture development is needed to promote urban-rural social equality

The urban-rural divide is a serious issue in the Chinese economy. The differences in income, as well as in quality of life between urban and rural populations, are wide. The *12th Five-Year Plan* includes measures to improve incomes – in rural as well as urban areas. China also plans to provide greater access to health services for the rural population, establishing a basic national medical insurance system, especially to cover non-working urban residents and rural households. Improvements have been achieved by, for instance, increasing government subsidies for basic medical insurance and reimbursement rates for hospitalisation and outpatient care. The government has also expanded the rural co-operative medical care system to cover a higher number of rural residents.

Agricultural and rural development, too, is crucial if inequality is to be reduced. Improvements to agricultural productivity are therefore needed to increase production and rural incomes, although the medium-term plan does not set any explicit targets towards these ends. Agricultural modernisation and infrastructure upgrades could help to boost incomes in rural areas, as could widening access to healthcare, education and other services that enhance productivity and well-being.

Environmental degradation remains a major issue despite efforts to reduce pollution

Industrialisation has grown fast and, with it, energy demand – total energy consumption increased by 2.7% *per annum* between 1990 and 2001, and has climbed by 7.9% *per annum* on average since 2001 (ABB, 2011). China has struggled to balance pollution reduction with rapid growth and the consequently burgeoning energy demand. Addressing environmental challenges has now become a long-term focus. The 12th Five-Year Plan reflects the continuing commitment to addressing the issue of environmental degradation and outlines ambitious targets. It targets reduced emissions of major pollutants – carbon dioxide (CO_2), chemical oxygen demand (COD), sulphur dioxide (SO_2), nitrous oxide (NOx) and ammonia nitrogen. The plan also aims to increase forest cover.

Despite these efforts, pollution remains a major issue. China is still the world's largest emitter of CO_2, the principal greenhouse gas, with a 29% share of global CO_2 emissions in 2012 – considerably larger than the shares of either the United States (16%), the European Union (11%) or India (6%). China's CO_2 emissions from fossil fuel and cement production increased by 3.3% between 2011 and 2012, although the rise was actually lower than the annual increases of around 10% over the previous decade. Nevertheless, it was still higher than the growth in the European Union (1.3%) (Figure 2.7.1).

The bulk of China's carbon emissions originate in manufacturing, while emissions in most advanced economies are more mixed between manufacturing, transport-related, commercial and residential sources. To curb emissions, China will therefore have to focus on industry and ease the power and manufacturing sectors away from their dependence on coal consumption.

China is also the largest emitter of SO_2 and NOx, pollutants that are generated by coal-fired power plants and cause environmental damage like acid rain (Figure 2.7.2). The country emits more than the United States and the European Union combined (OECD, 2013b).

To address its multiple pollution issues effectively, China must promote investment in carbon capture, clean-up technologies and green energy. It also needs to further strengthen the enforcement of environmental law and supervise the environmental authorities more closely. To those ends, co-ordination between central and local government should be improved.

Figure 2.7.1. Trends in CO_2 emissions, 1990-2012

Billion tonnes of CO_2

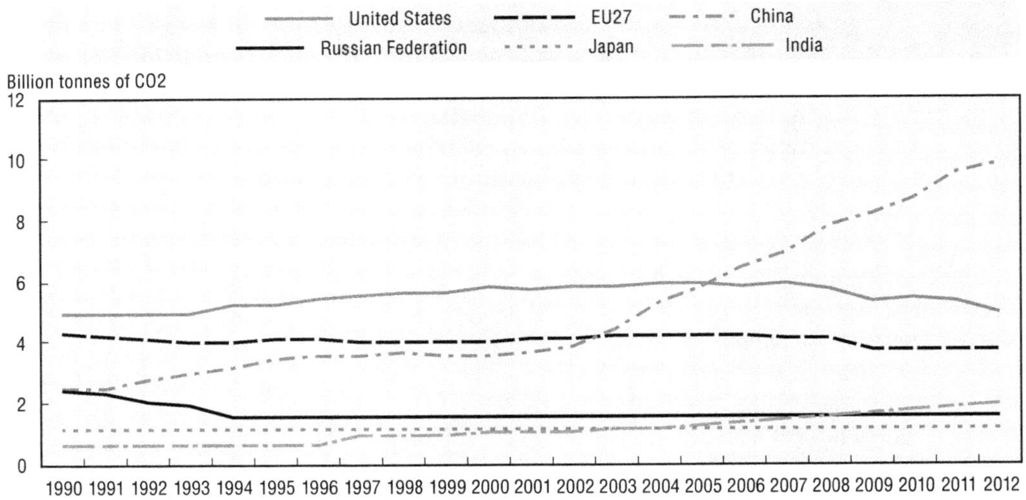

Source: Oliver, J. et al. (2013), *Trends in Global CO_2 Emissions*; 2013 Report, Background Studies, PBL Netherlands Environmental Assessment Agency and European Commission's Joint Research Centre, The Hague.

StatLink http://dx.doi.org/10.1787/888933179751

Figure 2.7.2. SO_2 and NO_x intensity in selected OECD countries

Tonnes per million USD

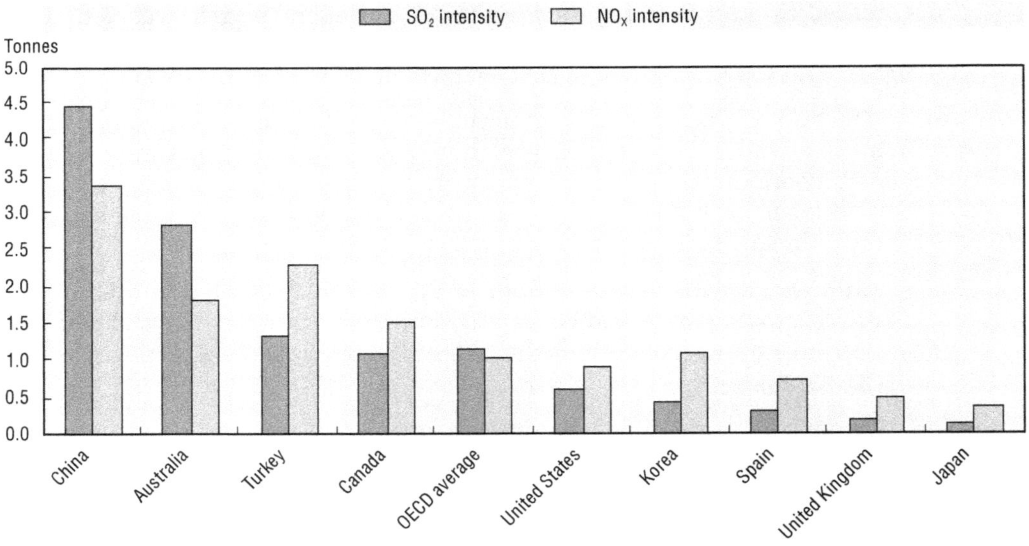

Source: OECD (2013b), *OECD Economic Surveys: China*, OECD Publishing, Paris.

StatLink http://dx.doi.org/10.1787/888933179769

Further efforts on energy efficiency are required to achieve sustainable development

In order to achieve its carbon-intensity and energy-intensity targets, China should encourage clean energy use by championing non-fossil fuel and renewable energy, as coal remains the country's main source of energy. Under the *12th Five-Year Plan*, China aims to achieve that goal by supporting the development of hydropower construction and nuclear energy. To achieve sustainable growth, though, China should strive not only to reduce carbon intensity, but to improve energy efficiency, too. Through the 12th plan, it is seeking to reduce energy consumption per unit of GDP.

Accordingly, the government has earmarked USD 372 billion for energy conservation and anti-pollution projects. Liberalising energy prices may also contribute to meeting the energy efficiency target. Nevertheless, China is still less energy efficient than most OECD countries and some other large emerging economies. Further encouraging initiatives to improve the energy standards of buildings and consumer goods could help boost energy efficiency.

Further development of the services sector is important

While it has been eclipsed by the rapid expansion of manufacturing in China, the services sector has great potential to drive future growth. The 12th Plan reflects China's attempts to boost its services sector's share of GDP to 47% as it seeks to restructure the economy. Although the figure would be a major improvement, it is still low compared to other countries (Roach, 2011), since China's services account for a smaller share of national income than in many other developing countries (Liping and Evenett, 2010). China has plenty of room for improvement in developing its services sector. Doing so would support the objective of a greener economy, as the service industry is more environmentally friendly than resource-intensive manufacturing. And it would help absorb the country's labour surplus.

Distributive services, like the wholesale and retail trade, have employment potential and can help absorb the new rural workforce that growing urbanisation draws to the cities. Micro, small and medium-sized firms (MSMEs) with fewer than 250 employees account for 43% of China's employment in services (Figure 2.7.3). SOEs still account for a sizeable share of total firms (20%) and employment (19%) in the services sector, and tend to be larger than their private sector peers, on average. The development of the services sector is therefore likely to benefit from the creation of a business environment supportive of dynamic, innovative SMEs.

Figure 2.7.3. **MSMEs make a significant contribution to China's services sector**

Shares of services firms and employment by firm size

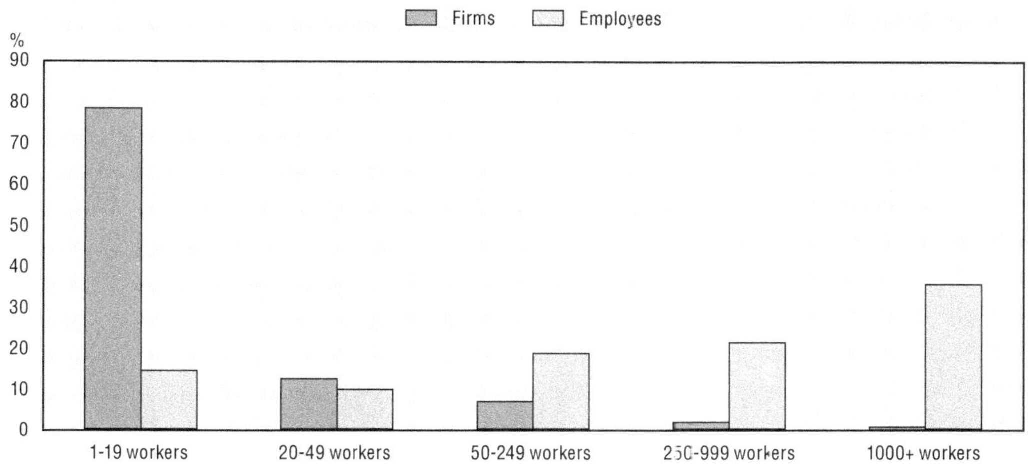

Sources: National statistics; OECD Development Centre's calculation.

StatLink http://dx.doi.org/10.1787/888933179774

Greater access to education is needed to support inclusive growth, particularly in the services sector. Modern and high-technology services with the greatest potential to drive future growth – such as telecommunications, financial and business services – require highly-trained workers. To be sure, China has made great advances in education: Shanghai's students topped the 2012 PISA rankings in mathematics, with a mean score of 613 points – 119 points above the OECD average. Nevertheless, many children and young people in China face barriers in accessing education, particularly among poor and rural households and rural migrants to the cities. In 2010, only 18% of Chinese adults aged between 25 and 64 had reached at least the upper-secondary level, still far below the OECD average of 74%.

A continued emphasis on economic reform can be expected from the government in the future

The March 2013 Chinese People's Political Consultative Congress (CPPCC) and National People's Congress (NPC), the first such meetings held under the premiership of Li Keqiang, highlighted priority areas for reform. While some attention was paid to decentralisation and other limited political reform, the stress was on the need to further liberalise the economy – including the financial sector. Furthermore, government reforms are intended to bolster the market, with fiscal and tax system reforms and the opening of SOEs to mixed-ownership structures planned.

Such plans echoed the outcomes of the Third Plenary Session of the 18th Central committee of the Communist Party of China, held in November 2013. While the plenum stated its commitment to the "dominant role" of public ownership in the economic system, it focused much of its attention on deepening economic reform and allowing market mechanisms to allocate resources efficiently.

India

A. Medium-term economic outlook (forecast, 2015-19 average)

GDP growth (percentage change):	6.7
Current account balance (% of GDP):	-2.3
Fiscal balance (% of GDP):	-7.2

B. Medium-term plan

Period: 2012-17

Theme: Faster, more inclusive and sustainable growth

C. Basic data (in 2013)

Total population:	1 243 million*
Population of NCT of Delhi:	16.79 million (in 2011)
GDP per capita at PPP:	4 077 (current USD)**

Note: * Total population data for 2013 are estimates.
** IMF estimate.
Sources: OECD Development Centre, MPF-2015, national sources and IMF.

GDP growth rates (percentage change)

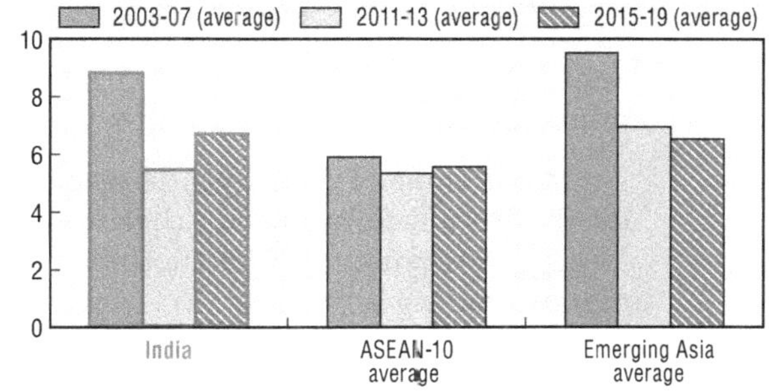

Source: OECD Development Centre, MPF-2015.

GDP per capita, 2013 (PPP, current USD)

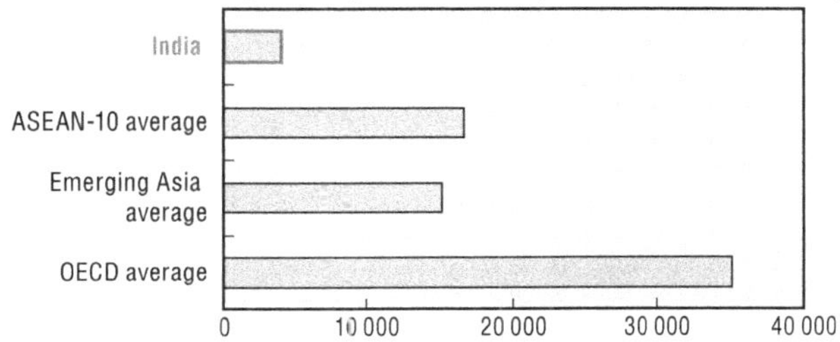

Source: IMF.

Composition of exports, 2013
(percentage of total exports)

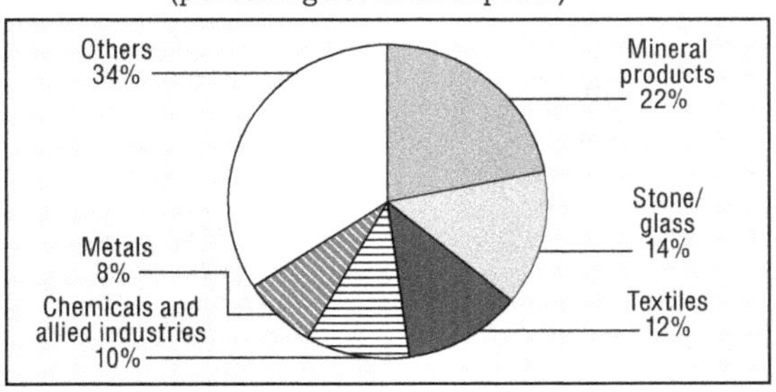

Source: Trademap.

Composition of imports, 2013
(percentage of total imports)

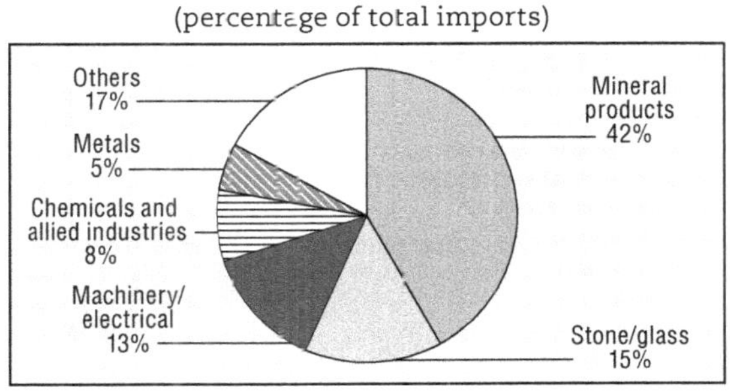

Source: Trademap.

Summary of the medium-term development plan: Towards faster, more inclusive and sustainable growth

India's *Twelfth Five-Year Plan* began in 2012 and will last until 2017. The weakening macroeconomic conditions in developed economies in the last years of the Eleventh Plan, together with domestic constraints like deepening fiscal and current account deficits, saw India's growth slip to below 5% at the inception of the Twelfth Plan. Its response has been to prioritise the restoration of rapid growth and ensure it is inclusive and sustainable.

The Planning Commission co-ordinates the process of defining the Plan's targets and main strategies after consulting widely with other stakeholders, such as central and state governments, experts, economists, political scientists, and civil society organisations.

The *Twelfth Five-Year Plan* puts the emphasis on inclusion and sustainability. It also trains its sights on social sectors, taking into account their impact on human development and the quality of life. It covers a wide range of programmes in many sectors – health, education, water and sanitation, infrastructure, and the environment – as well as programmes to support disadvantaged sections of the population such as Scheduled Castes and Scheduled Tribes (SCs and STs), Other Backward Classes (OBCs), minorities, and other marginalised groups.

In the wake of the May 2014 elections, the government of Prime Minister Modi finds itself with a reform agenda that seeks to improve the business climate, domestic and foreign investment, infrastructure, and India's overall competitiveness, particularly in manufacturing activities.

Table 2.8.1. **India's key medium-term development targets, 2012-17**

	Initial status (2011)	Current status (2013)	Target (2017)
Economic growth			
Real GDP growth rate (%)	4.5 (2012-13)	5 (2013-14)	8 (2012-17, average)
Agriculture growth rate (%)	1.4 (2012-13)	4.7 (2013-14)	4 (2012-17, average)
Manufacturing growth rate (%)	1.1 (2012-13)	-0.7 (2013-14)	7.1 (2012-17, average)
Poverty and Employment			
Head count ratio of consumption poverty	People living below poverty line in 2009-10: 29.8% (Tendulkar method)	21.9% (2011-12, Tendulkar method)	Reduced by 10 percentage points over the preceding estimates by the end of 12th plan
Generate new work opportunities in non-farm sectors and provide skill certification to equivalent numbers	0	n/a	50 million
Education			
Mean years of schooling	4.2 (2000)	5.1 (2010)	7
Enhance access to higher education by creating additional seats for each age cohort aligned to the skill needs of the economy	0	n/a	2 million seats
Gender and social gap in school enrolment	Gender parity index in 2010-11: 0.99 (elementary), 0.87 (secondary), 0.86 (higher education)	n/a	Gap eliminated by the end of the 12th Plan
Health			
Infant mortality ratio per 1 000 live births	44	42 (2012)	25
Maternal mortality ratio per 100 000 live births	212 (2007-09)	178 (2010-12)	100
Total fertility rate	2.5 (2010)	2.5	2.1
Child sex ratio (0-6 years) (number of girl children per 1 000 male children)	914 (2011), 927 (2001)	n/a	Improve to 950
Under-nutrition among children aged 0-3	40% (NFHS-3)	n/a	Rduced to half of the NFHS-3 levels (20%)

Table 2.8.1. **India's key medium-term development targets, 2012-17** *(cont.)*

Infrastructure			
Investment in infrastructure (% of GDP)	5.4 (2006-07)	9.3 (2011-12)	9
Gross irritated area (hectare)	86.4 (2009-10)	90 (2012)	103 million
Electricity provision	n/a	n/a	Electricity to cover all villages; 20% of AT&C losses
All-weather roads	n/a	n/a	All villages connected
National and state highways improvement	9 220 km of NHs having less than 2-lane standards at the beginning of 12th Plan (estimate)	n/a	Upgrade national and state highways to the minimum two-lane standard
Eastern and Western Dedicated Freight Corridors	n/a	n/a	Completed
Increase rural tele-density (%)	37.5 (December 2011)	41.7 (September 2013)	70
Water and sanitation	n/a	n/a	50% of rural population has access to 55 LPCD piped drinking water supply and 50% of communities meet standards (Nirmal Gram Status)
Additional capacity of electricity (MW)	0	28845 (March 2012 - September 2013)	88 000
Environment			
Additional renewable energy capacity (MW)	0	3681 (March 2012 - September 2013)	30 000
Increased green cover	692 027 sq km	697 898 sq km	1 million hectare every year
Reduced emission intensity of GDP	CO_2 emissions in 2005: 1.29 billion tonnes	CO_2 emissions in 2012: 1.97 billion tonnes	20-25% reduction by 2020 over 2005 levels
Service delivery			
Access to banking services (% of households)	59	n/a	90
Subsidy and welfare payments	n/a	n/a	Major subsidies and welfare related beneficiary payments to be shifted to a direct cash transfer, using the Aadhar platform with linked bank account

Source: OECD Development Centre's compilation based on national sources.

India's development plan and implementation

Policy challenges of implementing the national plan in India

- Restore growth to reverse the slow-down – even negative growth in 2013-14 – in manufacturing over the last few years.
- Widen access to secondary education in order to meet the goal of universal secondary education by 2017.
- Strengthen the public sector health system. Improve access to curative and preventive healthcare facilities.
- Accelerate the development of infrastructure, especially in rural areas.

GDP growth has been slowing down compared to the previous medium-term plan

The *Twelfth Five-Year Plan* targets average real GDP growth of 8%. It is a somewhat ambitious target based on the Eleventh Plan (2007-12) which, despite the global crisis, reached the 8% growth rate, the highest achieved in any of India's five-year plans. However, GDP growth has been slowed since the inception of the Twelfth Plan by domestic constraints, such as slow structural reform progress. In 2012-13, the country recorded growth of 4.5%, down on the 6.2% in 2011-12. Although growth bounced back to 4.7% in 2013-14, the 8% target is still far off.

Economic activity was boosted by the agriculture sector, which grew from 1.4% in 2012-13 to 4.7% in 2013-14. Manufacturing, by contrast, has slowed down in recent years. In 2009-10, it outstripped growth in services, but fell behind in 2011-12 (Figure 2.8.1), and even went into negative growth in 2013-14, slipping even further short of the 7.1% growth targeted. The slowdown mostly affects capital goods and high technology sectors such as machinery and equipment, where growth has been negative since 2011-12. Growth has also been sluggish in office, accounting and computer machinery; motor vehicles; and other transport equipment. Medium-to-low technology products and labour-intensive sectors like leather goods and textiles have been more buoyant, however.

Dwindling investment has been one chief reason for slack growth, while low standards of technology and poor infrastructure have also weighed heavily. Accordingly, it is important to address infrastructure bottlenecks and revitalise the investment climate to boost manufacturing.

The reform agenda of newly-elected Prime Minister Modi was initially well received by the market (as of November 2014). However, there are many intertwined structural challenges to contend with – including the complexity of the country's federal system, which makes reforms more difficult to undertake in key areas such as tax, product and labour market regulation, water, and infrastructure (see Chapter 1).

Reducing poverty and increasing employment

Although it is declining, India's poverty rate is still high. In 2012, it reached 22%, higher than in Brazil (16%) and Indonesia (12%) (World Bank, 2014). Poverty persists, especially in rural areas, with Uttar Pradesh, Bihar, Madhya Pradesh, Maharashtra, West Bengal and Odisha among the poorest parts of the country (Figure 2.8.2). Poor access to education, healthcare and finance are some causes of rural poverty in India. Certain social groups, such as SCs and STs, are more vulnerable to poverty. In 2005, 80% of the country's rural poor came from such groups.

The government is seeking to bring down poverty by strengthening economic growth and implementing programmes that specifically address rural poverty, such as the 2005 National Rural Employment Guarantee Act (NREGA). However, another poverty-related issue is rapid urbanisation. The manufacturing sector is not vibrant enough to absorb migrant labourers; unemployment and poverty have mounted in cities. Any anti-poverty policy must entail programmes that consider the poor in both rural and urban areas.

Burgeoning employment is a daunting challenge in a country of more than 1.2 billion inhabitants and around 12.8 million new labour market entrants every year. There is indeed concern that recent growth has not created jobs as expected, particularly in the formal sector and manufacturing. In addition to concerns of exclusion and social stability, productivity catch-up may also be affected, as excessive informality and working poverty are often barriers to sustainable productivity gains. The challenge of meeting the Twelfth Plan's target of 50 million new work opportunities in the non-farming sector has been further exacerbated by the manufacturing slow-down. Under the Eleventh Plan, the government created three institutional structures as a part of its national skill development mission:

- The Prime Minister's National Council on Skill Development;
- The National Skill Development Co-ordination Board (NSDCB), which is under the aegis of the Planning Commission and co-ordinates skills development programmes in different ministries or states; and
- The National Skill Development Council (NSDC), which answers to the Ministry of Finance. It encourages the private sector's involvement in skills development activities such as training and certification.

The programmes that are undertaken, however, need to be aligned with market needs. What is more, labour market rigidities hamper job creation and do not provide workers with efficient protection due to the size of the informal sector. Making regulations more flexible and enforceable may help foster job creation, as does further encouraging entrepreneurship.

Improving access to secondary education

The government runs strategic programmes to increase access to education, especially at the primary level. Among such schemes are the Right to Free Education (RTE), which was launched in April 2010 with the aim of making eight years of elementary education a fundamental right for all children. As a result, primary school enrolment rates have risen and now take in more than 90% of children in most states (OECD, 2013a). However, the country's educational system still faces many challenges.

Access to secondary and tertiary education needs to be improved and special efforts will be needed to meet the country's goal of universal secondary education by 2017. Although the secondary school gross enrolment rate increased from 58.6% in 2007 to 68.5% in 2011, it still lags behind the OECD averages of 98.1% and 99.1% for those years, and is low compared even to China's 71.2% and 86.6% and Indonesia's 72.4% and 81.2% (World Bank, 2014). India addresses the issue through its National Mission for Secondary Education (Rashtriya Madhyamik Shiksha Abhiyan [RMSA]). The RMSA was introduced in 2009 to provide facilities, including libraries and toilets, and improve the quality of education through teacher training and curriculum reform. Nevertheless, dropout rates between elementary and secondary schools remains high, especially for girls (Planning Commission, 2013), which reflects another challenge for the country's educational system: gaps in access to education between the genders and among social groups and regions.

Strengthening the public health system

The public health system needs to be strengthened, especially for the underprivileged who cannot afford private healthcare. It is also important to improve access not only to curative treatment, but to provide facilities such as sanitation and clean water that ensure basic health. Better nutrition for children, especially the poor in rural and urban areas, to reduce the country's infant mortality rate of 42 per 1 000 live births in 2012, still well short of the target of 25.

Only around 240 million people were covered in 2010. Government-sponsored health insurance schemes have improved matters and private insurance has helped to widen coverage to 300 million people (La Forgia and Nagpal, 2012). Yet, the vast majority of the population are still not insured. An increase in public health spending is needed to help achieve the long-term objective of universal health coverage. Effective co-ordination of public and private health service providers is also important, as is addressing the shortage of healthcare personnel, especially in rural areas.

Accelerate the development of infrastructure

The Eleventh Plan tackled the issue of inadequate infrastructure as one of the main constraints on economic growth (Planning Commission of India, 2008). However, the problem remains. Greater improvement is necessary, not only in transport infrastructure such as roads and railways, but also in electricity capacity (where the increase of 28 845 MW still falls short of the Twelfth Plan's 88 000 MW target), health facilities, and schools and other education facilities. Poor infrastructure is a particular issue in rural areas, where only 41.48% of schools were connected to the power grid in 2011-12, compared to 81.13% in urban areas (NUEPA, 2013). It is important not only to build new but also to maintain existing transport infrastructure, as properly functioning infrastructure helps to improve the investment climate.

Greater investment is needed. Public funds are the biggest source of infrastructure financing in India, but public resources are limited and the country's infrastructure consequently fails to meet demand. Alternative financing options need to be found. One such option is the involvement of the private sector through PPP projects. By March 2012, 390 PPPs had been approved for projects in transport, healthcare and education (Planning Commission of India, 2013). Nevertheless, implementation frequently comes up against issues like land acquisition delays and uneven risk sharing. Co-ordination between central and state governments can also be an obstacle and cause of delays. The newly-elected administration has thus sought to upgrade the infrastructure framework and reach out to the state governments run by its political allies to resolve land acquisition problems related to large projects.

Renewable energy for the future

The country's energy demand has increased with economic growth. The power supply is limited, however, which led to a large 9.2% supply shortfall in December 2012, with the greatest shortage reaching 16.8% in southern India. Although the Twelfth Plan has targeted electricity provision for all villages by 2017, shortages are likely to be an impediment to meeting the target. Only greater investment can meet the country's high electricity demand, which in turn requires new and upgraded energy infrastructure – in generation, transmission, distribution, transportation and equipment. Each of those sectors – distribution as much as generation and transmission – requires careful, improved management to avoid bottlenecks in supply.

A further imperative is to make greater use of renewable energy sources to reduce dependency on limited fossil fuel resources. These accounted for more than 72% of India's total energy consumption in 2011, up from 2004's 67% (World Bank, 2014). Coal remains the single most widely used fuel in India despite slowed mining development stemming from such obstacles as slow land acquisition and strict environmental protections (IEA, 2012). For long-term sustainability, alternative energy resources – like wind, solar and hydro power – need to be developed and encouraged.

Increasing access to finance

Financial inclusion is another challenge. In India, 41% of households do not have any access to banking services, according to the 2011 Census. Access to banking services is lower in rural areas, particularly in the states of Assam, Bihar, Odisha and Madhya Pradesh. The government has set itself the target of making banking services accessible to 90% of households by 2017. The issue of access to finance, though, concerns not only households, but firms, too, particularly MSMEs. Only between 33% and 34% of MSMEs have access to banks and institutional financing channels (ASSOCHAM and Resurgent India, 2013). Limited access to finance can prevent smaller firms from growing to their full potential.

The government and Reserve Bank of India (RBI) have striven to expand the reach of banking services. In 2011, the government issued the *Strategy and Guidelines on Financial Inclusion*, advising banks to open branches in under-serviced districts, expand their ATM networks and ensure that every household had at least one bank account. Banks have been given permission to appoint intermediaries – business facilitators and correspondents – to provide financial and banking services. In another move, the government launched the so-called "Swabhimaan" Financial Inclusion Campaign in 2011. Banking services help deliver the access to finance that is necessary to developing businesses and encouraging entrepreneurship. Nevertheless, alternative business financing practices like rural credit cooperatives should also be further encouraged.

India's banking sector liberalisation, associated with trade liberalisation, has contributed to reallocating funds to the most productive firms (Bas and Berthou, 2012). However, the lack of access to credit may inhibit many SMEs that are not yet productive. Although credit guarantee schemes do ease such constraints, the government should monitor the situation in order to avoid financial risks.

Figure 2.8.1. **Growth in manufacturing and services, 2009-10 to 2011-12**

Manufacturing and services growth rate and share to GDP

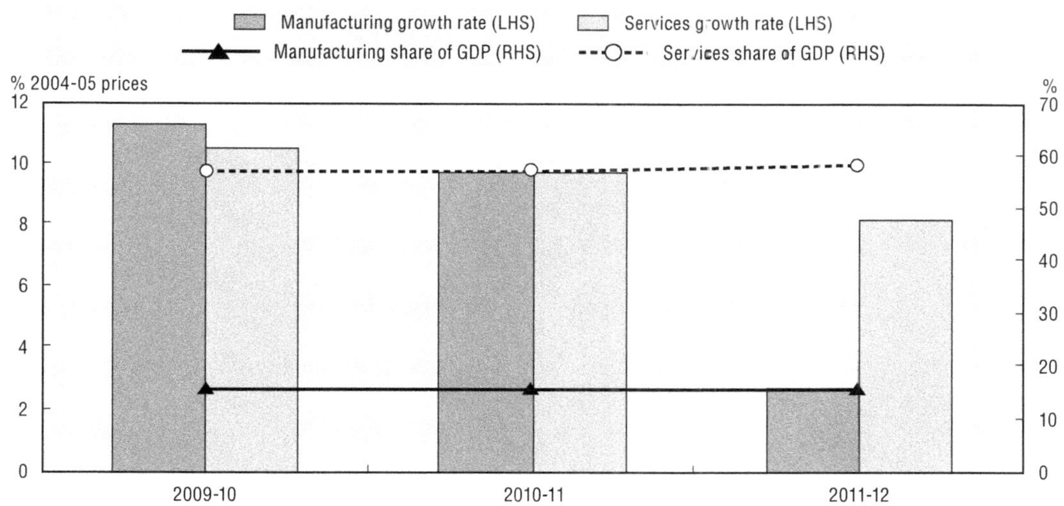

Source: Planning Commission of India (2013), *Twelfth Five-Year Plan (2012-2017): Faster, More Inclusive and Sustainable Growth*, 3 vols., Planning Commission, Government of India.

StatLink http://dx.doi.org/10.1787/888933179788

Figure 2.8.2. **Population below poverty line by state, 2011-12**

Millions of people in poverty (Tendulkar methodology) in selected states

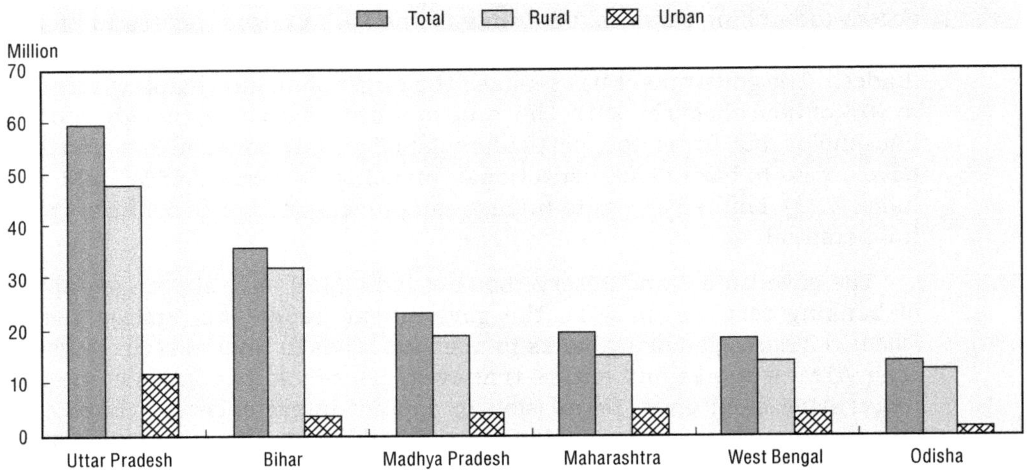

Note: Tendulkar methodology is adopted by the government of India based on recommendations of an expert group in 2009. In addition to food, the method also includes spending on education and health.

Source: Planning Commission of India (2013), *Twelfth Five-Year Plan (2012-2017): Faster, More Inclusive and Sustainable Growth*, 3 vols., Planning Commission, Government of India.

StatLink http://dx.doi.org/10.1787/888933179794

References

ABB (2011), *China: Energy Efficiency Report*, ABB Country Report, http://www05.abb.com/global/scot/scot316.nsf/veritydisplay/63246e62080610aec12578640050f217/$file/china.pdf.

Agarwala, R. (1983), "Planning in developing countries: Lessons of experience", *World Bank Staff Working Papers*, No. 576, World Bank, Washington, DC.

ASSOCHAM (Associated Chambers of Commerce and Industry of India) and Resurgent India (2013), *Indian Banking Industry: Sustaining Growth with Equity*, ASSOCHAM and Resurgent India, September.

BAPPENAS (2013), *Evaluasi Paruh Waktu RPJMN 2010-2014 (Mid-term Evaluation of the RPJMN 2010-2014)*, BAPPENAS, Jakarta.

Bas and Berthou (2012), "The unequal effects of financial development on firms' growth in India", *Centre d'Etudes Prospectives et d'Informations Internationales Documents de Travail*, No. 2012-22, CEPII, Paris, October, http://www.cepii.fr/PDF_PUB/wp/2012/wp2012-22.pdf.

BSP (Bankgo Sentral ng Pilipinas) (2013), *Report on the State of Financial Inclusion in the Philippines – 2013 Data Updates*, Inclusive Finance Advocacy Staff Supervision and Examination Sector, Bankgo Sentral ng Pilipinas, Manila.

BSP (Bankgo Sentral ng Pilipinas) (2012), *Report on the State of Financial Inclusion in the Philippines – 2012 Data Updates*, Inclusive Finance Advocacy Staff Supervision and Examination Sector, Bankgo Sentral ng Pilipinas, Manila.

Cornell University, INSEAD and WIPO (2014), *The Global Innovation Index 2014: The Human Factor in Innovation*, Fontainebleau, Ithica and Geneva, https://www.globalinnovationindex.org/userfiles/file/reportpdf/GII-2014-v5.pdf.

DOSM (Department of Statistics Malaysia) (2012), *Economic Census 2011: Profile of SMEs*, Department of Statistics Malaysia, Putrajaya.

EPPO (2013), *Annual Report 2012*, Energy Policy and Planning Office, Energy Ministry of Thailand.

General Statistics Office of Vietnam (2014), *Report on Labour Force Survey 2013*, Ministry of Planning and Investment, Ha Noi.

Government of Malaysia (2010), *Tenth Malaysia Plan 20112015*, Economic Planning Unit, Prime Minister's Department, Putrajaya, www.epu.gov.my/epu-theme/RMKE10/rmke10_english.html.

IEA (International Energy Agency) (2012), *Understanding Energy Challenges in India: Policy, Players, and Issues*, International Energy Agency, Paris.

IMF (2013a), *Energy Subsidy Reform: Lessons and Implications*, International Monetary Fund, Washington, DC.

IMF (2013b), *Myanmar 2013 Article IV Consultation and First Review Under the Staff-Monitored Program*, International Monetary Fund, Washington, DC, August.

Kornai, J. (1970), "A general descriptive model of planning processes", *Economics of Planning*, Vol. 10, No. 1-2, pp. 1-18.

La Forgia, G. and Nagpal, Somil (2012), *Government-Sponsored Health Insurance in India: Are you covered?*, World Bank, Washington DC.

Liping, Zhang and S.J. Evenett (2010), *The Growth of China's Services Sector and Associated Trade: Complementarities between Structural Change and Sustainability*, International Institute for Sustainable Development (IISD), Winnipeg.

MADB (Myanmar Agriculture Development Bank) (2013), *Welcome to MADB* (presentation), MADB, Yangon.

MNPED (Ministry of National Planning and Economic Development, Myanmar) (2013), *Framework for Economic and Social Reforms – Policy Priorities for 2012-2015 towards the Long-Term Goals of the National Comprehensive Development Plan*, Ministry of National Planning and Economic Development, Nay Pyi Taw, January.

MPC (Malaysia Productivity Corporation) (2013a), *Productivity Watch*, Malaysia Productivity Corporation, Petaling Jaya, June, www.mpc.gov.my/Publication/ProductivityWatch1.pdf.

MPC (Malaysia Productivity Corporation) (2013b), *Productivity Report 2012/2013*, Malaysia Productivity Corporation, Petaling Jaya, www.mpc.gov.my/publication/APR2013.pdf.

Mudiarasan, K., M. Raman and G. Lee (2009), "Whose ICT investment matters to economic growth: private or public? The Malaysian perspective", *Electronic Journal on Information Systems in Developing Countries* (EJISDC), Vol. 37, No. 7, pp. 1-19.

Munusamy, M. (2008), "Development of SMEs in Malaysia", presentation at the Joint Regional Workshop on SME Development and Regional Economic Integration, Tokyo, 22-27 September.

Myanmar Development Research (2014), *Draft Preliminary Social Assessment: Myanmar Decentralizing Funding to Schools Programme*, World Bank, Washington DC, www-wds.worldbank.org/external/default/WDSContentServer/WDSP/IB/2014/04/24/000371432_20140424102207/Rendered/PDF/E45170V20P14630Box385202B00PUBLIC0.pdf.

NEDA (National Economic and Development Authority) (2014), *Philippines Development Plan Midterm Update with Revalidate Results Matrices*, NEDA, Manila.

NEDA (National Economic and Development Authority) (2011), *Philippines Development Plan 2011-2016*, Results Matrices, NEDA, Manila.

NESDB (National Social and Economic Development Board) (2013), *First Year Progress Report*, National Economic and Social Development Board Office of the Prime Minister, Bangkok.

NESDB (2011), *Eleventh National Economic and Social Development Plan 2012-2016*, National Economic and Social Development Board Office of the Prime Minister, Bangkok.

NSDC (National SME Development Council) (2013), *SME Annual Report 2012-13: Embracing Changes*, NSDC, Kuala Lumpur, www.smecorp.gov.my/vn2/node/717.

NSDC (National SME Development Council) (2012), *SME Masterplan 2012-2020: Catalysing Growth and Income*, NSDC, Kuala Lumpur, www.smecorp.gov.my/vn2/node/190.

NSDC (National SME Development Council) (2008), *SME Annual Report 2007*. NSDC, Kuala Lumpur.

NUEPA (National University of Education Planning and Administration) (2013), *Elementary Education in Urban India: Where do we stand? Analytical reports 2011-12*, National University of Education Planning and Administration, New Delhi.

OECD (2013a), *Economic Outlook for Southeast Asia, China and India 2014: Beyond the Middle Income Trap*, OECD Publishing, Paris. http://dx.doi.org/10.1787/Saeo-2014-en

OECD (2013b), *OECD Economic Surveys: China*, OECD Publishing, Paris.

Oliver, J. et al. (2013), *Trends in Global CO_2 Emissions: 2013 Report*, Background Studies, PBL Netherlands Environmental Assessment Agency, The Hague.

Planning Commission of India (2013), *Twelfth Five-Year Plan (2012-2017): Faster, More Inclusive and Sustainable Growth*, 3 vols., Planning Commission, Government of India, New Delhi.

Planning Commission of India (2008), *Eleventh Five Year Plan (2007-2012): Inclusive growth, Volume 1*, Planning Commission, Government of India, New Delhi.

Roach, S. S. (2011), *China's 12th Five Year Plan: Strategy vs. Tactics*, Morgan Stanley Asia, April.

Sapie, N.M. (2014), "Government Incentives for Innovation Development of Small and Medium Sized Enterprises (SMEs) in Malaysia", *ASIAN Journal of Multidisciplinary Studies*, Vol. 2, Iss. 5, pp. 90-95, May.

Social Weather Stations (2013), "Third Quarter 2012 Social Weather Survey: 72% believe the K to 12 Program will give students more sufficient knowledge and preparation", Social Weather Stations website, www.sws.org.ph/pr20121106.htm (accessed 17 October 2014).

State Bank of Vietnam (2014), *Statistics on the Performance of Credit Institutions*, State Bank of Vietnam, Hanoi, www.sbv.gov.vn.

Suharyadi, A. and P. Sambodho (2013), "Assessment of policies to improve teacher quality and reduce teacher absenteeism", SMERU Working Paper, Jakarta, December.

Turner, M. and D. Hulme (1997), *Governance, Administration and Development: Making the State Work*, MacMilan, Basingstoke.

Waterston, A. (1966), "A hard look at development planning", *Finance and Development*, Vol. 3, No. 2, June, pp. 8591.

World Economic Forum (2013), *WEF Global Competitiveness Report 2013-2014*, World Economic Forum, Geneva, www3.weforum.org/docs/WEF_GlobalCompetitivenessReport_2013-14.pdf.

World Bank (2014), *World Development Indicators* (database), World Bank, Washington, DC.

World Bank (2013), *Skilling up Vietnam: Preparing the Workforce for a Modern Market Economy*, World Bank, Washington, DC, November.

World Bank (2012), "PKH Conditional Cash Transfers", *Social Assistance Programme and Public Expenditure Review*, No. 6, World Bank, Washington, DC.

Chapter 3

Key factors to succeed with public sector reforms across Emerging Asia

Recognising the importance of good institutions, recent decades have seen countries in Emerging Asia and around the world take an increased interest in public sector reform. Efforts to improve public financial management (through expenditure and tax administration reforms) and reform government administration (through anti-corruption initiatives, civil service reforms, and restructuring and decentralisation) can help to make government more efficient in using scarce resources and more responsive in providing public goods and services. The results of these reforms have varied with circumstance and the ways in which they were implemented. Generally, it can be concluded that public sector reforms are gradual processes that cannot be isolated from broader developments in the public and private sectors. At the same time, good design alone is not usually a guarantee of success, as political economy factors, such as the interests of influential stakeholders, often have considerable influence on the outcomes of reforms.

Introduction

Since the 1970s, Emerging Asian countries – like developed and developing countries in other regions – have been particularly active in reforming their public sectors. These public sector reforms (PSRs) are motivated by the recognition that the effectiveness and efficiency of the public sector in managing its finances, implementing government programmes and delivering public services are critical to the success of overall development and the achievement of key development objectives. The rapid growth and profound transformation that Emerging Asia has undergone have made PSRs of special importance to the region.

The scope, extent and sophistication of PSRs have increased considerably over time as best practices – and, in some areas, models for their pursuit – have developed out of country experiences and the support of major multilateral organisations. However, despite progress and many instances of tangible benefits, the overall experience has been somewhat disappointing. The implementation of PSRs has all too often been uneven or incomplete, and the benefits often not sustained. Civil service reforms and efforts to combat corruption have proved particularly difficult to carry out successfully.

This chapter examines the state of public sector institutions in ASEAN countries, China and India and the lessons to be drawn from their public sector reform experiences. One key lesson is that the effectiveness of PSR depends not only on the design of reforms, but on political economy factors – particularly the degree to which reforms align or conflict with vested interests inside and outside government. Country experiences also underscore that PSRs are best viewed as evolutionary processes requiring on-going development, refinement, and correction. They need to be skilfully sequenced in line with the development of key support capacities and institutions within the government and across the economy. Two factors seem to be particularly important to success:

- sustained commitment from the most senior echelons of government to the implementation of reform; and
- an institutionalised process of reform in a self-reinforcing progression from basic to more sophisticated measures.

Political and bureaucratic cultures have widely proved to be considerable constraints on what can be accomplished with PSRs, particularly in certain areas.

Taxonomy of public sector reforms and their broader implications

Public sector reform comprises measures to determine how government should best organise to carry out its policies. It can be divided broadly into two categories: **public financial management reforms** (PFM) and **administrative reforms** (Table 3.1).

Table 3.1. **Types of public sector reforms**

Reform	Key elements	Key objectives	Potential economic/social benefits
Public financial management			
Tax administration	Reorganisation of tax authority; reform of procedures for collection and compliance; upgrading of information systems, including introduction of ICT	Increased revenue yield and efficiency; reduced burden on private sector; improved government credibility	Improved resource allocation and productivity; enhanced growth potential; private sector development; improved public trust and accountability
Public expenditure management (PEM)	Budgeting reforms; incorporation of planning goals in budgets; improved monitoring, transparency and accountability	Fiscal soundness; alignment of expenditures with national objectives; improved delivery of public services	Poverty reduction and other social needs; enhanced potential growth; public trust and accountability
Administrative reforms			
Civil service	Merit-based and inclusive recruitment; reformed pay scales; performance based monitoring and career advancement	Increased efficiency, integrity and credibility; quality of services	Poverty reduction and progress on other social issues; improved public trust and accountability
Anti-corruption	Strengthening of legal/ regulatory frameworks; establishment of anti-corruption agencies; measures to improve transparency and accountability to the public	Increased efficiency, integrity and credibility	Public trust and accountability
Organisational reforms	Streamlining of tasks; improved matching of competencies and responsibilities	Increased efficiency and quality of services	More efficient use of resources and more responsive government
Central government	Reorganisation of ministries and other agencies	Improved alignment of spending with needs; efficiency in implementation of programmes	Improved policy formulation and implementation; greater efficiency in the use of government resources
Decentralisation	Political, administrative devolution of responsibilities and powers to sub-national governments; expenditure and revenue assignments and inter-government transfers	Greater local autonomy; improved programme/service delivery	Services better tailored to local needs; more effective poverty reduction and inclusive economic growth; greater national cohesiveness

Source: OECD Development Centre.

Public financial management and administrative reforms cover six areas of public sector organisation and activities that all contain sets of interdependent policies.

- **Public expenditure management reforms** involve measures to improve the coherence and comprehensiveness of budget formulation and its responsiveness to government objectives; to strengthen budget execution and control; and to improve budget accountability and transparency through reforms to accounting, reporting and auditing systems (Allen and Tommasi, 2001; WB-IEG, 2008).
- **Tax administration reforms** focus chiefly on the organisation and powers of the government bodies responsible for collecting revenues; rules and other arrangements governing the interaction of government bodies with taxpayers; and personnel training, IT development and other measures to improve the institutional capacities of the organs.
- **Central government organisational reforms** have typically focused on restructuring government ministries and major departments and their responsibilities, mechanisms for determining the allocation of resources across and within ministries, and co-ordination among ministries and their oversight by government political authorities and legislatures.

- **Decentralisation reforms** involve the reorganisation of political powers and responsibilities across government levels, with a special focus on the division of expenditure, tax and other fiscal functions (including, where applicable, their sharing); and mechanisms for co-ordinating their policies. For example, the 2008 Constitution of Myanmar established a Financial Commission as the body that co-ordinates budgeting between the Union Government and the governments of the states and regions (OECD, 2014).
- **Civil service reforms** typically focus on procedures and criteria for recruitment, performance evaluation, career development and the promotion of government employees, including senior civil servants. These reforms may also include the introduction of mechanisms for ensuring the integrity and reasonable consistency of personnel policies.
- **Anti-corruption** reforms address the legal definition and enforcement of rules governing corruption within the civil service and among political officials, as well as (in some countries) broader abuses in the relations between government bodies and non-government interests and actors (e.g. state capture).

There are a number of elements common to all the above areas of reforms. The use of ICT to improve information systems has become an increasingly important focus of PSR, particularly reforms that address public expenditure management, tax administration and the civil service. Performance evaluation and other reporting systems (e.g. to flag violations of expenditure or personnel management procedures) are important components of all reforms, especially where these systems are most advanced. As discussed further below, the themes of shifting the focus of public sector management, particularly in public expenditure management and civil service reforms, toward results rather than inputs and the gradual replacement of command and control mechanisms with incentives and other market type mechanisms have had considerable influence on the design of PSRs, although their feasibility and cost-effectiveness remain controversial.

Historical country experiences have led to the development of best practices and models for PSR in certain areas. Some important examples are:

- medium-term budget frameworks (MTBFs) to replace the year-by-year budgeting that has been most common in developing countries;
- the development of single treasury accounts for public expenditure management reform; and
- the organisation of tax administration bodies along functional lines (instead of by type of tax) and the establishment of large taxpayer units to focus on the biggest taxpayers who typically account for a sizeable share of total tax revenue.

Experience has shown that such models and best practices need to be adapted to countries' existing institutional capacities. For example, there are several kinds of medium-term budget framework, ranging from frameworks emphasising the definition of and imposition of aggregate resource constraints in budgeting that are most suitable for countries in an early stage of development to more sophisticated frameworks including results-oriented budgeting techniques (WB-IEG, 2008). Best practices and models are less well-defined or accepted in other areas of PSR, particularly in civil service and anti-corruption reforms. For example, whether to concentrate anti-corruption efforts in a single agency or to divide them among several agencies remains controversial (World Bank, 2012a; WB-IEG 2008; Meagher, 2002).

Public sector reform has wide-reaching implications and potential benefits for economies and societies

The direct objective of public sector reform is to improve the formulation of government policy and the effectiveness and efficiency of its implementation. Countries with efficient public sectors are more likely to achieve government goals with lighter tax and other burdens for the public than those whose public sectors do not perform well.

Beyond the immediate benefits for government performance, public sector reform delivers a wide range of economic and social improvements, some of which are more easily quantified than others. Among the most easily identified economic effects are those on the climate for domestic and foreign private investment. The quality of public governance affects the investment climate in a number of ways:

- The efficiency of tax administration and government regulation directly affect the costs of forming and operating a business. For example, improvements in auditing and other compliance procedures reduce the time and number of separate steps businesses (and individuals) must go through to meet their tax obligations. Indeed, indicators of the costs of paying taxes are components of international rankings of country business climates and competitiveness, such as the World Bank's annual *Doing Business* reports. Successful efforts to improve the quality of the civil service and to combat corruption also help to reduce business costs by reducing the complexity of dealings with the government.
- PSR also helps to ease uncertainty in the business climate by making it easier for businesses and individuals to understand their legal obligations and by reducing arbitrariness in their implementation. The transparency and predictability of tax obligations and government regulations is an important element in calculations of domestic and foreign businesses' potential returns to investment in a country and the attendant risks.
- PSR's potential benefits for the investment climate also help to foster private sector development, particularly in countries in transition and those where the private sector has been severely constrained. Similarly, reforms to improve tax administration and to combat corruption have an important part to play in bringing informal business activities back into the formal sector.

Effectively functioning public sectors are equally important to the achievement of government development and social welfare goals. Poorly organised government activities, weak civil service quality, and the poorly managed formulation and execution of government expenditure are all likely to both waste scarce government resources and to impair the effectiveness of government programmes and services. For example, confusion and overlapping and conflicting responsibilities in government efforts to improve vocational education and training have severely damaged their effectiveness and become an important focus of reforms in a number of ASEAN countries, such as in Indonesia and Myanmar (OECD, 2013). Problems in managing infrastructure spending also blunted the effectiveness of fiscal stimulus programmes in Emerging Asia in the wake of the global financial crisis and, in some countries, delayed the alleviation of electricity shortages (OECD, 2012). Inconsistencies in the division of fiscal and other responsibilities between central and local governments have distorted expenditure decisions, reduced the overall effectiveness of government programmes and undermined control of public sector debt in many countries, a particularly notable example being China. They have also interfered with efforts to achieve more inclusive growth and to reduce poverty.

Public financial management reforms have important macroeconomic benefits for fiscal soundness and stability. As discussed below, improved revenue yields from tax administration reforms have helped to bolster fiscal positions in a number of developing Asian countries. The effective management of public expenditure is essential to ensuring that government spending and deficits are reasonably predictable and remain within sustainable levels. Transition countries face particularly serious risks to fiscal stability arising from the greater but incomplete autonomy accorded to state-owned enterprises (SOEs) and to financial institutions and, in the case of Myanmar, fiscal decentralisation. It is largely for that reason that budget reforms to keep public expenditure within available fiscal resources have been given high priority in transition countries such as Myanmar.

Beyond their potential economic impacts, public finance reforms are important for improving interactions between the government, political representatives and society. Greater transparency in disclosing the rationale behind government policies and the implications thereof is critical both to strengthening trust in governments and to the effectiveness of the policies themselves. Perceptions of a government's competence in pursuing its objectives and its freedom from corruption are critical to its overall credibility. In turn, credible governments are more likely to be able to sustain the public consensus needed to implement policies that are critical to development but take a long time to materialise. They are also better equipped for making the difficult, sometimes painful decisions required to deal with crises or other critical issues. A government's transparency and its adherence to the rule of law are also essential to its sustained accountability and to the effective participation of citizens and civil society organisations in the formulation and implementation of government policies.

Box 3.1. **The new public management paradigm**

New public management (NPM) reforms refer to public finance reforms that seek to incorporate market mechanisms in the formulation and implementation of government policies. The underlying principles are that government management should be oriented towards servicing the needs of citizens and be held accountable for results (Manning, 2000). Although there is considerable variation, NPM reforms are generally characterised by:

- the use of resource constraints and other incentives in place of command and control rules to manage government organs and to ensure that they act in accordance with overall government goals;
- the extensive use of objective indicators of performance and results in decisions on government programmes and on government personnel as regards hiring, compensation and advancement; and
- the introduction (in certain areas) of competition between government agencies and between government agencies and private sector entities.

Results-based budgeting, contracting for services from government bodies, and the linking of civil service promotions and compensation to objective performance indicators are all policies characteristic of NPM even though they are often used more widely in other contexts as well. NPM reforms have also typically involved decentralisation and the deconcentration of government activities to smaller, more autonomous units, often together with the extensive privatisation of government activities.

Box 3.1. The new public management paradigm (cont.)

OECD countries began ushering in NPM reforms in the 1980s. They were deployed most extensively in English-speaking countries, particularly the United Kingdom under the Thatcher government and New Zealand, where NPM reforms have arguably been the furthest-reaching and most durable. Most other OECD member countries – including the United States, most of continental Europe and Asian countries – have applied NPM more selectively and narrowly.

Developing countries in Asia and elsewhere have undertaken NPM sparingly. Indeed, many of those that have officially instituted NPM-type reforms have not applied them in practice (Polidano, 1999). The limited role for formal NPM reform in developing countries is largely a reflection of its need for relatively sophisticated organisational, technical and other capacities.

However, the influence of the basic concepts underlying NPM has been much more widespread than the formal adoption of NPM reforms would suggest. Among the NPM tenets that have influenced the design of PSRs in developing countries are: the desirability of results-based PFM over mainly input-based management, the building of civil service personnel management on principles applied in the private sector and the need to confine government functions (as far as possible) to those that cannot be carried out efficiently by the private sector.

Political economy factors as well as design shape public sector reform outcomes

A recent stocktake by the World Bank found that civil service reforms and anti-corruption reforms improved performances in less half and barely more than half, respectively, of the programmes it supported in these areas (Table 3.2) (WB-IEG, 2008). Outcomes were somewhat better for public financial management reforms, but even in these cases major improvements occurred in only one-third of the programmes.

Table 3.2. Results of public sector reforms carried out with World Bank support

Number of countries and percentage

Frequency of improvements according to Country Policy and Institutional Assessment (CPIA) indicators	Total number of countries	Share of countries by reform type	Share of countries with major improvement (>0.5)
Quality of budget and financial management (CPIA 13)			
Any public sector reform - public finance management lending	87	62%	28%
No public sector reform - public finance management lending	48	25%	10%
Quality of public administration (CPIA 15)			
Any public sector reform - civil service and administration lending	71	42%	10%
No public sector reform - civil service and administration lending	64	33%	16%
Efficiency of revenue mobilisation (CPIA 14)			
Any public sector reform - tax administration lending	44	70%	32%
No public sector reform - tax administration lending	91	52%	21%
Corruption, transparency and accountability (CPIA 16)			
Any public sector reform lending	93	53%	26%
No public sector reform lending	42	40%	7%

Notes: CPIA refers to the Country Policy Institutional Assessment Indicators used by the World Bank to assess public sector quality. Entries show the percentage and the number of countries that register an improvement in CPIA scores between the years 1999 and 2006 (or closest year available). Rows show this figure for subsets of countries based on the number and type of investment loans approved or active fiscal 1999-2006 and development policy loans approved fiscal 1999-2006.

Source: World Bank Independent Evaluation Group (WB-IEG) (2008), *Public Sector Reform: What Works and Why? An IEG Evaluation of World Bank Support*, World Bank, Washington, DC.

These mixed outcomes demonstrate that PSRs are difficult processes and raise the question: what makes them more or less successful? Two general observations drawn from historical experience can be made about the nature of public sector reforms that have important implications for the conditions under which they may be more or less effective.

First, PSRs are **longer-term evolutionary processes** whose fruits generally materialise gradually over the long term. Reforms require a process of learning within government before their benefits can be fully reaped. PSR design needs to be based on and evolve with broader institutional capabilities such as: accounting, legal and regulatory infrastructure; private sector development; the rule of law; and institutional arrangements for civil society and interactions between citizens and government. For example, the design of budgeting system reforms depends on broader accounting, legal and information systems that condition what the reforms can accomplish. Thus, PSRs are rarely capable of being effectively implemented in the short term and, even when they are initially successful, the adage, "good work leads to more work", applies.

Second, **good design alone is not usually a guarantee of success**: PSR also depends critically on key political economy factors specific to the country in which they are undertaken (Bunse and Fritz, 2012; World Bank, 2013a). Most important is the degree to which reforms are perceived as being in the interests of, or conflicting with, those of key stakeholders within the political sphere and government bureaucracy, as well as business and other outside stakeholders. Some political and bureaucratic cultures have proved especially difficult environments for PSR, particularly those where formal lines of authority within the government and civil service exist alongside informal and unsanctioned, yet strong, relations, such as those of the patron-client kind.

Stocktaking of public sector reform progress in Emerging Asia

Before considering the lessons from past public sector reforms in Emerging Asia, it would be useful to examine the current states of the major public sector functions discussed earlier. They may be viewed partly as the reflection of PSR outcomes and partly of other factors. However, any evaluation is necessarily a very crude and tentative undertaking, so the measurements presented below should be regarded as indicative only (Box 3.2). Indicators of civil service or organisational quality are especially limited, so the discussion focuses on public financial management and corruption.

Box 3.2. **Limitations of indicators of public sector performance**

Substantial effort has been made over the past two decades by the World Bank, the IMF and a number of international forums to develop objective indicators of the quality of public sector functions. These indicators have been developed to allow those working on public sector reforms and those affected by them to make cross-country comparisons of public sector quality. The indicators are also designed to enable changes in quality to be tracked over time – in part to facilitate evaluation of the effectiveness of specific types of PSRs.

The resulting indicators fall into three basic types. The first are measures, typically from surveys, of perceptions by businesses, the public and experts of the quality of some aspect of public sector governance. An example is the *Perceptions of Corruption Index* published by Transparency International that is based on surveys of the public in each country.

The second type of indicator focuses on whether or not certain facets of public sector functions thought to be important to their effectiveness are present or not, and to what degree. The scores used by the World Bank to evaluate PFM performance and track its progress over time are primary examples of this type of indicator.

Box 3.2. **Limitations of indicators of public sector performance** (*cont.*)

The third type of indicator is a more direct measurement of an aspect of public sector performance in specific areas. For example, figures for the amount of time required to pay taxes and the number of procedural steps involved – both of which are reported in the World Bank's *Global Competitiveness* surveys – are fairly direct measures of the performance of tax authorities.

All three sets of indicators are subject to limitations. Perceptions of public sector quality tend to be backward-looking and slow to reflect the effects of recent PSRs. They may also be blunt in the sense that they are often affected by other conditions that are not related, or only tangentially, to public sector performance. Indicators of formal government structures and arrangements, which make up most of the second set of indicators, measure the effectiveness of the outcomes of public sector functions seldom directly, or at best imperfectly. For example, an indicator showing that a country has some process for multi-year budgeting does not by itself reveal whether the process is effective. The third set of indicators often provide a more direct indicator of the effects of public sector functions but they have been developed for a relatively limited array of functions. Furthermore, none of the three sets of indicators can directly measure the broader effects of PSRs on economic growth or other development objectives. Equally, most of the indicators are available only for a limited number of recent years, so cannot yet paint a clear picture of how the effectiveness of public sector governance has evolved over time.

Public governance quality is roughly correlated with level of development

Various indicators suggest that the overall quality of public governance tends to be positively correlated with countries' level of development. The pattern is illustrated by the *Government Effectiveness Index*, a composite measure of public perceptions produced by the World Bank from a wide range of sources of the quality of public services and the civil service, the effectiveness of policy formulation and implementation, and the credibility of the government in carrying out its policies. The government rankings of developing Asian countries with low *per capita* incomes are generally lower than those higher-income countries and well below the scores of major OECD member countries (Figure 3.1).

The positive association between income and effectiveness largely reflects the fact that the sophistication and effectiveness of public sector functions rest on broader institutional capacities that develop over time along with the economy and society at large. However, the correlation is only rough. According to the *Government Effectiveness Index*, some countries, such as the Philippines, appear to perform somewhat better than their *per capita* incomes might suggest, while some other countries seem to underperform.

A broadly similar pattern holds for another set of indicators – the *Institutional Policy Profiles* of public governance published by the French *Centre d'Études Prospectives et d'Informations Internationales* (CEPII). They are based on a variety of survey and other indicators. As with the World Bank's aggregate indicators, lower income countries tend to score less well than countries with higher *per capita* incomes on the overall quality of public services, the capacity for structural reform and the effectiveness of the policy making process (Figure 3.2). Again, however, the association is only approximate. China, for example, seems to score somewhat more favourably than some of its higher-income regional peers, notably Malaysia and Thailand.

Figure 3.1. **Indicators of overall governance quality in 2012**

Government Effectiveness Index percentile rankings

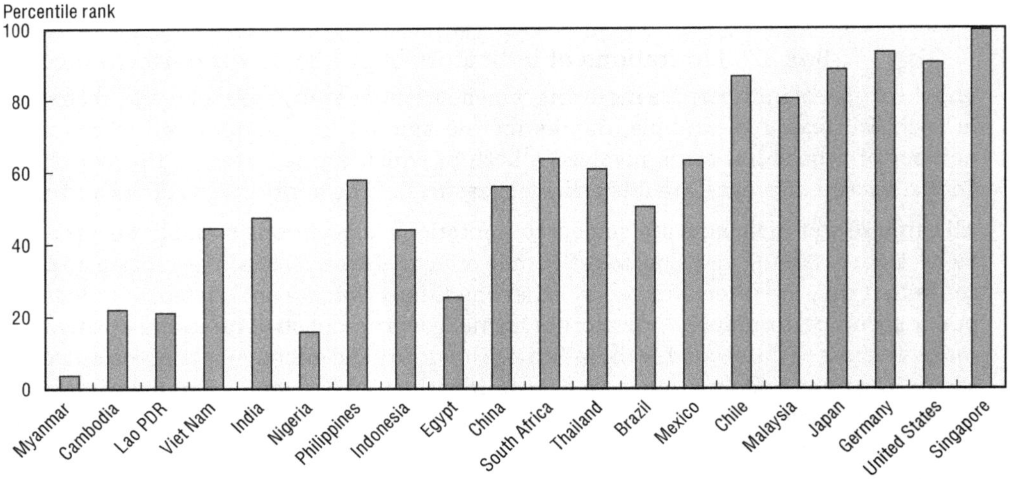

Notes: Figure shows percentile rank among all countries (ranging from 0 [lowest] to 100 [highest] ranks). Countries are arranged from lowest to highest *per capita* income at purchasing power parities. It reflects perceptions of the quality of public services, the quality of the civil service and the degree of its independence from political pressures, the quality of policy formulation and implementation, and the credibility of the government's commitment to such policies.

Source: World Bank (2014a), *World Governance Indicators* (database), World Bank, Washington, DC.

StatLink http://dx.doi.org/10.1787/888933179801

Figure 3.2. **Detailed indicators of government capacity in 2012**

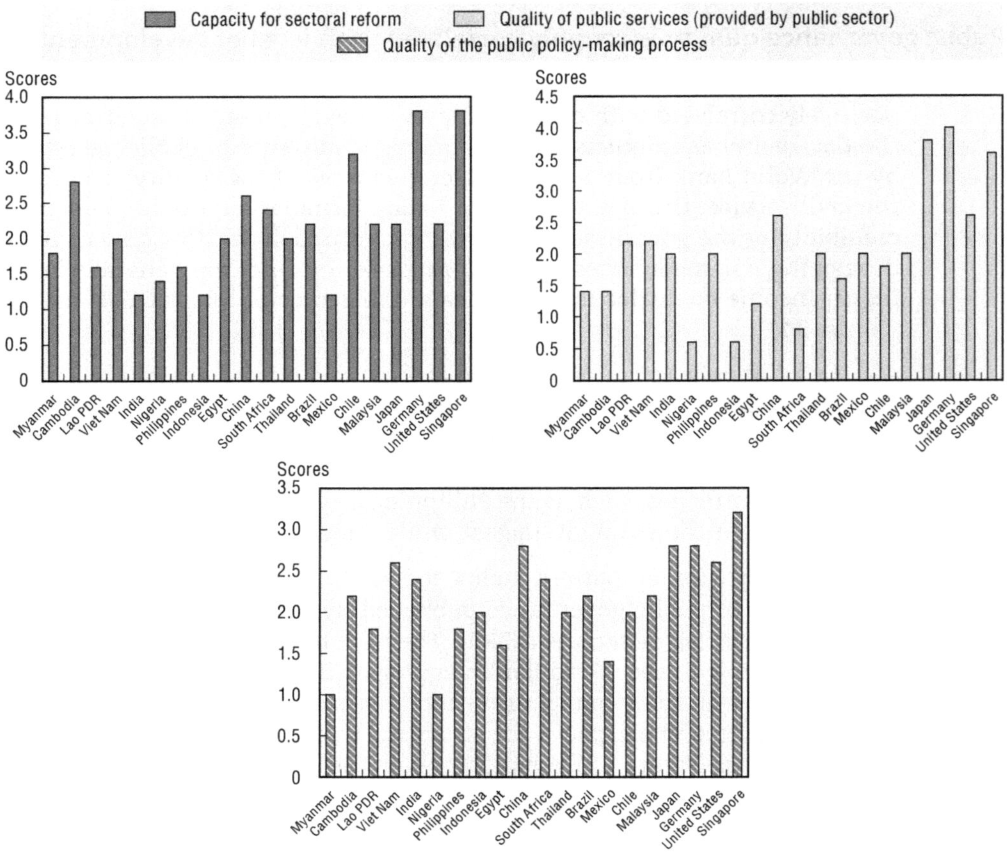

Notes: Scores range from 0 = very low to 4 = very good. Countries are arranged in ascending order of *per capita* income from the left.

Source: CEPII, *Institutional Profiles Database* (database), Centre d'Études Prospectives et d'Informations Internationales, Paris, http://www.cepii.fr/institutions/EN/ipd.asp.

StatLink http://dx.doi.org/10.1787/888933179811

Information on trends in indicators of overall public sector quality is fairly limited, chiefly because most were developed only relatively recently. The World Bank's *Government Effectiveness Index*, however, which goes back to 1996, does not show any clear trend among ASEAN member countries, except for Myanmar, whose score has fallen since 2000 (Figure 3.3). The index rose noticeably for China and India through the middle of the last decade, but has since fallen back. The lack of a clear upward trend in the indicator in most ASEAN countries should not be taken as necessarily indicating that PSRs have been unsuccessful, or that public sector governance has not improved in absolute terms. It should be seen more as a reflection of perception indicators' tendency to be based on comparisons with country peers rather than comparisons with idealised benchmarks of optimal governance. Similarly, the recent apparent declines in the standing of China and India may simply be that their reform efforts have slowed more sharply than elsewhere.[1]

Figure 3.3. **Trends in the Government Effectiveness Indicator in ASEAN countries, China and India**

Government Effectiveness Indicator score (estimate)

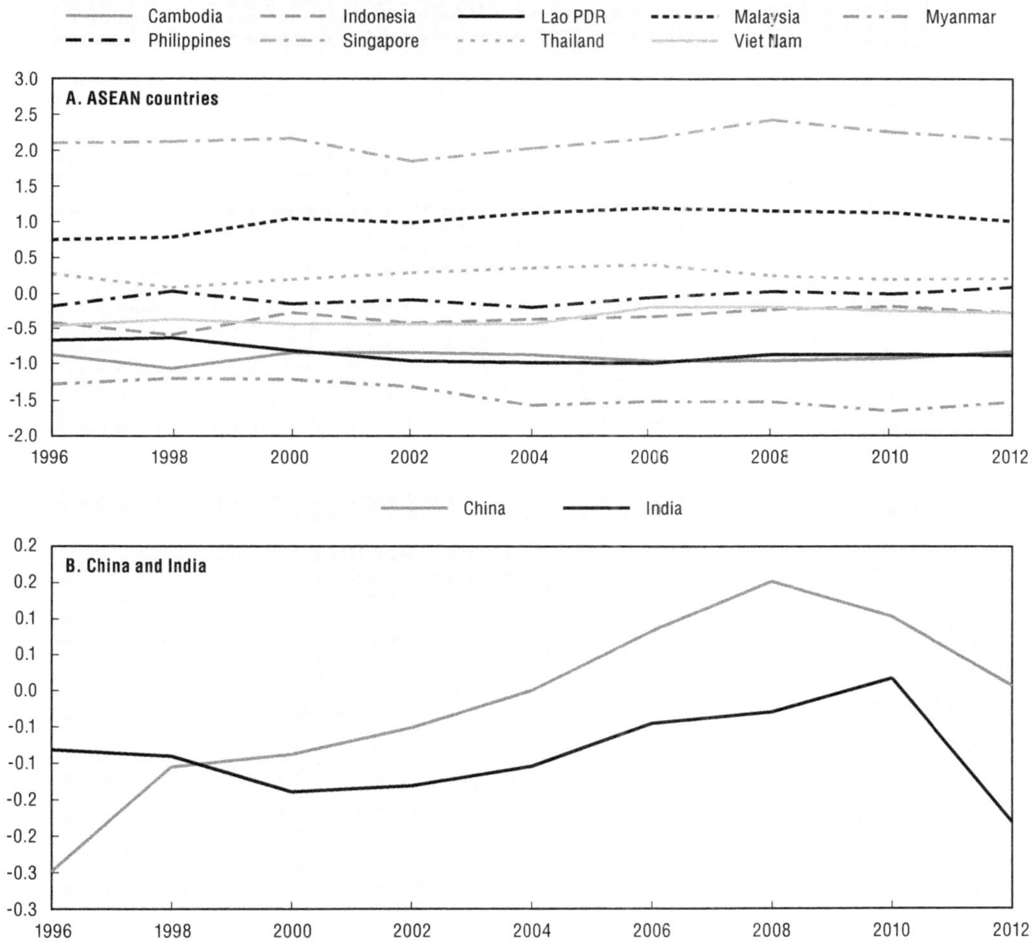

Notes: Higher scores indicate greater effectiveness. Scores are graded along a standard normal distribution, for approximately -2.5 to 2.5.

Source: World Bank (2014a), *Worldwide Governance Indicators* (database), World Bank, Washington, DC.

StatLink http://dx.doi.org/10.1787/888933179821

Overall, these aggregate measures do highlight the complex, multi-dimensional nature of public sector governance. While rough and tentative, they at least underscore the fact that the quality of public sector institutions in the ASEAN countries, China and India will need to continue to improve if they are to reach the levels that prevail in most developed countries.

Progress in implementing public financial management reforms has been varied

Public expenditure management and tax administration functions are both made up of many dimensions that together determine their overall effectiveness (Allen and Tommasi, 2001; World Bank, 2012a). The most effective public expenditure management systems all share certain key components: multi-year rather than annual budgeting, the use of single treasury accounts rather than multiple accounts to pay government bills and control expenditure effectively, and the integration of the budgeting for current and capital expenditures. The most advanced public expenditure management systems also use results-based budgeting, in which expenditure allocations are linked to programme outcomes and their contributions to government objectives rather than to inputs (Asia Pacific COP and MFDR, 2011).

All those PEM components offer yardsticks for evaluating the state of development of individual countries' public expenditure management systems. Most countries in Emerging Asia have adopted some of them, albeit to varying degrees (Table 3.3). All the middle-income ASEAN countries, together with China and India, have single treasury accounts, which are also under development in Cambodia and Lao PDR. In fact, nearly all countries in the region now have or are developing early-stage systems for medium-term budgeting.

In Cambodia, Lao PDR, Myanmar and Viet Nam, the focus is on ensuring that budgeted expenditures are compatible with medium-term aggregate fiscal frameworks, while some middle-income ASEAN countries and China also seek to align budgets with medium-term national and sector priorities. No country, however, has yet developed comprehensive medium-term frameworks based on performance measures and in which expenditure allocations are explicitly linked to results – a budget system that requires advanced institutional capabilities most likely to be found in the highest-income countries. Although some countries such as Indonesia, Malaysia and Thailand have introduced some initial elements of performance-based budgeting, most of Emerging Asia continues to separate budgeting for current and capital spending. These three countries integrate the two kinds of expenditure, and even then only partially.

Table 3.3. **Selected public expenditure management benchmarks in Emerging Asia**

Country	Medium-term budgeting	Treasury single account	Integration of current and capital budgeting*
ASEAN countries			
Cambodia	Medium-Term Budget Framework (MTBF)	Yes - developing	No - separate
Indonesia	Medium-Term Fiscal Framework (MTFF)	Yes	Partial
Lao PDR	None	In process of implementation	No - separate
Malaysia	Medium-Term Fiscal Framework (MTFF)**	Yes	No - separate
Myanmar	None	No	No - separate
Philippines	Medium-Term Fiscal Framework (MTFF)	Yes	No - separate
Singapore	Medium-Term Performance Framework (MTPF)	Yes	Partial
Thailand	Medium-Term Budget Framework (MTBF)	Yes	Partial
Viet Nam	Medium-Term Fiscal Framework (MTFF)	No	No - separate
China and India			
China	None	Yes	No - separate
India	Limited	Yes	No - separate

Notes: * Indicator P1-12(IV) from World Bank PEFA scores. ** A medium-term budget framework (MTBF) is in the process of being developed.
Source: World Bank (2013a), *Beyond the Annual Budget: Global Experiences with Medium-Term Expenditure Frameworks*, World Bank, Washington, DC.

Under the framework used by the World Bank,[2] the quality of country public expenditure management systems is collectively determined by institutions and arrangements to:

- formulate budgets coherently and consistently;
- ensure that budgets reflect national planning and other objectives;
- provide control and predictability of budgeted expenditures;
- ensure that budgets are comprehensive and transparent; and
- ensure the budget decisions and related PFM processes are accountable to legislators, outside auditors and the public.

The scores in these areas from the latest World Bank country PEM assessments further highlight the fact that PEM systems in Emerging Asian countries are more advanced in some areas than in others, with some lower-income countries sometimes out-performing their higher-income peers (Table 3.4). About half of the countries recorded deviations between aggregate budgeted and realised government spending exceeding 10% in two or more of the three years leading up to the assessment, and substantially higher rates of deviations in individual spending components. While the expenditure deviations are partly attributable to unpredicted outside economic and other circumstances, the much smaller deviations between budgeted and realised revenues suggest that much is due to weaknesses in internal control systems.

Table 3.4. **World Bank public expenditure and financial assessment evaluations in Emerging Asia**

Scores in the latest evaluation, 2009-13

Country	Year of latest evaluation	Aggregate expenditure out-turn compared to original approved budget (Performance Indicator-1)	Aggregate revenue out-turn compared to original approved budget (Performance Indicator-3)	Classification of the budget (Performance Indicator-5)	Comprehensiveness of information included in budget documentation (Performance Indicator-6)	Extent of unreported government operations (Performance Indicator-7)	Transparency of inter-governmental fiscal relations (Performance Indicator-8)	Orderliness and participation in the annual budget process (Performance Indicator-11)	Multi-year perspective in fiscal planning, expenditure policy and budgeting (Performance Indicator-12)	Effectiveness of internal audit (Performance Indicator-21)	Quality and timeliness of annual financial statements (Performance Indicator-25)	Scope, nature and follow-up of external audit (Performance Indicator-26)	Predictability of direct budget support (Donor Practices/D-1)
Cambodia	2011	B	A	C	B	C	C+	A	B	D+	D+	D+	C
Indonesia	2012	C	A	A	A	C+	B	A	C+	D+	B+	B+	B+
Lao PDR	2010	B	A	C	B	D+	D	C+	D+	D	D+	D+	D+
Myanmar	2013	C	B	D	D	D+	D	C+	D+	D+	D+	C+	NA
Philippines	2010	NR	A	D	B	A	B	B	D+	D+	D+	D+	NA
Thailand	2009	B	A	B	B	B+	D+	A	C	C+	C+	B	NU
Viet Nam	2013	C	A	NR	D	D	C+	B	C	A	B	C+	B
India	2010	C	A	A	A	A	B+	C+	D	D+	C+	D+	NU

Notes: Scores from D to A in ascending order of quality. NR denotes "not reported". NA denotes "not available". NU denotes "not used".

Source: World Bank, Public Expenditure and Financial Assessments (PEFA), World Bank, Washington DC, http://www.pefa.org/en/dashboard.

Most countries have scored relatively well for the overall comprehensiveness of their budgets, with the exception of Myanmar and Viet Nam. However, most also have substantial extra-budget and off-budget spending that is not included in the formal budget and which is often not as well controlled or integrated into overall budgeting as on-budget expenditure. In some cases, like Myanmar, extra-budget expenditure is as much as one-quarter of total spending (OECD, 2014; World Bank, 2013b). Generally speaking, internal and external auditing and reporting functions appear to be a relatively weak area of PEM management, with some exceptions. Most countries have developed their budgeting beyond the traditional year-by-year approach into a multi-year framework only to a limited degree – especially in incorporating multi-year fiscal projections and debt estimates and in linking current and investment expenditure.

The effectiveness of tax administration functions is shaped by:

- the way in which tax administration authorities are structured, which includes how they are insulated from undue interference from political or other outside influences;
- the coherence of taxpayer obligations and how transparent they are to taxpayers;
- the quality of systems for registering taxpayers; and
- the efficiency of systems for collecting taxes and ensuring compliance, which includes those handling tax arrears and tax appeals.

Taken together, these four elements largely shape the overall effectiveness with which taxes are collected and the costs to businesses and individuals of complying with their tax obligations.

More advanced and effective tax administrations are usually located in a body that is either separate from the main budget authority (usually the ministry of finance) or, if within that authority, has an explicitly independent status. These administrations also tend to be structured along functional lines rather than by kinds of taxes, often with units that deal with large taxpayers and, sometimes, other taxpayer segments. Tax administration offices in most Emerging Asian countries are still located within finance ministries, although those in Malaysia, the Philippines and Singapore are only affiliated with ministries and have a semi-independent status (Table 3.5). Only in China is there a separate body, the State Administration for Taxation.

Tax administration agencies in most countries are organised along functional lines, although less than half have yet established separate units to deal with large and other special taxpayer segments. Some countries, which include Myanmar, though, are currently developing large taxpayer units (OECD, 2014). There are substantial variations in the ratio of personal income taxpayers to the total labour force. They partly reflect the fact that lower *per capita* income countries have proportionately more households with incomes that are too low to be efficiently or fairly taxed.

The World Bank's tax administration scores are roughly comparable overall to those for public expenditure management (Table 3.6). Thailand scores comparatively well, while the rankings for Myanmar, at a much earlier stage of administrative development than other countries, are low. Most countries, except for Thailand, score relatively poorly in the overall effectiveness of tax collection.

Table 3.5. **Tax administration characteristics in ASEAN countries, China and India**

Country	Location of tax authority	Organisation of tax authority	Labour force/full-time equivalents in tax administration functions (2011)	Tax administration expenditures as percentage of net revenue collected (2011) (%)	Ratio of registered personal income tax payers to labour force (%)	Year-end tax debt outstanding to net revenue collected (2010) (%)	Tax debt collected to total debt outstanding (2011) (%)
ASEAN countries							
Cambodia	In Ministry of Finance (MOF)	Functional	5 809*	NA	NA	NA	NA
Indonesia	In MOF	Functional	3 737	0.55	17.2	6.0	NA
Lao PDR	In MOF	Functional	2 966*	NA	NA	NA	NA
Malaysia	Affiliated with MOF	Functional	1 242	1.09	53.8	10.3	36
Myanmar	In MOF	Functional	8 565	0.40	1.5	5.5	31
Philippines	Affiliated with MOF	Functional	3 851	0.71	28.8	6.5	21.8
Singapore	Affiliated with MOF	Functional; tax item based	1 741	0.87	53.4	1.7	NA
Thailand	In MOF	Functional; tax item based	2 004	0.76	23.7	6.8	8.9
Viet Nam	In MOF	Functional; tax item based	NA	NA	NA	NA	NA
China and India							
China	Independent	Functional; tax item based; taxpayer segment based	1 041	NA	NA	NA	NA
India	In MOF	Functional; taxpayer segment based	10 968	0.55	6.9	26	NA

Notes: *Population divided by full-time equivalents in tax administration functions. NA denotes "not available".
Sources: Araki and Claus (2014), *A Comparative Analysis of Tax Administration in Asia and the Pacific*, Asian Development Bank, Manila, April; and national sources.

Table 3.6. **World Bank indicators of tax administration effectiveness in Emerging Asia**

Scores in the latest evaluation, 2009-13

Country	Year of assessment	Transparency of taxpayer obligations and liabilities (Performance Indicator-13)	Effectiveness of measures for taxpayer registration and tax assessment (Performance Indicator-14)	Effectiveness in collection of tax payments (Performance Indicator-15)
Cambodia	2011	B	C	D+
Indonesia	2012	B	C	D+
Lao PDR	2010	D+	C	NR
Myanmar	2013	C+	D+	D+
Philippines	2010	C	C	D+
Thailand	2009	A	B	A
Viet Nam	2013	C+	C+	C+
India	2010	C+	B+	D+

Notes: Scores "A" to "D" where A is best and D worst. NR denotes "not reported".
Source: World Bank, Public Expenditure and Financial Assessments (PEFA), World Bank, Washington DC, http://www.pefa.org/en/dashboard.

Figure 3.4. **Overall tax effort in Emerging Asia and global aggregate income categories**

Estimated tax effort ratio

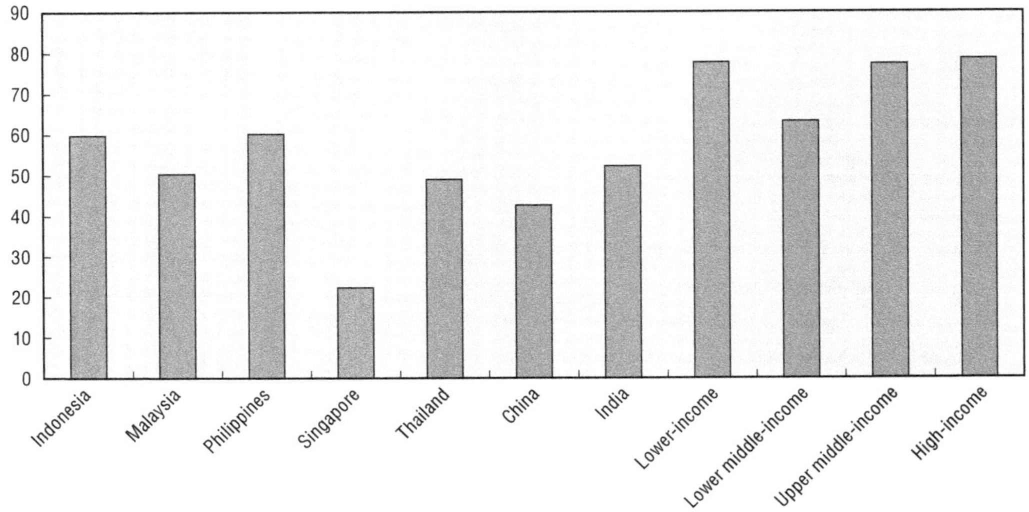

Note: The overall tax effort is the ratio of actual total tax revenues to the estimated amount of taxes owed if all provisions were fully complied with. Estimates are updated calculations based on Pessino and Fenochietto (2010). Countries are grouped according to the World Bank Atlas Method, which rates countries against the yardstick of their 2009 gross national income (GNI *per capita*). Low-income groups are USD 995 or less; lower middle-income, USD 996-3 945; upper middle-income, USD 3 946-12 195; and high-income, USD 12 196 or more. Information on estimated tax effort is the most recent year available.

Source: International Monetary Fund (2011), *Revenue Mobilisation in Developing Countries*, International Monetary Fund, Washington, DC, 8 March.

StatLink http://dx.doi.org/10.1787/888933179830

IMF estimates (Figure 3.4) suggest that Emerging Asian countries actually collect 60% or less of the taxes that are theoretically owed under existing tax laws, while in China the figure is barely more than 40% (IMF, 2011). The performance of Emerging Asian countries is, at best, comparable to and sometimes worse than the average of developing countries at their income level. Compliance burdens vary widely in the region, but are decreasing in a number of countries, such as China and Malaysia, where the number of required payments fell between 2006 and 2009, or Indonesia, Lao PDR and China, where the time taken to comply fell dramatically over 2006-14 (Figure 3.5). They rank relatively low for the overall time required to pay taxes and the number of procedures involved, both of which result in relatively high costs of compliance.

According to Transparency International's index, the general public in these countries believes corruption is at its most acute in the region's less-developed countries, with Myanmar bringing up the rear, Indonesia and Thailand next worst, and Malaysia and China slightly less bad. The perceptions of the business executives surveyed by the WEF are broadly similar, except that Lao PDR comes out of it better. The WEF rankings point to substantial petty corruption in the form of bribes for government favour and to corruption in the allocation of public funds.

Figure 3.5. **Costs to firms of paying taxes in Emerging Asia**

Number of payment and time required (in hours) per year, 2006-14

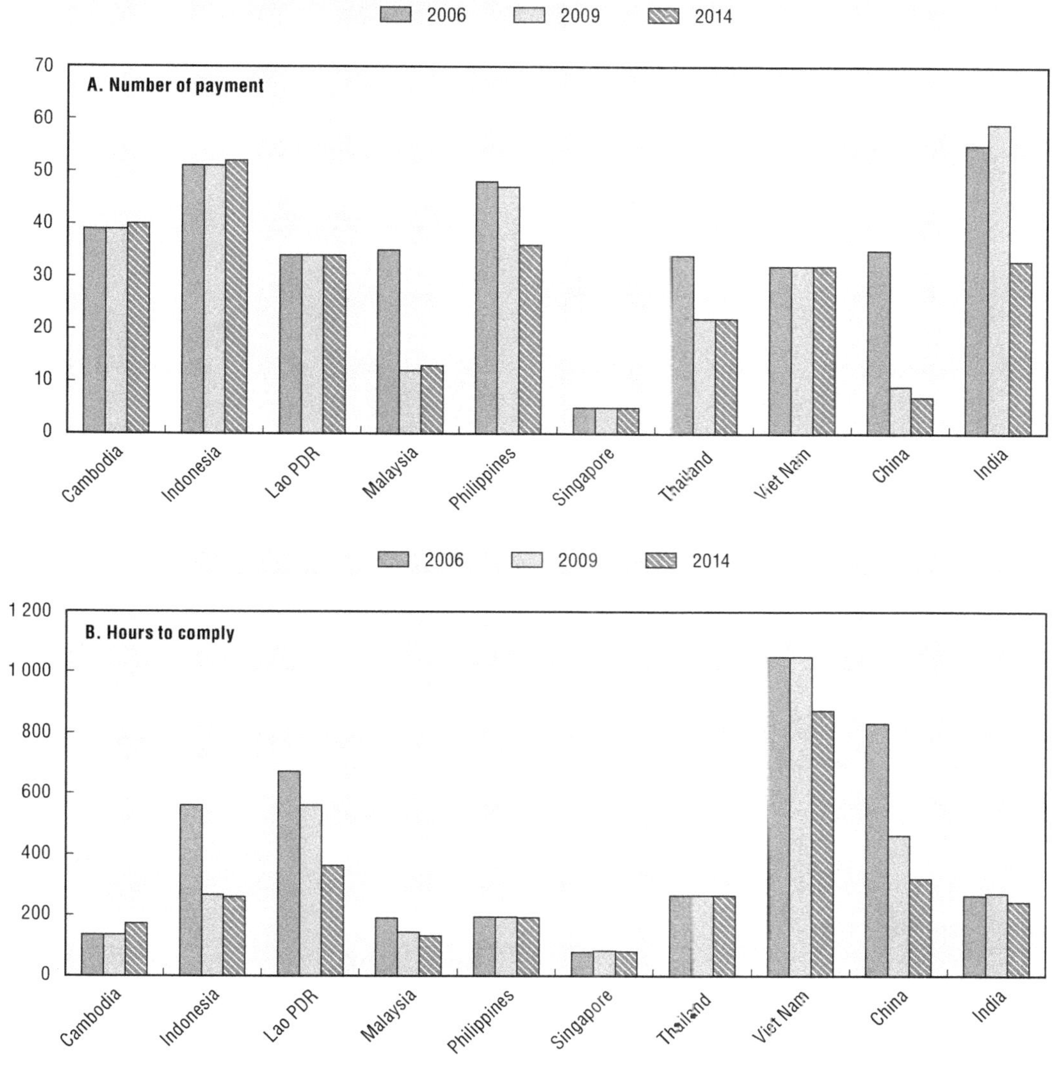

Source: World Bank (2014b), *Doing Business 2014*, World Bank, Washington, DC.

StatLink http://dx.doi.org/10.1787/888933179844

Corruption remains a significant problem with little improvement in most cases

As the next section states, corruption has been a principal focus of developing countries' efforts to reform and improve their civil services. The importance given to these reforms reflects the corrosive effects of corruption on the business climate and on public trust in government.

Large-scale surveys reveal that corruption continues to be a serious problem in nearly all Emerging Asian countries. Both the Transparency International *Corruption Perceptions Index*, based on extensive surveys of members of the public in the individual countries, and the corruption components of the World Economic Forum's *Global Competiveness Indicators*, drawn from surveys of business executives, place most Emerging Asian countries in the bottom half of their rankings (Figure 3.6 and Table 3.7).

Figure 3.6. **Perceptions of corruption in ASEAN countries, China and India**

Corruption Perception Index, 1995-2011

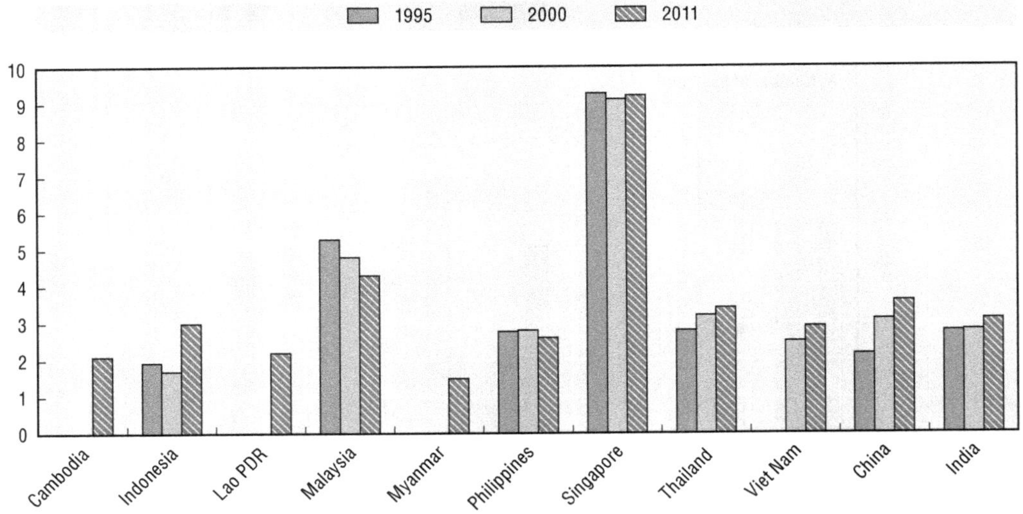

Note: The Corruption Perception Index ranks countries and territories based on how corrupt their public sector is perceived to be. A country/territory's score indicates the perceived level of public sector corruption on a scale of 0 to 10, where 0 denotes "highly corrupt" and 10 "very clean". A country's rank indicates its position relative to the other countries and territories in the index.

Source: Transparency International, *Corruption Perception Index*, Transparency International, Berlin.

StatLink http://dx.doi.org/10.1787/888933179853

Table 3.7. **Prevalence of types of corruption in ASEAN countries, China and India in 2013**

Scores and ranks

	Diversion of public funds		Irregular payments and bribes	
	Score	**Rank**	**Score**	**Rank**
ASEAN countries				
Cambodia	3.1	81	2.9	124
Indonesia	3.4	60	3.3	106
Lao PDR	3.7	54	3.7	85
Malaysia	4.2	42	4.7	44
Myanmar	2.3	128	2.3	145
Philippines	3.1	79	3.3	105
Singapore	6.1	5	6.5	3
Thailand	2.7	101	3.8	77
Viet Nam	3.2	74	3.1	116
China and India				
China	3.9	44	4	68
India	2.8	98	3.2	110

Note: "Diversion of Public Funds" shows the prevalence of the diversion of public funds to companies, individuals, or groups. "Irregular Payments and Bribes" shows how often firms make undocumented payments in respect of exports/imports; public utilities; taxation; the awarding of contracts; court decisions. Scores: [1 = very commonly occurs; 7 = never occurs]. Higher country ranks indicate greater frequency of diversion or irregular payments compared to lower ranks. Rankings are out of 148 countries.

Source: World Economic Forum (2013), *The Global Competitiveness Report 2013-2014*, World Economic Forum, Geneva.

The historical evolution of these indices also indicates that there has been little improvement in most countries in corruption perceptions since the mid-1990s. According to the Transparency International index, the most noticeable improvements have come in China and in Indonesia, which was last of the 41 countries ranked in 1995. By 2011, Indonesia had risen to near the middle of the entire group (100th out of 181), although it has since fallen back somewhat. The improvements in India, Thailand and Viet Nam have been modest.[3] The trends evidenced in the two indices underscore the difficulties countries have had in successfully combatting corruption.

Lessons from public sector reforms in Emerging Asia

Overall, public sector reforms in Emerging Asia can be said to have made significant but uneven progress, with more success in some areas of reform and aspects of specific reforms than in others. Such uneven progress squares with the evolutionary nature of PSR, reflecting its complex multi-dimensional character and its interdependence with institutional capacities, the degree of economic development, the political system and society. The question that naturally arises is thus: what circumstances seem to shape the likelihood that PSR achieves more or less progress? This section attempts to offer some insights drawn from a review of selected historical experiences of PSR efforts in the region.

PSR initiatives in Emerging Asia have typically been instigated and driven by internal and external circumstances that, in some instances, have had an important bearing on their outcomes. Many of the reform efforts in China and Viet Nam and, to a lesser extent, in other countries with a heritage of extensive state intervention in the economy – e.g. Indonesia and Malaysia – have been shaped by the need to adapt government organisation and functions to the growing importance of the market economy and the private sector. That need has been a key driving force in the successive waves of government reorganisations in China, for example. Economic crises and political upheavals have also been important in spurring and shaping PSR. Particular examples are the 1997 Asian Financial Crisis and the balance of payments crisis in India in the early 1990s.

Major political transitions, like those that followed the regimes of Marcos in the Philippines and Soeharto in Indonesia and, more recently, the advent of the Thaksin government in Thailand, have also sparked PSR – although their role in sustaining the reform momentum has been more problematic. The external forces of globalisation, particularly multilateral and regional trade and investment agreements and FDI have increasingly driven and influenced PSR processes since the 1990s. And their importance is likely to grow with the ASEAN Economic Community and other regional integration endeavours.

Historical experiences underscore the fact that PSRs are best viewed as long-term evolutionary processes whose payoffs are usually limited in the near term. A PSR is a complex undertaking whose design needs to be carefully tailored to and sequenced in line with institutional capacities in the government, the economy and society. Design matters greatly, although it is not alone sufficient for success. Sustaining reforms until their main objectives have been achieved has proved to be much more difficult than initiating them. With such general observations in mind, it is time to look at related lessons drawn from experience.

- Although economic and political upheavals have often triggered PSR by galvanising government, the public and outside actors to address the need for fundamental change, the window of opportunity they create does not guarantee that reforms will be sustained.

- Globalisation and the constituencies for reform in local business and foreign investment communities it has helped create have been major and increasingly important drivers of PSRs.
- Reforms are more likely to succeed and prove durable if they are institutionalised in a culture of reform where the long term objectives are widely accepted among the political elite and the public and early-stage reforms provide lessons and impetus for further action.
- There are both advantages and disadvantages to incremental or partial reform as opposed to comprehensive change. Incremental reforms often gain acceptance more easily and do not have the high costs of failure associated with more comprehensive reforms. However, they do run the risk of being overtaken by rapid economic and social change. Although consensus on the need for comprehensive reform may be harder to achieve and its implementation challenging, it may bring longer lasting and ultimately more effective solutions.
- Best practices and models developed from country experiences are a very useful resource for designing PSRs, although they are better developed in some areas than in others.
- PSRs are likely to encounter the greatest difficulties when they conflict, or are perceived to conflict, with the interests of key stakeholders. While such conflicts cannot always be avoided, they need to be taken into account when deciding the priorities of PSR.
- Sustained commitment by high-level political authorities and senior civil servants is very important to the success of PSRs. They are also critical to gain public support and to overcome resistance from stakeholders who perceive threats to their interests.
- Civil society and the general public can play key roles in sustaining PSR initiatives, provided government policies are sufficiently transparent and the legal/regulatory framework promotes strong accountability of the government to its citizens.

Tax administration reforms show the influence of globalisation and the need for high-level political commitment

Tax administration reform in Emerging Asia has focused on remedying common weaknesses that reduce revenue yields and increase compliance costs to taxpayers. The weaknesses include:

- the inefficient organisation of the tax administration itself and insufficient autonomy for it to effectively carry out its mandates;
- deficient procedures for registering taxpayers and for assessing and collecting taxes;
- lack of transparency and taxpayers' inadequate knowledge of their obligations;
- inadequate, opaque and often arbitrary mechanisms for dispute settlement and taxpayer appeal; and
- insufficient ICT and information systems.

A key overall objective is to strengthen voluntary compliance with tax obligations, which has proved to be as important in improving overall tax collection as measures to combat wilful non-compliance (OECD, 2001; Brondolo et al., 2008).

Some aspects of tax administration reform would seem, in principle, to make it easier to implement than some other PSRs. These reforms do not generally depend as much on extensive co-ordination between government organs as PEM reforms, for example.

Nor do they depend on reforms to the civil service as a whole, although they do require effective personnel policies from the tax authority itself. The benefits of effective tax administration reforms are also comparatively visible to key stakeholders in the public, particularly the business community.

As indicated below, a number of specific measures – like the introduction of large taxpayer units and the dissemination of ICT capabilities – have demonstrated significant benefits moderately soon time after their introduction and can help to create win-win situations. The international business community has become an increasingly influential constituency for tax administration reforms as competition in international trade and FDI has increased. However such advantages have not always brought success in tax administration reforms, as the case of the Philippines highlights.

Tax administration reform came to the fore in most Emerging Asian economies in the wake of a long period of tax structure reform that continues to this day. For example, tax reforms in China, India and the middle-income ASEAN countries from the 1970s and through much of the 1990s focused on modernizing and streamlining the income tax and the taxation of goods and services – notably through the development of systems for value-added taxation (Wong, 2007; Brys et al., 2013; Rao and Rao, 2005; Fabella and Chua, 2005; Brondolo et al., 2008). These reforms laid important foundations for tax administration reforms in that certain aspects of tax structures – e.g. threshold rates for sales taxes, VAT and income taxes – have a considerable impact on the efficiency with which taxes owed are collected.

Tax administration reform gained momentum during the 1990s with the increasingly acute need to raise tax yields while containing the burden on taxpayers and coping with the constraints on tax rates from international competition. Major tax administration reform in most of the less-developed countries only began recently – at the start of the millennium – due in part to their history of conflict and political upheavals (OECD, 2014; Pham and Engelschalk, 2011; Nguyen, 2011; Seiha, 2012).

The substantial drop in the costs of paying taxes for businesses in China is a fine illustration of the importance of globalisation in driving successful tax administration reforms. Much of the improvement reflects measures to streamline regulatory procedures for foreign-invested businesses in the special economic zones that China put in place in the late 1990s ahead of its accession to the WTO, and which it has partially extended to the rest of business community. China supported those measures with reforms to simplify tax policies that also helped to reduce compliance burdens (OECD, 2008). Major tax reform driving forces in China have been pressures from China's obligations under the WTO and from the active foreign business community, as well as from Chinese partners of foreign businesses and other firms involved in international trade and investment. The need to remain competitive in FDI has also been an increasingly important driver of reforms to both tax policy and administration in other countries in Emerging Asia (OECD, 2013).

Tax administration reform requires sustained support from senior levels

Reform to tax administration systems can be complex and may lend themselves to gradual, phased approaches to implementation. The sustained commitment from senior political and civil service staff is therefore a crucial element, as illustrated in the successes of Indonesia and challenges faced by the Philippines during their reforms.

Indonesia's relatively successful tax administration reforms in the wake of the 1997 Asian Financial Crisis highlight the value of effective design in phasing, of targets and other performance criteria, and of sustained political commitment at the highest levels. The country's reform drive was initially prompted by the critical need to raise government revenues in order to restore fiscal soundness. It was subsequently further shaped by the need to preserve and strengthen Indonesia's investment climate, which restricted the degree to which additional revenues could be raised through higher tax rates. Underpinning the need for substantial tax administration reform was an historical background of inefficient tax collection and high compliance burdens that reflected weaknesses in the legal and regulatory frameworks, taxpayer services, enforcement, and information systems (Brondolo et al., 2008). The overall effect was to weaken incentives for voluntary compliance while encouraging tax avoidance and evasion.

Indonesia phased in its tax administration reforms with a short initial stage beginning in 2001, followed by a second medium-term stage. The initial stage consisted of measures offering rapid benefits and deemed within the capabilities of the tax authority. There then came a medium-to-longer term phase of broader and more fundamental reform.

The short-term phase focused on the establishment of a pilot large taxpayer unit for the capital region, the introduction of computerised tax payment processing and measures to swiftly improve compliance in order to secure a near-term boost in revenues and improve perceptions of the direction of the investment climate.[4] The government set explicit targets for the number of reform actions to be undertaken and drew up projections of the amount of additional revenue it could generate. This phase also provided experience and practice for implementing the broader reforms with longer-term payoffs in the second phase that began in 2003.

Indonesia's medium-term reforms concentrated on gradually broadening the initial reforms while instituting legal and regulatory changes in the organisation of the tax authority which would take longer to implement and bear fruit. From 2003, the country extended large taxpayer units further into the country and launched reforms to establish dedicated units for medium and smaller taxpayers, again beginning with pilot projects. The government also made efforts to develop criteria for measuring the performance of tax administration systems and improving their staff's human capital and incentives. Tax administration reforms were accompanied by a broad review of tax structures, aimed at first simplifying VAT and other taxes in order to reduce compliance burdens.

The reforms had rapid, significant success in raising tax yields. According to estimates by the IMF, over half of the increase of overall government revenues (1.2% of GDP) between 2000 and 2006 was attributable to these reforms (Brondolo et al., 2008). And they probably accounted for much of the significant drop in the times required to pay taxes. Direct and indirect evidence also suggests that the reforms reduced tax arrears and improved compliance among large taxpayers. They very likely also contributed significantly to the noticeable improvement in Indonesia's investment climate rankings after 2000, even if they have dropped back somewhat in the course of the current decade. The impact of the broader, and often more difficult, medium-term reforms has been more mixed so far, due in part to delayed or incomplete implementation in some areas, particularly in enforcement, taxpayer services and tax simplification. The ultimate benefits are likely take some time longer to materialise.

Indonesia's tax administration reforms were not only well designed, they also enjoyed strong, on-going support from senior government officials that was critical to securing adequate resources and capable staff to carry out the reforms. The support was reinforced by the linkage of these reforms to the fiscal adjustment programme, which was at the top of the country's economic agenda. Initiatives by the tax authority to periodically consult with representatives of the business community further helped to strengthen the consensus behind the reforms and ensure that they were sustained (Brondolo et al., 2008).

The importance of sustained high-level political support is underscored by the less favourable experience of the Philippines in tax administration reform. Since the 1970s under the Marcos regime, the country has undertaken a series of tax administration reform initiatives. Most were, at best, partially implemented and of limited, purely short-term effectiveness. At worse, they were discarded or dismantled (Fabella and Chua, 2005; Diokno, 2005; Alonso i Terme, 2014). The most spectacular example was the failure of the ambitious reforms pushed through in 2001-02 by Rene Bañez, the Commissioner of the Bureau of Internal Revenue, which led to a tax collection strike, the withdrawal of the reforms and resignation of the Commissioner.

The failures of the Philippines' tax administration reforms are attributable more to lukewarm political support than to defects in their design. Arguably the most successful reforms were those carried out under President Marcos between 1975 and 1980 and President Aquino in the mid-1980s. They were driven in both cases by presidents with strong political standing and public backing (Fabella and Chua, 2005). Most other reforms received much less sustained high-level support, a problem compounded by the country's periodic political upheavals.

Without the backing of top politicians, reform initiatives in the Philippines have tended to be overwhelmed by strong vested interests and widespread corruption among tax authority bureaucrats, particularly at the local level. Limited public backing for reforms, reflecting a long-standing heritage of low government credibility, further undermined the necessary support for the reforms (Alonso i Terme, 2014).

Public expenditure management reforms highlight the importance of institutional capacity and the advantages and drawbacks of incremental approaches

Public expenditure management reform entails extensive changes in the relationship between the planning and finance ministries and government bodies of all levels; it also involves extensive changes in budget classification, information systems, and audit and other internal control mechanisms (see Shah, 2007). Even more than tax administration reforms, what PEM reforms can be expected to achieve at any one time depends critically upon the broader institutional capacities of the government and the economy. Successful PEM reform is an evolutionary process that begins with a focus in less developed countries on the most basic objectives necessary to control aggregate government finances and which then gradually gains in complexity as countries become more developed (World Bank, 2012a; Allen and Tommasi, 2001).

Extensive public expenditure management reform programmes in Emerging Asia have been undertaken since as early as the 1970s in Malaysia, for example. In the 1990s and 2000s the lower-income countries have followed suit. The impetus for PEM reforms intensified during the 1990s, especially after the 1997 Asian Financial Crisis. The need to better control overall government expenditure in order to contain budget deficits and better align spending with government objectives has been a leitmotif of PEM reforms in lower-income and some middle-income countries. At the same time, reforms to base budget formulation and implementation on results and performance criteria (i.e. outputs rather than inputs) have become increasingly important in higher-income countries such as Malaysia and Thailand. Some elements of PEM reform, like improvements in budget classification and better control of expenditure disbursements through a single treasury account, have been relatively successfully implemented in most cases. Others, however, like measures to achieve a full multi-year framework for budgeting and a linkage between development plans and the budget, have made less headway.

As the following examples highlight, factors restricting the pace and overall effectiveness of PEM reforms are: structural problems in the interaction between central and sub-national governments, the failure of PEM reforms to keep up with or adequately take into account rapidly changing economic conditions, and difficulties in changing the relationships between the traditional actors of public financial management. Isolated reforms in China have been of limited use (Box 3.3). Also, the more advanced PEM systems in the region point to the benefits of long-term continuity, with earlier reforms providing the foundation for subsequent more sophisticated reforms.

Box 3.3. **Public expenditure management reform in China has achieved less than originally hoped**

China's post-reform PEM process began with the adoption of a new budget law in 1994. The overall aim was to create a more modern budget formulation and control process in order to control overall expenditure and the budget deficit more effectively. A specific purpose was to rein in burgeoning extra-budget and off-budget activities.

There were two key planks of reform. One was the establishment of department budgeting in 2000 in place of traditional function-based budgeting which had led to opaque, fragmented spending that was difficult to monitor or control. The other was the introduction of a single treasury account in 2002 in order to further improve central control over spending (Wong; 2007, 2012b). There followed reform of the government procurement system in 2002, the introduction of a new budget classification system in 2005 that was broadly in line with international norms, and improvements to ICT capabilities. As part of the effort to make budgeting more comprehensive and transparent, fees and charges levied at the local level were prohibited unless they were explicitly authorised by the central government and measures were taken to bring the remainder onto the official budget.

There is general agreement that the Chinese budget reforms have resulted in substantial improvement in PEM processes (Wong, 2007, 2013; Brys et al., 2013; Deng and Peng, 2011). The measures have put in place the essential infrastructure for a modern budget system on which further reforms can be built (Wong, 2013). The overall budget now is more comprehensive, transparent, detailed and accountable to senior government and the National People's Congress.

However, the reforms have not improved overall budget control or curbed fragmentation as much as was originally hoped. Outcomes have deviated from budgeted revenues and expenditures much more substantially than can be explained by unanticipated developments (Deng and Peng, 2011). While earlier types of extra-budget transactions have been reduced and brought into the budget, there has been a proliferation of other non-tax revenues, mainly from land sales, profit remittances by SOEs, and social insurance contributions that have complicated budget formulation and control (Wong, 2007). Government ability to contain and control investment spending through the budget – the key to achieving more balanced aggregate growth – remains limited.

At least part of the reason for such shortcoming lies in the incremental nature of Chinese economic reforms (Wong, 2012a). The PEM reforms, although far-reaching, have still not addressed key areas. Budgeting for capital and current expenditures remains separate and, most importantly, relations between central and local governments have yet to be comprehensively overhauled. Growing pressures on sub-national governments, which in China account for a comparatively high share of total government spending, and the effects of incremental reform in other areas have complicated budget management and control. Indeed, they have partly offset the gains from the budget reforms. China's government has made extensive efforts to put in place performance-based management of government personnel and programmes. Yet, persistent shortcomings in auditing capabilities, in information systems and in the fiscal relations between different government levels have curtailed their effectiveness (Wong, 2012b).

Box 3.3. Public expenditure management reform in China has achieved less than originally hoped (*cont.*)

China's experiences offer useful insights for its lower-income neighbours now seeking to improve their PEM while moving toward less state-dominated, more market-oriented economies. Extensive PEM reforms have been underway in Lao PDR since the middle of the last decade. The country passed a new budget law in 2006 and brought in measures to strengthen its audit, treasury and other budget control functions. It followed those measures up in 2007 with further reforms that included launching the development of a medium-term budgeting framework (World Bank, 2010b).

Extensive PEM reforms are also planned in Myanmar as part of its broader reform programme (OECD, 2014). Viet Nam's PEM reforms have followed a similar path to those of China, with reforms of the budget laws in 1996 and 2002 that have improved budget management, decentralisation, flexibility and accountability. However, as in China, PEM reforms will probably need to go further as other reforms, like those to SOEs, proceed.

Note: Specific reforms include a central treasury management system for expenditure and the establishment of a state audit office to audit national budgets and, since 2005, the assistance of the National Assembly in budget execution and preparation. The reforms have strengthened transparency for the public as well as the legislature.

Results-based public expenditure management has yielded mixed results

The ultimate goal of PEM and public sector reform in general is to ground budgeting and public programme implementation in outcomes as measured by objective performance indicators. As noted above, effective, comprehensive results-based PEM frameworks require very well developed institutions for managing public programmes, a capable civil service, strong information management and considerable experience, all of which is typically found only in more advanced economies. However, some developing countries in Emerging Asia, e.g. India, Malaysia and Thailand, have been seeking to incorporate elements of results-based PEM in their budgeting systems.

In 1999, Thailand first implemented a results-based management system on a pilot basis. It was subsequently widened to all government departments by the middle of the last decade. The system involves performance contracts for services, performance indicators and, in principle, the extensive devolution of programme implementation to ministries (World Bank, 2009). However, while the system's formal elements are in place, implementation lags behind. Top-level officials have been reluctant to delegate the authority needed by lower levels under the system, ministries have balked at reallocating resources to their programmes in accordance with the performance criteria (Blondal and Kim, 2006), and the traditional patron-client relationships that hold sway in the Thai civil service have seen performance standards being widely bypassed and inconsistently applied (Mongkul, 2012).

Results-based management reform in Emerging Asia goes back the longest and has gone furthest in Malaysia. The country ushered in its reform process in 1969 with the Programme Performance Budget System (PPBS) and expanded it considerably during the 1980s and subsequent decades. The way the country has deployed its reforms is heavily influenced by the principles of NPM, as it seeks to foster a performance management culture. The NPM-inspired approach has also been a key factor in shaping other Malaysian public sector reforms, such as privatisation and the conversion of public sector entities into corporations (Sidiquee, 2014; Stiles et al., 2011). The current PEM processes centre around a robust set of programme agreements, performance indicators, expenditure targets and controls, and an evaluation cycle. In 2009, the evolution towards a fully results-based public sector received further impetus with the introduction of the Government Transformation Programme (GTP).

Malaysia's long experience of developing results-based PEM highlights both its strengths and limitations (Box 3.4). Reform has delivered significant improvement over time in Malaysia's public financial management, as suggested by its comparatively high ratings against the indicators discussed above (see Figure 3.3). Results-based PEM has effectively become institutionalised in the sense that, for some time, it has been the framework for reforms under a series of governments, with acceptance by outside stakeholders and the public. Such institutionalisation makes it more likely that lessons learned from earlier stages of development will provide a foundation for further refinement and corrections.

Box 3.4. Development of results-based public financial management in Malaysia

Malaysia began developing mechanisms for results-based financial management in the 1960s with the adoption of the Program Performance Budgeting System (PPBS) in place of its line item budgeting system. The PPBS was part of a broader reform effort that included the introduction of a goal-based management system for government personnel. The PPS required government departments to explicitly define their objectives and missions and to develop programmes accordingly (Sidiquee, 2014; Thomas, 2007).

Although the PPBS was only partially implemented and not integrated with other reformed public sector processes, it was further elaborated during the 1970s and 1980s, culminating in the introduction of the Malaysia Modified Budgeting System in 1990. The MBS was a response to budget reform trends in more advanced economies. It was heavily influenced by those developments and included key NPM elements (Sidiquee, 2014; Stiles et al., 2011). The MBS was a more comprehensive orientation of PFM/PEM towards results based on linkages between inputs and outputs and explicit performance criteria. The system evolved further with the introduction in 1999 of an integrated results-based management (IRBM) framework. The framework was designed to better link results-based budgeting to the performance management system for government personnel and to remedy other limitations of the original MBS (Thomas, 2007).

Under the MBS, all government bodies enter into contracts ("programme agreements") with the Treasury, specifying the inputs and expected results in quantity, quality, timeliness, costs and impacts (Sidiquee, 2010). A programme's progress is regularly measured against expected outputs and goals using objective-related indicators. Budgeting is embedded in a long-term macro-planning framework. In principle, the MBS and overall IRBM facilitate the linking of national development goals (which include the Millennium Development Goals) to the national strategic plan.

By the late 1990s, the IRBM gave Malaysia recognition as being in line with best international practices and a model for other developing countries (Thomas, 2007). However, with experience and as the tangible improvements in public sector performance proved to be less than originally hoped for, serious limitations also became evident. Malaysia introduced a number of stand-alone reforms in the early 2000s to remedy some of the weaknesses. They included a key performance indicator system in 2005, following successful experiences with a similar initiative in government-linked companies.

In 2009, the new Malaysian government introduced its Government Transformation Programme (GTP) as the next step toward transforming public sector management and the government relationship to the economy and society. The GTP seeks to root public management in performance assessment and to strengthen accountability for public service delivery (Sidiquee, 2014). As with earlier reforms, the GTP has shown promising initial results but considerably more time will be required before its ultimate effectiveness can be assessed.

However, despite the long process of development, results-based PEM is still hampered by significant limitations that reflect long-standing bureaucratic rigidities in the public service. The newer performance-based systems are more formally than practically effective in creating a performance culture across government departments. They have not fully replaced older input-oriented budget formulation and execution schemes. Instead, to a significant degree, they co-exist with the older systems, which continue to exert substantial influence on actual decisions (Sidiquee, 2010). As the example of Thailand shows, decentralised implementation of PEM can still be hindered by the heritage of a traditional top-down bureaucracy culture. These limitations should not be viewed as implying that results-based PEM has been unsuccessful, or that it is not applicable to developing countries. They do, however, highlight the fact that its development requires a sustained and long-term learning process, as seen in Malaysia (Box 3.4).

Civil service reform experiences reveal need for high-level political commitment to overcome rigidities

As with public sector reforms generally, civil service reforms in Emerging Asia have been driven by the tension between the underdeveloped capabilities of the civil service and the growing demands placed on it for more and sophisticated services prompted by rapid economic development. The success of reforms has been restricted by a bureaucratic reluctance to change, by cronyism and corruption, and by patron-client and other relations within the civil service and with outside actors. All these factors tend to weaken the responsiveness of civil servants to political leaders and, except when pushed by strong political leadership, have also restricted the penetration, implementation, and durability of civil service reforms. A further impediment has been the lack of well-defined models and operational indicators of civil service quality (Brosamle, 2012).

The comprehensiveness and continuity of reform have varied among the region's countries. In Malaysia, which has been conducting reforms for several decades and has taken them furthest, civil service reform has been part of broader, heavily results-oriented reforms to the public sector. The way in which the country has embedded CSRs in the on-going public sector reform process has almost certainly helped to enhance their effectiveness.

In India, the New Economic Programme of 1991 lent fresh impetus to civil service reform, as it did to public sector reform generally (Mishra 2014) Substantial reforms were also taken as part of the Integrated Reorganisation Plan introduced in the Philippines in 1972 and, again in the 1980s, under President Aquino. Little more was undertaken until after the 1997 Asian Financial Crisis (Tjiptoherijanto, 2012b).[5] A series of largely top-down technocratic reforms were carried out in Thailand during the 1990s but their effects, especially in making bureaucrats more accountable to elected governments, were limited (Painter, 2005; Tjiptoherijanto, 2012a). During the 1990s, Indonesian reforms initially focused on facilitating the broader process of government decentralisation. These were followed up in 2000 with reforms to the central government bureaucracy with the assistance of the World Bank and other multilateral organisations (Tjiptoherijanto, 2014). China and Viet Nam began to modernise their civil services in the 1990s in tandem with, and partly in order to facilitate, broader economic reforms. Lao PDR, Myanmar and Viet Nam have embarked on civil service reforms only recently (Burns, 2007; Poon et al., 2009; David, 2013).

The focus of those efforts across Emerging Asia has, to varying degrees, been on improving recruitment in order to improve qualifications; strengthening incentives and accountability through reformed pay, promotion and other personnel policies; increasing the overall responsiveness of the civil service to political authorities; and improving integrity and (especially) containing corruption.

On the whole, civil service reform seems to have had most success in improving the qualifications and skills of those recruited to government service. China's personnel management reforms between 1993 and 1997 greatly strengthened the civil service in key areas – e.g. competitive hiring, examinations, performance evaluations, compensation and career advancement criteria and procedures – and expanded them to the Communist Party and other political and government bodies. The reforms helped to reverse the deterioration in the civil service and over time have considerably improved overall qualifications and skills (Burns, 2007). Viet Nam began personnel reform in the late 1990s, shifting responsibility for hiring away from the universities to line ministries. The result has been in a significant improvement in skills and quality in much of the civil service (Hausman, 2009; Poon et al., 2009; Mukherjee et al., 2009).

Overall, though, progress towards better recruitment and qualifications has been somewhat uneven. In China, civil service skills and qualifications are noticeably lower in local government in provinces of the interior than in the central government and the governments of the more developed coastal provinces and cities. Substantial numbers of civil service appointments are still made through connections and other forms of patronage in Viet Nam (Hausman, 2009). In both countries, initiatives to place workers displaced by SOE reforms in government positions have temporarily run counter to efforts to promote strict merit-based recruitment. The diversity and representativeness of civil service hiring practices also remain limited in Thailand, where a substantial portion of new recruits come from families whose members have traditionally been employed in the civil service and from the military. In Malaysia, preference is given to ethnic Malays in recruitment.

Civil service reform seems to have been less successful in strengthening incentives for government staff to carry out government policies and serve the public effectively. Civil service compensation continues to be linked mainly to rank rather than responsibility or merit in most countries, including India and China. With the exception of Malaysia, performance evaluations and other explicit mechanisms to tie pay to performance have yet to be developed or are at very early stages of development. Even where such systems have been developed, they tend to be only partly or inconsistently applied.[6] There is little provision for addressing poor individual staff performance, especially as civil servants are typically subject to dismissal for cause only.

Such weaknesses in incentives and performance management capabilities have not infrequently made it difficult for government reformers to implement their policies effectively. Thailand is a classic example of a bureaucratic polity in which the domain of senior civil servants spills over into the political domain, eclipsing the powers of elected government officials and curbing their ability to implement new policy directions (Painter, 2005). The administration of Prime Minister Thaksin attempted to make the bureaucracy more responsive by reorganising government ministries and transferring civil servants, decentralising administrative functions, and creating a Senior Civil Service. However, the reforms were aimed chiefly at creating a senior corps of civil servants who would be more responsive to the Prime Minister. It failed to penetrate far into middle and lower ranks. The reforms also became highly politicised as a result of the controversy surrounding the Thaksin administration, which has probably constrained subsequent attempts to reform the Thai civil service.

Strong political support and a multi-pronged approach are needed to combat pervasive, historically rooted corruption

The threat posed by corruption to the legitimacy of governments and political elites and its cost to the public purse have spurred on-going, often vigorous efforts to combat it right across Emerging Asia. Yet the impacts seem limited in most countries and often short-lived.

The pervasiveness of corruption and the historical legacies underpinning it are serious challenges for anti-corruption reforms in the region and are compounded by limited geographic integration and ethnic diversity (David, 2013). Corruption in most Emerging Asian countries extends well beyond the core civil service and politicians. Police are often as or more widely viewed as corrupt than is the civil service. The judiciary is also widely viewed as corrupt in many countries, especially in Indonesia (Table 3.8).

Corruption takes many different forms. It includes government employees overtly soliciting bribes, the awarding of government contracts to businesses in which senior officials have a financial interest, and the bending of regulations and their implementation to favour those being regulated (i.e. state capture).

Table 3.8. **Corruption perceptions by sector in Emerging Asia**

Percentage of survey respondents who think of national institutions as "corrupt" or "extremely corrupt", 2013

Percentage of those surveyed believing sector is corrupt or highly corrupt	Political parties	Parliament/ legislature	Judiciary	Police	Public officials/civil servants
Cambodia	28	16	60	37	30
Indonesia	86	89	86	91	79
Malaysia	69	44	35	76	46
Philippines	58	52	56	69	64
Thailand	68	45	18	71	58
Viet Nam	27	28	53	72	55
India	86	65	45	75	65

Source: Transparency International (2013), *Global Corruption Barometer 2013*, Transparency International, Berlin, http://www.transparency.org/research/gcb/overview.

In part, corruption in the region is a reflection of historical practices and traditions. They include the widespread use of personal connections in social, business and public spheres and traditions of patron-client relations. However, the persistence of corruption is more fundamentally about incentives and opportunities for corrupt behaviour as opposed to weaknesses in institutional mechanisms for combatting it. The substantial impact that government officials' decisions have on the economic and social well-being of individuals and businesses gives rise to mutual incentives for illicit arrangements. Incentives tend to be magnified when government rules and regulations are opaque and ambiguous and give officials considerable discretion in applying them. Policies that overly limit government workers' pay also foster corrupt practices as a means of supplementing income. For example, bribing teachers to obtain grades or recommendations for admission to university is reportedly widespread in Thailand and a number of other countries in the region. Economic development also tends to create new opportunities for corruption where it expands the scope of government activities and increases the gains that can be obtained from selling government favours.

Experiences in Emerging Asia, together with some successful anti-corruption programmes elsewhere in Asia, suggest that the fight against pervasive corruption requires strong, on-going political commitment; effective legal and institutional frameworks; and a multi-pronged approach that extends beyond enforcement to address incentives and opportunities for corruption and which engages civil society. The importance of sustained high-level political commitment is underscored by the success of Hong Kong, China. Once one of the most corrupt economies in the world, it saw corruption fall dramatically after the Government established the Independent Commission Against Corruption in 1974 (Smith, 2012). Crucial to the success of the Commission – and of the multiple anti-corruption authorities in Singapore – has been constant oversight and commitment from the senior leaders, made possible in part by continuity in political orientation. Although there are many examples of vigorous campaigns against corruption in Emerging Asia, political shifts and, in some cases, corruption among top-ranking politicians have weakened their consistency over time.[7]

Effective formal anti-corruption frameworks incorporate laws, regulations and codes which not only define proper and improper official conduct and effective enforcement mechanisms, but which build transparency and accountability to the public, including provisions for civil society and the general public to monitor government activities. Good formal institutions are necessary to sustaining a strong internal culture of integrity and honesty among civil servants and politicians. Experiences in Asia indicate that dedicated anti-corruption agencies can help considerably in combatting corruption, provided that they have adequate legal authority and enforcement powers, clear mandates and adequate resources (Meagher, 2002).[8] However, effective formal arrangements for enforcing laws and rules against corruption are unlikely to be sufficient by themselves in an environment of pervasive corruption; even the strongest enforcement can apprehend and prosecute only a small portion of offenders. Ultimately, multi-pronged anti-corruption efforts that focus on reducing the opportunities and incentives for corruption as well as enforcing and punishing are likely to be the most successful.

Governments in Emerging Asia have been engaged in a variety of efforts to combat corruption over the past decades. Periodic campaigns to root out and punish particularly egregious offenders have been most common in China and Viet Nam, but they have been undertaken in other countries, too (Chan, 2010). Such campaigns have probably had some positive short-term benefits. However since they only can influence a very small portion of corrupt behaviour and do not typically address its root causes, their effects tend to be short-lived. Indeed, as corruption after campaigns is usually perceived to be as great as before, there is a risk of the public growing even more sceptical and cynical over government efforts.

Longer-term efforts against corruption emphasise the development of legal frameworks and institutions. Basic corruption laws were well-established in most countries by the 1990s although they have been further strengthened recently in Viet Nam (Formin-Finland, 2008) and, under its 2010 anti-corruption law, in Cambodia (David, 2013). There have been considerable efforts since the 1990s to set up or bolster formal anti-corruption institutions, inspired and, in some cases, modelled on anti-corruption agencies in Hong Kong, China and Singapore, which are widely viewed as effective (Meagher, 2002). In most Emerging Asian countries, responsibility is shared between several anti-corruption bodies (typically with one taking the lead), although Indonesia and Malaysia have established single agencies loosely in line with the model from Hong Kong, China.[9]

Anti-corruption reform has established formal institutions to address corruption in the middle-income ASEAN countries and India that, by international standards, are relatively strong (Nawaz and Bridi, 2009; Mutebi, 2008; Quah, 2010). However, the actual reduction of corruption, as measured by surveys and other indicators, has been noticeably less. The discrepancy highlights the fact that, especially in anti-corruption efforts good structures do not by themselves guarantee fundamental improvement, particularly when the culture of corruption is pervasive and historically deep-rooted. An apt illustration is provided by Indonesia's recently established Corruption Eradication Commission (KPK).

The KPK was established in 2002 after nearly 50 years of experimenting with task forces, commissions and other anti-corruption bodies. The KPK was endowed with extensive powers to investigate and prosecute corruption cases and monitor state activities. It was widely regarded as one of the formally strongest such bodies in the Asian region (Schutte, 2012).[10] In the years following its establishment the KPK brought numerous corruption cases before Indonesia's Anti-Corruption Courts. A number involved high-level government officials and nearly all resulted in convictions. The success of the Commission led to a noticeable improvement in Indonesia's standing in rankings like Transparency International's *Perceived Corruption Index*. However, in 2011, the Commission suffered a strong backlash from judicial and police officials, evidenced in a series of acquittals in cases brought by the KPK (Butt, 2012). Those setbacks have been followed by some slippage in recent years in Indonesia's standing in corruption rankings.

The difficulties encountered by strong formal institutions in an environment of pervasive corruption are hardly unique to Indonesia. Thailand's efforts in 2000-05 to control the bureaucracy and strengthen government facilitation of business led to pressures that threatened to overwhelm the formal anti-corruption institutions. Tensions were manifest in the resignation of nine members of the lead anti-corruption agency in the wake of their convictions for abuse of power in raising their own salaries (Quah, 2007).

Such travails do not indicate that strong formal institutions are ineffective, but that putting them in place is only the first step in the necessarily long and far-from-smooth process of reducing corruption.[11] Key to that process are addressing the root causes of corruption and engaging the public in efforts to combat it. Many countries have been, or are, moving to improve compensation for public employees in some sectors, partly to reduce incentives for bribery as a way to supplement income. Efforts to streamline procedures for business regulations like licensing, such as those in China, should also help to reduce opportunities for corruption and to reduce incentives for corrupt behaviour. Experiences in a number of Asian countries – like the Philippines, Malaysia and Singapore – also highlight the positive role that civil society organisations can play in monitoring government integrity and thereby strengthening accountability. However, protections for such organisations are noticeably stronger in some countries, such as the Philippines, India and Malaysia, than in others, such as China and Viet Nam.

Generally speaking, initiatives that seek to address the root causes of corruption and engage the public in the fight against it are less well developed than formal enforcement institutions. They need to be taken further.

Decentralisation has been the most difficult aspect of government reorganisation

Changes prompted by economic development necessitate periodic reorganisation in order to reallocate and streamline government functions. In advanced economies and developing ones with well-established market systems, restructuring at the central government level has usually been partial. Reforms of that kind seek, for example, to establish bodies that promote environmental objectives or to modernise financial regulatory institutions. Many countries in emerging Asia have reorganised financial regulatory functions to deal with the pressures of globalisation. Particularly in countries in which NPM has influenced PSR, such as Thailand and Malaysia, the reorganisation of functions has included transferring some to autonomous corporations or agencies, either to carry out traditional government duties or to establish special commissions (Government of India, 2009).[12] The transition from central planning to a market economy in some countries, notably China, has also spurred more extensive restructuring (Box 3.5).

Box 3.5. China's administrative reorganisation reforms

Frequent extensive government administrative reorganisation has been a hallmark of Chinese reform in the post-Mao era. The first major reform came in 1982 and was followed by further measures roughly every five years in tandem with the five-year plans. The frequency of reform can be attributed to the rapid, profound changes the country has undergone in its transition to a market economy and opening up to foreign investment and trade. But it also stems from the need to address problems arising from earlier reforms (Wang, 2010).

A major objective of reform into the mid-1990s was to streamline government functions in order to reign in and reverse the mushrooming of government bodies and workforce that was partly the result of the incremental and, to some degree, *ad hoc* nature of the overall reform process. The 1982 reform reduced the number of state council organs from 100 to 61 together with significant cuts in the number of agencies at the provincial, city, town and autonomous region levels (Wang, 2010). However, the reductions were short-lived as the forces of development and ensuring policy responses led to renewed proliferation of agencies and civil servants, which necessitated further streamlining and downsizing in the reforms of 1988 and again in 1993. This waning and waxing pattern in restructuring highlights how the incremental approach to reform struggles to deliver lasting solutions in fast-changing circumstances.

The focus of China's reorganisation reforms began to shift in the late 1990s toward adapting government structures to its ever more open economy and impending accession to the World Trade Organization. Since then they have thoroughly restructured the major planning agencies and related key bodies, reorienting their missions toward facilitating rather than directing market forces and businesses. Financial regulatory institutions have been reorganised, rationalised and modernised: bank regulation has been switched from the People's Bank of China to the China Bank Regulatory Commission and securities and the insurance regulatory commissions have undergone sweeping change. Such reforms have been a major step toward bringing China's financial regulatory capabilities up to the standard of the best international practices. Overall, organisational reforms since the 1990s have been more successful than previously in putting in place durable, adaptable structures. Pressures from the opening-up of the Chinese economy and the ability of government reformers to make productive use of international practices and experiences have been important factors in this success.

The decentralisation of functions to sub-national governments has proved to be the most complex and difficult form of government restructuring. Experiences in the region prompt three observations about the factors that affect reform success. First, decentralisation is a complex process, arguably the most complex in PSR. It involves many political, administrative, and fiscal elements that are highly interdependent but which have usually been developed independently. Inconsistencies and conflicts between them have weakened the overall effectiveness of decentralisation. Second, while often useful and effective in other areas, incremental approaches to decentralisation have tended to generate and accumulate problems. Decentralisation is likely to be more effective, proceed more smoothly and, ultimately, adapt more easily to changing circumstances when guided by comprehensive planning that takes into account major political, administrative and fiscal factors and constraints. Third, the need for a more comprehensive approach is particularly important for the design of fiscal transfer mechanisms, which need to do a better job of ensuring that expenditure needs at the local level are matched by available revenues.

Decentralisation involves the devolving of government powers and resources from central to sub-national levels. It can and does occur in both formally federal and unitary states.[13] It comprises up to three dimensions (Shah, 2004; Lin et al., 2003):

- political – the explicit transfer of authority over policies to sub-national governments;
- administrative – the shifting of policy implementation to local bodies under the supervision of central government agencies; and
- fiscal – the allocation of selected expenditure and revenue-raising powers to lower government levels.

In principle, decentralisation improves overall government effectiveness by allowing local officials and their constituents to better shape policies to local needs and conditions, about which the central government typically knows little. Decentralisation can also encourage innovation in the provision of government services by local governments and enhance policies to promote regional development and reduce poverty. Decentralisation may also improve government credibility and – under the right circumstances – accountability by bringing government functions closer to the populations they serve.

A general principle of decentralisation is that responsibilities should be allocated to the level of government that is best suited to carrying them out. For example, local authorities are typically responsible for the maintenance of local roads while monetary policy is left to the central government. The potential benefits of decentralisation are particularly great for countries with large, highly diverse regions and ethnic populations, as is true of most Emerging Asian countries. However decentralisation is a complex process with highly interdependent parts and presents especially difficult principle-agent problems in ensuring compatibility between national government objectives (acting as principles) and the incentives and decisions of local governments (acting as agents). Poorly constructed decentralisation structures can create adverse incentives and distortions that prevent the theoretical benefits from being realised and undermine key national goals.

Many countries in Emerging Asia have been pursuing extensive decentralisation reforms since the early 1990s. China began in the early 1980s as part of its move to reverse the centralisation of the Mao era, and has undertaken a series of further decentralisation reforms since then (Wong, 2007; Xu, 2011; Lin et al., 2003). The Philippines and Thailand introduced major decentralisation reforms in the early 1990s, and Indonesia followed suit in 1999 (World Bank, 2005; Capuno, 2005; Amornvivat, 2004; Green, 2005). Cambodia and Viet Nam also developed basic decentralisation frameworks in the 1990s, with Cambodia conducting major revisions in 2009 and Viet Nam in 2004. Myanmar has established a basic framework for a federal state and the decentralisation of government as part of the constitution it adopted in 2008 (Niazi, 2011; Bjornestad, 2009; OECD, 2014). These efforts have differed in emphasis, with decentralisation in China, Viet Nam and Cambodia, for example, stressing administrative and fiscal reform and Indonesia, the Philippines, Thailand and Myanmar also including elements of political decentralisation.

Decentralisation has brought both tangible benefits and significant problems. The Philippines reforms spurred local government innovation, increased public participation, and improved local governments' ability to respond more rapidly and appropriately to local needs (Capuno, 2005). Decentralisation in Viet Nam and Cambodia has also helped to improve service delivery and public participation and, at least in Viet Nam, has contributed to broader efforts to reduce poverty (Bjornestad, 2009; World Bank, 2005). By helping to extend the outreach of social services to poorer and more remote areas, decentralisation has very likely helped to improve health and education outcomes in recent decades (World Bank, 2005).

However, decentralisation seems to have had limited effects on narrowing disparities in income and living standards between regions and little or none on gaps in growth rates, which continue to be wide in China and a number of other countries.[14] Nor does decentralisation seem to have helped reduce corruption in most cases. In Indonesia, it seems to have aggravated problems of corruption by creating new opportunities (Green, 2005).

Co-ordination, accountability and fiscal transfers are key unresolved challenges

Two key, but not fully resolved, challenges of decentralisation in Emerging Asia have limited its benefits. The first is the challenge of creating effective co-ordination and accountability mechanisms to ensure that sub-national government policies are both responsive to local needs and consistent with national objectives. The challenge takes on different forms according to countries' political systems.

In unitary states with little or no mechanisms for the people to choose local officials, as in China, Viet Nam and, to a lesser extent, Cambodia, co-ordination and accountability are largely carried out administratively – through the formal relations between officials at different levels and the hierarchy of authority over policies specified in national legislation. In federal countries such as India, Malaysia and Myanmar, elections and participation are the key mechanisms in local accountability, while constitutional provisions establishing and limiting sub-national government powers, along with revenue sharing and other arrangements, help to align sub-national government policies with national objectives.[15] However, such arrangements have often needed to be augmented with other mechanisms to ensure that local government capacity is sufficient.

Nevertheless, the severe agency problems inherent in relations between levels of government can create and have created incentives for local officials to carry out policies and actions that are contrary to central government policies and laws. Such adverse incentives have long been evident in China in the persistent problem of local officials making illegal sales of land and other public property and levying unauthorised fees and taxes, particularly in rural areas, during the 1980s and 1990s. There are also difficulties in implementing central government rules and mandates in areas such as environmental protection. Despite considerable refinement over the years, performance criteria and evaluation mechanisms for local officials have proved insufficient for remedying conflicts. They may even have worsened them in some ways – e.g. by giving too much prominence to local investment and growth as criteria for performance has encouraged excessive and inefficient investment at times. Other countries in the region have struggled with similar problems. In Indonesia, for instance, ambiguities in the powers granted to sub-national government have sometimes led to the passing of local laws that are inconsistent with national objectives or mandates (Green, 2005).

The control and accountability of sub-national governments have often been impaired by incentives arising from the gaps between their spending powers and their own revenue sources. Sub-national governments account for nearly 80% of total government expenditure in China, the most fiscally decentralised country in the region, and more than 40% in the next most highly decentralised countries, India and Viet Nam (OECD, 2014). Sub-national government shares of spending are smaller, but still substantial, in the other countries – around one-quarter in the Philippines, and nearly one-fifth in Indonesia and Cambodia.

However, taxes most appropriately assigned under fiscal decentralisation principles to central government – especially those with broad, mobile bases like VAT and business income taxes – tend to be the largest revenue sources. Sub-national governments' share of total revenues is therefore generally much lower than their share of expenditure. In China and a number of other countries, revenues explicitly allowed or assigned through tax-sharing or similar arrangements to sub-national governments are as much as one-quarter to one-third of total expenditure. Moreover, because the size of tax bases tends to vary far more widely between poorer and wealthier regions than spending powers do, the gaps between own-source revenue and spending powers in less well-off regions are generally greater than the national average. Indeed, disparities in own revenue are greater than those in *per capita* income in at least some countries. For example, the *per capita* revenues of the wealthiest province in China in the middle of the last decade were 15 times higher than those of the poorest province, and such gaps were as wide or wider in the Philippines and Viet Nam (World Bank, 2005). They have been further accentuated by differences in regional growth rates in some countries, such as China.

A key principle of effective fiscal federalism is that sub-national government revenues should be sufficient to cover their expenditure responsibilities (Shah, 2004). This principle implies that fiscal transfers from central to sub-national governments and between sub-national governments should fill the gap between sub-national governments' spending powers and their own-source revenues (including taxes shared with the central government). Such transfers include unconditional grants and various types of conditional grants that involve requirements such as matching from recipients (*ibid.*).

Total fiscal transfers account for a significant share of sub-national revenues; as much as 40-50% in some cases. In practice, however, fiscal transfer mechanisms in the region have not generally been enough to close the fiscal gaps at sub-provincial level, particularly in poorer regions, although they have narrowed disparities in pre-transfer revenues in China, Indonesia, the Philippines and Viet Nam (World Bank, 2005). The persistence of sub-national governments' fiscal gaps has led to or contributed to a number of problems in China – e.g. the squeeze on sub-national governments has fostered growth in local government debt and the proliferation of unauthorised fees and charges. Fiscal gaps in China and other countries have impeded national policies to improve education, health, and other human development conditions in poorer areas.

The inadequacy of fiscal transfer mechanisms partly reflects an incremental, *ad hoc* process of decentralisation in some countries. Decentralisation in China was essentially a move to adapt to broader economic reforms, rather than the result of a comprehensive plan, and used incremental approaches to the most pressing problems (Lin et al., 2003; Wong, 2013; World Bank, 2005). Decentralisation in Indonesia was carried out relatively rapidly in response to the situation after 1997, while in Thailand, the Philippines and Viet Nam it was governed by more systematic plans. However, in most cases, transfer mechanisms have tended to less developed and of limited responsiveness to differences in local expenditure needs and changing fiscal gaps. For example, only a low share of transfers to provincial governments in China is based on explicit formulas that include indicators of expenditure needs. What's more, there are no explicit rules for transfers from provincial to lower government levels, which spend the most on education and health (OECD, 2006). There are also few transfers based explicitly on measures of expenditure needs in Indonesia and Thailand. Needs-based transfers are somewhat more important (although still only part of overall transfers) in the Philippines and have become more important in Viet Nam as a result of reforms in 2004 (World Bank, 2005; Bjornestad, 2009).

Conclusion

Countries in Emerging Asia have pursued, and continue to pursue, extensive reforms in their attempts to improve the effectiveness of their public sectors in supporting development and providing services to the public. Their efforts have benefited considerably from the technical advice and support of multilateral and bilateral agencies and donors. And they have brought substantial benefits – public sector capacity has improved significantly in recent decades. Nevertheless, results have been uneven and public sector effectiveness in key areas is, according to wide-ranging indicators, still short of levels in more advanced economies in Asia and elsewhere. With the exception of Malaysia, the ideal of orienting public sector management towards results rather than input is still at a very early stage, as it is in most developing countries.

Countries' experiences with public sector reform across the region underscore that it is a long-term process that needs to be adapted to and evolve with broader institutional capacities such as legal frameworks, accounting systems, the rule of law and the development of markets. The design and implementation of PSR should also take into account political and bureaucratic cultures, particularly as they shape the perceived interests of stakeholders. Countries, particularly developing ones, cannot afford to undertake public sector reforms just once and then leave them unchanged. Nor can they simply import institutions and arrangements that have proved successful in more advanced countries without carefully adapting them to local capacities and constraints.

The evolutionary nature of public sector reform means that continuity and on-going high-level political support and public consensus are likely to be very important to its ultimate success. Lack of continuity and a tradition of reform underpinned by a consensus on objectives and basic orientation have tended to slow or even interrupt progress in public sector reform. Economic crises and political upheavals have often provided the impetus for reforms, but not nearly as often the sustained pressure required to ensure that they are fully carried out or their benefits realised. Coherent design that takes into account the interdependencies between the component elements of reform and broader institutional capacities and constraints has proved to be critical to the success of public sector reform. The difficulties of decentralisation reforms, which have tended to follow a more reactive, *ad hoc* course throw into relief the importance of coherent design. The availability of well-tested best practices and models, pressures for reform arising from globalisation, and on-going interest from domestic constituencies all help explain why tax administration and public expenditure management reforms have generally made more progress than civil service or anti-corruption reforms. However, that relative success is probably also a reflection of the fact that tax administration and public expenditure reforms usually, although not always, threaten entrenched stakeholder interests less and require less immediate change in bureaucratic traditions than the other reforms. Such interests and traditions have been key obstacles to progress in other areas, particularly anti-corruption reform. Sustained political longer-term support for reforms that address the incentives and opportunities for corruption as well as enforcement is likely to be key to further progress.

Notes

1. Indeed, the country percentile rankings corresponding to the patterns in Figure 3.3 show a similar pattern as the overall scores.
2. Indicators under the formal framework are divided into categories: Budget Credibility (1-4); Transparency and Comprehensiveness (5-10); Policy-based Budgeting (11-12); Predictability and Control in Budget Execution (13-21 – a number of these indicators apply to tax administration); Accounting, Recording and Budgeting (22-25); and External Scrutiny and Audit (26-28). See the Public Expenditure and Financial Accountability Portal at http://www.pefa.org/en/content/pefa-framework.
3. Although a time series of the Transparency International indicators is not available for Cambodia, Lao PDR and Myanmar, an alternative indicator, "Control of Corruption", from the World Bank's Governance Indicators shows a marked deterioration for Lao PDR and little change for Cambodia and Myanmar.
4. Measures to improve compliance included expanded taxpayer registration, strengthened audits, enforcement of filing requirements and collection of tax arrears.
5. IRP focused on rationalising and downsizing government bureaucracy. However, it also included measures to strengthen the merit system and professionalise the civil service, reform the Civil Service Commission and create a career executive service.
6. Indonesia has been piloting merit-linked pay systems in certain public sectors, notably education. The government has recently drafted a master plan for bureaucracy reform comprising nine elements. They include improving the structure of the bureaucracy; improving the quantity, distribution and quality of civil servants, and ensuring a transparent selection process and system of merit-based promotion.
7. Quah (2010) argues that political support for anti-corruption efforts, as measured by monetary and human resources allocated to anti-corruption agencies, has been stronger in Singapore and Hong Kong, China than in India, Indonesia or the Philippines.
8. There has been considerable debate about the relative merits of centralised anti-corruption authorities as opposed to distribution powers among several agencies (Meagher, 2002). There are examples of success for both approaches, such as the multi-agency approaches in the United States and Singapore. Multi-agency approaches are likely to require co-ordinating capacities that are weaker in developing countries than in advanced ones. However history – or other country-specific circumstances – may still make a multi-agency approach the most appropriate choice.
9. Sub-national governments also often have anti-corruption bodies, even in those countries with a single lead body at the central government level.
10. The Commission has legal power to demand information, institute wire taps and travel bans, demand financial information, and call upon the assistance of other law enforcement agencies in its investigations.
11. In the case of Thailand, the fact that the officials were convicted by the Supreme Court could be taken as a sign that pressures against corruption also remain strong.
12. In India, the report from the Second Administrative Reforms Commission noted the proliferation of government ministries and agencies, their often poor integration and co ordination, and an excessive number of levels (Government of India, 2009). The Commission recommended that the functions and activities of all ministries undergo detailed analysis with a view to reorganisation as part of a focus on core government functions and the principle of subsidiarity.
13. In the developing ASEAN+2 region, only India, Malaysia and now Myanmar are formally federal states, while the other countries are formally unitary. Except for the political dimension, the extent of decentralisation seems in practice to depend little – if at all – on whether a state is formally federal or unitary. As the text discussion indicates, China, a formally unitary state, is the most fiscally decentralised state in the region.
14. Literacy rates in China did improve more in poor than in wealthy provinces between 1982 and 1999. There was also a marked drop in infant mortality rate disparities between the provinces in the Philippines following decentralisation (World Bank, 2011). There was also some convergence in regional growth rates in the Philippines, although the extent to which decentralisation was responsible is unclear (Capuno, 2005).
15. An exception is the Financial Commission created by Myanmar's 2008 constitution to co-ordinate budgets among central and state/region governments (OECD, 2014).

References

Allen, R. and D. Tommasi (eds.) (2001), *Managing Public Expenditure: A Reference Book for Transition Economies*, OECD Publishing, Paris, http://dx.doi.org/10.1787/9789264192607-en.

Alonso i Terme, R.M. (2014), "What prevents the Philippines from undertaking tax reform: A story of the unraveling state", *International Centre for Tax and Development Working Paper*, No. 16, Brighton.

Amornvivat, S. (2004), "Fiscal Decentralization: The Case of Thailand", paper presented at the International Symposium on Fiscal Decentralization in Asia Revisited on 20-21 February, Hitotsubashi University, Tokyo.

Araki, S. and I. Claus (2014), *A Comparative Analysis of Tax Administration in Asia and the Pacific*, Asian Development Bank, April.

Asia Pacific CoP and MFDR (2011), *Framework for Results-Based Public Sector Management and Country Cases*, September.

Bjornestad, L. (2009), "Fiscal decentralization, fiscal incentives, and pro-poor outcomes: Evidence from Viet Nam", *Asian Development Bank Working Paper*, No. 168, July.

Blondal, J.R. and S. Kim (2006), "Budgeting in Thailand", *OECD Journal on Budgeting*, Vol. 5, No. 3, OECD Publishing, Paris, http://www.oecd.org/gov/budgeting/40140263.pdf.

Brondolo, J. et al. (2008), "Tax administration reform and fiscal adjustment: the case of Indonesia (2001-2007)", *IMF Working Paper*, Vol. 08, No. 129, May.

Brosamle, K.J. (2012), *Civil Service Reform in Developing Countries: We Do Not Really Know What We Are Doing*, August.

Brys, B. et al. (2013), "Tax policy and tax reform in the People's Republic of China", *OECD Taxation Working Papers*, No. 18, OECD Publishing, Paris, http://dx.doi.org/10.1787/5k40l4dlmnzw-en.

Bunse, S. and V. Fritz (2012), "Making public sector reforms work political and economic contexts, incentives, and strategies", *World Bank Policy Research Working Paper*, No. 6174, August.

Burns, J.P. (2007), "Civil service reform in China", *OECD Journal on Budgeting*, Vol. 7, No. 1, OECD Publishing, Paris, http://www.oecd.org/gov/budgeting/44526166.pdf.

Butt, S. (2012), "Anti-corruption reform in Indonesia: an obituary?", *Bulletin of Indonesian Economic Studies*, November.

Capuno, J.J. (2005), "The quality of local governance and development under decentralization in the Philippines", *UP School of Economics Discussion Papers*, Vol. 2005, No. 06, University of the Philippines.

CEPII, *Institutional Profiles Database* (database), Centre d'Études Prospectives et d'Informations Intenationales, Paris, http://www.cepii.fr/institutions/EN/ipd.asp.

Chan, W. (2010), "Considering the system: the search for an effective anti-corruption strategy in China", *Stanford Journal of East Asian Affairs*.

David, A.G. (2013), *One Size Doesn't Fit All: Tailoring Cambodia's Anti-corruption Strategy*, George Washington International Law Review, George Washington International Law School, Washington.

Deng, S. and J. Peng (2011), "Reforming the budgeting process in China", *OECD Journal on Budgeting*, OECD Publishing, Paris, http://www.oecd.org/gov/budgeting/49070820.pdf.

Diokno, B.E. (2005), "Reforming the Philippine tax system: Lessons from two tax reform programs", *UP School of Economics Discussion Papers*, No. 502, March.

Fabella, R. and K.K.T. Chua (2005), *BIR reform Initiatives: Why Is Success So Elusive?*

Formin (Ministry for Foreign Affairs Finland) (2008), *Anti-Corruption in Viet Nam: The Situation after Two Years of Implementation of the Law*, Hanoi, November.

Government of India (2009), "Organisational structure of government of India", *Thirteenth Report of the Second Administrative Reforms Commission*, April.

Green, K. (2005), "Decentralization and good governance: The case of Indonesia", *Munich Personal RePEc Archive Paper*, No. 10897, February.

Hausman, D. (2009), *Policy Leaps and Implementation Obstacles: Civil Service Reform in Viet Nam, 1998-2009*, Innovations for Successful Societies, Princeton University.

International Monetary Fund (2011), *Revenue Mobilisation in Developing Countries*, International Monetary Fund, Washington, DC, 8 March.

Lin, J.Y., R. Tao and M. Liu (2003), *Decentralisation, Deregulation and Economic Transition in China*, http://sticerd.lse.ac.uk/dps/decentralisation/china.pdf.

Manning, N. (2000), *The New Public Management and its Legacy*, World Bank, Washington, DC, http://www.mh-lectures.co.uk/npm_2.htm.

Meagher, P. (2002), *Anti-Corruption Agencies: A Review of Experience*, prepared for the World Bank IRIS Center, University of Maryland.

Mishra, R.A. (2014), *National Civil Service System in India: A Critical Review*.

Mukherjee, R. et al. (2009), *Implementation of Civil Service Legislation in Viet Nam: Strengthening Elements of a Position-Based System*, Princeton University.

Mutebi, A.M. (2008), "Explaining the failure of Thailand's anti-corruption regime", *Development and Change*, Vol. 39, No. 1.

Nawaz, F. and A. Bridi (2009), *Overview of Corruption and Anti-corruption in the Philippines*, U4 Anti-Corruption Resource Centre/Transparency International Report.

Niazi, T.H. (2011), *Deconcentration and Decentralisation Reforms in Cambodia, Recommendations for an Institutional Framework*, Asian Development Bank.

Nguyen, N.V. (2011), "Tax Reform in Viet Nam: Main Accomplishments and Lessons", Presentation, Tax Policy Department, Ministry of Finance of Viet Nam.

OECD (2014), *Multi-dimensional Review of Myanmar: Volume 2. In-depth Analysis and Recommendations*, OECD Publishing, Paris, http://dx.doi.org/10.1787/9789264220577-en.

OECD (2013), *Southeast Asian Economic Outlook 2013: With Perspectives on China and India*, OECD Publishing, Paris, http://dx.doi.org/10.1787/saeo-2013-en.

OECD (2012), *Southeast Asian Economic Outlook 2011/12*, OECD Publishing, Paris, http://dx.doi.org/10.1787/9789264166882-en.

OECD (2008), *OECD Investment Policy Reviews: China 2008: Encouraging Responsible Business Conduct*, OECD Publishing, Paris, http://dx.doi.org/10.1787/9789264053717-en.

OECD (2006), *Challenges for China's Public Spending*, OECD Publishing, Paris, http// 10.1787/9789264013728-en.OECD (2003), *China in the World Economy: the Domestic Policy Challenges*, OECD Publishing, Paris, http://www.oecd.org/investment/investmentfordevelopment/2075272.pdf.

OECD (2001), *Principles of Good Tax Administration – Practice Note*, OECD Centre for Tax Policy and Administration, OECD Publishing, Paris, May (amended).

Painter, M. (2005), "Thanksinocracy or managerialization? Reforming the Thai bureaucracy", *South East Asia Research Centre Working Paper*, No. 76, May.

Pessino, C. and R. Fenochietto (2010), *Determining Countries' Tax Efforts*, Hacienda Pública Española/Revista de Economía Pública, Vol. 195, pp. 61–83.

Pham, D.M. and M. Engelschalk (2011), "Tax administration", in Ganggada Prassad Shukla et al. (eds.), *Tax Reform in Viet Nam: Toward a More Efficient and Equitable System*, World Bank, Washington, DC, September.

Polidano, C. (1999), *The New Public Management in Developing Countries*, University of Manchester Institute for Development Policy and Management, November.

Poon, Y., N.K. Hùng and X. Truòng (2009), *The Reform of the Civil Service System as Viet Nam moves into the Middle -Income Country Category*, The United Nations Development Programme Viet Nam.

Quah, J.S.T. (2010), "Curbing corruption in Asian countries: The difference between success and failure", *Asian Journal of Political Science*, Vol. 16, No. 3, December.

Quah, J.S.T. (2007), "Anti-corruption agencies in four Asian countries: A comparative analysis", *International Public Management Review*, Vol. 8, No. 2.

Rao, M.G. and P.K. Rao (2005), *Trends and Issues in Tax Policy and Reforms in India*, India Policy Reform, NCAER and Brookings Institution, Vol. 2, 2005-06.

Schutte, S.A. (2012), *Against the Odds: Anti-Corruption Reform in Indonesia*, Public Administration and Development, Vol. 32.

Seiha, U. (2012), "Cambodia: Tax Revenue Reform Issues, Further Reforms", presentation to the IMF-Japan Conference on Emerging Tax Issues in Asian Countries, Tokyo, December.

Shah, A. (ed.) (2007), *Budgeting and Budgetary Institutions*, World Bank, Washington, DC.

Shah, A. (2004), "Fiscal federalism in developing and transition economies: Progress, problems, and the promise", *World Bank Policy Research Paper*, No. 3282, April.

Sidiquee, N.A. (2014), "Malaysia's Government Transformation Programme: a preliminary assessment", *Intellectual Discourse*, Vol. 22, No. 1.

Sidiquee, N.A. (2010), "Managing for results: lessons from public management reform in Malaysia", *International Journal of Public Sector Management*, Vol. 23, No. 1.

Smith, H. (2012), *Asia Anti-Corruption Report*, Issue 1.

Stiles, D.R., Y. Karbhari and M.H.S. Mohamad (2011), *The New Public Financial Management in Malaysia*.

Thomas, K. (2007), *Malaysia: Integrated Results-Based Management – the Malaysia Experience*.

Tjiptoherijanto, P. (2014), *Civil Service Reform in Indonesia: Racing with Decentralisation*.

Tjiptoherijanto, P. (2012a), "Civil service reforms in Thailand: Political control and corruption", *University of Indonesia Working Paper in Economics and Business* Vol. II, No. 1, Department of Economics, University of Indonesia.

Tjiptoherijanto, P. (2012b), "Civil service reform in the Philippines: Building strong governance", *University of Indonesia Working Paper in Economics and Business*, Vol. II, No. 2, Department of Economics, University of Indonesia.

Transparency International (2013), *Global Corruption Barometer 2013*, Transparency International, Berlin, www.transparency.org/research/gcb/overview.

Wang, Q. (2010), "Administrative reform in China: Past, present and future", *Southeast Review of Asian Studies*, Vol 32, Southeast Conference of the Association for Asian Studies.

Wong, C. (2013), "Reforming China's public finances for long-term growth", in R. Garnaut and L. Song (eds.), *China Update 2013*, Australian National University.

Wong, C. (2012a), "Rebuilding government for the 21st century: Can china incrementally reform the public sector?", *China Quarterly*, No. 200, December 2009.

Wong, C. (2012b), "Toward building performance-oriented management in China: The critical role of monitoring and evaluation and the long road ahead", *ECD Working Paper*, No. 27, World Bank, Washington, DC.

Wong, C. (2007), "Budget reform in China", *OECD Journal on Budgeting*, OECD Publishing, Paris, http://www.oecd.org/china/43412239.pdf.

World Bank (2014a), *World Governance Indicators* (database), World Bank, Washington, DC.

World Bank (2014b), *Doing Business 2014*, World Bank, Washington, DC.

World Bank (2013a), *Beyond the Annual Budget: Global Experiences with Medium-Term Expenditure Frameworks*, World Bank, Washington, DC.

World Bank (2013b), *Republic of the Union of Myanmar: Public Finance Management Performance Report*, World Bank, Washington, DC, May.

World Bank (2012a), *The World Bank Approach to Public Sector Management 2011-2020: Better Results from Public Sector Institutions*, World Bank, Washington, DC.

World Bank (2012b), *Indonesia: Public Expenditure and Financial Accountability (PEFA), Public Financial Management*, World Bank, Washington, DC, December.

World Bank (2011), "Cambodia More Efficient Government Spending for Strong and Inclusive Growth", *Integrated Fiduciary Assessment and Public Expenditure Review (IFAPER)*, World Bank, Washington, DC, November.

World Bank (2010a), *Philippines: Public Expenditure and Financial Management (PEFA)*, World Bank, Washington, DC, June.

World Bank (2010b), *Lao People's Democratic Republic: Public Expenditure and Financial Accountability (PEFA): Public Financial Management Assessment*, World Bank, Washington, DC, June.

World Bank (2009), *Thailand Public Expenditure and Financial Accountability*, Public Financial Management Assessment Report, Poverty Reduction and Economic Management Unit, East Asia and Pacific Region, October.

World Bank (2005), *East Asia Decentralises, Making Local Government Work*, World Bank, Washington, DC.

World Bank Independent Evaluation Group (WB-IEG) (2008), *Public Sector Reform: What Works and Why? An IEG Evaluation of World Bank Support*, World Bank, Washington, DC.

World Economic Forum (2013), *Global Competitiveness Report 2013-2014*, World Economic Forum, Geneva.

Xu, C. (2011), "The fundamental institutions of China's reform and development", *Journal of Economic Literature*, Vol. 49, No. 4.

Chapter 4

Strengthening institutions to address informality in Emerging Asia*

While it is difficult to accurately define and measure informal output and employment, these appear to be quite high in several countries in the region. Tax and regulatory burdens, along with cyclical and structural economic factors and social norms, contribute to this situation. Fundamentally, these factors and the degree of informality over the long run depend on government capacities in developing market-building institutions to support formality and in enforcing tax and regulatory requirements on firms and workers. Informality appears to have been declining recently in many Emerging Asian economies and provides employment for marginalised workers. Nevertheless, it remains an important policy challenge to be addressed to support government capacity and economic strength and flexibility. Reforms to improve capacities generally and target informality and the areas of the economy where it is often found therefore need to be included in the development strategies of many countries.

* The statistical data for Israel are supplied by and under the responsibility of the relevant Israeli authorities. The use of such data by the OECD is without prejudice to the status of the Golan Heights, East Jerusalem and Israeli settlements in the West Bank under the terms of international law.

Introduction

Informal firms and workers are found in all economies. The sheer extent of informality makes it a critical issue for policy makers to understand and address – particularly in emerging economies like those of Emerging Asia, which are undergoing significant structural transformation. Informal activities are more likely to arise in such countries, with serious effects on growth and inclusiveness.

Institutions and institutional capacity are central to understanding the causes and consequences of informality and to developing formal alternatives. While informality may be difficult to define and measure and has multiple overlapping causes, institutional factors are fundamental determinants of how prevalent informal output and employment are. Weak institutional capacity may, in turn, also be exacerbated by informality, as hidden activity lowers government revenue, its regulatory reach and its credibility. And although informality ensures the livelihoods of many, it harms growth and development when it replaces dynamic formal activities.

This chapter discusses the state, causes and consequences of informality in Emerging Asia. It then goes on to consider policy options for curbing informality while encouraging the dynamism of the formal business sector. Informal output and employment are more prevalent in some Emerging Asian countries than in others, although it is not surprising that in such a diverse region experiences of informality should vary widely. However, there are signs of its decline in terms of both output and employment, despite fluctuations over time. This chapter uses multiple direct and estimated measures of informality both to paint a more complete picture of the levels and trends of informal output and employment and to compensate for any weaknesses in a particular measurement.

The challenges in measuring informality further complicate efforts to understand its complex, overlapping causes. Excessive tax and regulatory burdens are commonly cited reasons for firms operating covertly and employers and their workers agreeing not to register their employment arrangement. Although taxation and regulation are the primary costs of formality, they are insufficient explanations in themselves for informality. Broader contexts are doubtless critical, too. Informality may be encouraged by high levels of poverty and inequality, by the processes of industrialisation, and by social norms that do not support trust in government or the willingness to pay taxes. While many such factors escape direct government control, long-term levels of informality are – fundamentally – driven by the quality of the institutions that underpin the formal sector and the capacity of government to enforce compliance with requirements on the private sector.

The consequences of informality can also be complex. Informal work and production tend to fare better than the formal economy during downturns, acting as buffers against shocks and offering much needed employment opportunities. However, informal firms are generally less productive because they lack access to formal institutions, which prevents them from obtaining finance and entering into contracts, among other benefits of formality. Moreover, they can slow economic growth with their low productivity and by using their cost advantages over formal firms to gain market share. And, of course, informality also robs the government of revenue and, accordingly, places greater tax burdens on compliant firms and workers.

Clearly, there is a call for policy solutions that encourage higher levels of registration and tax and regulatory compliance, while allowing the flexibility offered by informality in formal firms and employment. Comprehensive solutions are needed across a range of policy areas to strengthen the core institutions underpinning the formal market and to bolster enforcement capacities, particularly where informality is rife.

Informality in Emerging Asia

Diverse states and histories of economic and institutional development across Emerging Asia have produced different experiences of informality. While some evidence suggests it may be on the decline in most countries, it is still common in others. The region's rapid growth has indeed seen the expansion of the formal sector. However, remaining weaknesses in institutional capacity, combined with other social and economic factors, have continued to breed informality. Its persistence threatens development in some economies by further limiting government capacity and credibility and damaging productive potential.

Although understanding informality is of great importance to policy makers, its hidden, ill-definable nature make it hard to measure (Box 4.1). The simultaneous use of multiple definitions and measures allows a more accurate and nuanced understanding of how it varies across economies and over time.

Box 4.1. Discussion of informality requires clear definitions

A definition of informality is a prerequisite to any attempt to describe its causes and consequences and the policy responses that it ultimately prompts. Informal and formal production and employment may overlap in some cases, complicating discussion and measurement. Clarifying the dimensions of informality and how the terms are used is therefore necessary before data can be collected and understood.

Broadly speaking, the "non-observed", "hidden" or "shadow" economy may refer to all productive activities that escape government regulation, including the payment of taxes. In addition to productive activities overlooked as a result of deficiencies in the statistical system, *Measuring the Non-Observed Economy: A Handbook* (OECD, 2002) identifies four categories in the non-observed economy: illegal activities, household production for own use, hidden production by registered firms, and the informal sale of legal goods and services for and by unregistered firms. Discussions of the informal sector typically focus on the last of these categories, though companies' hidden production and tax evasion are closely related concerns. The non-observed economy complicates the production of national accounts. Although many national statistics offices make adjustments based on estimates and secondary data sources, these adjustments are not done consistently across countries and the methods that they use are not always disclosed publicly.

Informality also includes informal employment, which describes the employment of most workers of non-registered firms in the informal sector and those working informally for registered firms. Workers not covered by labour legislation, regular tax arrangements or social protection may be self-employed (providing goods and services directly to a firm or for the open market). Or they may be employed as non-registered employees in either the formal or informal sector. Just as the sources of informal output may range from completely hidden unregistered producers to registered firms, counting the number of informal workers comes up against ambiguity: for example, the self-employed may do some of their work off-the-books or workers may hold both formal and informal positions. In acknowledgement of the latter case, some more detailed surveys of informal employment count jobs instead of or in addition to workers.

Box 4.1. Discussion of informality requires clear definitions *(cont.)*

Definitions of informality that are both nationally relevant and internationally comparable enhance the value of data collected. Regular labour force surveys (LSFs) that include questions on the nature, remuneration, and health and safety of informal work may be particularly useful. Several countries in the region do not publish regular survey results, though improvements are being made. Lao PDR carried out its first LFS and National Child Labour Survey in early 2013, while Myanmar is poised for its first survey since 1990, which it plans to conduct in the wake of its 2014 National Population Census. Internationally comparable measures can further increase the value of LFS data by enabling cross-country comparisons. And they need not preclude flexibility in individual countries' definitions of informality. Indeed, the 15th International Conference on Labour Statistics outlined a definition of informality open to some adjustment by individual countries. The Philippines, for example, has decided not to include certain categories of firms, farms and domestic helpers in its definition of informality.

Source: OECD (2002), *Measuring the Non-Observed Economy: A Handbook*, OECD Publishing, Paris, http://dx.doi.org/10.1787/9789264175358-en.

Informal employment can be measured as the number of workers not covered by labour regulation or, more commonly but less accurately, as the number of self-employed workers not officially employed by a firm. Regardless of the definition, the informally employed account for a large share of total non-agricultural workers in a number of Emerging Asian economies and vary considerably in number across the region (Figure 4.1). There tend to be fewer in wealthier economies, though *per capita* income is not the only determinant. Informal employment is relatively high in India, Indonesia, Cambodia, the Philippines and Viet Nam, and low in Singapore and Malaysia. As is also true outside of the region, most informal positions are found in the informal sector, though there are many informal jobs in the formal economies of some countries. In China, for example, formal firms account for 38% of total informal employment, and in Viet Nam, 37%.

Figure 4.1. **Much of employment is informal across Emerging Asia**

Shares of total non-agricultural employment, by employment type

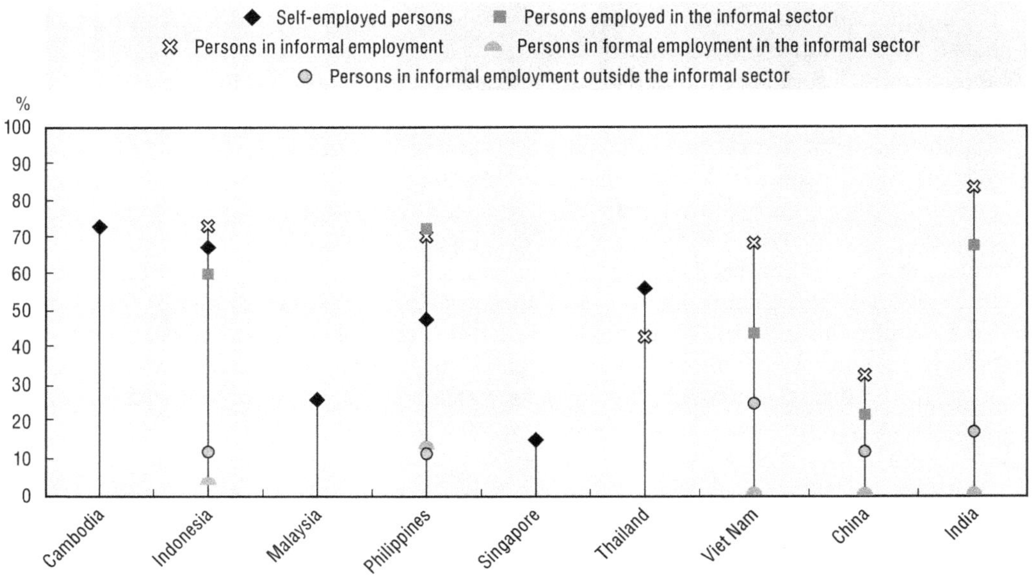

Note: All data from various years in 2008-10.

Sources: International Labour Organization (2010a), *LABORSTA* (database), ILO, Geneva, http://laborsta.ilo.org/.

StatLink http://dx.doi.org/10.1787/888933179860

Shares of informal output are somewhat different from those of informal employment in Emerging Asia, however. While the use of different methods of estimation yields considerable variations in the scale of informal production due to difficulties in obtaining reliable measures (Box 4.2), wealthier and more developed Singapore and Malaysia again appear to have smaller informal sectors and Cambodia, Myanmar, Thailand and Lao PDR larger ones (Figure 4.2).

Figure 4.2. **Estimates of informal output show some similar patterns**

Informal sectors' shares of total output, by type of estimation

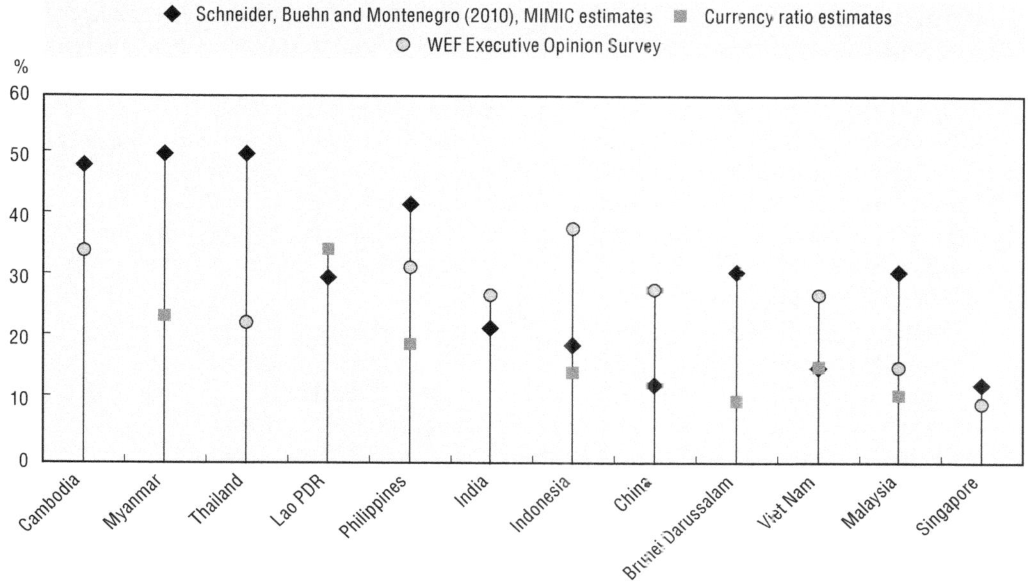

Note: Averages of 2000-07 values from MIMIC and currency ratio estimations and 2006 survey results.

Sources: Schneider, F., A. Buehn and C.E. Montenegro, "Shadow economies all over the world: New estimates for 162 countries from 1999 to 2007", *World Bank Policy Research Working Paper*, No. 5356, World Bank, Washington, DC; World Economic Forum (2006), *The Global Competitiveness Report 2006-2007*, World Economic Forum, New York; OECD Development Centre calculations.

StatLink http://dx.doi.org/10.1787/888933179878

Informality can be common in emerging economies and average levels in Emerging Asia are not out of line with those in other parts of the world. The region's countries have very different experiences, however. Among the 47 emerging economies for which the ILO has recently published figures on the informal share of total employment, India ranks highest and above those of lower-income countries such as Mali, while China's rate of informal employment is among the lowest, lying between those of South Africa and Turkey (Figure 4.3).

Box 4.2. **Estimations of informal output can produce useful indicators**

While household-level labour force surveys can systematically measure informal employment, it is not so easy when it comes to reasuring hidden output outside the formal sector. In the absence of registers of informal firms, surveys of limited geographic regions can sometimes help to obtain information about formal and informal firms' activities. Comprehensive measures of national-level informal output, however, have typically been forced to rely on subjective opinion surveys and macro estimations using observed proxy indicators. Opinion surveys that ask respondents about their thoughts on the size of the informal sector and econometrics-based estimations are problematic: the former are affected by individuals' perceptions and partial information, while the latter require strong assumptions about the relationships between the indicators used and informal output.[1] The best solution is therefore to compare the results obtained from multiple measures in order to develop an approximate understanding of the size of and trends in the informal sector. Accordingly, this chapter uses several indicators of informal output to estimate informal sector output in Emerging Asian economies:

- Schneider, Buehn and Montenegro's (2010) estimations of hidden economy output shares in 162 countries were created using the multiple indicators multiple causes (MIMIC) approach. This method uses monetary, labour market and income proxy measures of informality, and measures of tax and social security contributions, regulation intensity, public sector services, and the performance of the official economy as presumed causes of informality. MIMIC estimations produce indices of informal output that can be converted to shares of total economic activity through monetary estimation methods, such as the currency demand or currency ratio approaches.
- The currency ratio method uses the ratio of currency in circulation to the total money supply in order to estimate the share of activity in the hidden economy. This approach assumes that the hidden economy is motivated by a desire to avoid tax pressures, that transactions outside of the observed formal economy are carried out only with cash, and that the velocity of money is the same in the formal and informal sectors.
- The World Economic Forum's 2006-07 *Executive Opinion Survey* asked business leaders in 125 countries to estimate the size of the informal sector in their countries. Respondents were given ranges of options to choose from, with the largest equal to 50%. Average responses may therefore be understated.
- The physical input method uses the change in electricity consumption as a proxy for growth in the total economy after controlling for changes in industry structure and price level. Combined with information on the level of informal output from a base year, this method can be used to produce estimated time series on informal output. Such an approach has come in for a number of criticisms and may underestimate informal growth rates where improvements in energy efficiency decrease the GDP elasticity of electricity consumption.

Note: In addition, macro estimation methods typically assume that official GDP statistics exclude all transactions in the hidden economy. This assumption is also used here in analysis of trends in informality using the electricity consumption estimation method. National statistics organisations, however, typically include some form of estimate of informal output in their national accounts figures. As a result, the assumption that official GDP figures exclude the informal sector can create an upward bias in the estimates of its size and share of total output. Unfortunately, this bias is difficult to correct, as the decisions on what aspects of the hidden economy to include and how the methodologies used vary across countries are not usually published (Gyomai and van de Ven, 2014).

Figure 4.3. **Informal employment can be relatively high in Emerging Asian economies**

Informal employment as a share of total non-agricultural employment

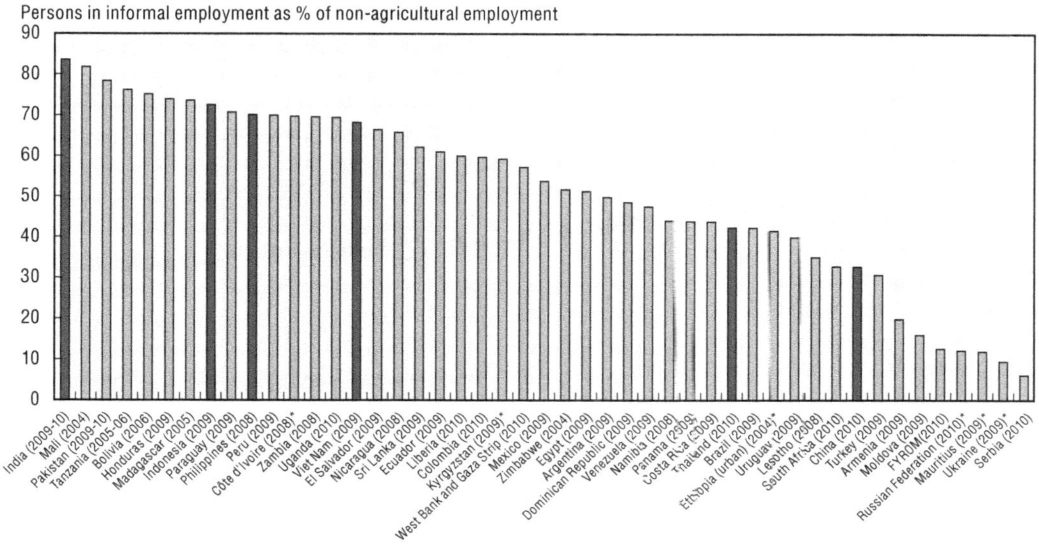

Notes: Countries selected based on the availability of data. Values for starred (*) countries indicate the share of persons employed in the informal sector.

Source: International Labour Organization (2010a), *LABORSTA* (database), ILO, Geneva, http://laborsta.ilo.org/.

StatLink http://dx.doi.org/10.1787/888933179886

Although informality is prevalent in some Emerging Asian countries, there have been falls in shares of employment over the recent past, as economies have gone through a period of growth, continued development (which includes slowing rates of structural transformation and urbanisation) and reform of governance. The nature and extent of the falls is not so clear, however, as different measures supply contradictory evidence. Self-employment accounts for a relatively low share of total non-agricultural employment in wealthier Singapore and did not change much between 1986 and 2012. However, it declined considerably in emerging Cambodia (from 87% to 64% between 2004 and 2012) and Viet Nam (from 83% to 65% between 1996 and 2012), both countries having undergone relatively greater economic and institutional development over the period 1986-2012 (Figure 4.4). Estimates of trends in informal output derived from electricity consumption rates indicate a similar decline in informality in most countries in the region for which data were available (excluding Brunei Darussalam, Lao PDR and Myanmar), and surprisingly, slight increases in Cambodia and Viet Nam (Figure 4.5). Currency ratio estimates, which are used to estimate levels of informal output rather than its change over time, have also declined in most countries. However, they show relatively constant shares of informal output in recent years in China and India, where estimates of informality based on electricity consumption show the steepest declines.

Figure 4.4. Self-employment is low or declining in many economies

Self-employment as a share of total non-agricultural employment, 1986-2012

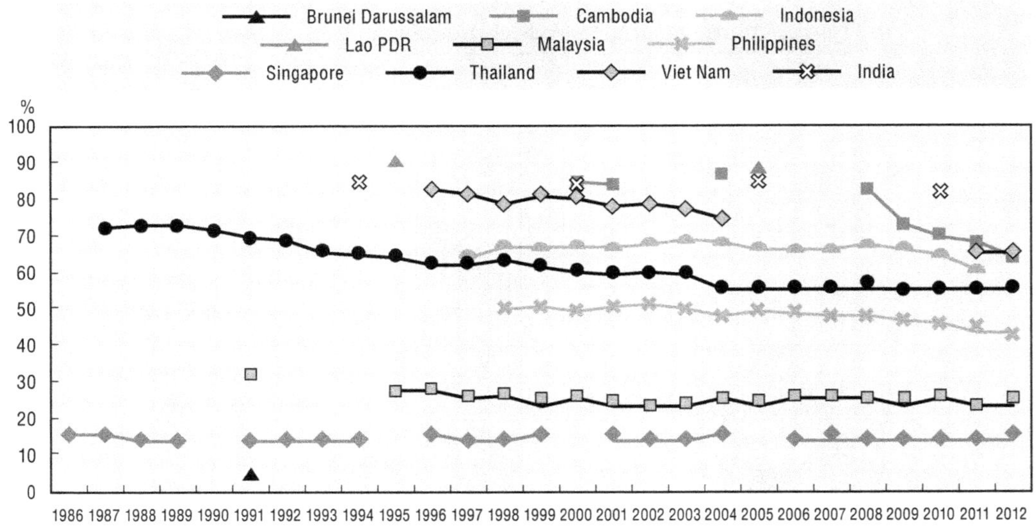

Source: International Labour Organization (2010a), *LABORSTA* (database), ILO, Geneva, http://laborsta.ilo.org/.

StatLink http://dx.doi.org/10.1787/888933179892

Figure 4.5. Estimated shares of informality are declining in most Emerging Asian economies

Informal sectors' shares of total output, 1995-2011

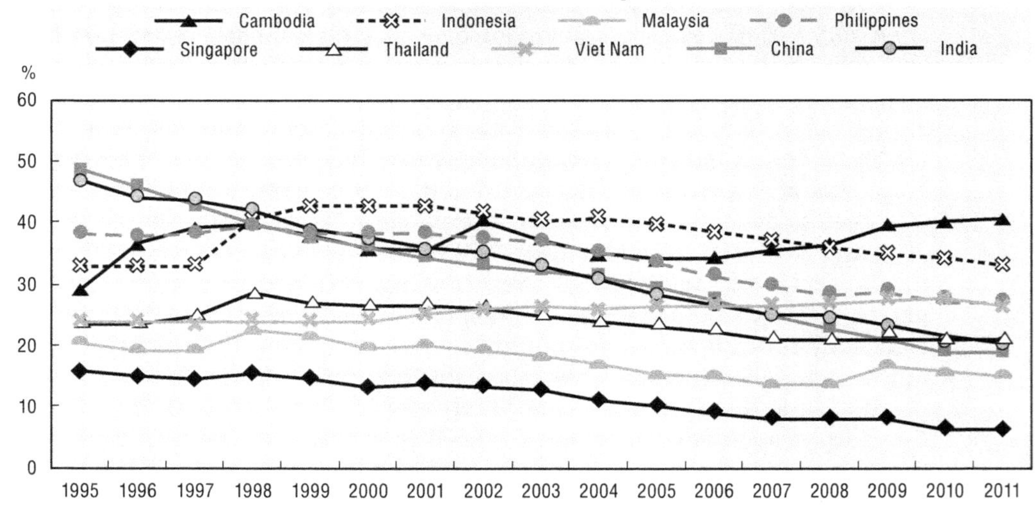

Note: Informal output shares estimated using WEF Executive Opinion Survey values for 2006, extended with growth rates estimated using the electricity consumption method. Estimates for Brunei Darussalam, Lao PDR and Myanmar are not available.

Sources: World Economic Forum (2006), *The Global Competitiveness Report 2006-2007*, World Economic Forum, New York; OECD Development Centre calculations.

StatLink http://dx.doi.org/10.1787/888933179903

The determinants of informality

Informal employment and output have multiple interconnected proximate and deep-lying causes. Tax and regulatory burdens and associated administrative costs, along with countries' economic and social contexts, play important parts in determining informality. Fundamentally, institutional capacity that is too weak to underpin the formal sector and enforce tax and regulatory compliance can encourage informality directly and indirectly through more proximate causes.

Tax and regulatory factors may contribute to informality

High levels of informality are often blamed on excessive tax and regulatory burdens on firms, though their influence is complex and also depends on the broader economic and institutional environment. While high taxes increase the direct costs of operating formally for firms and employees, their effects and willingness to pay may also be dependent on satisfaction with the government, as suggested by Cowell (1990). Indeed, limited institutional capacities and the revenue-draining effects of informality mean that tax ratios are often lower where informality is more common. On top of average tax rates, tax structures and administration may weaken compliance. Tax structures may do so when they place heavy burdens on small firms and discourage employees from reporting revenue, while complex tax administration procedures increase filing costs.

Product and labour market regulations can afford valuable protection to customers, employees and firms by promoting fair competition and correcting for externalities and market imperfections. By contrast, excessive regulation – in addition to increasing production costs and distorting firms' incentives – can also drive businesses out of the formal sector. The administrative formalities required to register and run a business, such as the red tape for costly licenses, are a particularly relevant factor in this regard. In an international study of emerging economies, Dabla-Norris, Gradstein and Inchauste (2005), for example, found that informality declines as the quality of the legal system improves, and that regulatory burdens appear to be less damaging to the formal sector in countries with strong rule of law.

High labour-market entry costs and overregulation are also often blamed for curtailing formal job opportunities and exacerbating informal employment. Given its low productivity levels, employment shares in the informal sector are often higher than its output shares. The wedge may even be thicker where informal employment in the formal sector is encouraged by taxes on labour and labour market rigidities such as high minimum wages or strict hiring and firing rules.

While restrictive labour markets may contribute to informal employment, they do not appear to be a sufficient explanation. Although Chinese labour protection indicators (the length of time, number of procedures and costs for employers of making individual and collective dismissals) top those of all other OECD member countries and are among the strictest in Indonesia and India, the differences between countries are not as great as may be expected (Figure 4.6). Moreover, in all three countries minimum wages as percentages of the median wage and average and marginal taxes on labour are mostly below or slightly above OECD averages (OECD, 2014a). Such simple comparisons do not necessarily take into account, however, that employers may place greater importance on flexibility in fast-changing, lower-productivity emerging economies.

Figure 4.6. **Labour protection provisions in China, Indonesia and India are somewhat higher than the OECD average and several other emerging economies**

Strictness of employment protection provisions for individual and collective dismissals of workers on regular contracts in OECD member and selected non-member countries, 2013

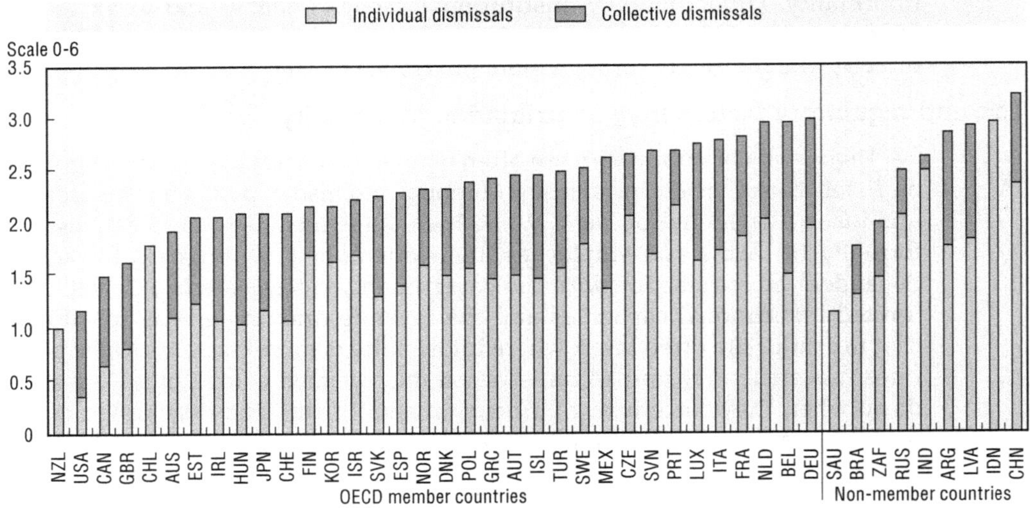

Notes: Data for OECD member countries are from 2013 and for non-members countries from 2012. The OECD employment protection indicators are compiled from information on the inconveniences and additional costs of individual and collective dismissals of workers with regular contracts. They are measured on a scale of 0 to 6, where 0 indicates a lack of restrictions and 6 indicates maximum restrictiveness.

The statistical data for Israel are supplied by and under the responsibility of the relevant Israeli authorities. The use of such data by the OECD is without prejudice to the status of the Golan Heights, East Jerusalem and Israeli settlements in the West Bank under the terms of international law.

Source: OECD (2014b), *Indicators of Employment Protection* (database), OECD, Paris, http://www.oecd.org/employment/emp/oecdindicatorsofemploymentprotection.htm.

StatLink http://dx.doi.org/10.1787/888933179919

Economic and social factors also affect informality

Factors beyond governments' market interventions also affect informality, as it tends to be higher in underdeveloped and industrialising economies and where social and cultural pressures to comply with laws are weaker. While policy does not easily affect such determinants, they remain relevant considerations for policy makers in formulating expectations about informality and designing appropriate strategies. A government can even influence them indirectly.

Informality tends to be associated with inequality and underdevelopment and is generally widespread among the poor and less well educated workers who face exclusion from the formal sector. As argued in the model put forward by Chong and Gradstein (2004), poor entrepreneurs operating in an economy with low-quality institutions are more likely to join an informal sector that offers free access to less productive technology rather than invest in the advanced technologies needed to compete in the formal economy. In such a context, high levels of poverty and inequality are likely to contribute to high levels of informality, as more firms are pushed out of the formal sector.

The process of transitioning from agriculture and traditional labour-intensive activities into more modern industries may also prompt a rise in informality and the proliferation of small firms and self-employment. According to such thinking, self-employed workers help to expand economic opportunities and are a sign of the growing importance of markets. In a study of self-employment in rural China from 1981 to 2000, for example, Mohapatra, Rozelle and Goodhue (2007) find that self-employed workers tend increasingly to operate in higher-productivity industries like trade and transportation. The inference is that self-employment may be more a sign of development than of exclusion in quickly developing economies. Similarly, the rural-urban migration that typically accompanies the shift away from agriculture can increase informality as institutional barriers and a slowly adjusting formal sector fail to create sufficient employment to absorb new migrants. A study of migrants in four major Indonesian cities found that recent arrivals were more likely to work informally and for lower wages than those who had been settled longer (Manning and Pratomo, 2013).

Although their effects are particularly difficult to measure, social and cultural factors may also foster informality where social norms do not strongly deter people from operating outside legal frameworks. While policy makers cannot directly influence these norms, Levi (1988) argues that self-motivated compliance is an outcome of two factors that they should consider. The first is exposure to compliance by others, the implication being that social norms may make informality self-reinforcing if its commonness increases its acceptability.

The second factor is government provision of services in exchange for tax collected. The argument is that the development of social and cultural norms is partly dependent on institutional settings, particularly with regard to tax payment, as tax morale – the motivation for paying taxes – is an outcome of good governance. People are generally more willing to pay tax where trust in government is higher. At the country level, responses to the *AsiaBarometer* survey generally indicate that higher levels of trust in the central government are associated with greater willingness to pay more tax so as to see more public spending (Daude, Gutiérrez and Melguizo, 2012).

Efficient formal markets rely on good institutions

At a more fundamental level, institutions influence levels of informality over the long term. Effective institutions encourage formality both through push factors – tax and regulatory enforcement and penalties for non-compliance – and pull factors – i.e. access to market-supporting public goods and institutions such as the rule of law; the protection of property rights; contract enforcement and closer interaction with formal sector financers, suppliers and customers.

Impartiality, respect for the rule of law, fair and timely enforcement of contracts, and the recognition and protection of property rights are particularly critical factors. In a study of 42 developing and advanced economies, Loayza and Rigolini (2006) find that self-employment (used as a proxy for informality) moves counter-cyclically over the short run, but declines in the long term with such institutional improvements as the more effective rule of law. Such patterns are also apparent among Emerging Asian economies. For example, estimated shares of total output in the informal sector are lower where the rule of law is stronger, as suggested in the PRS Group's *Rule of Law Index*, which rates countries on the impartiality of their legal systems and the extent of compliance with the law (Figure 4.7).

Figure 4.7. **Weaker rule of law is associated with higher informality**

Rule of law and estimated informal share of total output in selected countries, 2011

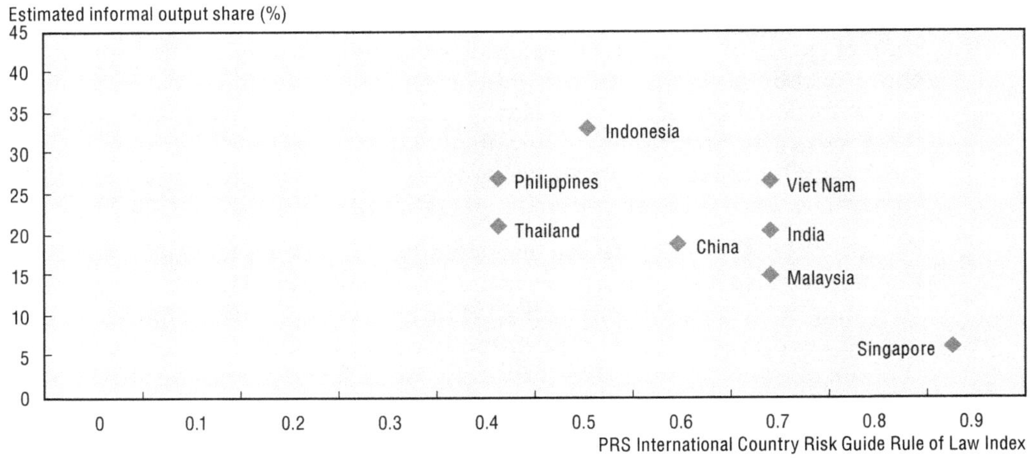

Notes: The PRS Rule of Law Index, which varies from 0 to 1, gives higher scores to countries where the legal system is strong and impartial and the law is popularly observed. Informal output shares estimated using WEF Executive Opinion Survey values for 2006, extended with growth rates estimated using the electricity consumption method.

Sources: Political Risk Services (2014), *International Country Risk Guide* (database), PRS, Syracuse; OECD Development Centre calculations.

StatLink http://dx.doi.org/10.1787/888933179920

At the same time, governments should enforce tax and regulatory requirements effectively if they are to have any influence on behaviour. Enforcement, in turn, requires the capacity to inspect firms and penalise those caught breaking the rules – a capacity that is often found wanting in Emerging Asian and other developing economies. Accordingly, Indonesia began planning a large-scale expansion of its tax collection efforts in 2013, aiming to almost double the number of tax office employees from 62 000 within five years and bringing in an additional 100 000 employees over ten years. To address the related issue of insufficient deterrence for breaches of tax law, Viet Nam introduced reforms in 2013 to amend the statute of limitations on firms' and individuals' tax procedure violations and doubled the size of maximum fines. While important, such changes will remain of little consequence without efficient legal systems that have the capacity to hear cases within a reasonable length of time.

The consequences of informality

While the consequences of informality are generally adverse, they can also be for the good in emerging economies where they make for greater economic flexibility. Informal firms create jobs for workers excluded from the formal economy, particularly during downturns, which has a buffering effect. However, that benefit is outweighed by downsides if better formal jobs could have been created in their place. Informality also stunts government capacity and reach and tends to be associated with low productivity, which can create unfair competition for the formal sector and harm growth.

The counter-cyclicality of informality can mitigate volatility

In general, fluctuations in informality are counter-cyclical, as tax and regulatory avoidance may help to lower costs during downturns and there may be differential income elasticities in demand for formal and informal products. By acting as a safety net, informality helps to smooth growth. Informal shares of employment and output often expand as growth in the formal sector slows thanks to increases in competitive pressures that make the cost advantages of informality more attractive. Formal firms go informal or hide more output and new and existing informal firms take greater market shares from their formal competitors. These changes are then reversed as the formal sector rebounds. The cyclicality of informality, however, is determined by its structure and the nature of the shock experienced. In a study of four Latin American countries, Fiess, Fugazza and Maloney (2009), for example, find that informal employment can sometimes move pro-cyclically when jobs are chiefly in non-tradable sectors and when demand shocks affect those sectors disproportionately.

Though it is an imperfect measure of true fluctuations in informal output (see Box 4.2), estimated growth rates in the absolute size of the sector suggest that its movements can be highly countercyclical (Figure 4.8). Short-term improvements in official GDP growth are often accompanied by falling growth rates in the informal sector, and *vice versa*. Growth in informal output rose considerably as official GDP growth fell below zero in 1998 in Indonesia, Malaysia, the Philippines, Singapore and Thailand, which were among the Emerging Asian economies worst affected by the 1997 Asian Financial Crisis. Informal growth rates are not a perfect mirror of formal sector growth, however, as a range of factors – including policy changes and differential exposure to demand shocks – can affect the informal sector differently in different countries.

Informality provides employment opportunities, particularly for the poor and marginalised

Difficulty in accessing formal positions and the pull of informal work mean that marginalised groups are often overrepresented in informal jobs. Poorer and less-educated entrepreneurs and workers are likely to be attracted by the relative ease of operating informally and may see fewer benefits from the network, finance, and scale opportunities that formalisation brings. While the implication may be that informality provides job opportunities, the jobs tend to be of lower quality and offer fewer benefits.

A recent Thai labour force survey found that, while only 13.9% of formally employed workers in the country had less than an elementary level education or no formal education at all, the proportion of informal workers was 58%. Not surprisingly, the wage gap between the two groups of workers was also wide. On average, formal workers earned 2.5 times more per month, even though informal workers were more likely to work in excess of 50 hours per week. The same disparity was found in all identified industries, although it was typically at its narrowest in labour-intensive activities like household employment, agriculture, and accommodation and food services.

Immigrants may also face economic, regulatory and social barriers to formal work, even when they have crossed borders legally. Together with domestic rural-urban migrants, they may outnumber available jobs and find themselves unemployed or in informal work, at least temporarily, as originally suggested by Todaro's (1969) development model. For example, *China Urban Labour Survey* data show that, while 32.6% of established residents worked informally in 2005, the figure was 84.3% among migrants.

Figure 4.8. The informal sector can act as a buffer against formal sector downturns

Annual growth rates in official GDP and estimated informal output, 1996-2011

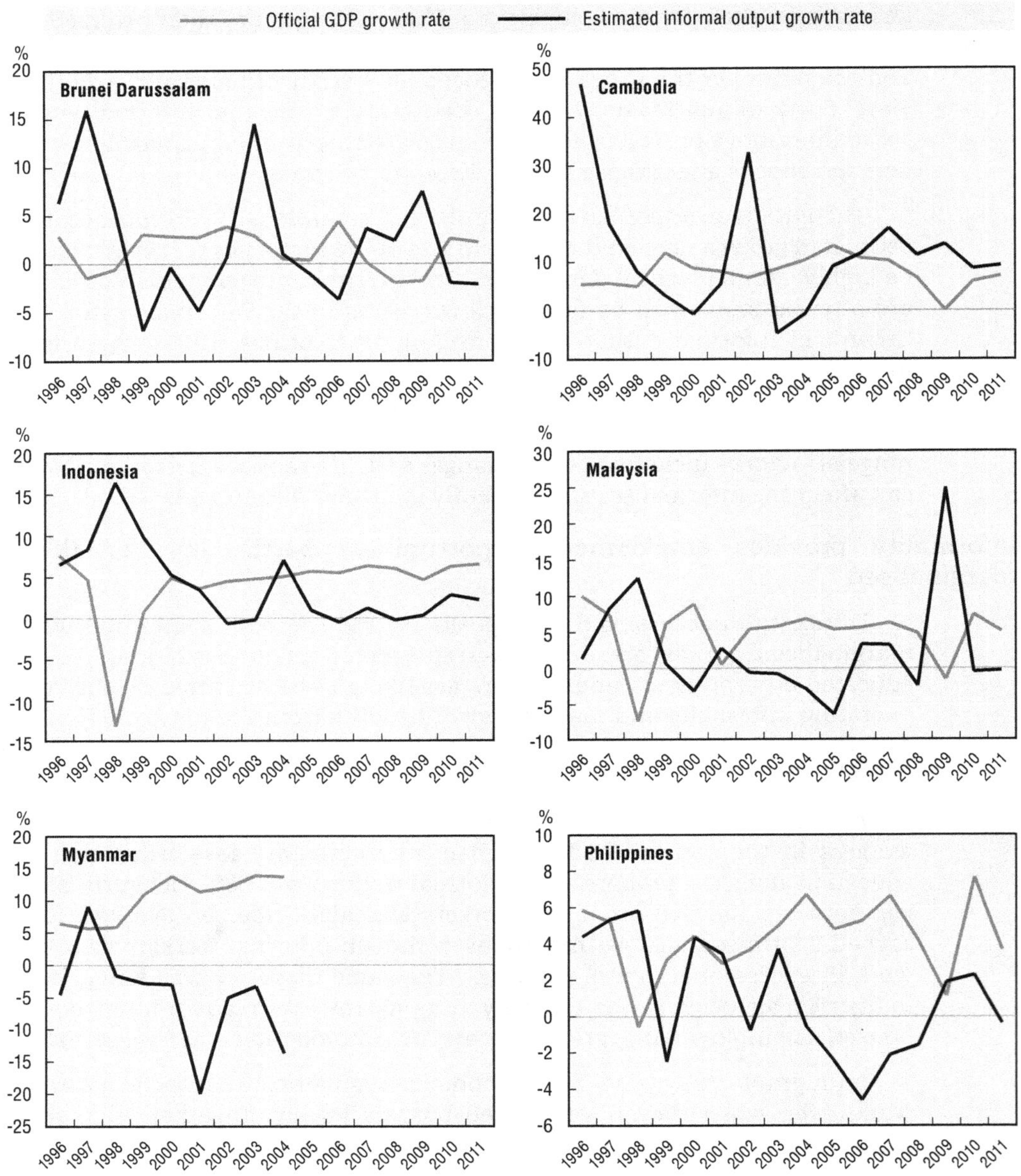

Notes: Informal sector growth rates were estimated using the electricity consumption method. Estimates for Lao PDR and Myanmar 2005-11 were not possible due to data limitations.

Sources: World Bank (2014a), *World Development Indicators* (database), World Bank, Washington, DC; OECD Development Centre calculations.

StatLink http://dx.doi.org/10.1787/888933179934

Figure 4.8. The informal sector can act as a buffer against formal sector downturns *(cont.)*

Annual growth rates in official GDP and estimated informal output, 1996-2011

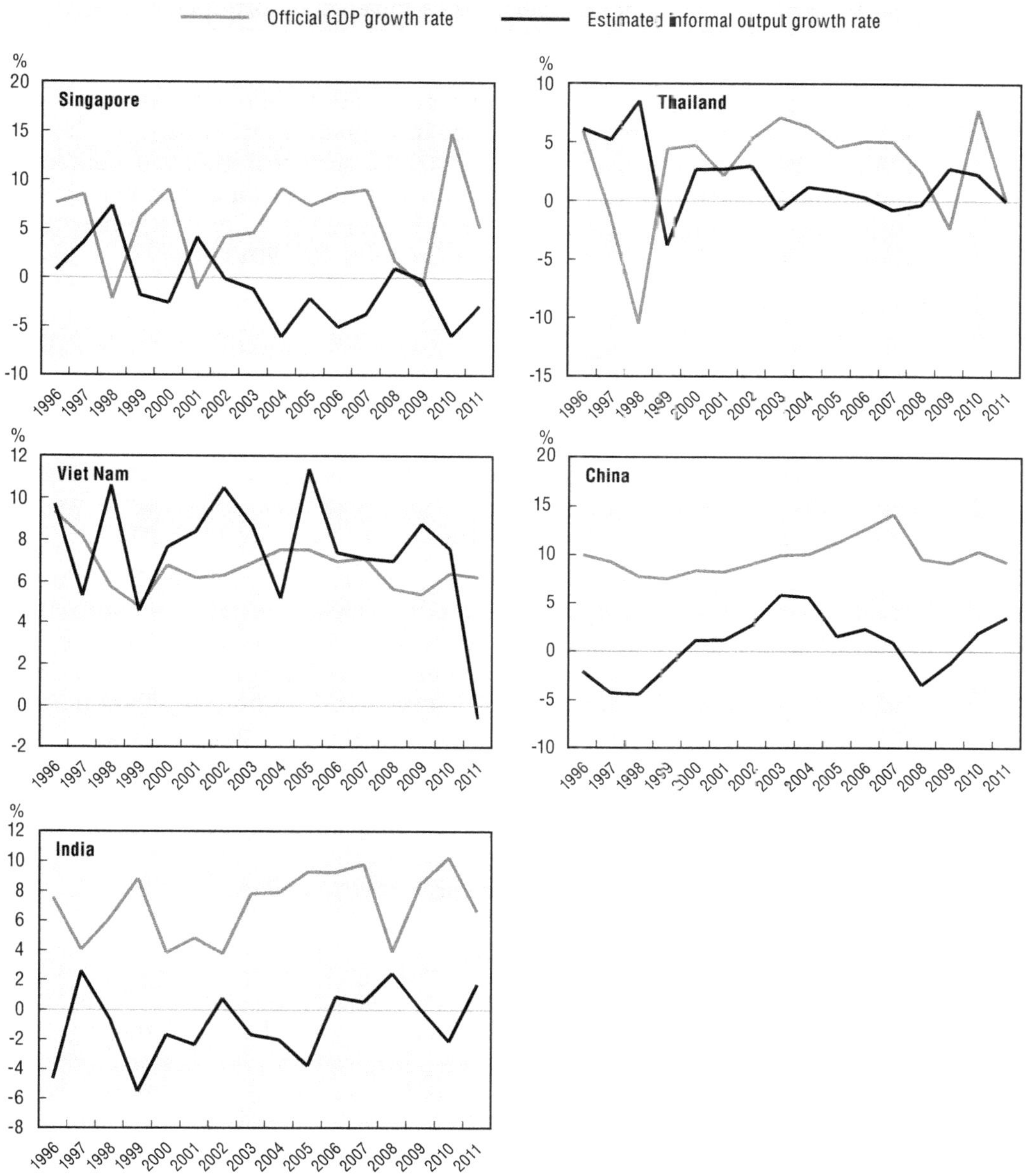

Notes: Informal sector growth rates were estimated using the electricity consumption method. Estimates for Lao PDR and Myanmar 2005-11 were not possible due to data limitations.

Sources: World Bank (2014a), *World Development Indicators* (database), World Bank, Washington, DC; OECD Development Centre calculations.

StatLink http://dx.doi.org/10.1787/888933179934

Women also tend to be overrepresented in informal employment – attributable to factors that include social norms, insufficient women's rights, limited access to education and other resources, and gender differences in both types of work performed and in migration patterns (Jütting and Laiglesia, 2009). The gender gap is wide in China, where 35.7% of women working in the non-agricultural sector are employed informally, compared with 30.1% of men. Disparities are similar, though narrower, in India, Indonesia, the Philippines and Thailand, and actually reversed in Viet Nam, where 66.8% of women and 69.4% of men who are not employed in agriculture work informally. Women working informally tend to be overrepresented in lower paid occupations like industrial outworking.

Informal employment is a flexible, inclusive source of labour. Yet it comes at a cost to workers: not only are their wages lower, they often lack access to basic social protection. Although they may enjoy some forms of social assistance targeting the poor, such as cash transfers, they are widely excluded from contributory programmes like unemployment benefits and health and workplace injury insurance and pensions. Schemes aimed at informal workers also have great trouble raising their awareness and building the capacity to reach them. A 2009 ILO survey of informal workers in Indonesia found that 86% had no formal or informal form of social security apart from reliance on family, even though almost 60% knew about the country's Jamsostek scheme for informal workers (International Labour Organization, 2010b).

Informality can limit government capacity

The most immediate negative consequence of informality is that it robs governments of revenue, which in turn affects the private sector. The problem can be serious, and the free-riding issue of non-payment of taxes either increases the burden on the formal sector or impairs the provision of public goods and services. Along with other forms of tax avoidance, informality contributes to low tax ratios. The *Revenue Statistics in Asian Countries* report shows that tax-to-GDP ratios in Indonesia and Malaysia were respectively 12.8% and 15.7% in 2011 – well below the OECD average of 34.1% (OECD, 2014c).[1]

Informality may also weaken state effectiveness by diminishing the credibility of government and the legal system generally. Legal and regulatory requirements of firms and employees are, of course, less influential where they are widely ignored without consequence. Because informality accounts for such a large share of employment in India, for example, most workers are not covered by labour legislation. At the extreme end, an estimated mere 5% in agriculture are covered (NCEUS, 2008). Indirectly, respect for and trust in government and the rule of law may be harmed by exposure to unaddressed informality if firms that break one law or regulation are then more likely to break others. At the same time, by providing an exit option, informality also imposes pressure on governments to show restraint in the demands made on the formal sector, thereby potentially encouraging more pro-growth policies.

Informality can constrain firm productivity

Lower productivity can be both a cause and an outcome of firms' informality. As a cause, low-productivity producers who seek to avoid tax and the regulatory burdens of formality and do not intend to develop proprietary products or production methods are likely to remain informal. As an outcome, informal firms generally operate in labour-intensive and traditional activities, such as outsourced manufacturing activities, retail, and other low-productivity services. Most modern, high-tech, capital-intensive industries, such as rail and air transport, power generation, and telecommunications, preclude firms from doing business informally.

More importantly for growth, operating informally limits the productivity potential of firms, as they cannot easily access the efficiency-raising institutions available to the formal sector. Public services like training and trade fairs often fail to reach informal firms. Instead, they rely on limited markets because they use personal relationships with suppliers and customers instead of legally enforced contracts.

Because they lack collateral and do not enjoy a legal status, informal firms tend not to borrow through the formal financial system. Instead, they use alternatives that increase costs or provide lower funding, which limits their ability to invest in productivity-enhancing machinery, equipment and technology (Box 4.3). Financial access can be particularly challenging in emerging economies where formal firms also have trouble borrowing. In China, for example, large, profitable firms with better credit histories and ratings can borrow from banks relatively easily, while the rest rely on retained earnings and informal sources for their financing needs (Tanaka and Molnar, 2008). While big firms are not always the most productive, informal businesses may be forced to operate on smaller scales than would otherwise be efficient because of insufficient financing, less efficient production technologies and the need to remain hidden.[2]

Box 4.3. **Informal firms' access to finance in Myanmar**

The formal financial sectors in many emerging economies are underdeveloped and, in any case, difficult for informal firms to access without clear legal status and proof of property ownership they can use as collateral. The informal sector is therefore more likely to rely on alternative sources of finance, such as retained earnings, personal savings, loans from family and friends, microcredit organisations, and informal lenders. Such funding arrangements typically offer limited credit or, in the case of informal lenders, loans at high interest rates. Widespread reliance on informal financing prevents the financial system from developing as a means of improving overall economic efficiency and may also bring systemic risks into the broader financial system. Although the severe banking crisis in Myanmar in 2003 was a result of weaknesses in the broader system and mounting panic, it began with the collapse of informal finance companies before spreading to formal banks that incurred direct losses.

Although both formal and informal firms may look beyond banks and the formal financial sector to borrow – particularly in countries with highly regulated or underdeveloped financing – such alternative sources are generally more important to informal firms. In Myanmar, most informal firms only use their own funds to cover overheads and finance investment in fixed assets (Figure 4.9). While more financing or better terms may be available from microfinance institutions and banks, Myanmar's informal sector avails itself of them very little, which suggests low levels of access.

Figure 4.9. **Few informal firms in Myanmar rely on formal sources of finance**
Percentage of informal firm respondents making recent use of finance sources, by type of financing need

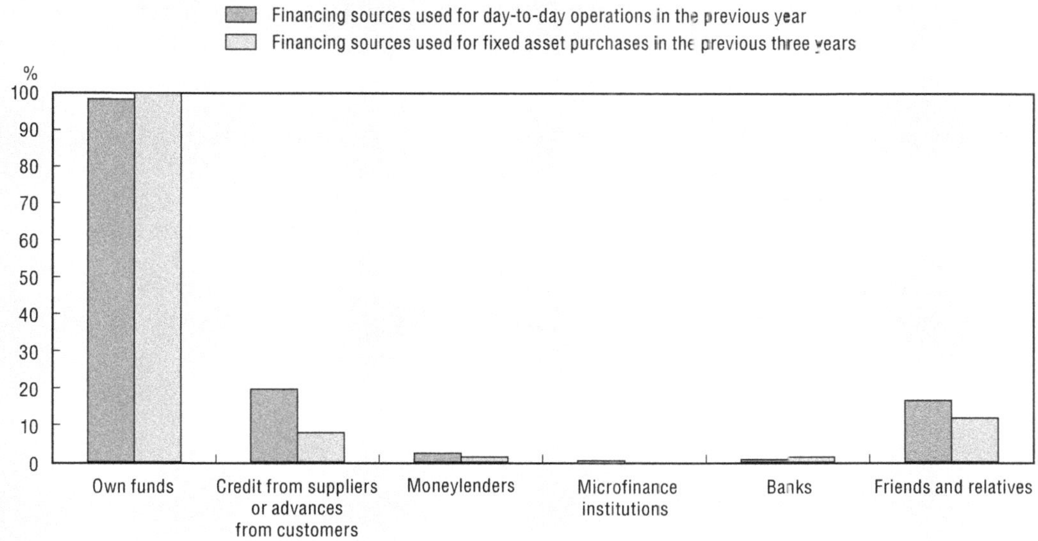

Sources: World Bank (2014b), *Enterprise Surveys* (database), World Bank, Washington, DC, http://www.enterprisesurveys.org; OECD Development Centre calculations.
StatLink http://dx.doi.org/10.1787/888933179948

Unfortunately, there have been but few large-scale surveys of the informal sector that collect information on productivity. A 2009 study by the Asian Development Bank and Statistics Indonesia (Badan Pusat Statistik) surveyed formal and informal workers in two Indonesian provinces: Yogyakarta and Banten. Though the degree of informality varied between the more agricultural Yogyakarta and urbanised Banten, informal sector productivity in both was considerably lower than in the formal sector. Value added per job in Yogyakarta's informal sector was found to be about half of the total level in the province, while in Banten it was only one-third. Accordingly, wages and earnings were also considerably lower in informal jobs.

Formal firms are also negatively affected by informality

The informal sector constrains productivity not only directly, but indirectly, too. In part, indirect effects are manifest in the greater relative tax burden on compliant formal firms while a related impact is to be found where formal firms share markets with informal producers. They may well find themselves at a disadvantage – even when they are more productive – because of the lower production costs of informal firms who avoid taxes and compliance with other laws and regulations. Even though the informal sector tends to produce goods for lower-income customers than the formal sector, the two may come into competition where they produce similar products. Customers are sensitive to price as much as quality, and the small scale and flexibility of informal firms enable them to offer customers convenience and additional services (Mazumdar, 1989). Competition of this type can slow growth as informal firms claim market shares, thereby displacing more productive formal activity.

Informal competition is seen as a serious constraint by many formal firms, though a number of contextual factors influence that perception. The World Bank's Enterprise Surveys of Emerging Asian countries asked registered firms whether they faced informal competition and how serious an obstacle they perceived it to be to their business. Over 30% of respondents in every country surveyed recently in the region stated they had to contend with informal competition. And a number of firms were indeed found to feel exposed to and worried about the competition (Figure 4.10), although findings varied widely: 7% of respondents in Lao PDR in 2009 and 34% in Indonesia perceived competition from the informal sector as a "moderate", "major" or "very severe" obstacle.

These responses are without doubt influenced by multiple factors beyond the size of the informal economy, such as the extent to which the informal economy resembled and competed with the formal sector and respondents' subjective views of how a serious problem informal competition was. Such additional factors may explain why exposure to informal competition does not appear to be closely linked to a country's level of informality and why more firms in Lao PDR reported exposure to and concern about informal competition in 2012 than in 2009. In addition to price competition in overlapping markets supplied by both sectors, informal firms may hinder innovation and profitability in the formal sector by violating the intellectual property rights of their competitors (Box 4.4).

Figure 4.10. **Informal competition is experienced and seen as a constraint by many formal firms**

Percentage of registered firms

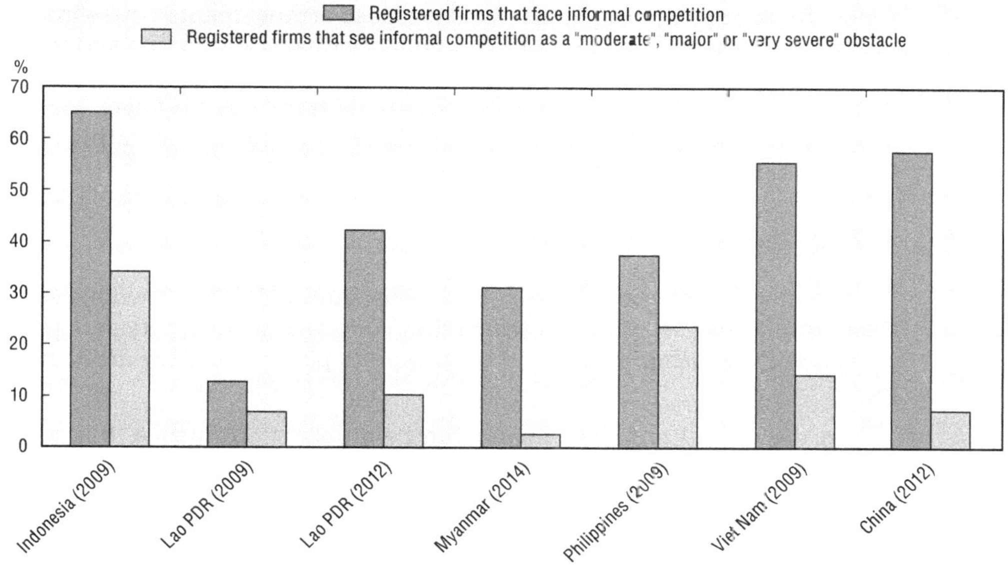

Sources: World Bank (2014b), *Enterprise Surveys* (database), World Bank, Washington, DC, http://www.enterprisesurveys.org; OECD Development Centre calculations.

StatLink http://dx.doi.org/10.1787/888933179957

Box 4.4. **Intellectual property, counterfeiting, piracy and informality**

Businesses hidden from tax and regulation not only rob formal competitors of market shares. They also pose more direct challenges when they make use of other firms' intellectual property. Counterfeit and pirated production is often seen as being particularly problematic in China, India, and Southeast Asia, as illegal producers take advantage of institutional weaknesses in enforcement and access to strong manufacturing bases and global supply chains. Such activities may take place more commonly in high-tech sectors like electronics or pharmaceuticals or brand-based consumer product industries, like footwear and apparel. And they may be carried out by formal subcontractors as well as by informal firms.

Informal firms can discourage competitors' R&D efforts. By ignoring the exclusive rights of their formal competitors, undercutting prices or producing inferior products, firms making use of others' intellectual property lower the returns to them. The result may be to deter formal firms from investing in R&D or to make innovation more costly. Furthermore, informal production that escapes inspection and is performed by firms without brands to protect can pose threats to consumer health and safety. Counterfeit pharmaceuticals, which are a particular risk if they contain unsafe additives or insufficient drug dosages, can also secure strong footholds on markets: India's pharmaceutical companies suggested in 2002 that counterfeit medicines accounted for about 20% of sales in major cities and were gaining market share. Appropriate general policy options for addressing informality – such as entrenched rule of law, stronger legal systems, and greater tax and regulatory enforcement – should also help to limit counterfeiting and other violations of intellectual property rights. Additional measures are also likely to be needed, though.

Most importantly, a strong system of safeguarding intellectual property rights is needed – one that encourages firms to register their innovations, balances incentives for R&D with consumer interests and is revisited over time to ensure it remains relevant to fast-changing technology. International co-operation, through forums such as the World Trade Organization, World Intellectual Property Organization and World Customs Organization, is also a necessary component of strategies to tackle the trade in counterfeit goods.

Of course, informal firms and employees also co-operate with formal firms through supplier-customer relationships – be they loose arrangements where informal suppliers sell through the open market or through individual transactions and value chains that directly connect informal producers to formal customers. Although the formal firms that make use of such arrangements benefit from having lower-cost suppliers, the practice still constitutes competition for those formal firms operating at the same level of production as these informal suppliers.

Policies to address informality

The adverse effects of informal activities outlined in the previous section highlight the multiple channels through which they constrain productivity and growth generally, put a strain on formal firms, and contribute to poverty and the creation of low-quality jobs.

On the other hand, informality can be a positive influence. It is a safety net that provides employment and livelihoods for excluded workers and, through its flexibility, helps to buffer negative shocks and so allow formal firms to adjust to changing conditions more quickly. A more inclusive, dynamic formal sector would, however, yield the same benefits without the concomitant drawbacks. Governments should, therefore, work to limit the size of the informal sector by including formalisation and inclusive growth of the formal sector in their policy making.

Emerging Asia's experience in promoting formalisation varies widely from country to country. In 2009 the World Bank's *Enterprise Surveys* showed that, compared to the rest of the region, late registration rates were very high in Indonesia, where 71% of registered firms were not registered when they began their operations (Figure 4.11). While the country's late registration rates may point to effective formalisation, they are also likely due to administrative barriers keeping many new firms from registering at their inception.

Figure 4.11. **Most Indonesian formal firms registered after they began operating**

Percentage of registered firms that were not registered when they began their operations

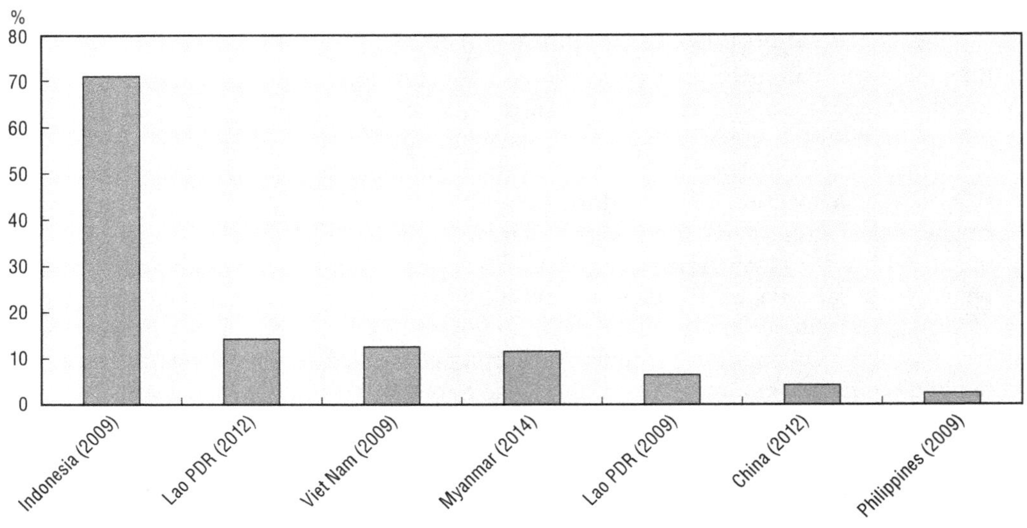

Sources: World Bank (2014b), *Enterprise Surveys* (database), World Bank, Washington, DC, http://www.enterprisesurveys.org; OECD Development Centre calculations.

StatLink http://dx.doi.org/10.1787/888933179967

Economic growth and industrialisation alone cannot be relied upon to reduce informality, particularly as informality itself already slows growth. Apart from low-income levels, institutional and other factors are conducive to the rise of informality. What is needed are comprehensive policy responses that deter disruptive informality without affecting the livelihoods of the poor and marginalised workers who depend on informal income sources. Responses may include elements of reform that address four policy areas:

- judicial institutional capacities;
- investment in formal sector productivity and assistance for SMEs;
- the tax and regulatory environment; and
- targeted enforcement and concessions.

Responsible reform can encourage informal employees and firms similar to their formal peers to formalise. It should provide poor and marginalised workers excluded from the formal sector with basic social protection and opportunities to improve their productivity.

Institutional and judicial reforms can help strengthen the formal sector

Informal activities can be curbed if formality is made a more attractive proposition. To that end, policy makers should improve governance and administration, particularly with respect to the rule of law and the judicial system as a whole; contract enforcement; and the protection of property rights. The strengthening of such fundamental institutions may, in turn, require legislative and organisational change. Broad-based reforms may also help to boost tax morale, as an improved image of effective, credible government is more likely to coax individuals and firms into paying their taxes. Generally speaking, the rule of law depends on clear and consistently applied laws and regulations. As for informality in particular, it requires the effective enforcement of corporate contracts and protection of property rights. Addressing corruption at all levels through strengthened government oversight bodies and civil service reforms is also important to ensuring the rule of law and improving the public image of government.

Unfortunately, fundamental market-building institutions are underdeveloped in a number of Emerging Asian economies. Even countries that perform fairly well overall in the World Bank report, *Doing Business 2014*, are ranked low in areas of critical importance when it came to addressing informality. Brunei Darussalam, where resolving a standardised commercial contract dispute takes an average of 540 days and costs 36.6% of the debt's value in court and attorney fees, for instance, is ranked 59th overall out of 189 countries, but 161st on enforcing contracts. Cambodia, India and Myanmar also perform poorly on contract enforcement, coming 162nd, 186th, and 188th, respectively. And in Indonesia (with 139.4%) and Cambodia (103.4%) the average cost of enforcing contracts exceed the value of the claim, which is the case in only five other countries. Case administration reform, like the introduction of electronic filing and management systems, has helped improve contract enforcement, however. The establishment of specialised courts and alternative mechanisms of dispute settlement such as arbitration, mediation and conciliation hearings have also proven effective where they have expanded capacities and enabled the training of specialised judges, mediators and other officials and administrators. In some cases, new and amended legislation may help to streamline legal proceedings. A case in point is China's Civil Procedure Law, which was passed in 2012. The extensive reforms it introduced helped to clarify all aspects of court procedure.

The ease with which property ownership can be registered is a crucial element in any system of property rights. In *Doing Business 2014*, even the lowest-ranked Emerging Asian economies perform relatively better against the yardsticks of numbers of procedures and the time and cost of registering immovable property purchased from another business. There is nevertheless room for improvement, particularly in Brunei Darussalam (116th), Cambodia (118th), the Philippines (121st) and Myanmar (154th). The legal provision of property rights protection can be further supported by streamlined administrative procedures – e.g. the computerisation of records – to facilitate the registration and transfer of property. The importance of ownership rights extends to other forms of tangible and intangible property as well, and the formal sector is made more attractive and innovative when it is easy for firms to register and legally protect their property and brands.

Encouraging formality through policies supportive of SMEs

SMEs offer considerable potential for growth in Emerging Asia. Their contribution has been recognised by legislators and policy makers who have responded by developing comprehensive strategies. Myanmar, for example, recently passed a new SME law, created a Central Department of SME Development in the Ministry of Industry, and looked into developing SME clusters and improving access to finance. As most informal firms are small, strengthening the SME sector will help them improve their productivity and give them incentives to formalise in order to access training, finance and technical assistance programmes.

Expanded access to training and finance is particularly important for SMEs. Broadly speaking, they thrive where there are strong financial and education systems, though they may also benefit from additional SME-specific schemes like targeted programmes and indirect financial support such as loan guarantees. The establishment of business incubators or development centres can further help to improve firm productivity, particularly for new and small businesses. Business associations can provide similar services by themselves or in co-operation with government-led programmes. Singapore's SME Centres are useful examples from the region of services that can be offered to assist firms. These are one-stop shops managed by the Standards, Productivity and Innovation Board of Singapore are staffed by business advisors who offer assistance on legal matters, finance, innovation, expansion and other topics.

Efforts to increase SME awareness of the costs of informality and opportunities to formalise through public information campaigns complement broader policy reforms. Effective awareness campaigns should employ moral suasion to highlight the importance of formalisation as well as providing information on how to register and access other public services. Various forms of information campaigns and communication strategies have been used to target informality in a number of OECD countries, including Denmark, Estonia, France, Sweden and the United Kingdom.

Tax, regulatory and administrative reforms can lower the cost of operating and working formally

As part of efforts to discourage informality, some countries should give thought to the direct costs, levels of taxation and regulations that weigh on the private sector. They may well have to reform the nature and administration of companies' legal obligations in order to encourage the growth of the formal sector.

For the same average tax rate, changes in the structure of taxation and reforms benefitting smaller firms – such as tax exemptions on re-invested earnings or tax credits for investment and job creation – could be part of a comprehensive strategy to reduce informality. While progressive systems of taxation can complicate filing and administration, their application to individual earnings, as in the United Kingdom and Nordic countries, provides incentives for firms and households to declare larger numbers of employees (OECD, 2004). Tax compliance may be further facilitated by administrative reforms, such as simplified rules and filing procedures like the electronic filing system introduced by Malaysia's Inland Revenue Board in 2004. As illustrated in Chapter 3, Emerging Asia has recently made great progress in improving tax administration, although much remains to be done.

Providing one-time amnesties for firms that register but have previously avoided tax may be useful as part of broader strategies to encourage formalisation. However, this ploy should be employed carefully and sparingly. Regular amnesties in Turkey, for example, are often described as ineffective or even counterproductive in encouraging formalisation, as taxpayers come to expect that further amnesties will be offered in the future. In Emerging Asia, income tax has been the focus of amnesties, such as Indonesia's 2008 Sunset Policy. Tax amnesties for informal firms and workers, be they full or partial, may be justified as one component in a broader push for formalisation, but they do not replace the need for other policy tools.

Regulatory and administrative barriers are high in several Emerging Asian economies, though performances range widely. While Singapore was ranked first in *Doing Business 2014* (World Bank, 2014c), Myanmar was near the bottom, the 182nd out of 189 countries. Seven other countries in the region (China, Viet Nam, the Philippines, Indonesia, India, Lao PDR and Cambodia) were also in the bottom 50%. Emerging Asian countries tend to be ranked relatively high on the "getting credit" sub-index and low in "starting a business". Similarly, China, India and Indonesia, along with the rest of the BRIICS, tend to be more restrictive than the OECD member-country average in barriers to entrepreneurship as well as the other subcategories measured by the OECD's Indicators of Product Market Regulation.

Reforms could give particular focus to lowering the barriers that new and small firms have to negotiate. Administrative costs are more of a strain for start-ups and SMEs, which may see smaller sacrifices in operating informally to avoid taxation. The use of a lighter touch on SMEs should not suddenly cease, however, when they reach a certain size, as threshold effects can discourage firm growth or push them out of the formal sector.

Alternative approaches to motivating and facilitating SME registration have been deployed in OECD member countries. In France, Belgium, Italy and in some sectors in Ireland, new employees are required to be declared immediately in order to discourage employers from delaying the process indefinitely. UK firms have been similarly required since 2000 to register with the Inland Revenue when they begin business, rather than after a grace period. Some countries have introduced unique firm identifying codes and information sharing to improve administrative efficiency. The 1998 *Koppelingswet* (Linking Law) in the Netherlands, for example, requires the use of unique Social Fiscal Numbers to connect social security, social services, revenue and healthcare client files.

A combination of increased flexibility in labour markets and the provision of protection for informal workers may also help to close the regulatory requirement gap between the formal and informal sectors. Employee rights in Japan and France stipulate that even undeclared workers are entitled to some protection – when they are laid off, for example – so that they enjoy at least some assistance and dare report their former employers.

The problem of low-level corruption among public officials is related to and often a result of complex administrative barriers. The need to pay bribes in order to secure permits within a reasonable time or to complete other formalities increases firms' cost in a similar way to red tape. Reforms to increase enforcement capacity, provide better incentives and training for public officials, and make rules more transparent should help government run more efficiently and reduce opportunities for corruption.

Emerging Asian economies perform relatively poorly in international comparisons on low-level corruption. *Enterprise Surveys* carried out by the World Bank asked registered firms whether they had received requests for a "gift or informal payment" by tax officials during an inspection. Of the 169 surveys of emerging economies where responses to the question were available, Myanmar, Viet Nam, Lao PDR (in 2009 and 2012), the Philippines and Indonesia were all in the bottom half of countries, with a high prevalence of bribery. The lowest ranked was Myanmar, where 35% of respondents stated that they had been asked for a bribe, which put the country in the bottom 8th percentile of countries surveyed (Figure 4.12). While firms also contribute to corruption when they agree to pay bribes – a factor not addressed by the surveys – it is telling that bribe requests tend to be less common where governance in general and legal and judicial systems in particular are more effective.

Figure 4.12. **Bribery of tax officials is relatively common in several countries in the region**

Percentage of registered firms asked for bribes by tax inspectors

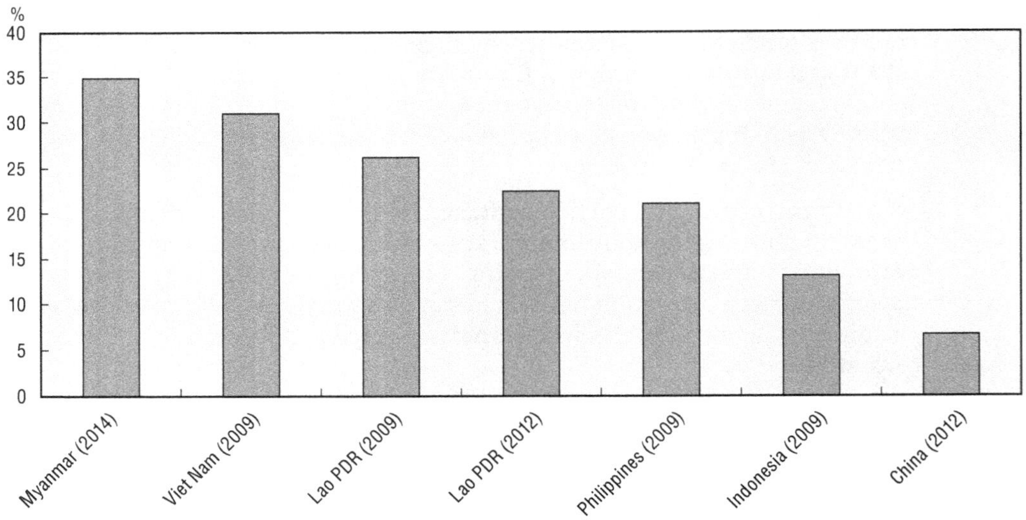

Sources: World Bank (2014b), *Enterprise Surveys* (database), World Bank, Washington, DC, http://www.enterprisesurveys.org; OECD Development Centre calculations.

StatLink http://dx.doi.org/10.1787/888933179975

Policies targeting informality should also be considered

Along with broad reforms to the judicial system, assistance for SMEs, and tax and regulatory reforms, policy strategies that target informal firms and workers through tighter enforcement and concessions for compliance have a role to play in comprehensive responses to informality. They can be particularly effective where resources are limited and a more nuanced approach to reducing informality is needed. Targeting productive informal firms that compete with the formal sector and formal firms employing informal workers are the most beneficial for growth when combined with the institutional and productivity-enhancing reforms described above. Targeted strategies should also seek to simultaneously formalise firms, their competitors, suppliers, customers and even lenders from the informal financial sector. Such an approach would help to alleviate concerns over lost cost competitiveness and offer opportunities to formalise business-to-business and financial relationships. Targeted approaches to enforcement and tax concessions for sensitive sectors have been among the approaches to tackling informality in OECD member countries (Box 4.5).

Box 4.5. **Creative, targeted policies for reducing informal output and employment in the OECD**

While it tends to be less common in wealthier countries, informality is everywhere. There are large economic, social and institutional differences between Emerging Asian economies and most OECD member countries. Yet the latter still face challenges in addressing informality and tax compliance. Their policy responses might therefore be lessons that could also be applied by, or at least inspire, the region's policy makers. The *OECD Employment Outlook 2004* provided an overview of policies to curb the size of the informal sector and the prevalence of undeclared work. It shows that several countries have used sector-specific targeted policies and enforcement (among other approaches) to address informality. Some examples of interesting solutions include:

- **Liability for subcontractors**: To prevent the use of informal workers as external subcontractors, firms in several sectors (commonly including construction) in France, Germany, the Netherlands and the United Kingdom acting as chief contractors are legally responsible for subcontractors' tax and regulatory compliance.
- **Alternative tax administration procedures**: In the United Kingdom, inspectors may investigate suspicious firms and attempt to reconcile observed cash transactions with a firm's activities, its size and its number of customers to determine whether their declared income is reasonable.
- **Tax rates to encourage compliance**: A range of tax measures are used to encourage firms to declare their income and employees. Tax concessions in sensitive sectors – such as domestic work in Germany and some construction work in Sweden, France and Italy – attempt to boost compliance in sectors with widespread informal employment.

Source: OECD (2004), *Employment Outlook 2004*, OECD Publishing, Paris, http://dx.doi.org/10.1787/empl_outlook-2004-en.

Informal competition with the formal sector tends to be fiercest among smaller firms operating away from the modern, international sectors of the economy – sectors that may be useful targets of anti-informality policy reforms. In Indonesia, Lao PDR (in 2009), Malaysia and Viet Nam, the smallest firms are those most likely to compete with informal firms (Figure 4.13). The trend is hardly surprising: informal firms are also likely to be small and to share the technological and financial constraints of smaller formal firms. In all countries in the region for which data were available, however, exporters were less likely to compete with informal firms. The reason is that they tend not to export because administrative, financial, business and technical barriers prevent them from doing so (Figure 4.14). Informal firms avoid the administrative formalities that exporting requires, have less access to finance, are smaller, have fewer opportunities to develop international connections (or to secure them through contracts) and are more likely to fall short of customers' product quality expectations.

Figure 4.13. Smaller firms are often more likely to experience informal competition

Percentage of registered firms experiencing informal competition, by firm size

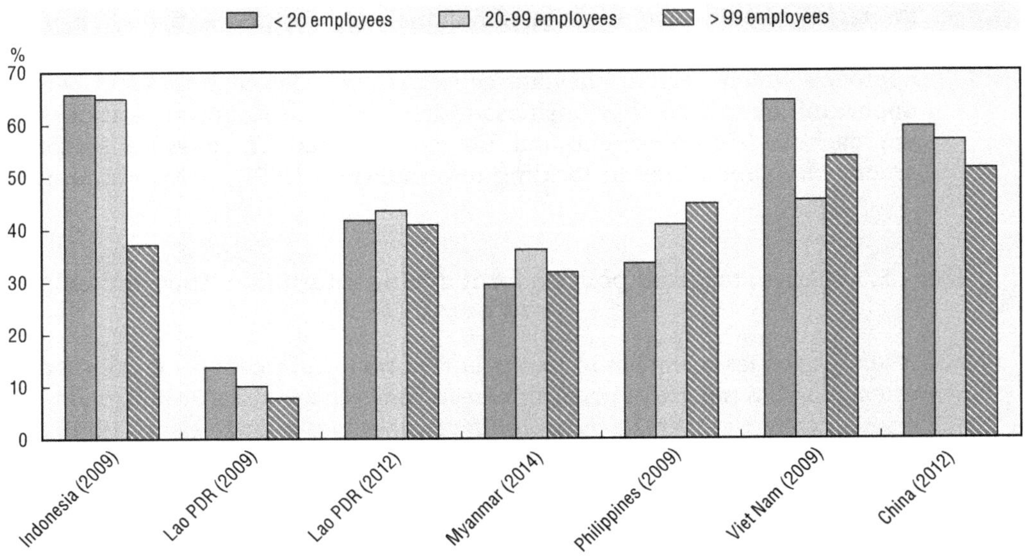

Sources: World Bank (2014b), *Enterprise Surveys* (database), World Bank, Washington, DC, http://www.enterprisesurveys.org; OECD Development Centre calculations.

StatLink http://dx.doi.org/10.1787/888933179982

Figure 4.14. Exporters tend to be considerably less likely to experience informal competition

Percentage of registered firms experiencing informal competition, by firm exporting

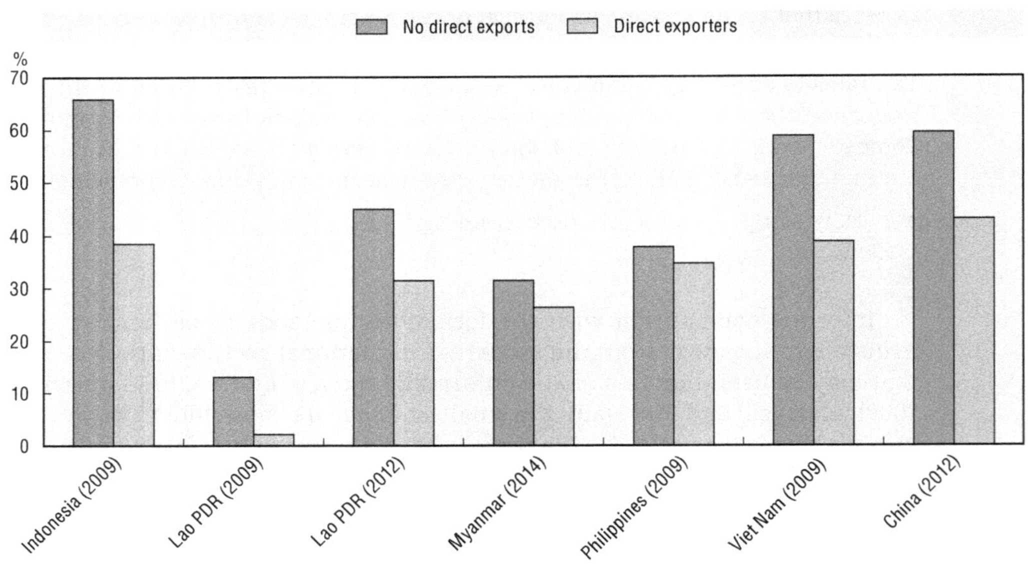

Sources: World Bank (2014b), *Enterprise Surveys* (database), World Bank, Washington, DC, http://www.enterprisesurveys.org; OECD Development Centre calculations.

StatLink http://dx.doi.org/10.1787/888933179995

Conclusion

Informality can present serious challenges to policy makers in emerging economies. While informal output and employment appear to be declining across most of the region, both remain at high levels in a number of Emerging Asian economies. They are a serious threat to development in that they rob governments of revenue, limit regulatory reach, and directly and indirectly impede growth. The challenge for policy makers in the region is therefore to curb informality while not jeopardising the livelihoods of marginalised workers and promoting the flexibility of the formal sector. They can rise to that challenge by designing and instituting comprehensive reforms that address the interconnected economic, social and institutional roots of informality.

Comprehensive strategies to address informality should, at the very least, consider issues relating to the legal and judicial system, support for SMEs, the tax and regulatory environment, and the use of targeted enforcement and concessions. A number of Emerging Asian countries need to strengthen the rule of law and property rights and enforce contracts more efficiently if they are to improve the attractiveness of the formal sector.

Training, technical and financial assistance, together with public awareness campaigns targeting SMEs, can further help pull firms into the formal sector and do viable business. At the same time, more efficient tax structures and administrative procedures, streamlined product and labour market regulations, and reduced corruption can also help to make the formal sector more efficient and easier to join. Finally, enhanced enforcement and, in some cases, concessions may help to discourage informality in sectors of the economy that are particularly prone to non-compliance.

Annex 4.A1: Informality estimations methodologies

Currency ratio estimation of informal share of output

The predicted ratio of currency in circulation to money supply (M2) without fiscal pressure is subtracted from the original estimation to determine the share of currency used in the informal sector. The size of the informal sector is then estimated, assuming that informal transactions are carried out with cash only, that the velocity of money in the informal sector is the same as in the formal sector and that official GDP measures only the formal sector.

The approach is based on that of Tanzi (1980), although it omits the labour compensation share from the estimation and uses tax revenue shares instead of weighted average tax rates due to limited availability of those data.

$$\ln(C/M2)_t = a_0 + a_1\ln(1+T_t) + a_2\ln Y_t + a_3\ln R_t$$

Where C is currency in circulation, *T* is tax revenue as a percentage of GDP, Y is real *per capita* income and R is the nominal interest rate on savings deposits in year t. This is estimated separately for each country. Results with negative coefficients for the fiscal variable are omitted.

Electricity consumption estimation of growth in informal output

After controlling for price fluctuations (using the CPI inflation rate) and the share of industry in GDP through the following estimation, change in total electricity consumption by country is taken as a proxy for change in total economic activity:

$$\Delta E_{it} = a_{0i} + a_1 I_{it} + a_2 \Delta S_{it}$$

Where E is electricity consumption, *i* is CPI based inflation and S is the share of industry in official GDP in country *I* and year t.

Following Kaufmann and Kaliberda (1996) in assuming the elasticity of electricity consumption to total economic activity to be one and that official GDP records only activity in the formal sector, the annual growth in the informal sector is estimated as the growth of filtered electricity consumption minus the annual growth rate of official GDP. Informal output shares for 2006 taken from the WEF Executive Opinion Survey are used as the base year, and extended using the estimated change in informal output.

Notes

1. Low tax ratios and large gaps between potential and actual tax collection are often seen in emerging economies due to factors such as pervasive illegal tax evasion, legal tax avoidance, exemptions and inefficient tax collection.
2. These observations apply to labour productivity, and so may partly be the result of low capital-labour ratios in informal firms. Alternative measures of productivity that take these ratios into consideration, such as multifactor productivity, may therefore show less of a productivity gap between the formal and informal sectors, and would be worth exploring further in future research.

References

Chong, A. and M. Gradstein (2004), "Inequality and institutions", *Inter-American Development Bank Research Department Working Paper No. 506*, Inter-American Development Bank, Washington, DC, http://www.iadb.org/res/publications/pubfiles/pubWP-506.pdf.

Cowell, F. (1990), *Cheating the Government: The Economics of Evasion*, Massachusetts Institute of Technology Press, Cambridge, MA.

Dabla-Norris, E., M. Gradstein and G. Inchauste (2005), "What causes firms to hide output? The determinants of informality", *IMF Working Paper*, IMF Institute, Washington, DC, August.

Daude, C., H. Gutiérrez and Á. Melguizo (2012), "What drives tax morale?", *OECD Development Centre Working Paper*, No. 315, OECD, Paris, http://www.oecd.org/dev/latinamericaandthecaribbean/WP315%20AE.pdf.

Fiess, N.M., M. Fugazza and W.F. Maloney (2009), "Informal self-employment and macroeconomic fluctuations", *Journal of Development Economics*, Vol. 91, pp. 211-226.

Gyomai, G. and P. van de Ven (2014), "The non-observed economy in the system of national accounts", *OECD Statistics Brief*, No. 18, OECD, Paris, June, http://www.oecd.org/std/na/Statistics%20Brief%2018.pdf.

International Labour Organization (2010a), *LABORSTA database*, ILO, Geneva, http://laborsta.ilo.org/.

International Labour Organization (2010b), *Social Security for Informal Economy Workers in Indonesia: Looking for Flexible and Highly Targeted Programmes*, ILO, Jakarta, www.ilo.org/wcmsp5/groups/public/---asia/---ro-bangkok/---ilo-jakarta/documents/publication/wcms_142763.pdf.

Jütting, J. and J. de Laiglesia (2009), "Is informal normal?: Towards more and better jobs in developing countries", Development Centre Studies, OECD Publishing, Paris, http://dx.doi.org/10.1787/9789264059245-en.

Kaufmann, D. and A. Kaliberda (1996), "Integrating the unofficial economy into the dynamics of post-socialist economies: A framework of analysis and evidence", in B. Kaminski (ed.), *Economic Transition in Russia and the New States of Eurasia*, M.E. Sharpe Inc., Armonk, NY.

Levi, M. (1988), *Of Rule and Revenue*, University of California Press, Berkeley.

Loayza, N. and J. Rigolini (2006), "Informality trends and cycles", *World Bank Policy Research Working Paper* 4078, World Bank, Washington, DC.

Manning, C. and D.S. Pratomo (2013), "Do migrants get stuck in the informal sector? Findings from a household survey in four Indonesian cities", *Bulletin of Indonesian Economic Studies*, Vol. 49, No. 2, pp. 167-192.

Mazumdar, D. (1989), "Microeconomic issues of labour markets in developing countries", *EDI Seminar Paper*, No. 40, World Bank, Washington, DC.

Mohapatra, S., S. Rozelle and R. Goodhue (2007), "The rise of self-employment in rural China: Development or Distress?", *World Development*, Vol. 35, No. 1, pp. 163-181, January.

NCEUS (2008), "Contribution of the unorganised sector to GDP report of the Sub-committee of an NCEUS Task Force", *National Commission for Enterprises in the Unorganised Sector Working Paper*, No. 2, New Delhi.

OECD (2014a), *Economic Policy Reforms 2014: Going for Growth Interim Report*, OECD Publishing, Paris, http://dx.doi.org/10.1787/growth-2014-en.

OECD (2014b), *Indicators of Employment Protection* (database), OECD Publishing, Paris, http://www.oecd.org/employment/emp/oecdindicatorsofemploymentprotection.htm.

OECD (2014c), *Revenue Statistics in Asian Countries 2014: Trends in Indonesia and Malaysia*, OECD Publishing, Paris, http://dx.doi.org/10.1787/9789264210691-en.

OECD (2004), *OECD Employment Outlook 2004*, OECD Publishing, Paris, http://dx.doi.org/10.1787/empl_outlook-2004-en.

OECD (2002), *Measuring the Non-Observed Economy: A Handbook*, OECD Publishing, Paris, http://dx.doi.org/10.1787/9789264175358-en.

Political Risk Services (2014), *International Country Risk Guide* (database), PRS, Syracuse.

Schneider, F., A. Buehn, and C.E. Montenegro, "Shadow economies all over the world: New estimates for 162 countries from 1999 to 2007", *World Bank Policy Research Working Paper*, No. 5356, World Bank, Washington, DC, http://www-wds.worldbank.org/external/default/WDSContentServer/IW3P/IB/2010/10/14/000158349_20101014160704/Rendered/PDF/WPS5356.pdf.

Tanaka, K. and M. Molnar (2008), "What is different about informal finance?: Financing of private firms in China", *Revue Économique*, Vol. 59, No. 6, pp. 1131-1143, November.

Tanzi, V. (1980), "The underground economy in the United States: Estimates and implications", *Banca Nazionale del Lavoro Quarterly Review*, No. 135, pp. 427-453, December.

Todaro, M.P. (1969), "A model of labour migration and urban unemployment in less developed countries", *The American Economic Review*, Vol. 59, No. 1, pp. 138-148.

World Bank (2014a), *World Development Indicators*, World Bank, Washington, DC.

World Bank (2014b), *Enterprise Surveys* (database), World Bank, Washington, DC, http://www.enterprisesurveys.org.

World Bank (2014c), *Doing Business 2014: Understanding Regulations for Small and Medium-Size Enterprises*, World Bank, Washington, DC.

World Economic Forum (2006), *The Global Competitiveness Report 2006-2007*, World Economic Forum, New York.

Statistical annex

Table A.1. **Real GDP growth of Southeast Asia, China and India**

Annual percentage change

Country	2013	2019	2000-07	2011-13	2015-19
ASEAN 10 countries					
ASEAN-5 countries					
Indonesia	5.8	6.3	5.5	6.2	6.0
Malaysia	4.7	5.6	6.0	5.2	5.6
The Philippines	7.2	6.3	5.7	5.9	6.2
Thailand	2.9	4.6	5.6	3.2	4.1
Viet Nam	5.4	5.8	7.2	5.6	5.7
Brunei Darussalam	-1.8	1.9	1.7	0.9	1.6
Cambodia	7.5	7.3	10.6	7.3	7.1
Lao PDR	8.0	7.7	7.1	8.1	7.6
Myanmar	7.5	7.8	-	6.9	7.8
Singapore	3.9	3.6	7.9	4.1	3.5
Two large economies in the region					
China	7.7	6.6	11.7	8.2	6.8
India	5.0	6.8	3.8	5.5	6.7
Average of ASEAN 10 countries	5.2	5.8	5.9	5.4	5.6
Average of Emerging Asia (*)	6.5	6.5	9.5	7.0	6.5

Notes: The cut-off date of data is 6 October, 2014. Emerging Asia denotes ASEAN-10 countries plus China and India. ASEAN-5 includes Indonesia, Malaysia, Thailand, the Philippines and Viet Nam.

Source: OECD Development Centre, MPF-2015 (Medium-term projection framework). For more information on MPF, please see www.oecd.org/dev/asiapacific/mpf.

Table A.2. **Current account balance of Southeast Asia, China and India**

Percentage of GDP

Country	2013	2019	2000-07	2015-19
ASEAN economies				
ASEAN-5				
Indonesia	-3.3	-2.9	2.8	-3.3
Malaysia	3.8	4.0	11.8	4.3
Philippines	3.5	1.5	1.0	2.1
Thailand	0.5	0.6	3.0	0.5
Viet Nam	6.5	3.4	-1.9	3.8
Brunei	46.0	39.2	-	42.0
Cambodia	-10.8	-7.1	-2.3	-7.9
Lao PDR	-29.5	-18.5	-13.4	-20.0
Myanmar	-4.8	-5.5	-	-5.1
Singapore	18.1	16.4	13.5	17.5
Two large economies in the region				
China	2.0	2.4	4.6	2.6
India	-1.7	-2.3	0.0	-2.3
ASEAN 5 average	2.2	1.3	3.3	1.5
ASEAN 10 average	3.0	3.1	2.0	3.4
Emerging Asia average	2.5	2.6	2.0	2.9

Notes: The cut-off date of data is 6 October, 2014. Emerging Asia denotes ASEAN-10 countries plus China and India. ASEAN-5 includes Indonesia, Malaysia, Thailand, the Philippines and Viet Nam.

Source: OECD Development Centre, MPF-2015 (Medium-term projection framework). For more information on MPF, please see www.oecd.org/dev/asiapacific/mpf.

Table A.3. **Private consumption in Southeast Asia, China and India**

Percentage changes

Country	2013	2000-07	2015-19
Indonesia	5.3	3.7	5.5
Malaysia	7.2	8.0	6.8
Philippines	5.7	4.9	6.3
Thailand	0.3	4.6	4.0
Viet Nam	5.2	7.1	6.4
China	7.7	6.7	8.4
India	4.9	6.3	6.8
ASEAN-5 average	4.7	5.7	5.8
Emerging Asia average	5.2	5.9	6.3

Source: OECD Development Centre, MPF-2015.

Table A.4. **Gross fixed capital formation in ASEAN-5, China and India**

Percentage changes

Country	2013	2000-07	2015-19
Indonesia	4.7	8.3	8.0
Malaysia	8.5	6.7	6.8
Philippines	11.9	4.2	6.0
Thailand	-2.0	6.8	4.8
Viet Nam	5.3	12.5	8.3
China	9.2	12.2	7.0
India	-0.1	11.8	7.2
ASEAN 5 average	5.7	7.7	6.8
Emerging Asia average	5.4	8.9	6.9

Source: OECD Development Centre, MPF-2015.

Table A.5. **Public finances of Southeast Asia, China and India**

Fiscal balances (central government)

Country	2000-07	2015-19
Indonesia	-1.6	-1.7
Malaysia	-4.7	-4.0
Philippines	-3.4	-1.6
Thailand	-1.1	-2.9
Viet Nam	-2.8	-3.4
China	-	-1.2
India	-7.3	-7.2
ASEAN 5 average	-2.7	-2.7
Emerging Asia average	-3.5	-3.1

Source: OECD Development Centre, MPF-2015.

ORGANISATION FOR ECONOMIC CO-OPERATION AND DEVELOPMENT

The Development Centre of the Organisation for Economic Co-operation and Development was established in 1962 and comprises 26 member countries of the OECD: Austria, Belgium, Chile, the Czech Republic, Denmark, Finland, France, Germany, Greece, Iceland, Ireland, Israel, Italy, Korea, Luxembourg, Mexico, the Netherlands, Norway, Poland, Portugal, Slovak Republic, Spain, Sweden, Switzerland, Turkey and the United Kingdom. In addition, 21 non-OECD countries are full members of the Development Centre: Brazil (since March 1994); India (February 2001); Romania (October 2004); Thailand (March 2005); South Africa (May 2006); Egypt and Viet Nam (March 2008); Colombia (July 2008); Indonesia (February 2009); Costa Rica, Mauritius, Morocco and Peru (March 2009); the Dominican Republic (November 2009); Senegal (February 2011); Argentina and Cabo Verde (March 2011); Panama (July 2013); and Côte d'Ivoire, Kazakhstan and Tunisia (January 2015). The European Union also takes part in the work of the Centre.

OECD DEVELOPMENT CENTRE

The Development Centre occupies a unique place within the OECD and in the international community. It provides a platform where developing and emerging economies interact on an equal footing with OECD members to promote knowledge sharing and peer learning on sustainable and inclusive development. The Centre combines multidisciplinary analysis with policy dialogue activities to help governments formulate innovative policy solutions to the global challenges of development. Hence, the Centre plays a key role in the OECD's engagement efforts with non-member countries.

To increase the impact and legitimacy of its work, the Centre adopts an inclusive approach and engages with a variety of governmental and non-governmental stakeholders. It works closely with experts and institutions from its member countries, has established partnerships with key international and regional organisations and hosts networks of private-sector enterprises, think tanks and foundations working for development. The results of its work are discussed in experts' meetings as well as in policy dialogues and high-level meetings, and are published in a range of high-quality publications and papers for the research and policy communities.

For more information on the Centre, please see *www.oecd.org/dev*.

OECD PUBLISHING, 2, rue André-Pascal, 75775 PARIS CEDEX 16
(41 2014 05 1 P) ISBN 978-92-64-21086-8 – 2015-06

www.ingramcontent.com/pod-product-compliance
Lightning Source LLC
Chambersburg PA
CBHW061207240926
51846CB00006B/1134
* 9 7 8 9 2 6 4 2 1 0 8 6 8 *